AMERICA'S MOST
SPECTACULAR
DRIVES

Louis Weber, CEO
Publications International, Ltd.
8140 Lehigh Avenue
Morton Grove, IL 60053

ISBN: 978-1-64558-262-5

Manufactured in China.

8 7 6 5 4 3 2 1

Let's get social!

 @Publications_International

 @PublicationsInternational

www.pilbooks.com

CONTENTS

MIDWEST 63

SOUTH 138

Along Alaska's Marine Highway, tourists encounter fjords, glaciers, mountains, waterfalls, and whales—all from the water. On Maine's Acadia Byway, a whirl of forests, lakes, marshes, coastal islands, and the highest rocky headlands on the Atlantic shore of the United States combine to produce a visual feast.

From the Northeast to the West Coast, the Mountain region to the South and Midwest, *America's Most Spectacular Drives* presents a diverse and distinctive collection of roadways that will transport you from the Atlantic to the Pacific, the Great Lakes to the Gulf of Mexico, and to the vast landscapes of mountains, hills, prairies, farmlands, woodlands, valleys, canyons, deserts, and communities large and small that lie between.

The roadways in this book are more than just scenic; the following destinations also combine unmatched beauty with recreational, natural, historical, cultural, or archaeological significance. These drives all represent classic journeys—places where America's story continues to unfold along unending ribbons of blacktop.

So warm up your car—or just pull up an armchair—and get ready for the adventure of experiencing America along *America's Most Spectacular Drives*. America's byways are journeys into the beauty and freedom of the open road, weaving a rich tapestry of the country's diversity and accomplishments—and, always, unforgettable scenery.

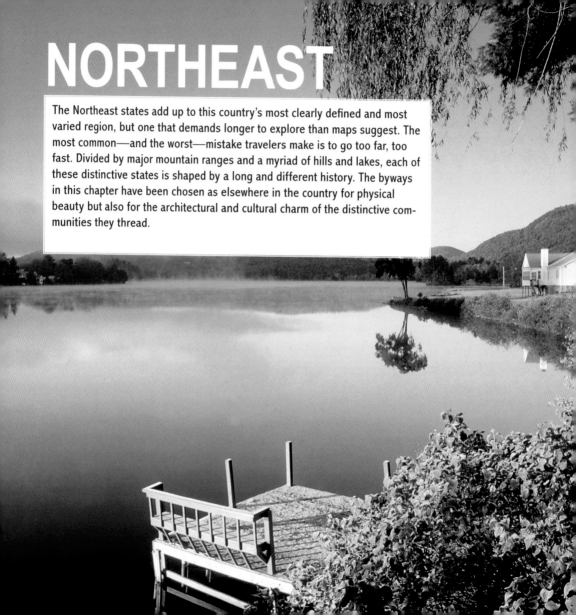

NORTHEAST

The Northeast states add up to this country's most clearly defined and most varied region, but one that demands longer to explore than maps suggest. The most common—and the worst—mistake travelers make is to go too far, too fast. Divided by major mountain ranges and a myriad of hills and lakes, each of these distinctive states is shaped by a long and different history. The byways in this chapter have been chosen as elsewhere in the country for physical beauty but also for the architectural and cultural charm of the distinctive communities they thread.

Acadia Byway

Acadia National Park spreads across much of Mount Desert, a mainland-hinged island known for its many rounded mountains rising abruptly from the sea. The Loop Road circles both ocean and shore, accessing hiking trails, bicycle paths, and the top of Cadillac Mountain.

Quick Facts

Length: 40 miles

Time to Allow: Three hours

Consideration: Mount Desert Island has a free seasonal bus service that visitors are encouraged to use; the central terminal is in downtown Bar Harbor. The buses stop at many of the hotels and campgrounds along the way. They also stop anywhere that offers adequate space to pull over. You can easily flag them down. The Park Loop Road is closed from late November to mid-April. Other roads can be closed during extreme weather conditions. You must pay a car toll to get on Park Loop Road at the national park.

As the name suggests, the Acadia area was French before it was American. French explorer Samuel de Champlain sailed into Frenchman Bay in 1604, naming the area Mount Desert Island because of its landmark bare top.

Today, the National Park Service owns approximately half of the island that makes up Acadia National Park. The island boasts lush forests, tranquil ponds, and granite-capped mountains, where exploring is made easy by an extensive system of carriage roads and hiking trails. This alternate transportation network provides access to all areas of the park for walkers, equestrians, bicyclists, and cross-country skiers.

Villages on Mount Desert Island present a variety of lifestyles. Bar Harbor offers many accommodations and amusements. Northeast Harbor shelters sailboats, both large and small, and a summer colony.

Cultural: While Maine is rich in culture, perhaps the best-known sights along the coast are the lobster

traps and colorful buoys. Catching lobster has been a profitable activity in Maine since the 1840s. Today, the sight of a lobster fisher reeling in a trap is common.

While the lobster boats are not the same wooden dories originally used, they are still a unique sight along the waters. They generally have a round bottom and a double wedge hull, ranging from 20 to 40 feet. The actual

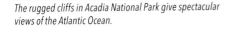

The rugged cliffs in Acadia National Park give spectacular views of the Atlantic Ocean.

lobster traps come in various designs. Two of the best known are the parlor trap and the double-header trap, and they're set anywhere from 50 feet to miles apart. During the summer, lobster can be found in shallow waters (60 to 100 feet), but during the winter, lobsters descend to depths of more than 200 feet.

Historical: Acadia's long history of settlement and colonization began with Samuel de Champlain, who led the expedition that landed on Mount Desert on September 5, 1604. Because de Champlain, who made the first important contribution to the historical record of Mount Desert Island, visited 16 years before the Pilgrims landed at Plymouth Rock, this land was known as New France before it became New England.

The land was in dispute between the French to the north and the English to the south. After a century and a half of conflict, British troops triumphed at Quebec, ending French dominion in Acadia. Hence, lands along the Maine coast opened for English settlement. Soon, an increasing number of settlers homesteaded on Mount Desert Island. By 1820, farming and lumbering vied with fishing and shipbuilding as major occupations. Outsiders—artists and journalists—revealed and popularized the island to the world in the mid-1800s.

Painters, then called rusticators, inspired patrons and friends to flock to the island. Tourism became a major industry.

For a handful of Americans, the 1880s and Gay Nineties meant affluence on a scale without precedent. Mount Desert, still remote from the cities of the east, became a retreat for prominent people of the times. The Rockefellers, Morgans, Fords, Vanderbilts, Carnegies, and Astors chose to spend their summers on the island. They transformed the area with elegant estates, euphemistically called "cottages." For more than 40 years, the wealthy held sway at Mount Desert until the Great Depression, World War II, and the fire of 1947 marked the end of such extravagance.

Although the wealthy came to the island to play, they also helped to preserve the landscape. George B. Dorr, in particular, was a tireless crusader for conservation. Dorr and others established the Hancock County Trustees of Public

Bar Harbor was once known as Eden, and is now known for its Maine lobster and unique ambiance.

Reservations. This corporation's sole purpose was to preserve land for the perpetual use of the public, and it acquired some 6,000 acres by 1913. In 1916, the land became the Sieur de Monts National Monument, and in 1919 it became the first national park east of the Mississippi, with Dorr as the first park superintendent. The name changed to Acadia in 1929, and today the park encompasses 35,000 acres of land.

Recreational: Relatively small at only 13 miles wide and 16 miles long, Acadia National Park offers a multitude of activities. Acadia maintains 45 miles of carriage roads for walking, riding, biking, and skiing and more than 100 miles of trails just for hiking. Situated right along the coast, the area is perfect for boating, sailing, and kayaking.

Hiking is one of the best ways to see all that Acadia has to offer. Trails crisscross the entire island. Take time to steal softly through a still forest, skip along the thundering coast, or meander through a swaying meadow. Up Cadillac Mountain is a particularly inspiring hike; its summit is the highest point on the Atlantic coast north of Rio de Janeiro. If you reach it before dawn and stand at the summit, you will be the first person in the continental United States to see the sun begin its journey across the sky and witness the beginning of a brand-new day.

For water enthusiasts, Acadia offers a number of alternatives. Ocean canoeing and kayaking are drawing new converts every day. The thrill of gliding on the surface of the rolling sea is an experience never to be forgotten. You can immerse yourself more fully in the ocean experience by swimming at one of the beaches, although water temperatures rarely exceed 55 degrees.

Highlights:

While traveling this byway, take your time. Because this route is on the coast and in a national park, you'll find no end to the brilliant views. Although the byway runs just 40 miles, you can spend several days here.

Bar Harbor: Spend time in the city of Bar Harbor, soaking in the relaxed atmosphere, eating at a fine or charming local-flavor restaurant, and exploring a few of the hundreds of specialty shops. You can seek out plenty of nightlife: bars, clubs, concerts, and specialty movie theaters.

Dorr and Champlain Mountains and The Tarn: Spend the day hiking around Dorr and Champlain Mountains and The Tarn. Explore off-road Acadia National Park on a mountain bike; take the 45 miles of carriage roads that are safe, serene, and gorgeous.

Thunder Hole, Otter Cliffs, Otter Point, and Cranberry Islands: Make sure to hit Thunder Hole (and its associated historical ranger station). Otter Cliffs and the adjoining Otter Point are simply remarkable. You may want to don a jacket as you sit on the rocks and have a picnic lunch. Hop a ferry out to the Cranberry Islands to explore or take a ferry to whale-watch.

Old Canada Road Scenic Byway

U.S. 201 runs north from the long-settled village of Solon along the Kennebec River. Beyond the hydro dam in Bingham it widens into shimmering Wyman Lake, then narrows again, churning through Kennebec Gorge to the delight of white-water rafters. Follow Benedict Arnold's lead, continuing north through Jackman and on to Quebec City.

Quick Facts

Length: 78 miles

Time to Allow: At least 2.5 hours

Consideration: Try to avoid coming during the Fourth of July and Labor Day weekends when the byway is really packed. Also, when driving the byway, be careful of moose in the road. Be aware of narrow passages of roads. Logging trucks are also frequent on the byway.

Find a snapchat of the past on the Old Canada Road Scenic Byway. Pass through villages and outposts that are much as they were at the turn of the 19th century. Remote and unspoiled, this neck of the Maine woods is a unique and beautiful place, where people live, work, and visit. The byway is in one of the most picturesque roads in the Northeast. It winds right alongside the Kennebec River, Wyman Lake, the Dead River, and vast forests. Rivers dominate the southern half of the route, while forests command the northern section.

The Kennebec River offers a mix of unending scenery, thrilling roller-coasterlike white water, and superb fishing opportunities, all in a remote setting.

The southern half of U.S. 201 is where you will first encounter old-time villages such as Solon and Bingham. Vernacular architecture contributes to the feel of an earlier time. Moscow gives way to the steep shoreline of Wyman Lake. Your drive hugs the shore, revealing undeveloped ridges on the opposite shore and islands framed by dramatic stands of white birch.

North of the West Forks, you'll see mountains and ridges, and an occasional moose or deer.

Cultural: The Old Canada Road, which runs from the Canadian border to Solon, Maine, is rich in history brought by the French that settled the area in the 1600s. The byway served as a route for loggers, but the area was virtually uninhabited with the exception of a few sporadic villages. Today, evidence of the influence of French and English culture is found in language, music, community celebrations, and food.

The folk culture and regional identity come in part from the immigration of people from French-speaking Canada. This influence is especially strong in the northern portion of the route, where many residents are bilingual. Many occupants of the area speak what is known as "Valley French," which is a combination of French, Quebecois, and English.

Throughout the year, communities along the byway celebrate their culture permitted migrants to disperse along the route throughout New England.

The road began as settlers from the Kennebec Valley moved northward into Somerset County. The Yankee pioneers found themselves closer to the markets of Quebec City than to those of Boston. In the early 19th century, Quebec was a growing lumber and ship-building port, as well as a military and administrative center, and it needed provisions. So Yankee drovers took livestock north, through the woods on a trail they built between the roads that lay alongside the Kennebec and Chaudière Rivers (the Chaudière River is in Canada). It became obvious that it was to almost everyone's advantage to "close the gap" between these two road systems.

In 1815, the road Chemin de la Chaudière along the northeast shore of the Chaudière River was extended to the fork of the DuLoup River and continued up the northeast shore of the DuLoup to just below the frontier. This 28-mile roadway was almost 18 feet wide and followed the earlier drover's trail.

In 1817, the legislature authorized construction of a "traveled path" to be

made suitable for the passage of loaded carts, sleds, and other such conveyances. It was to largely follow the old cattle drover's trail. Almost 25 miles in length, it ran from the north shore of Parlin Pond to the Canadian line. The next year Somerset County had the final 43 miles of road built between Concord and Parlin Pond along the west side of the Kennebec River.

By 1830, the dream of commercial profit finally drove government officials to upgrade the Canada Road into a carriageway that would accommodate drovers, entrepreneurs, government and military officials, laborers, couriers, hikers, sailors, farmers, and their families. Infrastructures began to develop in response to the increase in traffic, as post offices, inns, stage lines, and customs houses were established.

Recreational: Hunting, fishing, and camping are the main attractions, but whitewater rafting in this area of Maine is a thrill throughout the summer and fall. Winter offers the solace of silent trails or the invigoration of a lengthy snowmobile ride to distant towns and Canada.

Traditional sporting camps are plentiful and provide unique experiences in rustic accommodations. Hotels in Solon, Bingham, Caratunk, The Forks, West Forks, and Jackman provide lodging

through festivals that honor French music and traditions. Because many of the French continued south to what is now Louisiana, both old French and Creole music are often celebrated in the area.

Historical: The Canada Road served as the primary link between Lower Canada and Maine from about 1820 to 1860. The various east–west linkages, as well as the southern connections that allowed detours off the Canada Road, throughout the year.

Camping is available at a number of isolated public sites and private campgrounds, many near some of Maine's beautiful lakes and ponds. Canoeing is enjoyed on numerous lakes, ponds, bogs, and rivers. Enjoy birding from the serenity of a canoe floating in the lake. Drop your line in the water to lure tasty brook trout. Travel by canoe to untracked shores. For a unique experience to remember, visitors can enjoy the Moose River Bow Trip, a three- or four-day canoe or kayak trip of the Moose River that starts and ends at Attean Pond near Jackman.

The Appalachian Trail, one of the most famous multistate hiking trails in the United States, crosses the byway in Caratunk. The trail's 270-mile terrain throughout Maine is considered some of the most difficult of the 14 states the trail runs through, but the scenery is breathtaking. This rugged trail takes hikers through waist-high bogs, up steep inclines, and across the Kennebec River, which can only be crossed by ferry.

Highlights:

The byway starts where Route 151 intersects with U.S. 201 north of the town of Lakewood and ends near the Canadian border.

Solon and Bingham: Drive north on U.S. 201, which passes through two old-time villages, Solon and Bingham. Both are bounded on the west by the Kennebec River. Solon has wintertime snowmobiling trails.

Wyman Lake: Just north of Bingham is 13-mile-long Wyman Lake, a fishing hot spot for perch, bass, and sunfish. In January, there's ice fishing for land-locked salmon and trout.

Appalachian Trail: Farther north, the 2,160-mile-long Appalachian Trail crosses the byway at Caratunk. While the trail runs from Maine all the way to Georgia, day hikes are popular through the rugged terrain here. To cross the Kennebec River at Caratunk, hikers can use a free ferry service that runs from late May to mid-October.

Kennebec and Dead Rivers: Continuing north, the Kennebec River meets the Dead River at The Forks. Both rivers offer thrilling whitewater rafting. The Kennebec heads through remote wilderness and the beautiful Kennebec River Gorge and produces huge roller-coaster waves, with many class IV or higher rapids along 12-mile runs. Along the route, watch for

deer, river otters, and eagles. In late spring and early fall, the Dead River has the longest continuous class III–IV white water in New England. It offers milder rapids for much of the summer.

Moxie Falls: Also from The Forks, a short drive and less than a mile walk leads through the pines to the 90-foot-high Moxie Falls, which makes a nice picnic spot. From U.S. 201, turn east onto Lake Moxie Road and follow it to the sign-posted trailhead for the waterfall.

Jackman: North of The Forks, the Jackman area is a recreational mecca. In winter, a huge network of snowmobile trails includes thousands of miles of groomed crisscrossing trails leading up to Canada and across to New Hampshire.

An eagle's-eye view shows the Old Canada Road snaking its way between the Kennebec River and quaint villages.

Rangeley Lakes Scenic Byway

Wind through the western mountains of Maine on the Rangeley Lakes Scenic Byway. Trail your way through richly wooded forests, brisk mountain streams, farm fields, and a chain of lakes and ponds. Nature is all around you!

The Rangeley Lakes Region, the byway's namesake, was settled by a small number of hardy pioneers in the early 1800s. Rugged and remote, this region grew slowly, while sustaining about a dozen family farms and lumber mills throughout the first half of the century. In the 1860s, the small community began to change when vacationers from cities along the Eastern Seaboard discovered 10- to 12-pound brook trout swimming in the region's pristine waters. As word spread about the unparalleled fishing and the unspoiled beauty of the region, large numbers of anglers and their families began an annual trek to the region. By 1925, the Rangeley region had become a premier destination resort area that attracted visitors, as well as a host of U.S. Presidents, from all corners of the nation.

Today the region's cultural history and outstanding scenic, natural, and recreational resources offer local residents and visitors an array of activities that extend throughout the year. During the summer months, treat yourself to a host of festivals, concerts, and museums as well as boating, hiking, fishing, bicycling, and wildlife watching. When autumn paints the hillsides in red and gold, come enjoy leaf watching, hiking, and hunting in the crisp Maine air. A cup of fresh squeezed cider from the Apple

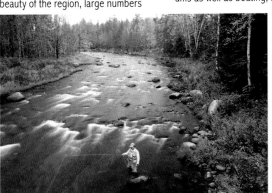

Excellent fly-fishing attracts people to the scenic Kennebago River. Nearby trails provide ample opportunities for hiking and wildlife viewing.

Festival, a tour of the Wilhelm Reich Museum, or a drive along the bronzed byway will round out your autumn day in Rangeley. Winter arrives early, cloaking the region in 12 feet of snow. Between Christmas fairs, concerts, and the annual Snodeo festival, join skiers, snowmobilers, and ice skaters and take to the slopes, trails, and lakes. Then, as temperatures rise and the days increase in length, spring ushers in the annual "ice out contest."

Cultural: Responding to the sudden flood of anglers (or "sports" as they were affectionately called) in the late 1800s, the local residents built rustic sporting cabins along the shores of the region's lakes. Equipped with beds, gas lamps, and fireplaces, these simple but comfortable structures offered a welcome alternative to a lumpy bedroll and canvas tent.

With an intimate knowledge of the lakes, the locals acted as guides, using the famed Rangeley Boat to row their clients to the best fishing holes in the region. Equally adept with a skillet and a campfire, the guides treated the sports to lakeside dinners of fresh trout, locally grown vegetables, and hefty mugs of coffee. The tradition of sporting cabins and guiding continues today, as anglers cast for the "speckled beauties" throughout spring and summer months.

Over the years, technological advances slowly replaced the handsaws, oxen teams, and axes. As a result, the physical demands of the job were reduced while the overall productivity was increased. Today the highly advanced mechanical harvester and 18-wheeler have replaced the double-bladed axe and river drive. Two-person crews have replaced the lumber camp and the storytelling, joking, and camaraderie that rose among the fallen trees as the loggers labored through the frigid winter months toward a common goal. Fortunately this unique story of the industry and the changing cultural landscape has been preserved at the Rangeley Lakes Logging Museum. Open on weekends in the summer, the muse-um captures the past and brings it forward to the future to be relived a few hours at a time.

Historical: Long before settlement of the region by pioneers from the south, two Native American nations made the lakes area their home during the warmest months of the year. The St. Francis nation from the north and the Abenakis from the south hunted game and fished for trout in the many lakes and rivers. Archae-ologists have uncovered evidence of campsites and arrowheads near the outlet of Rangeley Lake indicating that this was one of their favorite sites to spend the summer.

The region was first "discovered" by British lieutenant John Montresor in 1760. However, it was not until 1794 that the region, as part of the Common-wealth of Massachusetts, was surveyed and mapped.

In 1796, four investors, including Philadelphian James Rangeley, Sr., pur-chased nearly 31,000 acres of land in the western mountains for timber and mineral rights. However, it was nearly 26 years before any of the owners set foot on their land. In 1817, Luther Hoar and his family of eight established the region's first substantial and permanent settlement. The following year, two other families settled near the lake. When James Rangeley, Sr., died, his son inherited the land and bought out the remaining partners. James, Jr., and his family decided to make this wild place their home. Only 12 years later, the area was officially renamed Range-ley, and by 1840 the population had increased to 39 families.

In the 1880s, the region was prominently featured at several National Sporting Expositions, as well as in newspapers up and down the East Coast. As a result, outdoor enthusiasts arrived in throngs, and by 1900 there were more than 200 fishing guides in the area. The state's most famous and first registered Maine guide was Cornelia "Fly Rod" Crosby. Certified by the state in 1898, Crosby was not only a superb angler, but also the individual who first pioneered and promoted the now fashionable policy of "catch and release" and the adoption of fishing seasons.

By 1909, the population had swollen from a mere 238 in 1860 to nearly 1,400. The region boasted a number of five-star resorts and sporting camps, among them the Mooselookmeguntic House, Rangeley Lake House, and Grant's Kennebago Camps. A number of wealthy and influential families from New York, Philadelphia, and Boston owned many of the private camps, and the late 1920s and '30s became known as the "Golden Age." Entire families boarded trains to escape the heat and smog of the big cities for a summer of leisure and sport at their favorite resort. Upon arrival they were treated to exquisite dining, ballroom dancing, golf, casino gambling, moonlight boat rides, and a "Boston orchestra."

Following the outbreak of World War II, the travel and leisure habits of the nation changed. Reservations at the grand hotels declined dramatically, and by 1958, the famed Rangeley Lake House was razed. Fortunately, Rangeley is able to adapt to the changing demands of vacationers, and today is an extremely popular summer resort and summer home destination. Several historic sporting camps are still thriving as public resorts for outdoor recreationalists, and the more-than-90-year-old Rangeley Inn (once part of the Rangeley Lake House) continues to stand as a testament to the grand Hotel Era.

Recreational: Blessed with an abundance of natural resources, the Rangeley region provides four seasons of recreational treats. During the summer, this region comes alive with activities such as Fourth of July picnics and fireworks, blueberry and logging festivals, auctions, concerts, and stage performances.

Fall attracts many travelers because of the brilliant foliage and is a great time to hike. Since 1933, the famous Appalachian Trail has crossed both Routes 4 and 17 and leads to many of the region's highest peaks. A strenuous, but very rewarding, hike is along the trail northward to the summit of Saddleback Mountain. This hike is ten miles roundtrip and offers exceptional scenery along the way. Hikers should be prepared for sudden shifts in weather and high winds

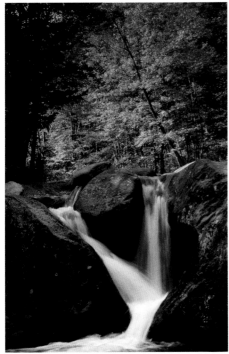

Water cascading from high ledges and a rest area with hiking trails and picnic tables make Small's Falls popular.

that rake the open ridgeline. An easier hike is the one-mile trek to Bald Mountain. The trailhead is a mile south of Haines Landing on Bald Mountain Road in the picturesque village of Oquossoc. A viewing platform at the peak offers spectacular 360-degree views of Mooselookmeguntic Lake, Rangeley Lake, Gull Pond, and Richardson Pond.

Spring and winter in Rangeley blend together until mid-April, allowing snow sport enthusiasts to play for a month longer than their neighbors to the south. When the ice finally goes out on the lakes and the green buds begin to swell on the trees, Rangeley's famous fishing season kicks into high gear.

Highlights:

The byway begins on Route 4 just west of the town of Madrid. Alternatively, you can start at the opposite end of the byway, which starts on Route 17 a few miles north of the town of Byron. If so, simply reverse the order of this itinerary.

Small's Falls: Start at Small's Falls, a waterfall and roadside picnic area on Route 4. The 54-foot waterfall has swimming and wading pools at the bottom, with rock waterslides.

Sandy River: The cliff-lined Sandy River begins at Small's Falls and runs west alongside the byway, with put-ins for canoes. The section of the river from Small's Falls to Phillips (15 miles) has class I–III rapids, best suited to expert canoeists when water flows high in the spring.

Appalachian Trail: The rugged Appalachian Trail, which runs more than 2,000 miles from Maine south to Georgia and provides access to many of the area's mountain peaks, crosses Route 4 near Piazza Rock, an enormous, overhanging ledge. The rock may be accessed via a clearly marked side trail near the Appalachian Trail.

Rangeley Lake: The byway skirts the eastern shores of Rangeley Lake, which has boat launch sites, camping, and good fishing (for landlocked salmon and brook trout) before entering the lakeside village of Rangeley, a center for outdoor sports.

Wilhelm Reich Museum: About three miles west of Rangeley on Route 4 is the Wilhelm Reich Museum, devoted to the controversial Austrian psychotherapist and scientist who had a home and laboratory here.

Mooselookmeguntic Lake: At Oquossoc, turn south onto Route 17 and follow it along Mooselookmeguntic

Rangeley Village and Haley Pond are in the foreground of this aerial view, while on the far side of the village Rangeley Lake stretches out.

Lake (an Indian word meaning "portage to the moose feeding place"), Maine's second largest. The lake is known for fishing, hiking trails, campsites, and great scenery.

Height of Land: Just southeast of Mooselookmeguntic is the Height of Land, considered one of the top scenic overlooks in all of New England, with views of the lake, forests, and mountains. The Appalachian Trail crosses the byway again here.

Swift River: The byway ends north of Byron. Accessed from Byron, the Swift River offers another good challenge for experienced canoeists (with class I–III white water) and is known for its scenic, natural, and recreational splendor.

Schoodic Scenic Byway

This little traveled stretch of Route 1 runs along the far, eastern rim of French-man Bay, with spectacular views back across the water to Mount Desert's mountains. Follow the Bay down the Schoodic Peninsula, through Winter Harbor to the open ocean at Schoodic Point, known for a great view of the high waves.

Looking for the "real" Maine? Flee tourist attractions and national chains, and come here, to a landscape and lifestyle that residents want to preserve and you will want to experience. Wake from a good night's sleep at a historic bed-and-breakfast and spend the day lobstering, clamming, and picking blueberries, and walking in vast timberland. Stop and shop at small shops and yard sales where local artisans and craftspeople sell their wares.

Nature and scenery along the byway match its cultural heritage for richness and beauty. As you travel this route, look sea- and skyward for glimpses of soaring animal life. Ducks, eagles, and osprey are plentiful near the many lakes, rivers, and coastlines along the byway. View gorgeous landscapes of mountains, islands, and fields of blueberries and wildflowers, historic buildings and lighthouses. Discover one of the last frontiers of the eastern seaboard on the Schoodic Scenic Byway.

Cultural: This region of Maine is unique because of its local Downeast culture. The term Downeast has been around for a long time. Years ago, when sailors hauled cargo to the northeast of New England the prevailing wind came from the southwest, pushing their schooners downwind in an easterly direction. While other areas of the state market this idiom, they fail to capture the essence of real

Maine living. The true Downeast Maine is an untouched jewel. The people of Maine, true Mainers (pronounced "May-nuhs"), want to keep their treasure a secret. Consequently, only the adventurous have stumbled upon the delights tucked away in the jagged coastline around the Schoodic Peninsula. The people of this area really do make a living off the sea and work primarily as anglers, shipbuilders, seafarers, and tradespeople. They only farm as a supplement to these other businesses and occupations.

The Schoodic Scenic Byway provides visitors with a beautiful way to explore the Downeast countryside. Take time to enjoy the many festivals and activities. Winter Harbor is a busy fishing port where a lobster festival is held every August with lobster boat races and

Mount Desert Island is home to Acadia National Park where this cobblestone arched bridge blends perfectly with the stunning scenery.

good food. Schoodic Arts for All, a group of local artists and community members, features a number of different activities such as the community steel band, traditional old-time string-band music, dancing, and more. Locally produced goods made by artisans and crafters are sold through small shops and yard sales year-round. Downeast clam bakes and lobster festivals are true traditions in this area, as well as summer "coasting" on a schooner.

Historical: The earliest Europeans here may have been the Vikings who briefly visited about a thousand years ago. The first documented visits were those of Portuguese, English, Spanish, and French explorers who mapped the coast in the early 1500s. Frenchman Bay, between Mount Desert Island and Gouldsboro Peninsula, got its name when English sailors saw (and avoided) a French man-of-war moored there.

Settlers from southern Maine, New Hampshire, and Massachusetts began moving into this area to harvest trees that were turned into lumber and shipped to Boston. During the 1880s, John G. Moore, a wealthy New Yorker from Steuben, Maine, purchased most of the land on Schoodic. In 1897, he put in a road and welcomed the public to visit. After Moore's death, the land eventually passed to George B. Dorr, a conserva-

tionist, who donated it to the Interior Department as an addition to Acadia National Park.

Recreational: The Schoodic Peninsula has plenty of recreational opportunities. Recreation varies from outdoor activities, such as hiking and walking, to browsing through galleries. There are also three picnic areas along the byway that provide access for sea kayaking and tidal pool combing. Bicycling is very popular

around Schoodic Point Road. The drive along the byway is recreation itself, with wonderful views that provide places for sightseeing and contemplation.

The easygoing Schoodic Head Trail takes travelers through striking landscape. Stands of northern white cedar, red and white spruce, paper birch, and jack pine tower over the rocky terrain. Vibrant green patchworks of a myriad of moss species meander across the pink granite boulders. Lichen patterns of silver and purple adorn rocks along the banks of the stream that parallels the trail. Charming small pools and miniature waterfalls gurgle above the sound of the crashing surf on the point. Schoodic Head Trail brings visitors onto a dirt road that connects with the Alder Trail, a southeasterly trail favored by woodcocks, spruce grouse, chickadees, and many small song birds. The Alder Trail takes travelers back to the Park Loop Road.

The Schoodic Peninsula offers biking enthusiasts an enjoyable 13-to 29-mile ride, depending on how far the visitor wants to go. The loop meanders through picturesque fishing villages and along a dramatic section of rocky shoreline. A short side trip to the fishing village of Corea is only six miles out and well worth the trip. Other side trips include a shorter ride to Lighthouse Point just 1/2 mile off of the main ride.

Highlights:

The byway begins at the west end of the Hancock–Sullivan Bridge about eight miles east of the village of Hancock on U.S. 1. It's best to start at this end of the byway because the most scenic stretch, which runs through a section of Acadia National Park, runs one way going west to east.

Sullivan: At West Sullivan, follow U.S. 1 east along the upper reaches of Frenchman Bay to Sullivan. Sullivan has Downeast-style architecture set around a central common with outstanding views south to Frenchman Bay and Mount Desert Island (site of the main section of Acadia National Park near Bar Harbor).

Winter Harbor: Just west of the town of West Gouldsboro, take Route 186 south, passing through South Gouldsboro and the resort town of Winter Harbor, where there are lodgings and restaurants.

Acadia National Park: East of Winter Harbor, go south onto Moore Road, which leads to the Schoodic Peninsula and the mostly undeveloped Schoodic section of Acadia National Park. The one-way Schoodic Drive then leads a bit more than seven miles along the park shoreline. Watch for deer, moose, seals, eagles, ospreys, herons—and bicyclists—along the way.

Frazer Point Picnic Area: After entering the park, the first turnout is for the Frazer Point Picnic Area, which features barbecue and picnic facilities with scenic views of Winter Harbor and its nearby islands, coves, and rocky beaches.

Winter Harbor Lighthouse: Continuing down the one-way road, watch to the west for Mark Island and the 1856 Winter Harbor Lighthouse. With Mount Desert Island's Cadillac Mountain rising in the background, it's considered the most photogenic lighthouse along the byway.

Schoodic Point: At Schoodic Point, the southernmost tip of the peninsula, Atlantic Ocean waves crash to the shore against granite rocks. The pounding surf can sometimes reach heights of 50 feet.

Blueberry Hill: A mile northeast of Schoodic Point, stop at Blueberry Hill to picnic, hike, and take pictures of offshore islands. This is one of the best vantage points for viewing 123-foot Petit Manan Lighthouse, Maine's second tallest, which dates from 1817.

The southern tip of Schoodic Point has massive granite outcroppings and pounding surf.

Kancamagus Scenic Byway

An east–west shortcut through the heart of White Mountains National Forest, Kancamagus Scenic Byway accesses otherwise remote waterfalls, swimming holes, hiking trails, and campgrounds.

Enjoy what many consider one of the top fall foliage trips in the world when you drive the Kancamagus Scenic Byway. Undoubtedly one of the most scenic routes through the White Mountains of New Hampshire, the "Kanc," as locals call it, climbs to nearly 3,000 feet on the flank of Mount Kancamagus. You can meander through beautiful forests, follow old logging roads, and cross American Indian hunting paths. In the fall, these woods yield a stunning array of colors that underscore the area's great natural beauty. Be sure to take the time to pull off the road and enjoy the hiking trails, waterfalls, and scenic overlooks this byway offers.

On the eastern section of the byway, you can visit the Rocky Gorge Scenic Area, and see where the Swift River has, over time, worn a narrow cleft through solid stone. Here you can appreciate nature's handiwork at its best while you wander through the woods and over the gorge to lovely Falls Pond.

The Kancamagus Scenic Byway was named for an early Indian Chief of the Penacook Confederacy. Called "The Fearless One," Chief Kancamagus tried to keep the peace between his people and the white settlers. However, repeated harassment by the English ended his efforts, bringing war and bloodshed. In the early 1690s, Kancamagus and his followers moved to northern New Hampshire and Canada.

Cultural: The first thing someone might say when describing this area's culture is that it is simply "New England." It can be generalized that the people of the area are peaceful, high-class, old-fashioned, friendly, and that they savor the simpler pleasures of life. Here are a few details, presented in a chance fashion, as one would discover them if they were actually traveling the byway: The area's people cherish their historic homes which are nestled in the quiet and stately White Mountains; they restore and keep well

The Albany Covered Bridge, built in 1858, is a Paddleford truss style with added arches. It spans the scenic Swift River.

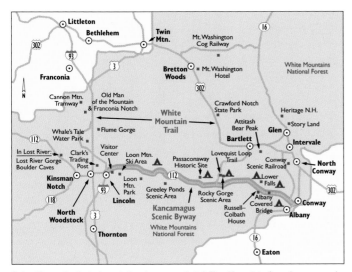

their whitewashed, clapboard churches and farmhouses; they enjoy their several local festivals and events; and they stroll unhurried on their tree-lined main streets, browsing leisurely among the specialty shops. And, perhaps, after a day of farming or logging (or maybe even after a "hard" day of skiing or backpacking, if they're on holiday), they might stop in to see a show at their town's old-fashioned movie theater, or have a superb meal at one of the old "grand hotels" of which they're so proud. And you really get the feeling while you're on this byway that you're welcomed just like any other returning guest at The Balsams (one of the area's famous and historic "grand

hotels"): with a pint of maple syrup and "welcome back" note.

Historical: The town of Passaconaway, settled in about 1790, is named after Passaconaway, who, in 1627, united more than 17 central New England nations into the Penacook Confederacy. The byway was named for his grandson, a great chief of this Confederacy, Kancamagus. Both Passaconaway and Kancamagus also have mountains named after them.

More recent history can be found at the Russell–Colbath House, the only remaining 19th-century homestead in the area. (It is now a U.S. Forest Service

information center.) The name memorializes the house builders and Ruth Colbath who, on a fall day in 1891, was told by her husband Thomas that he would be going out for a "little while"—which turned out to be 42 years. Every night during those years, Ruth placed a lamp in the window to welcome her husband. When he finally returned in 1933, Ruth had died, and the property had been sold. It is not known why her husband was gone so long.

Recreational: Hiking, snowshoeing, backpacking, and cross-country skiing are the most popular activities on this route. This forest's hundreds of miles of such trails range from easy family jaunts to some of the nation's most famous and challenging excursions. Some of these trails have great fishing.

An example of a very easy hike is the Rail 'n' River Trail, which is a flat, one mile round-trip along the river. It is wheelchair and stroller accessible, and you get to it from the Russell–Colbath House. For something a little more difficult, there's the Greeley Ponds Trail, which is about five miles long and features two ponds, the Upper Greeley Pond (dark aqua-green, and surrounded by old growth timber and towering cliffs) and the Lower Greeley Pond (shallow and more typical of a beaver pond). Both ponds offer trout fishing and an enjoyable place to have a picnic lunch. Find the Greeley Ponds trailhead nine miles east of exit 32 on I-93. A difficult hike is the four-mile trail to the summit of 2,660-foot Mount Potash. This trail hikes along somewhat dangerous cliffs, but it affords excellent, panoramic views of the Swift River Valley and the surrounding mountains (the trailhead is 13 miles west of the Saco Ranger Station).

Highlights:

Aside from the incredible scenery of the White Mountains National Forest, this itinerary highlights things to see and do for the entire family along the Kancamagus Scenic Byway.

Lost River Gorge and Boulder Caves:
Beginning in the town of North Woodstock, the Lost River Gorge and Boulder Caves invites visitors to, indeed, find the Lost River, as it seems to play hide-and-seek, meandering in and out of the granite outcroppings of Kinsman Notch. Boardwalks give easy access into most areas, or slightly more strenuous trails are available to lead adventurers into caves, as well as along the gorge and into the Nature Garden at the end of the self-guided tour.

Clark's Trading Post:
Clark's Trading Post at the western edge of the Kancamagus Scenic Byway near Lincoln isn't quite what the fur traders of frontier days would recognize, but it has got a history and tradition all its own and is certainly a must-see along the byway. Run by the Clark family as a roadside attraction since 1928, highlights of Clark's Trading Post include the trained black bear show, the Seiranian Family Circus, bumper boats, a climbing wall, several historical displays and museums, and the White Mountain Central Railroad.

Loon Mountain:
Just east of Lincoln, Loon Mountain adventures await. Gondola rides to the summit give a bird's-eye view of the entire area and surrounding mountains. Once at the summit more adventures begin, including exploring glacial caves, hiking an interpreted nature trail, visiting with local artisans as they create their wares, and climbing a four-story observation tower to behold some of the most sublime scenery you will ever see.

Passaconaway Historic Site:
The early days of the mountain lifestyle can be studied at the Russell–Colbath House just 12 miles west of Conway at the Passaconaway Historic Site. Built in the early 1800s, it is the area's only

Rocky Gorge has been managed for the safeguarding of its scenic features ever since its designation as a Natural Scenic Area in 1937.

remaining 19th-century homestead. Furnished as it would have been in the early days, the home is listed on the National Register of Historic Places. The U.S. Forest Service also has an information center located here, and the Rail 'n' River Hike is an easy half-mile trail that begins at the historic home.

Rocky Gorge Scenic Area and Lovequist Loop Trail:
Three miles east of the Passaconaway Historic Site is Rocky Gorge Scenic Area and Lovequist Loop Trail. The superb scenic quality of Rocky Gorge has been preserved ever since its designation as a National Scenic Area in 1937. An impressive waterfall, the narrow gorge, and an easy walking trail around Falls Pond make this the perfect place to relax and enjoy the natural serenity.

White Mountain Trail

This is the historic tourist trail through the White Mountains, accessing resort towns and a variety of ways to waterfalls, woodland trails, and mountain peaks.

Take a drive through a landscape unspoiled by overdevelopment when you travel the White Mountain Trail of New Hampshire. Enjoy the uninterrupted mountain and river views, wetlands, and woodlands that captured the imagination of writer Nathaniel Hawthorne and inspired landscape artist Thomas Cole. Despite the passage of time since the days of Hawthorne and Cole, this rural New England area remains beautiful.

Silver Cascade Falls in Crawford Notch State Park is easily accessible just off Route 302.

Take time to discover the history of the White Mountain Trail. Parts of it have been used for centuries, as attested by the charming 18th- and 19th-century buildings you will see along the way. The railroad also helped to shape this area and made possible the lumber industry, which spurred the development of many towns in the region, such as Bartlett, Conway, and North Conway. Be sure not to miss the amazing Frankenstein Trestle, which supports railroad tracks below the cliff in Crawford Notch.

Toward the beginning of the 20th century, the creation of the national forests coincided with the dawning of the automobile age, assuring Americans an opportunity to vacation a world away from the "citied world," yet within driving distance of the great Eastern cities. Since then, recreational pursuits enjoyed here have grown from hiking, fishing, and sightseeing to include downhill and cross-country skiing, camping, mountain biking, leaf-peeping, and antique hunting. You can also enjoy just about anything "outdoorsy" under these towering granite cliffs and soaring mountains.

Quick Facts

Length: 108 miles

Time to Allow: 3 hours

Consideration: The White Mountain Trail can safely and conveniently accommodate two-wheel-drive vehicles with standard clearance. It is also safe for tour bus travel. Except for Bear Notch Road, the highway is maintained year-round, including snow plowing during the winter months. There are several safety hazards relating to winter driving conditions due to winter storms, collision of vehicles with moose, and improper parking along the highways. Although moose present one of the most exciting viewing opportunities along the highway, they can cause traffic control and safety problems as people stop to view and take pictures.

Cultural: The influx of tourism and the development of the lumber industry spurred the development of many towns throughout this region. The history of this growth is found in the historic structures that remain in towns such as Bartlett, Conway, and North Conway. Along the trail there are numerous sites that are already on the National Register of Historic Places or are eligible to be placed on this National Register. These sites represent a range of different cultures and time periods. Examples include the Mount Washington Hotel, the Abenaki Indian Shop and Camp, the Crawford House Artist's Studio, and the North Conway Depot and Railroad Yard.

Historical: There are many historical events associated with the White Mountain Trail. Some of these events include the creation of towns, villages, national forests, resorts, hotels, and the railroad.

The White Mountains were originally home to the Abenakis and other Native Americans. At the beginning of the 19th century, the White Mountains were a place for artists and others. The White Mountain School of Art was a group of landscape painters that included Thomas Cole, Benjamin Champney, and Frank Shapleigh. Also during this era, Nathaniel Hawthorne and Reverend Thomas Starr King captured readers' imaginations with tales of the White Mountains.

By 1891, Crawford Railroad Station stood at the top of Crawford Notch. This railroad was a magnificent feat of engineering given the region's terrain, climate, and isolation. The Frankenstein

Trestle, which supports railroad tracks below the cliff in Crawford Notch, still makes observers gasp!

As access to the White Mountains improved, a series of ever-grander inns, hotels, and resorts was constructed to meet the needs of an increasingly affluent clientele. The most elegant of these, the Mount Washington Hotel, was the setting of the historic Bretton Woods Monetary Conference in 1944. It was at this conference where the dollar was set as the standard of international currency, earning the hotel a place on the list of National Historic Landmarks. This event, combined with the hotel's spectacular setting, contributed to its success as a thriving resort and stunning landmark.

The 1923 demise of another grand hotel, the Profile House, and the subsequent sale of its land to the Society for the Protection of the New Hampshire Forests and the State of New Hampshire, resulted in the creation of Franconia Notch State Park. More than 15,000 people, including children, contributed funds to make this purchase possible.

Recreational: There are plenty of places to hike, fish, sightsee, downhill and cross-country ski, camp, and mountain bike along the White Mountain Trail. Hiking trailheads dominate the roadway on both sides. There are great hiking trails for families, day hikers, and back-packers. The Crawford Path is the oldest (1819) continually maintained footpath in the United States. Twenty 4,000-foot mountains are located along this byway as well.

Fly-fishers can find heaven if they hike a bit to mountain lakes and streams. This wilderness also offers some of the most breathtaking ski slopes in the East.

Highlights:

Rambling through the White Mountains National Forest and connecting at each end of the Kancamagus Scenic Highway, the White Mountain Trail has an abundance of things to see and do, a few of which are highlighted below.

Clark's Trading Post: For more than 70 years, the Clark family has entertained visitors at Clark's Trading Post. At this site they have a museum, a fire station, a steam locomotive, and trained black bears.

Franconia Notch State Park:

Franconia Notch State Park is home of Old Man of the Mountain Historic Site, Cannon Mountain, New England Ski Museum, and Flume Gorge. Also in the park are the Basin waterfall, the Cannon Mountain Aerial Tram taking visitors to the 4,180-foot summit of the mountain, recreation trails, and Lafayette campground. Be sure to stop by the visitor center at Flume Gorge for a 15-minute film, maps, and interpretive exhibits.

The Rocks Estate: Located off Route 302, The Rocks Estate just outside Bethlehem is a historic working Christmas tree farm owned and operated by the Society for the Protection of New Hampshire Forests. Picnic areas, six miles of self-guided scenic and educational trails, and 55,000 Christmas trees make this a unique place to visit year-round.

Mount Washington Cog Railway: For a truly unforgettable way to ascend Mount Washington, try the world's first mountain-climbing cog railway. On especially clear days the vista from the summit allows for glimpses of four states, the Canadian province of Quebec, and the Atlantic Ocean. A round trip on the historic railway takes about three hours and allows for a 20-minute stop at the summit.

Mount Washington Observatory and Museum: Mount Washington Observatory and Museum, located at the summit of the mountain, is accessible by the Mount Washington Cog Railway, the Mount Washington Auto Road, or via several trails in the area. Definitely a must-see, the museum features displays about the brutal meteorological conditions on Mount Washington, exhibits on the geological history of the Presidential Range, and a unique presentation of alpine flowers that have been preserved in synthetic resin.

Glen: The village of Glen has two attractions side-by-side geared to families with young children. Story Land, a vintage theme park, opened in 1954 with a fairy-tale theme. Those who visited as children in the early days of the park are now returning with their kids and grandkids and still finding the theme park as enchanting as they remembered.

The steam-powered Mount Washington Cog Railway has been taking passengers to the summit since 1869.

Smugglers' Notch

Vermont's most dramatic road winds up from Stowe, the state's most famous resort village, and over a shoulder of Mount Mansfield, its highest mountain. Scenic pull-offs invite access to rock formations and hiking trails.

Native Americans traced the path over this high pass, but its name dates from use during the War of 1812 as a supply line to the British army in Canada, which happened to be fighting the U.S. Army at the time. In 1807, President Thomas Jefferson had imposed an embargo against trade from Canada, a hardship for Northern Vermonters for whom Montreal was a prime market. The first carriage road through the pass wasn't opened until 1894, and the present Route 108 dates from 1910. It was improved in 1922 in time for Prohibition, during which "Smugglers' Notch" took on new meaning, this time with contra-band flowing south from Canada.

Route 108 links Stowe with a town north of the notch that's called Jeffersonville after President Jefferson. In Stowe, where most travelers begin, it's known as "The Mountain Road."

Smugglers' Notch has been consid-ered a State Scenic Road since 1978 under the Vermont Scenic Roads Law. Breathtaking forests and amazing rock outcroppings beckon visitors to hike through and climb them. Or guests might be just as happy driving and stopping at the numerous pull-offs and just taking in the gorgeous scenery.

Highlights:

Begin your tour in Stowe, and end in Jeffersonville.

Stowe: One of Vermont's oldest and most famous ski towns, Stowe, actually attracts more visitors in summer and fall, luring them out of their cars and onto their feet and bicycles. The Stowe Recreation Path parallels the Mountain Road for its first 5.5 miles, run-ning through cornfields and meadows.

Quick Facts

Length: 18 miles

Time to Allow: One hour

Consideration: The eight-mile stretch within Mount Mansfield State Forest that's officially a state scenic road is closed December through mid-May, when it's reliably snow-covered and popular with cross-country skiers.

There are two Moss Glen Falls in Ver-mont: One is in Stowe, and the other is near Granville. Be sure to visit the one on this route in Stowe.

The alpine tundra atop the summit of Mount Mansfield offers a command-ing view of Mount Mansfield State Forest.

Mount Mansfield: Since the mid-19th century locals have been enticing visitors up to the heights of Mount Mansfield, a distinctive mountain with a series of peaks resembling the upturned profile of a man's face. Mount Mansfield is the highest point in Vermont. In 1858 an inn was built under "The Nose," along with an amazingly steep access road (now a ski trail in winter). The inn is long gone, but in summer and fall this toll road is still a local attraction, along with Stowe Mountain Resort's eight-passenger gondola that operates, weather permitting, to the Cliff House, a ski station with a view down the narrow valley to the east. It's still, however, a half-hour trek below "The Chin," a peak that on a clear day offers a truly spectacular view west across the Champlain Valley to the Adirondack Mountains.

Mount Mansfield State Forest: For its first seven miles Route 108 is lined with lodging places, shops, and restaurants but beyond the turnoff to the toll road and then the gondola, the road enters the Mount Mansfield State Forest and steepens to an 18 percent grade. Smugglers' Notch State Park offers tent and trailer campsites.

Big Spring: Beyond this park the full meaning of "Notch" becomes apparent. While the road is paved, it winds around boulders and beneath 1,000-foot high cliffs that hem it down to one-lane.

The turnoff beyond the height-of-land (at 2,161 feet)— with an information booth that's usually staffed in summer and fall—is the obvious place to stop. The Big Spring is here, an ideal brookside site for a picnic (there are even grills). Ask about hiking distances to natural rock formations with names like Elephant Head, King Rock, the (amazing) Hunter and His Dog, and Smugglers' Cave.

Smugglers' Notch Resort: The road continues to wind on for eight miles, down through more cliffs and boulders and just as it straightens and drops through woodland, motorists are startled by a condominium town rising out of the trees. This is Smugglers' Notch Resort, a self-contained and family-geared village. Route 108 continues spiraling downward, finally leveling in the village of Jeffersonville that is a different place than the resort country south of The Notch.

Middlebury Gap

Must-stops on the Middlebury Gap Road (Route 125) include Texas Falls and a wooded walk keyed to poems by Robert Frost, who spent 23 summers in a nearby cabin.

Vermont is a long, thin state, and most of its highways run north/south or take the low, lazy way along rivers. The exceptions are the high roads that cut east/west across the state, climbing up one side of mountain ranges, then plunging down the other. These high mountain passes are generally known in Vermont as "gaps," and cresting gaps is a bit like surfing. The Middlebury Gap is a fine example. It climbs, levels, and then drops down into the next valley.

Highlights:

Begin this route in beautiful Texas Falls, and end in the village of Ripton.

Texas Falls: Pick up Route 125 at its junction in Hancock with Route 100, the scenic old road that runs up the middle of the state. The turnoff for Texas Falls comes so quickly that you may miss it, but don't. A quarter-mile north of the road a series of shoots and pools is rimmed by interesting rock formations, viewed from footbridges.

Long Trail: Route 125 climbs up into Middlebury Gap itself, marked at 2,149 feet in altitude by a sign for the Long Trail, the 255-mile-long trail running high up in the Green Mountains, the spine of the state. You enter the Green Mountain National Forest and seem to be striking deeper into woodland when a big yellow, 1860s hotel suddenly appears.

Robert Frost Wayside Area: Less than a mile west of Bread Loaf the Robert Frost Wayside Area offers picnic tables, grills, and a map of the neighboring Moosalamoo Wilderness Area with its campsites and mountain biking trails.

Robert Frost Interpretive Trail: A bit farther west, past a classic old Vermont cemetery, is the Robert Frost Interpretive Trail. A path leads across the brook and into the pines. The trail is salted with Frost poems.

Ripton: Next comes the small mountain village of Ripton with its white clapboard meetinghouse and post office/general store. Here Route 125 begins its descent, dipping ever-downward along the Middlebury River.

The Green Mountain National Forest follows the backbone of Vermont and is a breathtaking sight no matter what season of the year.

Lakes to Locks Passage

Running along Lake Champlain, east of the Adirondacks, the Lakes to Locks Passage transports visitors through a land rich in old history and new adventures. Come by car, but carry your bike, kayak, or hiking boots.

Driving through the villages and hamlets of Lakes to Locks Passage, travelers are swept into a place of history. State parks and preserves offer hiking trails, lakeside beaches, and wildlife-spotting opportunities. Paralleling Lake Champlain and the Champlain Canal, the byway promises scenic views mixed with plenty of history.

Pre-colonial history is woven throughout the names of places and historic sites. The French explorer Samuel de Champlain named Lake Champlain in 1609. The struggle between nations and people occurred here between the Huron, Algonquin, and Iroquois. During the French and Indian War, the French and British built settlements and fortifications all along the passage. Since then, many changes have moved through the Lakes to Locks Passage, but the natural beauty remains as a constant appeal to new explorers and visitors.

Explorers along the Lakes to Locks Passage travel the road by car, but those who know a little bit about the area bring a bicycle along, too. Lake Champlain Bikeways are known as some of the best cycling roads in the country. But whether you travel by bicycle, on foot, or in the car, all the routes along the byway offer access to unique points of interest.

Cultural: Residents along the Lakes to Locks Passage look at their part of the country as a working land; the seasons harmonize with the agricultural activities that take place along the byway. From sugar in the winter to strawberries in the summer, the land along the passage is continually productive. This productivity began long ago with the Iroquois and Abenaki, who were able to develop strategies of survival there.

With bountiful harvests of fresh-cut hay and ripening tomatoes and gardens, life along the byway is bright and thriving. The people who live and work here enjoy the lakes, rivers, and forests as much as travelers do. During the Industrial Revolution, the rich iron deposits and the forests of the Adirondacks fueled the country. Later, another resource was discovered. Remember that yellow pencil you chewed on in elementary school? Ticonderoga

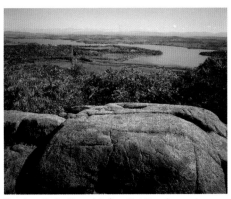

The view of Lake Champlain from Fort Ticonderoga gives little wonder why this location was chosen for a strategic military fortress.

was the name written on the side of the pencil, and it was made from the rich graphite deposits found along the shores of Lake Champlain and Lake George. In fact, the region is known as the paper and pencil capital of America.

Historical: Lakes to Locks is a passage of early American history. From the first Native Americans to the European explorers to the colonists, the geography and history of the land has played an important part in creating a passageway along the corridor that is now a byway. Expeditions and battles have been carried out on its soil. The growth and development of a new nation has also occurred along the byway, making it the well-known passage that it is today. The many historical sites along the byway are evidence that it has always been a land much sought after.

When Samuel de Champlain arrived in the area in 1609, he found people there who loved the land and who struggled for it. The Iroquois were battling with the Algonquins and Hurons, who were joined by the French. As de Champlain explored the area with the Algonquins and Hurons, they reached a beautiful lake with four islands and mountains in the distance. The lake was beautiful and, being the traditional explorer that he was, de Champlain called it "Lake Champlain." Meanwhile, an English sea captain named Henry Hudson anchored his ship in what is now Albany on his journey to find the legendary Northwest Passage to China. His naming of the upper Hudson River through Lake George and Lake Champlain later influenced trade routes and Dutch settlements in the New World. By 1709, the British had settled the southern end of the passage, while the French had settled the northern end. Eventually, this separation determined the boundary of New York and Canada.

The French and Indian War continued for seven years until 1763, when the French ceded Canada to Great Britain. For 15 years, the passageway that is now the Lakes to Locks Passage was under the control of Great Britain, but another war was about to take place. In 1775, American colonists began the Revolutionary War that changed the country forever. The American Navy gathered at the south end of Lake Champlain to delay British invasion. A year later a victory at Saratoga won French support and further control of the area. The battles at Saratoga are now considered the turning point of the Revolutionary War as the rebels gained control and a new country was formed.

A new country meant new growth, and settlements were founded all along the Hudson and Champlain Valleys. But the peace and prosperity were interrupted once again by war. This time, the War of 1812 set the British against the Americans once again. At the end of the war, the border between the United States and Canada was finally drawn, and peace and growth returned to the area. As the nation expanded, road and canal building became important endeavors. The Champlain Canal allowed movement of mineral and timber resources from the Adirondacks throughout New York. Drivers can see the history of a nation in the communities, forts, and battlefields all along the Lakes to Locks Passage.

Recreational: The land that surrounds the Lakes to Locks Passage has

The privately owned Ausable Chasm has numerous rapids, waterfalls, and rock formations for visitors to enjoy.

been a vacation destination since the early 1800s, when it was part of "The Northern Grand Tour." Artists, writers, and the elite of the time would enjoy the scenery on a train ride or from a canal boat. Today, gazing out the car window is only the beginning. The Lakes to Locks Passage is a place for boating, bird-watching, biking, and diving beneath the surface of Lake Champlain. The waterways are the center of recreation here, but even if you don't like the water, you'll find plenty to do.

The sights beneath the surface of Lake Champlain also interest visitors to the byway. America's best collection of freshwater shipwrecks can be found at the bottom of Lake Champlain, and diving is the best way to see them. You can find diving services as well as information on which sites are accessible. The Lake Champlain Underwater Historic Preserve and the Submerged Heritage Preserve are the places to start when searching for an exciting dive. Your dive may even include Champ, the legendary Lake Champlain Monster.

Part of the fun of driving the Lakes to Locks Passage is the variety of landscapes and terrains you pass along the way. Lakesides and forests are accented by historic buildings and quaint towns of America's early days. In the setting of lakes and agricultural countryside, the occasional colonial building or fort can be spotted. Meanwhile, the open valleys and rolling landscape of the passage provide a route for cyclists and visitors.

The passage begins in a place where canals and rivers converge, and then it follows the path of the Champlain Canal where visitors and residents are boating and canoeing. You will definitely want to stop at Fort Ticonderoga and, before you leave, obtain directions to nearby Mount Defiance, where an incredible vista of Lake Champlain, Fort Ticonderoga, and Mount Independence in Vermont are visible. At the north end of Lake Champlain, you can catch glimpses of Valcour Island and drive to Plattsburgh for a historic tour and scenic views of the lake. At Point Au Roche State Park, enjoy the Lake Shore Road that guides you through scenic farmland and views of the northern lake islands in Vermont.

Highlights:

Begin the Lakes to Locks Passage in Waterford, and make your way north to Plattsburgh and Rouses Point.tt

Waterford Historical Museum and Cultural Center: Head north from Troy on Route 4. At the town of Waterford, stop at the Waterford Historical Museum and Cultural Center, located in an 1830 Greek Revival mansion overlooking the Mohawk River and the old Champlain Canal. The museum has exhibits about Waterford, the oldest continually incorporated village in the United States.

Saratoga National Historical Park: About five miles north of the town of Stillwater, watch for Saratoga National Historical Park, site of a 1777 American victory that marked the key turning point of the Revolutionary War. A ten-mile auto tour runs through the battlefield.

Saratoga Springs: To visit the historic resort town of Saratoga Springs, take Route 29 west from Route 4 a few miles farther north. Saratoga Springs is the site of the beautiful Saratoga Race Course, the nation's oldest thoroughbred racetrack, and a public spa where the rich and famous have long taken the waters.

Adirondack Park: Continue north on Route 4 to Route 22 north. Off to the left are the southeastern fringes of 6.1-million-acre Adirondack Park, the largest park in the lower 48 states. The multi-use park covers much of eastern upstate New York, encompassing dozens of towns as well as recreational lands that include 46 mountain peaks more than 4,000 feet high, some 1,000 miles of rivers, and more than 2,500 lakes and ponds. The byway passes near the eastern shores of resort-lined Lake George, and then continues north along the eastern edges of the park for much of the rest of the route.

Fort Ticonderoga and Mount Defiance: Occupying a strategic location at the outlet of Lake George and above the southern tip of Lake Champlain is Fort Ticonderoga, built in 1755 by the French. Americans later captured it from the British in 1775, the first major victory of the Revolutionary War.

Lake Champlain: East of the byway lies Lake Champlain, the sixth largest freshwater lake in the United States. The byway continues along its western shores for most of the rest of the route. The lake is a natural wonderland, ideal for fishing, boating, scuba diving, bird-watching, and bicycling.

Both the British and the French claimed Crown Point in their struggle to dominate North America. Much later the Americans gained control of the location.

Crown Point State Historic Site: Farther north just off Route 9N/22 is Crown Point State Historic Site, where the ruins of two Colonial era forts, St. Frederic and Crown Point, are preserved. They were occupied by a succession of French, British, and American soldiers during the French and Indian and Revolutionary wars.

Ausable Chasm: Continue north (following Routes 22 and 9) to Ausable Chasm, a tourist attraction since 1870. The chasm, more than a mile long and up to 50 feet wide and 200 feet deep, was carved by the Ausable River, which plunges in falls and rapids past sandstone cliffs and huge rock formations. Paths and bridges crisscross and line the chasm, and river rafting trips are available.

Seaway Trail

Following the shores of two Great Lakes and the St. Lawrence Seaway, the ever-scenic Seaway Trail leads to Niagara Falls, the Thousand Islands, historic lighthouses, intriguing museums, and waterside fun in far upstate New York.

Quick Facts

Length: 454 miles

Time to Allow: A four-day tour is the suggested minimum.

Consideration: Parkway through mid-trail prohibits motor coaches without permits. Bicycling is possible in areas where shoulder width allows use.

The Seaway Trail brings the nation's earliest days to life and makes the nation's present days livelier. Follow this 454-mile byway paralleling the St. Lawrence River, Lake Ontario, Niagara River, and Lake Erie and discover historical scenery that is anything but sleepy.

Delight in this drive through naturally scenic landscapes, welcoming harbors, city skylines, and quaint villages. Plan time to pause at fresh fruit and vegetable stands or sample apple pie and the sweetest corn in the country at farmers'

markets, country fairs, and u-pick farms. You'll find festivals from Chautauqua's vineyards to Niagara Falls celebrating every season. Beyond the flavor of the rural community, travelers will find high culture in the cities along the byway as well. Cities such as Rochester and Buffalo offer a myriad of museums and a slew of historic sites.

With some of the world's best year-round sportfishing, anglers looking to catch the big one just may find it along the Seaway Trail. The shores of Lake Ontario and Lake Erie present plenty of options for water recreation. Historic lighthouses also line the trail, creating stops for further exploration. And if you enjoy a picnic in the park, there are many sites to choose from at the state parks lining the byway.

Cultural: The state of New York has been developing its culture for hundreds of years. Cities and towns

Though spanning the border of two countries, the misty thundering waters of Niagara Falls are accessible on the American side from Niagara Falls State Park.

along the Great Lakes and the St. Lawrence River add flavor not only to the Seaway Trail, but to the nation as well. As you travel this National Scenic Byway, spend a night in a cozy bed-and-breakfast, or tour a historical site from the War of 1812. Whatever you do, you will become acquainted with the culture of the Seaway Trail. It is a culture immersed in history and at the cutting edge of change.

The cultures of the Iroquois and the Mohawk leave an intriguing legacy that reflects an America of the past. These cultures can be rediscovered on the Seaway Trail in places like the Seneca Iroquois National Museum in Salamanca or the Akwesasne Cultural Center in Hogansburg. Businesses all along the trail display the crafting of the past in beautiful beadwork, cornhusk dolls,

The Rainbow Bridge straddles the Niagara River connecting Canada (on the left of the photo) and the United States (on the right of the photo).

historic sites significant to the Mormon Church. These cultures have been mixing over the years to form the diversity of festivals and monuments along the trail today.

and silversmithing. The presence of these cultures is also apparent in their seasonal festivals and powwows.

Eventually, these cultures mixed in with the British and the French as they arrived to stake their claim in the New World. The roots of these lasting European influences are commemorated at Old Fort Niagara as well as many other historic sites. As the country opened up to other European cultures, Italian and Greek immigrants made their way to New York as well. Their mark can be seen in the Old World architecture and woodcarvings in towns along the way. The cultures of a few religions also have roots on the Seaway Trail. Travelers on the trail will be able to visit Amish farms, remnants of Shaker heritage, or

One of the best places to experience the culture of the Seaway Trail is in the local restaurants and bed-and-breakfasts. Here, you will discover an old-fashioned hospitality that has been preserved and handed down from eras that came before. In the towns and the cities on the trail, historic buildings have been converted to places to rest and enjoy the local cuisine. The people of the Seaway Trail are just waiting to share their heritage in their architecture and their recipes.

Historical: Sea captains and military captains have created legacies along the Seaway Trail. Their stories are told, sometimes recreated, and sometimes only imagined all along the byway in the 42 different historic sites. Learn about

the history of the war that inspired the "Star-Spangled Banner." Many sites from the War of 1812 are located all along the byway and marked for visitor convenience. Quiet towns along the way offer a portal into the past where sea captains built their homes and simple businesspeople lived and worked. Visit America's oldest freshwater port in Oswego, and see if you can spot all 28 lighthouses located along the way. The ghosts of a maritime culture still haunt this byway.

Old forts and battle structures still remain all along the byway, one of which is Old Fort Niagara. This fort is located close to the famous falls of the same name and boasts 300 years of history of being passed from the French to the British and finally, to the Americans. As a gateway to the Great Lakes, the St. Lawrence River, and thus, the interior of the country, the Fort was situated in an extremely strategic position. As a result, it has a colorful history of battles and wars. Travelers will encounter a different world as they step through the gates of the fort. Soldiers and townspeople "from" 300 years ago are roaming about the area, ready to explain a black-powder rifle or the history of a battle.

Other structures along the byway leave more a sensation of mystery than of history. Visit Boldt Castle of the Thousand Island Region for a glimpse of true love and tragedy at the turn of the 20th century. The magnificent stone structures located in this area will transport travelers to another time and country through the architecture that is found only in the castles of Europe. All along the shores of the Great Lakes, lighthouses spring up to lure visitors to get out their cameras to capture their picturesque quality.

Recreational: With state parks and bustling cities all along the route, the Seaway Trail is not lacking in the selection of activities it offers visitors. Throughout the year, visitors to the byway enjoy shorelines and waterways with plenty of access. In the winter, when water sports might be less appealing, there is always the draw of both downhill and cross-country skiing. There are more than 30 state parks just along the byway. Detour off the road a bit and you'll find a few more. Little villages and points of interest lure visitors all along the trail. The natural beauty of the Finger Lakes is almost as enticing as the legend behind them.

Highlights:

Covering both urban and rural, inland and waterfront areas, the Seaway Trail has a plethora of pleasurable places

awaiting travelers. This listing of highlights captures just a bit of the flavor of this unique byway.

Frederic Remington Art Museum: On the northeast end of the byway in the town of Ogdensburg is the Frederic Remington Art Museum, commemorating the life and work of the famed bronze sculptor and painter of western art. A majority of the museum's vast holdings came as a bequest from Remington's widow upon her death in 1918, and includes not only paintings and bronzes but also sketchbooks,

notes, photos, and even the cigars that were in his pocket before he died, giving a personal as well as professional view of the great artist.

Heart Island and Boldt Castle: Just off Alexandria Bay, Heart Island and Boldt Castle are intriguing monuments to love, loss, and luxury. Built in the early 1900s as a symbol of love for his wife by the proprietor of New York City's famous Waldorf-Astoria Hotel, George Boldt never returned to the island or the extravagant Rhineland-style castle after his wife died suddenly in 1904. Acquired and rehabilitated by the Thousand Islands Bridge Authority, the island and its various buildings are now open to the public.

Seaway Trail Discovery Center:
For an overview of the Seaway Trail and complete information to take with you along your journey, a stop at the Seaway Trail Discovery Center in Sackets Harbor is a great idea. Located in the old Union Hotel in historic downtown along the waterfront, the Discovery Center has nine exhibit rooms featuring a lighthouse video display, animatronic and interactive exhibits, and abundant information about the history of the Seaway Trail.

Fort Ontario:
On Fourth Street in Oswego is the star-shaped Fort Ontario, restored to its mid-1800s appearance. An orientation exhibit tells the history of the fort from its beginnings in 1755, including its use as an emergency refugee center for victims of the World War II Holocaust. Costumed historians recreate the lives of military men, their families, and civilians from the mid-1800s.

Sodus Bay Lighthouse Museum:
Those lighthouses that do not provide overnight accommodations but do have tours provide wonderful experiences for visitors. One is Sodus Bay Lighthouse Museum. Multimedia exhibits present the early history of the area, early

railroading history at Sodus Point, and fishing here. And of course, a major attraction is the climb to the top of the lighthouse tower, 70 feet above the waters of the lake for a spectacular view.

Charlotte–Genesee Lighthouse and Museum:
In Rochester is the Charlotte–Genesee Lighthouse and Museum. The keeper's house has exhibits about lighthouse lore, local history, and navigation, while the adjacent building has exhibits focused on the early history of the site. And visitors are welcome to climb the tower.

Old Fort Niagara:
Old Fort Niagara is a National Historic Landmark belonging to the United States now, but it wasn't always so. With history reaching back into the 1700s, the fort has been in the hands of both the French and the British as well eventually the Americans. Visitors can explore 16 points of interest on the self-guided tour, including several buildings, monuments, earthen fortifications, and the lighthouse.

Niagara Falls:
The finale to this itinerary is the sublime Niagara Falls, accessible in Niagara Falls State Park. Though the falls straddle the border

of America and Canada, the American side has retained much of its natural environment while still having plenty for visitors to do. You'll want to begin your journey at the Niagara Gorge Discovery Center, showcasing the natural history of Niagara Falls and the Gorge with interactive displays and a 180-degree multi-screen theater presentation.

Observation Tower:
Also at the Niagara Falls State Park, the Observation Tower at Prospect Point gives a commanding view of the American Falls and the churning waters in the gorge below. An elevator ride to the bottom of the Observation Tower takes you to the dock where you can board the Maid of the Mist for a boat ride to the swirling basin of the Horseshoe Falls. The Cave of the Winds trek takes you down 175 feet into the Niagara Gorge and within 20 feet of Bridal Veil Falls.

Built as a tribute to love, Boldt Castle on Heart Island was never occupied by its owner. It is now a major landmark on the St. Lawrence River.

Mohawk Trail

The hilliest section of Route 2 runs through the Berkshire Hills in northwestern Massachusetts. Shadowing an ancient Native American path, it has been known as the Mohawk Trail since it was formally declared one of the country's first scenic "auto routes."

Quick Facts

Length: 38 miles

Time to Allow: One hour

Consideration: From mid-October through early May conditions may be treacherous due to ice and snow, but the road never closes. It's most beautiful late May through mid-October and usually crowded only on weekends during foliage season (late September through early October).

In 1914 the most mountainous miles of the Mohawk Trail were graded and specifically dedicated to "auto touring." This stretch begins in the small city of North Adams and zigzags its way up the "Hairpin Turn" to the western summit of Hoosac Mountain. It runs eastward along heavily wooded ridges, then drops into the long-settled Deerfield Valley, and finally descends into the broad Connecticut River Valley.

The sight forms a ridge above the town of Greenfield-inspired poet, Frederick Goddard Tuckerman, a writer admired by Hawthorne, Tennyson, and Emerson.

In 1914 the fastest way from North Adams to Boston was by rail, via the 4.5-mile Hoosac Tunnel, itself considered a wonder when it opened in 1875. By 1914, however, cars were becoming affordable and folks were eager to break away from the dictates of the rails, to stop and go where they wished. The challenge of driving over rather than riding through Hoosac Mountain drew families—driving their first cars—from throughout the Northeast. Recognized as a destination in its own right from the 1920s through the 1950s, this initial stretch of the Mohawk Trail sprouted tea shops and motor courts, trading posts and campgrounds, both private and state.

In the 1960s vacation patterns and highway routes changed. The 1965 opening of the Massachusetts Turnpike (Route 90) knocked an hour off the time it takes to cross the state and Route 2. The Mohawk Trail's vintage lookout towers, motor courts, tearooms, and trading posts faded.

For a decade or so now the tourist tide has once more been turning. Whitewater rafters on the Deerfield River are filling the old roadside lodging places, and bed-and-breakfasts draw travelers into the surrounding hills. The village of Shelburne Falls, long known for its Bridge of Flowers, has become a showcase for the area's many craftspeople and chefs. Once more the Mohawk Trail is becoming a destination, this time for travelers who appreciate its history as well as its natural beauty.

Highlights:

Start in North Adams, and end in Greenfield.

Massachusetts Museum of Contemporary Art: North Adams boomed into existence with the construction of the Hoosac Tunnel in the late 19th century, and its mills prospered until the 1970s, a period when much of its fine Victorian-era downtown was razed in the name of urban renewal. Thanks to the Massachusetts Museum of Contemporary Art, which now fills four large former mill buildings with changing exhibits and performances, the state's smallest city once more offers quality lodging and dining.

Natural Bridge State Park: The centerpiece of 49-acre Natural Bridge State Park is a white-marble formation bridging a gorge, a tourist attraction since the 1830s, and a popular picnicking and fishing spot.

Savoy Mountain State Forest: The forest's 11,118 acres are largely mountainous and wooded. Within Savoy Mountain State Forest, take a drive to North Pond, which is good for swimming, trout fishing, boating, and camping.

Whitcomb Summit: The highest point on the route (2,173 feet) is marked by a steel version of a wooden tower placed here in 1915. It commands an amazing view of waves of

hills. The cottages and café here date from the 1920s.

Tannery Falls: Be forewarned that this turnoff is unmarked. Just east of the bridge that marks the town line between Savoy and Florida, turn south on Black Brook Road and then on Tannery Road into the Savoy Mountain State Forest. From the parking area a trail follows a narrow stream steeply down to the bottom of a glorious cascade.

Zoar Gap: Zoar Gap is a dramatic gorge best viewed from a whitewater raft on the Deerfield River. Zoar Outdoor, based in a 1750s house on Route 2 in Charlemont, pioneered rafting to take advantage of

timed hydro releases on the Deerfield.

Charlemont: Here the Deerfield River slows, widens, and turns east, flanked by broad fields that have been farmed, judging from the vintage of the farmhouses, since the 1770s. The hospitable Charlemont Inn has been feeding and housing travelers since the 18th century. The Bissell Covered Bridge spans Mill Brook just north of Route 2, and the white-steepled Federated Church is known for the quality of its acoustics and of the Mohawk Trail Concerts held here in July and August. Also in Charlemont is the Indian Plaza Gift Shop, the site of periodic powwows.

Connecticut State Route 169

The Norwich–Woodstock Turnpike, as it was originally known, links 18th century villages in the Quinebaug and Shetucket Rivers Valley, better known as Connecticut's Quiet Corner. State parks and forests abound, along with prep-school campuses and antiques shops.

Consider everything you know about New England—spectacular autumn color, historic buildings, charming cities—and you will have an idea of what you will find on Connecticut State Route 169. Much has changed over the years on this byway, but the history and traditions of the area are still very much a part of the lives of the people who belong to the communities.

Take the opportunity to experience some of the sights along this historical stretch of road. Visit the beautiful churches in Pomfret that date back to the 1800s. Or find out what life was like for a prosperous family in the mid-19th century at the Roseland Cottage/ Bowen House Museum in Woodstock. Or simply explore some of the towns at your leisure, admiring the distinctive architecture and well-kept parks.

As you travel the byway, you will visit many wonderful communities. The route crosses through Lisbon, where the feeling of an early American community is still evident. Explore Canterbury, where

Connecticut's interpretation of Georgian architecture is prominent. Then you will find yourself in Pomfret, once known as "the other Newport" for its strong influx of wealthy summer vacationers. Finally, you will pass through Woodstock, with its many architectural surprises clustered around a town common. Traveling this byway, you will sense an area that is moving ahead in the times while still maintaining a sense of pride in its history.

Cultural:

The historic and cultural significance of this area was recently spotlighted by its designation as a National Heritage Corridor. The Quinebaug and Shetucket Rivers Valley National Heritage Corridor (Q-S NHC) recognized the great potential for recreation and site interpretation due to the byway's abundance of outstanding 19th-century mills, mill villages, and beautiful landscapes.

The salmon-colored Roseland Cottage has stunning original furnishings for the public to view.

State Route 169 forms the western edge of the Q-S NHC and is considered an important element in the Heritage Corridor, especially as a means for linking its many diverse historic sites.

In addition to two National Historic Landmarks (Prudence Crandall Museum and Roseland Cottage), there are more than 175 historic sites and districts recognized by local and state surveys and/or the State or National Registers of Historic Places. The National Register of Historic Places lists two districts along State Route 169 (Bush Hill and Brooklyn Green, both in Brooklyn), as well as individual properties. The rich architectural heritage of villages, such as Brooklyn, Pomfret, and Woodstock, is representative of the hill town communities that settled this part of Connecticut and are still very much intact.

Historical: The history of this ancient road is inextricably tied to the history of the hill towns of northeastern Connecticut. Since prehistoric times, the route has wound its way along, up, and down the spines of age-old hills in a north-south direction. Windham County historian Ellen Larned tells us that a "Nipmuck Trail" ran from Wabbaquasset (i.e. the Woodstock area) to the seashore. If some parts of that trail and today's State Route 169 are not the same, there were undoubtedly footpaths of American

Indian origin that took much the same course. On the northern end, it seems certain that John Eliot and Daniel Gookin crossed portions of this route in 1674 as they made their way to what is now Woodstock. During the decade that followed other people made forays into Wabbaquasset territory, burning cornfields and American Indian forts. It is only logical to assume that they used American Indian trails and perhaps some part of what is now State Route 169.

The first improvements by Europeans most likely occurred after the settling of Norwich in 1659; Lisbon was then a part of Norwich. However, the course of the lower portion of the highway was changed sometime after 1854,

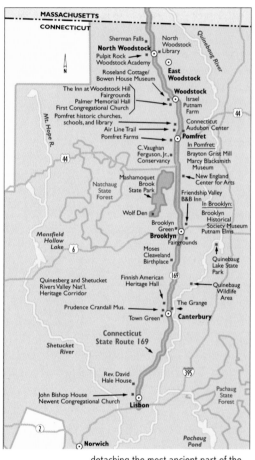

detaching the most ancient part of the road in that region. At present, there is no documentation for the road at the southern end. At the northern end, the Proprietor's Records of Woodstock record the laying of a road from North Running Brook, north of the village of Woodstock, to Sawmill Brook, in South Woodstock, by the first "Goers" during the summer of 1686. The public right-of-way was eight rods wide in some parts, and six rods wide in others (the rod used was probably 11 feet).

The Woodstock portion of the Norwich and Woodstock Turnpike was made free in 1836, while the rest of the road remained a toll road for another ten years. In 1846, the corporation persuaded the Connecticut assembly to relieve it of its obligations on the grounds that the cost of the road had been more than 14,000 dollars and that no "considerable profit" had ever been realized. Since the operation of the Norwich and Worcester Railroad, the income had not been sufficient to provide for the necessary repairs and no dividends had been paid for six years. Consequently,

The grounds of Roseland Cottage feature a 150-year-old boxwood parterre garden, bowling alley, and ice house.

the railroad was blamed for the demise of the 19th-century turnpike era.

Railroads also had other effects on the hill towns. To Pomfret, where the railroad passed over the highway, it brought summer tourists and a grand way of life; to other towns bypassed in favor of the thriving mill towns along the Quinebaug, it brought a long, slow decline. The period of dormancy is in large part the reason why so much of the path of this historic highway has remained unchanged throughout the years. As for the Norwich and Woodstock Turnpike, it undoubtedly remained much the same until the advent of the automobile and the development of the state highway system in the 20th century, when it was first given the number 93, which was later changed to 169. Early photographs are plentiful, showing portions of the road as a narrow, graded, and crowned dirt road. It has grown somewhat wider through the years, has been blacktopped along its entire length, and in recent years has been very well maintained. Even with all these improvements, one can still feel the bumps and turns of the ancient road, see the horizon ahead disappear and reappear, and feel a continuity through time with all who have traveled this beautiful road.

Highlights:

The spectacular views that travelers witness from State Route 169 are owned by the thousands of individual property owners that live along the corridor. The attractive pattern of land use that has evolved over many centuries is the result of the individual actions of the residents of the five towns that the corridor traverses. State Route 169 traverses the physiographic region of Connecticut known as the "Eastern Uplands." Within the eastern uplands there are three distinct landscape types: Glacial Till Uplands—the ridge tops and side hills, Drumloidal Glacial Till Uplands—the more rounded and oval shaped uplands, and Glacial Outwash Plains—the bottomlands.

This itinerary covers some of the natural and historic highlights of your journey along Connecticut State Route 169 as you travel from north to south.

Roseland Cottage: Begin at the Roseland Cottage/Bowen House Museum in Woodstock. This home with Gothic Revival architecture was constructed in 1846 and hosted elegant soirees attended by the elite of the day, including numerous Presidents. The cottage features original furnishings, bowling alley, and garden.

Connecticut Audubon Society:
Though Pomfret has many historic churches and homes, it is the natural features of the area that are highlighted at one of northeastern Connecticut's newest attractions. The Connecticut Audubon Center offers educational programs and bird walks. It is also the gateway to the adjoining 700-acre Connecticut Audubon Bafflin Sanctuary.

Brayton Grist Mill and Marcy Blacksmith Museum: Just west of Pomfret on Route 44 is the Brayton Grist Mill and Marcy Blacksmith Museum, located at the entrance to the Mashamoquet Brook State Park. It is an 1890s mill with the original equipment. The Marcy Blacksmith Museum has exhibits that detail more than a century of blacksmithing and three generations of the craft.

Mashamoquet Brook State Park:
This park offers camping, hiking, and picnicking. The most famous feature is the Wolf Den into which, on a night in 1742, Israel Putnam crept and shot a wolf that for years had preyed upon local sheep and poultry. Putnam later gained fame as a major general in the Continental Army during the Revolutionary War. Near the Wolf Den are the Table Rock and Indian Chair natural stone formations.

Brooklyn Historical Society Museum: This museum houses a collection of 18th- and 19th-century artifacts and Brooklyn memorabilia. Additionally it features historic items about the life of Revolutionary War hero Israel Putnam and special annual exhibits. The law office of Putnam's great-grandson, Daniel Putnam Tyler, is also open to the public.

This cemetery in Canterbury called the Carey Cemetery has headstones dating before 1800.

Putnam Elms: Yet another Putnam family site is Putnam Elms. Constructed in 1784 by the Putnam family and still maintained by Putnam descendants, the house is open for tours and contains exhibits about the history of Colonel Daniel Putnam and his father, General Israel Putnam.

Finnish American Heritage Hall:
Built in the 1920s, the Finnish American Heritage Hall in Canterbury is not only a social hall for those whose families immigrated and contributed to the melting pot of America; it is also the site of the Finnish American World War II memorial dedicated to Americans, including all the Finnish Americans, who fought in the war. On April 10, 1998, the Finnish Hall, along with numerous other buildings and residences on the Canterbury Green, was entered onto the National Register of Historic Places.

Prudence Crandall Museum: This museum is located on the site of Prudence Crandall's home, the first academy for black women in New England. Crandall's activities were not without controversy. Admitting Sarah Harris, a young black girl, to the women's academy outraged parents and townsfolk and caused an angry mob to ransack the school. Fearing for the safety of her students, Crandall closed the academy. Today this National Historic Landmark features three period rooms, changing exhibits, and a research library.

Merritt Parkway

Built with pride in the 1930s as a "Parkway," Merritt Parkway is more sinuous than modern highways, winding its way through parklike landscaping and under Art Deco bridges. It's an alternative to I-95 through Connecticut to New York City.

The Merritt Parkway is one of the only roads listed on the National Register of Historic Places, a distinction usually reserved for buildings or battlefields. Drive Merritt Parkway, and see for yourself why it inspires both reverence and devotion among fans and supporters, many of whom use it daily or live near its winding path through Connecticut's Fairfield County. Built in the 1930s to cope with America's new fascination with the automobile, this byway is enshrined in the hearts of many as an icon of the automobile age and a model of highway planning.

Cultural: As a scenic byway, Merritt Parkway has won national acclaim. From political leaders to talk show hosts, everyone has something to say about this parkway, and it always has something to do with the beautiful scenery visitors will experience on the prettiest drive in Connecticut. The road is half a century old and is traveled daily by at least 60,000 vehicles, but it remains a perfect combination of nature and industry. Perhaps it is because of the amount of travel that occurs on the road that it has become part of our nation's cultural heritage. Whatever the case, people inside and outside of Connecticut know about the Merritt Parkway.

Historical: On July 1, 1934, Oscar Tuthill, the First Selectman of

Greenwich, turned a spade of earth at King Street near the Connecticut–New York border to begin construction of the Merritt Parkway, which was among the first parkways in the nation and the first median-divided, limited-access highway in Connecticut. Its name was changed from Merritt Highway to Merritt Parkway one year after construction began. On September 2, 1940, just more than six years later, the final section of the roadway was completed and the entire parkway opened to traffic.

Described by one historian as "one of the most beautiful and best-engineered highways of the time," the parkway was built to solve traffic problems in the state. Before the parkway, local

Putnam Cottage was originally built in the 18th century. Since then, it has undergone many changes and has recently been restored to its colonial appearance.

In New Canaan:
New Canaan Nature Center
John Rogers Studio & Museum

In Stratford:
Boothe Memorial
Park & Museum

motorists and long-distance travelers were forced to compete for the same highway space. Drivers could move only at slow speeds, and merchants in communities along the route were upset because their customers were unable to find convenient parking.

The Merritt Parkway was a direct product of a period in American road-building history when there was a great deal of interest in linking urbanized regions with graceful highways set in natural surroundings. This parkway quickly emerged as a national model. To ensure a natural appearance, long, gradual, vertical curves were designed. Rock cuts were rounded and landscaped to produce a natural setting. The Merritt Parkway's designers attempted to integrate the traveled way into the roadside and its surroundings. The landscaping of the parkway followed closely upon completion.

In addition to the roadside beauty that can be viewed while driving along the Merritt Parkway, motorists are also treated to a unique exhibition of ornamental bridges. These structures were the creation of George Dunkelberger, an innovative bridge designer and architect. There were originally 69 bridges, with some carrying the parkway under intersecting roads and railroad tracks and others carrying the parkway over intersecting roads and rivers. These bridges were designed primarily in the Art Moderne and Art Deco styles, with no two alike. In the more than 75 years since the parkway's completion, three of the original bridges have been replaced and a number of others have been altered in response to needed maintenance or repair, but the bridges still remain a scenic element of the byway.

The 37-mile roadway now stretches

across Fairfield County from the town of Greenwich to the Housatonic River in the town of Stratford. The stately, neatly landscaped parkway connects the Hutchinson River Parkway at the New York state line with the Wilbur Cross Parkway at Stratford. Together, the Merritt and Wilbur Cross Parkways form part of Route 15 in Connecticut. In 1991, the parkway was listed on the National Register of Historic Places, a statement of its role as a nationally recognized cultural resource as well as a valued part of Connecticut's heritage. It is also a critical transportation facility for the southwestern part of the state. Six decades since its creation, millions of motorists from all over the nation still enjoy the scenic beauty of the parkway, especially its brilliant spring displays and rich autumn foliage.

Recreational: The Merritt Parkway was designed and built as a driver's road. Efficiency and speed took a back seat to the enjoyment of those who would sit in the front seat, especially the driver. Understandably, the primary form of recreation that is available is simply driving the Merritt Parkway. With an engaging variety of twists and turns, intriguing highway architecture, and lush, native surroundings, the Merritt Parkway has become a popular route for tourists and commuters alike. Due to its popularity, morning and afternoon rush hours are not the most pleasant times to travel the route and should be avoided if possible. At other times, a drive down the Merritt Parkway is a memorable driving experience that anyone can appreciate.

Highlights:

A scenic alternative to other north-south corridors, the Merritt Parkway gives easy access to some of the activities and attractions listed here.

Boothe Memorial Park and Museum: Near the northern end of Merritt Parkway, in the town of Stratford is the Boothe Memorial Park and Museum. The Boothe Family resided on this 32-acre estate from the mid-1600s to 1949. Ten of the 20 historic buildings have been restored at this National Historic Landmark. Displays include early farm equipment, carriages, trolley history, and more. The site also has a beautiful rose garden, an observatory and educational center, picnic facilities, and playground.

New Canaan Nature Center: Taking exit 37 off the Merritt Parkway and passing through the center of New Canaan, the New Canaan Nature Center is just a mile north on Route 124. The center has 40 acres of habitat diversity and walking trails, an apple cider house, and a maple sugar shack. The nature center also

features a visitor center with natural science exhibits, a Discovery Center, a solar greenhouse, an arboretum, and various gardens. To go back to Merritt Parkway, return back through New Canaan.

Silvermine Guild Arts Center: Just outside of town is the Silvermine Guild Arts Center. It began more than a century ago as a colony for artists and writers founded by sculptor Solon Borglum, brother of famed Mount Rushmore sculptor Gutzon Borglum, in 1895. Today the Silvermine Guild Arts Center features a gallery of changing exhibits with works from both local newcomers and nationally renowned artists.

Bush–Holley Historic Site: Connecticut's first art colony was in the town of Greenwich at the southern end of Merritt Parkway. Now a National Historic Landmark from around 1730, the Bush–Holley Historic Site features the Bush–Holley home, an 1805-period visitor center housed in a former post office, and the Hugh and Clair Vanderbilt Education Center, set in the historic barn and artists' studio. The grounds and gardens

have been restored to the appearance they had when the Cos Cob Impressionist Art Colony thrived with more than 200 students here between 1890 and 1920. Tour guides enhance your visit to the house, and you may explore the grounds at your leisure.

Putnam Cottage: Known as Knapp's Tavern during the Revolutionary War, Putnam Cottage was a popular gathering place for patriot leaders and ordinary travelers along the Boston Post Road. General Washington was even known to have eaten lunch here. Putnam Cottage is a repository of Colonial artifacts and is open to the public as a historical museum.

The New Canaan Historical Society is a haven for those who love history. You can find preserved items, dating back to 1713, concerning New Canaan.

Coastal Rhode Island

From Narragansett Bay to the Atlantic, this scenic route showcases the Ocean State's coastline, passing through its capital city and its ritziest resort on the way to its beach-lined southern shore.

The most scenic alternatives to the interstate—specifically I-95—are U.S. 1 and its offshoot 1A. However, they are not the quickest routes for driving through Rhode Island. The smallest state in the Union, just 37 miles wide by 48 miles long, Rhode Island is nonetheless blessed with some 400 miles of coastline, counting its many coves, bays, and islands. Much of the coastline is lined with beaches that are open to the public. Driving U.S. 1 and U.S. 1A—with a side trip over to the resort town of Newport—is the best way to experience the coast, although short side trips are necessary to access many of the beaches and small coastal resort areas.

This route provides a capsule viewing of much of the best of Rhode Island, including the lively capital city of Providence and the tony bayside resort of Newport, where some of America's wealthiest families built mansions on or near the water. It also passes through small, picturesque towns with colonial- or Victorian-era homes and little coastal villages that are a pleasant place to spend a weekend getting away from it all. Historic lighthouses line the route.

Small as Rhode Island may be, this route could easily take several days to explore if you linger in Providence and Newport or in one of the small resort towns or villages along the way.

Highlights:

Begin in Pawtucket, a blue-collar city in the state's Blackstone Valley.

Slater Mill Historic Site: Pawtucket is home to the Slater Mill Historic Site, the nation's first water-powered cotton spinning mill, dating from 1793. Its success at spurring mass production effectively ushered in the Industrial Revolution.

Providence: Drive south to Providence, the capital city of more than 175,000 people, built along the Providence River and situated on the northern lip of Narragansett Bay. Plan to spend some time in the city enjoying the history, the greenery, and the flourishing music and

The Newport Bridge brought an end to the official duties of the Rose Island Lighthouse. But today the lighthouse is active again as part of an environmental education program.

art scenes. A huge marble dome tops the Rhode Island State House; inside the Capitol is a famous Gilbert Stuart portrait of George Washington. Don't miss Benefit Street, with its many houses dating from the 18th and 19th centuries.

Wickford: Drive south from Providence on U.S. 1 and 1A to Wickford, where the route once again meets up with Narragansett Bay. Wickford is a pretty village dating from the early 1700s. Explore Main Street for a taste of the waterfront and the town's colonial-era homes.

Newport: A few miles south of Wickford, take Route 138 east toward Newport, crossing Narragansett Bay via the Jamestown and Newport bridges and Conanicut Island. After the Newport Bridge, the road enters Aquidneck Island. Reaching Newport, on the southern tip of Aquidneck, follow signs downtown to the waterfront (typically jammed with yachts, sailboats, and other craft). The Long Wharf area is good for lunch. Nearby Bellevue Avenue is lined with "summer cottages" (as the rich called their palatial mansions) built by old-money families in the 1890s, America's Gilded Age. Along Bellevue Avenue are Beechwood (home of the Astors), Rosecliff (used as a set in the film *The Great Gatsby*), and Belcourt Castle, home of the Belmonts. Ochre Point Avenue is the site of the Breakers (the 70-room Vanderbilt "cottage"), while Ocean Drive harbors Hammersmith Farm, where John and Jackie Kennedy were married.

Saunderstown: Now head back on Route 138 to U.S. 1A, and go south along the coast a short distance to Saunderstown, site of Gilbert Stuart's birthplace (located between U.S. 1 and 1A). Stuart, best known for painting more than 100 portraits of George Washington, lived in the house until age seven. Also the site of the first snuff mill in America, it has been restored and furnished in the mid-18th-century style and contains reproductions of some of Stuart's works.

Point Judith: Farther south on 1A is Narragansett, a Victorian-era resort town located at the point where Narragansett Bay meets the Atlantic Ocean. Continue south from there to Point Judith, site of a historic lighthouse at the tip of a peninsula and several beautiful beaches, including Scarborough State Beach, which has a beachside boardwalk. The village of Galilee on Point Judith is the embarkation point for ferries to Block Island, an unspoiled resort island with wonderful beaches, scenic walking trails, lighthouses, cliffs, and several wildlife refuges, about 12 miles off the coast.

East Beach and Misquamicut State Beach: Returning to U.S. 1, head west along South County and Rhode Island's southern coastline. Short side trips south of U.S. 1 lead to salt ponds, piney woodlands, and miles of wide, flat, whitesand beaches. Among the best beaches are East Beach, south of Charlestown, and Misquamicut State Beach, near the western tip of the state.

Historic National Road

Follow in the footsteps of George Washington and Daniel Boone over one of the most historic transportation corridors in America. Once a buffalo trace through southwestern Pennsylvania's Laurel Highlands, the National Road became the nation's first interstate route.

As America entered the 19th century, the young nation faced one of its first challenges: how to link the people and cities along the Eastern Seaboard to those on the frontiers west of the Allegheny Mountains. Settlers moving west faced perils aggravated by the lack of a well-defined roadway. And easterners were unable to take advantage of the abundant produce and goods from the western frontier without a road to transport them over the Alleghenies. The solution was the National Road, America's first interstate highway, and the only one constructed entirely with federal funds.

Construction began in 1811, and by 1818, the road stretched from Cumberland, Maryland, to what is now Wheeling, West Virginia. In time, the National Road ran the whole way to Vandalia, Illinois, a distance of 600 miles.

For three decades, the history, influence, and heritage of the National Road have been celebrated at the annual National Road Festival, held on the third weekend each May. The festival features memorable festivities and a wagon train that comes into town.

Cultural: The National Road was developed from existing Native American pathways and, by the 1840s, was the busiest transportation route in America. Over its miles lumbered stagecoaches, Conestoga wagons with hopeful settlers, and freight wagons pulled by braces of mules, along with peddlers, caravans, carriages, foot travelers, and mounted riders. In response to demand, inns, hostels, taverns, and retail trade sprang up to serve the many who traveled the

In the highlands of southwestern Pennsylvania is Fallingwater, one of the most famous homes in America, designed by renowned architect Frank Lloyd Wright.

road. Today, reminders of National Road history are still visible along this corridor, designated as one of Pennsylvania's heritage parks to preserve and interpret history throughout the region.

Historical: The first cries for a "national road" were heard before there was even a nation. Such a road would facilitate settlement and help the budding nation expand in order to survive and flourish. Economic considerations weighed heavily in favor of a national road, which would be a two-way street, allowing farmers and traders in the west to send their production east in exchange for manufactured goods and other essentials of life. In May 1820, Congress appropriated funds to lay out the road from Wheeling to the Mississippi. Construction in Ohio did not commence until 1825. Indiana's route was surveyed in 1827, with construction beginning in 1829. By 1834, the road extended across the entire state of Indiana, albeit in various stages of completeness. The road began to inch across Illinois in the early 1830s, but shortages of funds and national will, plus local squabbles about its destination, caused it to end in Vandalia rather than on the shore of the Mississippi River.

Highlights:

This tour begins in picturesque Falling-water and ends at the lovely Pennsylvania Trolley Museum.

Fallingwater: One of the most cele-brated buildings of the 20th century, architect Frank Lloyd Wright's Falling-water perches dramatically above a small waterfall on Bear Run. Completed in 1937 as a vacation retreat for the wealthy Kaufmann family of Pittsburgh, it aptly illustrates Wright's concept of "organic architecture"; that is, it was built to fit into the surrounding land-scape of rocky, tree-shaded hillsides. Escorted tours reveal some of Wright's idiosyncrasies; he was short in height, so ceilings are low—he designed to his own personal scale.

Kentuck Knob: Near Fallingwater, another wealthy family hired Wright. More modest in scope, their home sits high on a hillside hidden by trees as you drive onto the encircling 80-acre estate. From the outside, the house fits unobtrusively into its woodland setting, lacking the dazzle of Fallingwater. But the visual rewards, the magical spaces, are inside. The living room appears large, a look enhanced by a long wall of floor-to-ceiling windows. The ceiling is of polished wood, which reflects the light. In the evening, the glow is said to be very romantic. Though the house is luxurious, it boasts only a carport, not a garage. Wright, it seems, hated the clutter that a garage often generates.

Ohiopyle State Park: Just outside Fallingwater, Ohiopyle State Park and the village of Ohiopyle form a center for whitewater rafting and float trips. Several licensed outfitters offer trips of varying degrees of difficulty from gentle floats to daring, white-knuckle challenges. The outings take place on the Youghiogheny River, which is also known as the "Yock."

The Youghiogheny River winds through the heavily-forested Ohiopyle State Park.

Fort Necessity National Battlefield: Fort Necessity is the site of George Washington's only military surrender. Though the rebuilt fort is only a modest ring of stakes thrusting from the earth, it marks an important lesson for Washington that surely must have aided him two decades later in the American Revolution.

Braddock's Grave: A simple stone marker at Fort Necessity National Battlefield indicates the presumed gravesite of British General Edward Braddock. At the time of his death, he was commander of all British forces in North America.

In 1755, a year after Washington's surrender to the French, Braddock led a snail's pace march against the French, who were instigating Native American attacks on settlers from Britain's American colonies. Failing to heed Washington's advice on wilderness tactics, Braddock was fatally wounded. His army of 1,400 suffered 900 casualties.

Pennsylvania Trolley Museum: Preserving some 45 trolleys dating from the 1880s, the Pennsylvania Trolley Museum in Washington recreates the trolley era on the early 20th century. Visitors can learn about the evolution of

transportation and ride the museum's carefully restored trolleys on a four-mile track into the past.

Revolutionary War Trail: Washington's New Jersey Campaign

New Jersey's Revolutionary War Trail is a winding path that links four of General George Washington's most important victories in the early years of the Revolutionary War. An unofficial route, it travels some of the state's prettiest scenery, a rumpled green landscape where small streams tumble beneath stone bridges.

Historians have termed New Jersey the "Cockpit of the American Revolution" because so much of the battle raged within its borders. For much of the war, it was the front line. This 90-mile drive, beginning in Trenton and ending to the east in Freehold, tells an inspiring story. Against all odds, George Washington and his ragged, ill-equipped, and untrained band managed to outwit and outmaneuver their British and Hessian adversaries and ultimately carry the fight for liberty to victory.

As you follow Washington's footsteps, he and his soldiers seem almost to come alive, stepping for the day from the pages of a history textbook. You will visit well-preserved houses where Washington stayed while on the march and where he plotted his risky and desperate strategies. In museum displays, you will see such war-related items as an original war document signed by Washington, the authentic red tunic of one of the Redcoat enemy, and tools and equipment used by citizen soldiers in their daily life.

Beyond the colonial history, you can stroll the trendy streets of historic

This colonial gambrel-roofed house was likely used briefly by General George Washington and other officers at the time of their famous Christmas crossing of the nearby Delaware River.

Lambertville, lined with hip craft shops, contemporary art galleries, and fine antique houses. Take time out to hike a mile or two along the shady towpath of the Delaware and Raritan Canal, a state park.

Highlights:

Here are some points of interest along the Revolutionary War Trail: Washington's New Jersey Campaign.

New Jersey State Museum: View a replica of the famed painting Washington Crossing the Delaware. Standing in stalwart pose, Washington and his officers are being rowed through storm-tossed waves on the Delaware River to the New Jersey shore. Though of doubtful historical accuracy, it does help you imagine that fateful night.

Old Barracks Museum: Costumed interpreters recreate the life and living quarters of British and Hessian troops stationed in Trenton in the early months of the Revolutionary War. The anniversaries of the Battles of Trenton are celebrated the weekend after Christmas each year, and birthday cake is served yearly on President's Day in honor of George Washington.

Washington Crossing State Park: Sprawling across 841 acres of fields and woodlands, the park preserves the site at Johnson's Ferry where Washington's troops landed on the New Jersey shore. The Johnson Ferry House, dating to 1740, may have served briefly as Washington's headquarters during the crossing. Across the road, Continental Road, a six-foot wide wooded path, is believed to be the place where Washington's Continental Army began its march to Trenton.

Lambertville: Once a major industrial river town, Lambertville has become a chic weekend getaway destination. Visitors browse its well-preserved Victorian-era streets in search of fine antiques and artwork by local painters.

Princeton Battlefield State Park: Part of the Princeton Battlefield is contained within the Princeton Battlefield State Park. Every January, a reenactment of the Battle of Princeton occurs here. The visitor center exhibits detail the American victory here. The center occupies the Thomas Clarke House; he was a Quaker farmer who built the two-story whiteframe structure in 1772. During the fight, it served as a hospital for the Americans.

Princeton: Famed as the location of Princeton University, it is a pretty city with a cluster of fine shops near the campus. Two sights not to miss are the soaring Princeton Battle Monument, depicting a road-weary Washington on horseback, and the lovely stained-glass windows of the university's chapel. President James Madison, class of 1771, is pictured in the Window of the Law.

Monmouth Battlefield State Park: The park encompasses miles of spectacular landscape, a restored farmhouse, and a visitor center. The visitor center displays artifacts from the Battle of Monmouth. The exhibits also recall legendary Mary Ludwig Hays, who gained immortality as Molly Pitcher. Troops gave her the name when she carried water to them during the dreadfully hot day of battle. As the legend goes, she took over loading a cannon when her husband dropped from heat exhaustion.

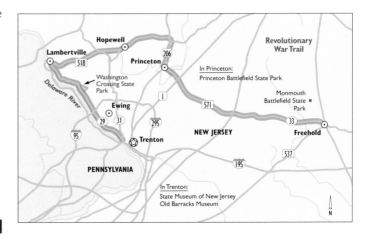

Map labels: Hopewell; Lambertville, 518; 206; Princeton; Revolutionary War Trail; Delaware River; Washington Crossing State Park; In Princeton: Princeton Battlefield State Park; Monmouth Battlefield State Park; Ewing; 1; 571; 29; 31; 295; 33; Freehold; 95; Trenton; NEW JERSEY; 537; PENNSYLVANIA; 195; In Trenton: State Museum of New Jersey, Old Barracks Museum; N

54 NJ

Chesapeake Country Scenic Byway

Find quiet relaxation among serene water views as you ease through the historic port towns of the Chesapeake Bay's eastern shore. Learn about the hardworking waterpeople, whose harvest of crabs and oysters is a staple at picturesque cafés.

There's a story around every corner of the Chesapeake Country Scenic Byway. As you drive this beautiful route, historic towns and buildings transport you to a new time. Nearly 15,000 years ago, American Indians began to cluster along the coast, thriving on the abundant wildlife. When the settlers from Europe came, many saw the Chesapeake Bay as an ideal spot to colonize.

If you enjoy bird-watching, be prepared for a treat. Rare and endangered species such as the colonial waterbird can be seen in wetlands along the byway. As a significant stop in the Atlantic Flyway, the region provides a tremendous number of critical waterfowl staging areas. Regional bird clubs sponsor a full schedule of bird walks and oppotunities to view migrating waterfowl, neotropical birds, hawks, eagles, and vultures. If you enjoy hunting, waterfowl hunting opportunities abound.

Cultural: As travelers explore Chesapeake Country, they will notice the relationship that people still have with the waterways that surround them. More than just recreational areas, the rivers and inlets of the area support a seafood economy, and as early as the 1600s, the settlers of the area were dependent upon the rivers and Chesapeake Bay for transportation. Travelers to the byway will likely see several different forms of watercraft from schooners and sloops to skiffs and canoes.

Not everyone was or is an angler along the byway. The success of Chesapeake's civilization rests on agriculture as well. Colonial families settled farms on the coastline while more recent farmsteads are located inland on rich soil. Towns formed where farmers would sell their goods and buy supplies. The historic towns of the byway reflect the way life has changed and remained the same in

The Chester River stretches 60 miles across Maryland. It is a hub of activity: boating, fishing, and even serving as a stop for migrating fish and wildlife.

Chesapeake Country Scenic Byway

N

Chesapeake City
Chesapeake & Delaware Canal
Cayots
Old Bohemia Church
Mt. Harmon Plantation   213   282
Cecilton
Betterton Beach
Sassafras River
Turner's Creek Path   292   Georgetown
Galena
Kennedyville   213
Kent Farm Museum   301
Schooner Sultana   Chester River
Chestertown
Washington College   Kingstown   300
20   Chesapeake Farms
Rock Hall Beach   Church Hill Theater
Rock Hall   Waterman's Museum   Church Hill
445   213   St. Luke's Episcopal Church
Eastern Neck NWR   Queen Anne's County Courthouse   313
Centreville   Queen Anne's Museum of Eastern Shore Life
Christ Church   18   Wright's Chance
301   304
Stevensville   50   Narrows   Queenstown
301
Grasonville

this corner of Chesapeake Bay. Buildings and districts on the National Register of Historic Places remind visitors and residents of the way things once were.

Travelers will not find a lack of places to visit on the byway. Churches and walking tours are found in nearly every town along the way. Museums collect the stories of the past to tell to curious visitors, and the stories of the present are readily available through residents at local festivals or fishing tournaments. The thread that connects the past with the present is the culture that still exists along the Chesapeake Country Scenic Byway.

Historical:

All along the Chesapeake Country Scenic Byway, towns and buildings from the bustling colonial period still stand with the same charm they had when they were first erected. This corner of Chesapeake Bay has been settled since the 1600s as a major port and commercial area. Central to many of the nation's most significant turning points, the byway can tell stories from the Revolutionary War and the War of 1812.

As travelers study the map of the byway, names such as Queen Anne's County, Georgetown, and Kingstown all reflect the beginnings of British colonialism in the New World. Many of the counties, towns, and buildings along the byway are named for their counterparts in England.

In the mid-1600s, a Dutch mapmaker named Augustine Herman proposed the construction of a waterway that would connect the Delaware River and Chesapeake Bay. The waterway would reduce the time it would take to transfer goods to and from the Chesapeake Bay area. Nearly 200 years later, in 1804, construction on the Chesapeake and Delaware Canal began. The canal is still in operation today—a piece of history that remains an important part of the present. It reduces the water route between Baltimore and Philadelphia by nearly 300 miles and is recognized on the National Register of Historic Places and as an Engineering Landmark.

Recreational:
If being in a boat on shimmering blue water sounds like fun to you, the Chesapeake Country Scenic Byway has much to offer. Recreation on the byway revolves around its water sources. Chesapeake Bay and all of its inlets provide great places for boating, fishing, or enjoying a sandy beach. If you keep your eyes open, you see that recreational opportunities are available all along the shore.

For sailing, Chesapeake Bay, the Sassafras River, and the Chester River are ideal spots to catch a bit of wind and glide across the water. Marinas and access points are located all along the shores and coasts, providing places for visitors to tie up their boats in the evening to go ashore for the nearest seafood restaurant. Fishing, crabbing, and oystering are a tradition on the Eastern Shore, so whether you participate in the catching or the tasting, it's a great tradition to get involved in. Charters for fishing are arranged in Narrows, Chestertown, and Rock Hall. Fishing from bridges or the shore can be as rewarding as a charter.

Two splendid beaches are available on the byway. Betterton Beach and Rock Hall Beach provide sandy shores and fresher water. Betterton Beach began as a resort area as early as the 1920s. Since then, families vacation there or just come for a day trip. At Rock Hall Beach, visitors are met with a great place for a beach cookout or swimming. But people aren't the only ones who enjoy the shores of the Chesapeake.

At refuges and wetlands along the byway, visitors have the opportunity to catch a glimpse of the waterfowl in the area. At Eastern Neck National Wildlife Refuge, Chesapeake Farms, Horsehead Wetlands Center, and Echo Hill Outdoor School, naturalists can get a taste of the native outdoors in Maryland. And the byway is one of the best ways to get to all of these places. Endangered bird species nest in refuges and the Atlantic Flyway brings many more species to

The manor house, separate kitchen, gardens, tobacco prize house, and wharf are open at Mount Harmon Plantation for tours.

the area. Make sure to bring a pair of binoculars for a closer look at some of the hawks, eagles, and neotropical birds in the wetlands.

Highlights:

Though there is a mix of pastoral scenery and rural bustle along the Chesapeake Country Scenic Byway that will entice you to stop and tour the tiny villages, browse in unique shops, and enjoy some tasty Maryland crabs freshly harvested from the bay, this itinerary gives the traveler a sampling of the agricultural and water-based heritage that has continued to sustain the area from the beginning.

Stevensville: Surrounded by the waters of the Chesapeake Bay, Kent Island is home to the quaint village of Stevensville where the tour begins. Stevensville's historic district has nearly 100 well-preserved buildings amidst quiet narrow streets. Among the historic structures worth noting are the Stevensville Train Depot, the Cray House, and the distinctly different Christ Church.

Centreville: Crossing over onto the Eastern Shore and traveling north on Maryland Route 213, Centreville captures the essence of small-town America with a distinctly colonial flavor. Wright's Chance is an early plantation house, circa 1744. Now home to the Queen

Anne's County Historical Society and open to the public, it has an exquisite collection of Chippendale and Hepplewhite furniture and Canton china.

Queen Anne's Museum of Eastern Shore Life: Also in Centreville is Queen Anne's Museum of Eastern Shore Life, displaying artifacts telling the story of the unique life of those who have called this area home. The collection includes antique farm implements, tools, and specialized equipment used to harvest the bounty of the Chesapeake Bay, Native American artifacts, and household items.

Chestertown: Farther north on the byway is the port town of Chestertown. Turn left onto Cross Street, and head into the heart of downtown, once a colonial port on the Chester River. In fact, Chestertown was the Eastern Shore's chief port for shipping both wheat and tobacco between 1750 and 1790. Wealthy merchants and planters built the elegant brick townhouses that dominate the historic district and waterfront. Be sure to stop by the Kent County Office of Tourism for information about Chestertown and Kent County.

Chesapeake Farms: Returning back the way you came on Maryland Route 20, turn right on Ricauds Branch Road to visit Chesapeake Farms. Though the history of the Chesapeake Country Sce-

nic Byway dates back to colonial times, the 3,300 acres of Chesapeake Farms is thoroughly modern in its techniques. It is a scientific area devoted to the development, evaluation, and demonstration of new and superior agricultural and wildlife management techniques. An extensive self-guided driving tour of the farm is available.

Turner's Creek Park: Return to Maryland Route 20 and back to Maryland Route 213, heading north. From Maryland Route 213 take Maryland Route 298 East to Turner's Creek Road. Turn right and follow the road to Turner's Creek Park. Here visitors can tour historic structures such as the Latham House, circa 1700. Also at the

park on the first and third Saturdays of the month, tours are available of Kent Farm Museum, where visitors can view antique farm machinery, a collection of antique implements from a variety of other occupations, and other artifacts of early rural life.

Mount Harmon Plantation: Continue north on Maryland Route 213 through villages full of charm and history. Just past the town of Cecilton, turn west on Maryland Route 282, and follow the road to Mount Harmon Plantation. Originally a thriving tobacco plantation shipping its bounty off to England, the property is bordered on three sides by water and offers a superb vista.

Mount Harmon Plantation's manor house dates back to 1730.

Historic National Road

A gateway to the West for thousands of settlers, the road cuts across Allegheny Mountain ridges dotted with historic communities, each with the look of a century past.

Many layers of urbanization have modified this historic route, but the diligent traveler still may follow the old Historic National Pike through the streets of Baltimore westward into the historic Maryland countryside. Today, with the construction of new roads, many historic towns and sites originally connected to the Historic National Pike lure modern travelers with rugged charm.

Cultural: As the first federally funded road, this byway blazed a trail for the emerging nation to follow. Maryland's Baltimore to Cumberland section of the Historic National Road was designated the Historic National Pike. Towns and cities along the pike began to spring up to provide comforts for weary travelers heading west.

Modern travelers of the Historic National Pike will find communities proud of their vibrant heritage. With Interstate 70 bypassing many of the original Historic National Pike cities, they have developed into artistic communities with a passion for diversity.

Historical: In the late 18th century, as the population of the United States began to grow, President Thomas Jefferson encouraged the development of a transportation infrastructure that would connect the Eastern Seaboard with points farther inland. The construction of the National Road westward from Cumberland was the first such investment by the federal government.

Recreational: Perhaps the most popular destination in all of Maryland is Baltimore's Inner Harbor, where you'll find outdoor performances, numerous eateries, the Baltimore National Aquarium and Marine Mammal Pavilion, the Maryland Science Center and Davis Planetarium, the MECU Pavilion, historic ships, shops, and much more.

If you love outdoor activity, this byway features fantastic biking, boating, hiking, and rock climbing. You can find numerous places to fish as well as hunt deer, turkey, grouse, squirrel, rabbit, quail, and waterfowl. If you like to view animals but not necessarily hunt them, you can also find excellent bird-watching areas.

Burnside Bridge, crossing Antietam Creek, was eventually taken by Union soldiers, in spite of the best efforts of greatly outnumbered Rebel troops.

Highlights:

Start your must-see tour in Baltimore at the B&O Railroad Museum.

B&O Railroad Museum:
The city of Baltimore was instrumental in the birth of passenger train service in 1830, an event commemorated by the B&O Railroad Museum. The museum is a storehouse of railroading lore, boasting a large collection of historic steam engines and restored passenger and freight cars.

Fort McHenry National Monument and Historic Shrine:
When the wind is calm, U.S. park rangers fly a replica of the giant "Old Glory" that Francis Scott Key saw when he was inspired to write what became America's national anthem. Exhibits at the massive, star-shaped fort overlooking Baltimore's harbor tell the story of that fateful dawn in 1814, when the fort's defenders survived an intense British bombardment in the War of 1812.

National Aquarium:
Two distinctive glass pyramids overlooking Baltimore's harbor house the National Aquarium. As you enter, the stingrays immediately capture your attention. From the pool, you ascend five levels. Level Two traces Maryland's waterways from the mountains to the sea. Level five is a recreated South American rain forest. Most spectacular of all is the descent through a giant circular tank, where sharks slip silently past.

New Market:
Step back in time in the historic village of New Market, which claims the title of "Antiques Capital of Maryland." Most of the old brick and wood-frame structures along a six-block stretch of Main Street display antiques of all kinds—from inexpensive knick-knacks to costly French furniture pieces. National Museum of Civil War Medicine: In the heart of Frederick, the National Museum of Civil War Medicine tells the story of how medical treatment improved radically in the four years of

the war as both sides coped with a flood of ill and wounded soldiers.

Antietam National Battlefield:
Fought on September 17, 1862, as Confederate General Robert E. Lee attempted to invade the North, the Battle of Antietam has entered the history books as the single bloodiest day of the Civil War.

Chesapeake and Ohio Canal National Historical Park:
A popular hiking and bicycling route, the towpath of the Chesapeake and Ohio Canal parallels the Potomac River for 184.5 miles from Washington, D.C., to Cumberland. Operating from 1828 to 1924, the canal was used primarily to haul coal from western Maryland to the port of Georgetown in Washington.

The Delaware Coast

From historic Lewes, a 17th-century Dutch colony, south to Fenwick Island, Delaware's Atlantic shore is a nearly nonstop stretch of inviting sandy beaches and popular beach towns with bustling boardwalks.

Nearly the entire length of this 25-mile drive down Delaware's Atlantic Coast is lined with sandy beaches that draw sun worshippers from all over the region. Twelve miles of beach are located within three state parks. They are quiet, only lightly developed oases between the more commercialized resort town beaches catering to visitors seeking boardwalk amusements and waterside lodging and dining.

Fortunately, the resorts—Lewes, Rehoboth Beach, Bethany Beach, and Fenwick Island—have resisted high-rise growth, and each retains a small-town charm. Victorian in look, they remain a nostalgic throwback to the beach vacations of that earlier time. The state parks preserve the landscape mostly as it might have looked a century or more ago. At dawn, shorebirds of all kinds scamper over the sand seeking breakfast, and majestic grass-topped dunes overlook pine forests and salt marshes.

Highlights:

This tour starts in the historic small town of Lewes and ends at the beautiful Fenwick Island Lighthouse.

Cape Henlopen State Park: A 5,000-acre natural area, the park thrusts between the Atlantic Ocean and Delaware Bay. Boardwalk steps ascend a high dune to reveal a long beach of golden sand. In season, lifeguards are on duty, and restroom and changing facilities are available. In addition to numerous swimming and sunbathing opportunities, Cape Henlopen State Park has many hiking and biking trails.

Lewes: Mostly overlooked by summer hordes flocking to Rehoboth Beach, just six miles

Quick Facts

Length: 25 miles

Time to Allow: 90 minutes

Consideration: July and August are high seasons, so advance reservations are essential if you plan to stay overnight—especially on weekends and holidays. September is a lovely time when the crowds are gone but the weather and water remain comfortably warm. Increasingly, beachgoers are visiting in winter to savor the quiet charm of the towns and the spectacle of roiling, storm-tossed waves on the beach.

Rising more than 80 feet above the shoreline, The Great Dune at Cape Henlopen State Park is the highest dune between Cape Cod and Cape Hatteras.

south, Lewes retains the look and charm of a small town of the past. In fact, it was the first town in Delaware. On Second Street, Lewes' "main" street, visitors can stroll beneath a canopy of giant old trees or sit on a bench and nibble cones from a nearby ice cream shop.

Zwaanendael Museum: Looking like a Dutch transplant of the town hall in Hoorn, Holland, the museum details Lewes' early Dutch heritage, recounts its modest role in the War of 1812, and more thoroughly explores its recent past as a headquarters for ship pilots on the Delaware River. Pick up printed walking tours of the town.

Rehoboth Beach: Founded by a Methodist church group, Rehoboth is a biblical term meaning "room enough." Rehoboth Beach is a very Victorian-looking town. It is Delaware's largest beach resort, and yet it is still very much a small, though very sophisticated, town. Many vacationers visit this beach from the D.C. area. In fact, Rehoboth Beach is sometimes referred to as the "nation's summer capital." Its shops display stylish beachwear, contemporary crafts, and antiques. Families return year after year, invariably spending part of each day strolling the mile-long wood boardwalk overlooking a wide beach.

Delaware Seashore State Park: A beachgoer's delight, the 2,825-acre park boasts six miles of ocean and bay shoreline. In season, lifeguards patrol, and restrooms and changing facilities are available. Shallow bay waters make the park a popular sailboarding and sailing destination. There colorful sails glide across the bay in a rainbow dance. Surf fishing on the ocean is a big sport here.

Bethany Beach: A pretty little family resort with a boardwalk, Bethany Beach got its start in 1901 as a church retreat. Even though times have changed, the town continues to bill itself as the "quiet" resort. It hasn't allowed liquor until recently, and liquor laws are still pretty strict. An amazing red cedar sculpture called Chief Little Owl, or Whispering Giant, is a landmark of Bethany Beach. This sculpture is a new incarnation of a previous version that was damaged. Both sculptures were created by artist Peter Toth.

Fenwick Island State Park: A three-mile-long barrier island with 344 acres of ocean and bay shoreline, Fenwick Island State Park claims description as the "quiet" beach. Here the white sand slopes gradually into the Atlantic Ocean, creating a vast swimming area families can enjoy. In season, lifeguards are on duty, and restrooms and changing facilities are available. A designated surfing area has been established. And at three dune crossings you can surf or fish after purchasing a vehicle permit.

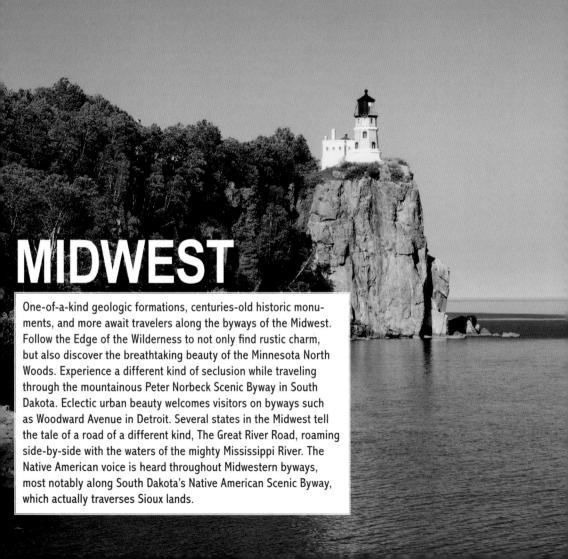

MIDWEST

One-of-a-kind geologic formations, centuries-old historic monuments, and more await travelers along the byways of the Midwest. Follow the Edge of the Wilderness to not only find rustic charm, but also discover the breathtaking beauty of the Minnesota North Woods. Experience a different kind of seclusion while traveling through the mountainous Peter Norbeck Scenic Byway in South Dakota. Eclectic urban beauty welcomes visitors on byways such as Woodward Avenue in Detroit. Several states in the Midwest tell the tale of a road of a different kind, The Great River Road, roaming side-by-side with the waters of the mighty Mississippi River. The Native American voice is heard throughout Midwestern byways, most notably along South Dakota's Native American Scenic Byway, which actually traverses Sioux lands.

Sheyenne River Valley Scenic Byway

The relatively new history of the rugged homesteaders and the ancient history of the Native Americans who first inhabited this area give this byway unique cultural diversity mixed with pastoral scenic attractions.

The Sheyenne River Valley Scenic Byway is distinguished by its small-town hospitality and a mixture of scenic hills and grassy flatlands. Pastoral scenery catches travelers' attention, featuring wildflowers, wild grasses, quaint farms, grassy hills, and wildlife. Old prairie churches, one-room schoolhouses, quaint farms, and historic towns allow the traveler to experience a little of the old frontier.

Cultural: The cultural heritage of the Sheyenne River Valley Scenic Byway has been strongly influenced by a mixture of customs and traditions passed on from the region's first settlers. The unaltered natural settings and rustic outdoor facilities of the region's most remote areas are a short distance from modern and sophisticated art centers, museums, restaurants, and hotels.

The cultural patchwork found in the Sheyenne River Valley Scenic Byway corridor is a result of this surprising diversity and contrast, as well as the number of cultural attractions and events. Among these cultural attractions are pioneer cemeteries, historic churches, antique shops, guest inns, museums, monuments, and community concerts and theaters. Cultural events include farmers' markets, horse shows and rodeos, county fairs, community days, antique and art shows, vintage tractor and car shows, and ethnic festivals.

Historical: About 15,000 years ago Native Americans began to filter from the north and west into the area east of the Rocky Mountains, foraging for food. The region's earliest inhabitants were members of these prehistoric cultures. The first written records of the region surrounding the Sheyenne River Valley came from the explorers Joseph Nicolas Nicollet and John C. Frémont, who noted the landmark Standing Rock on their maps during their exploration of 1839. They also recorded their experiences with the local Native Americans while camping in the area now known as Clausen Springs. The next written account from the area does not take place until James L. Fisk passed through, leading an emigrant train to the gold fields of Montana in 1862 and 1863. In 1867, the Fort Ransom military post was established on

Panoramic pastoral scenery abounds in the Sheyenne River Valley. The outstanding views are endless here.

Quick Facts

Length: 63 miles

Time to Allow: Nine hours

Consideration: Part of the road from Kathryn to Lisbon is a gravel surface (about 15 miles). The byway contains a total of about 26 miles of gravel roads. During the growing season, you may encounter minor changes in travel speeds when meeting or passing agricultural equipment. Spring sometimes brings closures due to flooding and excessive rainfall.

of a stream of mostly Norwegian immigrants.

Dramatic changes to the Sheyenne River Valley landscape resulted from the agricultural activities, urban development, and construction of transportation routes that accompanied the region's settlement. Sections of the river were dammed for mills, water supply regulation, pollution abatement during low-flow periods, and recreational purposes; and dikes were constructed to reduce flooding in river valleys. But through it all, the Sheyenne River Valley, its many historical structures, and its citizens have continued to share the valley's rich history and to provide visitors with memorable experiences.

Recreational: Activities include hiking, biking, and horseback riding all along the byway in spring, summer, and fall. The area's river and lake provide great opportunities for canoeing, boating, and kayaking. In the winter, cross-country and downhill skiing, snowshoeing, and snowmobiling are popular. Fishing is a year-round pastime that can be enjoyed all along the corridor, as is bird-watching. The byway is also a great location for hunting, whether it be for waterfowl, upland bird, deer, moose, or fur-bearing species.

Standing out on the basically lakeless landscapes of the North Dakota plains, Lake Ashtabula in the Sheyenne River Valley has several resort areas located along its 27-mile length, providing a plethora of recreational opportunities There are resorts, camping areas, swimming areas, restaurants, fish-cleaning stations, boat-rental locations, and cabin rentals.

Fort Ransom State Park provides a wealth of outdoor activities, including educational programs, camping, fishing, picnicking, horseback riding, canoeing, cross-country skiing, hiking, birding, and nature photography. Amenities include an outdoor amphitheater, canoe landing, campsites, nature trails, playground, picnic shelters, visitor center, and horse corrals.

A ski resort, Bears Den Mountain, is not something you would expect to see on the flat plains of North Dakota, but you can find it at Fort Ransom. This site offers a chairlift and T-bar, two beginner rope tows, snowmaking, grooming, a cafeteria, and rental equipment. The 285-mile Sheyenne Valley Snowmobile Trail system has

the Fort Abercrombie to Fort Totten Trail, to protect wagon trains on their way to the gold fields of Montana and to guard pioneer settlers and railroad workers passing through. Today, the Fort Ransom Historic Site recalls the importance of the original outpost.

With the advance of the Northern Pacific Railroad in 1872 came the first permanent European settlers to the area. The Great Dakota Boom, beginning in 1878, marked the influx a wide variety of riding areas, such as flat ditches, shelterbelts, national grasslands, and the Sheyenne River bottom.

Highlights:

One of the fascinating things about the Sheyenne River Valley Scenic Byway is the array of attractions that offer a glimpse into how various groups have interacted with the land over the years. The following itinerary suggests some highlights of those attractions.

Baldhill Dam and Lake Ashtabula: Operated by the U.S. Army Corps of Engineers, Lake Ashtabula includes eight recreational areas with ample year-round opportunities. Stop by the Corps of Engineers office on the west side of the dam for maps and information.

Valley City National Fish Hatchery: Ashtabula means "fish river" in the local Native American dialect. In keeping with that, eggs are harvested from the lake for use in the fish hatchery operated by the U.S. Fish and Wildlife Service, with a subunit just south of the dam and the main hatchery a bit farther south at Valley City. The Valley City National Fish Hatchery is a popular area for hiking, fishing, and picnicking. The goose pond is a fishing pond for kids and an exclusive area attraction.

Rosebud Visitor Center: For maps, information, and a bit of railroad history, stop at the Rosebud Visitor Center, located on the I-94 business loop between exits 290 and 294. The building houses an 1881 railcar that is one of only eight of its type that were built. The railcar, known as "Rosebud," is the only one known to have its artifacts still intact. The Rosebud Visitor Center provides information about the entire Sheyenne River Valley.

Medicine Wheel Park: Another point of interest in Valley City and certainly not to be missed is the distinctive Medicine Wheel Park. The wheel, 68 feet in diameter with 28 spokes radiating from the middle, is on the campus of Valley City State University and is intended to pay homage to the spirit and purpose of the original Indian medicine wheels used for centuries by Native Americans of the Great Plains.

Plains Woodland Indian Burial Mounds: Just to the east of the Medicine Wheel are the Plains Woodland Indian Burial Mounds. These Sheyenne River mounds were used for centuries but were first charted in 1883.

The picturesque Fort Ransom Valley is located in Fort Ransom State Park.

Fort Ransom State Park: Continuing south 34 miles along the path traveled for centuries, first by Native Americans and then by fur traders and pioneers, your next stop will be Fort Ransom State Park. Though the fort itself was abandoned in 1872, Fort Ransom State Park offers ample recreational opportunities for history lovers as well as outdoor sports enthusiasts of all kinds.

Bjone Home and Sunne Farm: Fort Ransom State Park features two historic homesteads that reflect the life and times of the Norwegian homesteaders who settled this area. The Bjone Home is used as the visitor center and houses exhibits highlighting local tradition and Norwegian legends. The Sunne Farm is a living history farm used each year during the second full weekend in July.

Edge of the Wilderness

Rustic seclusion, breathtaking views, and a multitude of natural recreational opportunities greet travelers on the Edge of the Wilderness.

Celebrate northern hospitality, hometown pride, and the treasures of our natural heritage. Minnesota, midway between America's east and west coasts, is home to 12,000 lakes. It is filled with beautiful country and all the pleasures of the four seasons. The Edge of the Wilderness is the rustic slice of this great state, with more than 1,000 lakes and one mighty river, the Mississippi, all in landscapes of remarkable natural beauty. There are still more trees than people here, offering classic North Woods seclusion.

The Edge of the Wilderness begins in Grand Rapids with meadows and lakes, then winds through mixed hardwoods and stands of conifers and aspens in the Chippewa National Forest. Rounding bends and cresting hills, you will find breathtaking views that, during the fall, are ablaze with the brilliant red of sugar maples, the glowing gold of aspen and birch, and the deep bronze of oak.

The Edge of the Wilderness route offers some of Minnesota's most popular sporting and resorting opportunities in its unique environment of clear lakes, vast shorelines, and hills blanketed in hardwood forests and northern pines. Recreation seekers will find hiking, camping, fishing, cross-country skiing, and snowmobiling within the byway corridor. You will find that you are really living on the "edge."

Historical: At the height of the Great Depression, President Franklin D. Roosevelt formed the Civilian Conservation Corps (CCC) to provide jobs and restore the environment. CCC camp crews often were called the Tree Army. They were responsible for planting more than two billion trees across the United States in nine years. Other tasks included road construction; site preparation; surveys of lakes, wildlife, and streams; and even rodent control.

The Day Lake CCC Camp was one of 20 camps established in Minnesota

The winter months frost the trees that stand vigil on the banks of North Star Lake.

> ### Quick Facts
>
> **Length:** 47 miles
>
> **Time to Allow:** Three hours
>
> **Consideration:** The best time to drive this route is during the fall foliage season (end of September, beginning of October). High season includes July and August. Highway 38 courses up and down and curves often—that's part of its charm. Locals named it Highway Loop-de-Loop in the early days. As you drive the byway, be aware of the lower speed limits, other traffic on the highway, and weather conditions. This is a working roadway, with trucks carrying logs and other local products.

during the Great Depression. Day Lake was the only camp in the forest to host AfricanAmericans in the segregated CCC program, and was one of only six that lasted past the CCC era; it became one of four camps in the Chippewa National Forest that housed German prisoners of war during World War II (1943–1945).

Today, on the west side of Highway 38 are the remains of a concrete shower. East of the highway and up the hill are the outside stone stairway and a chimney that are remnants of the camp mess hall. Many old camp foundations and sites are also visible. After its closing, much of the Day Lake CCC Camp was replanted with red pine, hiding many of the signs of its history.

Recreational: Following World War II, northern Minnesota's tourist and resort industry grew rapidly. Itasca County had a peak of about 300 resorts in the 1940s and 1950s. Today, there are approximately 100 resorts and vacation sites in the area, many vacationers returning year after year. North Star Lake—at more than three miles long and about 1/2 mile wide—is considered one of the best fishing and recreational lakes in the area. It is representative of many of the lakes on the Edge of the Wilderness, with its scenic beauty, islands and bays, clear waters, and recreational offerings. The still-visible

remnants of the railroad trestle provide a good habitat for the lake's many fish. The lake is 90 feet deep and is managed for muskie. Visitors also catch walleye (the state fish of Minnesota), northern pike, largemouth bass, smallmouth bass, bluegills, and crappies.

With a wingspan of more than six feet, keen vision, and white head and tail feathers, the bald eagle is truly a magnificent bird. People often make a special trip to the Chippewa National Forest just to observe bald eagles. Spending time along the shorelines of the forest's larger lakes is the best way to treat yourself to the sight of an eagle in flight. Large, fertile lakes; towering red and white pines; and remote areas provide ideal nesting and feeding habitat for bald eagles. Nesting birds return in late February and early March, though a few

birds spend the entire winter in the forest. Eggs are laid in early April, and the young eagles leave their lofty nests in mid-July. Eagles occupy their breeding areas until the lakes freeze over.

The best opportunity for viewing bald eagles is from a boat; in fact, one of the best opportunities to see eagles is to canoe down the Mississippi River. You can search the lakeshore with binoculars to spot eagles that are eating fish on the beaches. These birds of prey often perch in trees found around the larger lakes,

Visitors can tour the grounds of Trout Lake's historic Joyce Estate and examine the rustic log architecture of the hunting resort's buildings.

such as Bowstring. The Bigfork River is also a favorite eagle area. However, if you do not have a boat, you can simply find an area along the beach with a good panoramic view of the lake. Campgrounds, picnic areas, and boat landings are good places to visit.

Highlights:

The Edge of the Wilderness officially begins in Grand Rapids, Minnesota. The byway proceeds north with sites of interest marked consecutively as follows.

Grand Rapids: Grand Rapids is in a historic logging and papermaking region. It is named for its strong

rapids on the Mississippi River. Other waterways, including lakes and forests, help make Grand Rapids's recreational opportunities great.

Black Spruce/Tamarack Bog Habitat: Black Spruce/Tamarack Bog Habitat is one of the largest and most mature bogs in the area. It began forming here some 16,000 years ago when the last of four glaciers covered this part of Minnesota.

Trout Lake and Joyce Estate: The Trout Lake area offers 11 lakes for outdoor enthusiasts. While fishing, visitors are likely to see loons, herons, and beavers. Joyce Estate is an impressive

1920s estate in the Trout Lake area.

Day Lake CCC Camp: Day Lake CCC Camp has a long and varied history of use as both a Depression-era work camp and a German POW camp during World War II.

Laurentian Divide: On the north side of this site, the divide directs the waters to empty into Hudson Bay and on to the Arctic Ocean. On the south, water flows into the Mississippi River and eventually into the Gulf of Mexico.

Scenic Overlook at North Star Lake: Years ago, loggers cut down trees around this potato-shape lake during winter then floated them downstream when the temperature rose.

Chippewa National Forest Ranger Station: The Chippewa National Forest encompasses 1.6 million acres of forest and lakes, providing ample opportunities for the outdoor adventurer.

Gut and Liver Line: Make a stop here to view the remnants of old lumbering operations. Locals share legends and tales about this line on the Minneapolis and Rainy River Railroad.

Grand Rounds Scenic Byway

Home to such diverse sites as St. Anthony Falls, the only natural falls along the Mississippi River, and an artistic rendering of a giant spoon capturing an enormous cherry, the Grand Rounds Scenic Byway is a unique urban journey.

Quick Facts

Length: 52 miles

Time to Allow: Three to four hours

Consideration: With only a few exceptions, the route is generally above local flood plains. During the winter, in addition to the roadway surfaces, a single paved trail is plowed throughout the system for shared use by pedestrians and cyclists. Truck traffic is prohibited from using all but several short segments of the byway.

Offering a unique byway experience, the Grand Rounds Scenic Byway is a continuous course of paved pathways. It encompasses more than 50 miles of parks, parkways, bike paths, and pedestrian paths that encircle the byway's host city, Minneapolis. The system includes the Chain of Lakes, Lake Nokomis, Lake Hiawatha, and the Mississippi River, as well as Minnehaha Creek.

Parks, recreation centers, historic districts, and lakes are all defining characteristics of the Grand Rounds Scenic Byway. Depending on the season, you interact with a landscape encompassing combinations of natural areas, historical features, and cultural amenities.

The Grand Rounds Scenic Byway has been the crème de la crème of urban byways for more than a century, being the longest continuous system of public urban parkways and providing motorists with access to an unprecedented combination of intrinsic qualities of the highest caliber.

Cultural: An urbanized culture originating in the early 1800s is what visitors to the Grand Rounds Scenic Byway will experience. However, amid this urban culture is a prominent appreciation for nature and the arts. This can be seen in the beautiful parkways, lakes, and parks on the Grand Rounds. Hiawatha Avenue and Minnehaha Park are examples of remnants of a culture that held a great respect for the waters of Minnesota.

Architectural styles ranging from fine to functional exist all along the byway. Unique bridges hold views to the old milling district of the city, where settlers made a living working in the sawmills. Modern art can be found in the uptown area of the byway as well as in the lakeside areas. This art is one contribution of a culture that has evolved from all the previous inhabitants of the Minneapolis area.

The new bandshell on Lake Harriet has architectural features that harken to the area's historic past.

Historical: The Grand Rounds Scenic Byway is one of the nation's longest and oldest connected parkway systems owned entirely by an independent park board. This road has many historical qualities. For example, the Stone Arch Bridge found along the byway is a National Civil Engineering Historical Landmark Site. Minnehaha Falls, also found along the byway, is immortalized in Longfellow's epic poem "The Song of Hiawatha." Master crafting is a significant element of the beauty of the Grand Rounds Scenic Byway, while other forms of architecture are being brought to the surface again. The St. Anthony Falls Heritage Trail offers a wide-ranging perspective on Minneapolis, exploring many highlights of the city's history.

Recreational: With such widely varied attractions in one city, you'll find many places to see and different activities to do at each of those places. Outdoor recreation is not out of reach, while touring historical buildings and parks is a possibility as well. Sailboats and canoes are seen every day on the Chain of Lakes, while bikers and hikers have miles of roads to enjoy. The byway is also host to many national running events; for example, the Twin Cities Marathon was named "the Most Beautiful Urban Marathon in the Country."

Highlights:

Drive the Grand Rounds Scenic Byway and you will see the following sites, and many more.

Theodore Wirth Park: Beginning at the northeastern terminus of the Grand Rounds on Highway 35 W, travel west and follow the byway as it winds around to Theodore Wirth Park. This park is well worth the visit and includes the Eloise Butler Wildflower Garden, with its spectacular display of wildflowers.

Loring Park/Sculpture Garden: Returning to the byway, follow it around Cedar Lake to Lake Calhoun. Here, turn northeast and travel around Lake of the Isles to Loring Park, home of the well-known Sculpture Garden. With its impressive display of sculpture and fanciful artwork, the Sculpture Garden is one of the highlights of the Grand Rounds.

Lake Harriet Refectory: Return in the direction you came, only continue to wind around Lake Calhoun to Lake Harriet to visit the Lake Harriet Refectory.

Minnehaha Park and Lake Hiawatha: Continue following the byway as it turns and travels east to Minnehaha Park, where you may view the falls, and Lake Hiawatha.

Nicollet and Boom Islands: From here, follow the byway north to its terminus at Nicollet Island and Boom. Both offer historic and recreational opportunities in downtown Minneapolis.

Great River Road

The source of the mighty Mississippi River is a must-see and is on the Minnesota section of the Great River Road. Don't forget to look for legendary Paul Bunyan and his blue ox, Babe, along the way.

The Great River Road offers the best of Minnesota. The route encompasses banks of the Mississippi River, 10,000 lakes, beautiful bluff lands, and a variety of outdoor recreation and wildlife. Brilliant wildflowers, evergreen forests, colored autumn leaves, rainbows, snowflakes, migrating birds, and waving fields of grain make this byway a photographer's paradise.

Recreational spots have taken over the land of the lumberjack, where Paul Bunyan and his blue ox, Babe, used to roam freely. State parks and lakeside resorts are all part of the fun that visitors will find on the Great River Road today. And then there is the river itself. Minnesota is where the mighty Mississippi begins. Its meanderings make up a trail of cultural, historical, natural, recreational, and scenic sites. Whether camping in the forested areas of the north or relaxing in a Minneapolis hotel, you will find accommodations in the perfect setting.

The Great River Road is an adventure along a myriad of quaint towns and urban cities. The Twin Cities metropolitan area offers the hustle and bustle of a city that is rich in history, culture, and recreational opportunities. Deep wilderness surrounds the river towns of Minnesota and offers relaxation and privacy.

Cultural: The Great River Road in Minnesota takes you along the southeast end of the state, providing a look at the culture that began and continued on the banks of the Mississippi. This is where you find the Great River and the source of the development of civilization in Minnesota. It began with the American Indian nations of the Sioux and Chippewa, who lived in the area for many years before they began to interact with the Europeans in fur trade. When wildlife grew scarce, new settlers began an industry of logging, which forced native nations out of the area so that logging could proceed.

Although many people initially came to the area for jobs in the logging industry, tourism also blossomed as people traveled to see the beautiful Minnesota forests. In

Leap the 15 or so stones that cross the Mississippi River at its headwaters in Lake Itasca.

the 1930s, people began to restore the once-great forests of giant red and white pines. An appreciation of nature is still part of the byway culture today.

Cultures of the past have left their traces. Native American languages can still be found in names like Lake Winnibigoshish and Ah-Gwah-Ching (Leech Lake), while the heritage of the European settlers resounds in the names of communities all along the road. You will also find more recent pieces of American culture in Lindbergh State Park and the Lindbergh home, a memorial and a glimpse at the boyhood of the famous pilot Charles Lindbergh.

In the Minneapolis to St. Paul area of the byway, you can experience 1840s food, dining, and preparation. Special events include Children's Day, Historic Mendota Days, the Mill City Blues Festival, the Capital City Celebration, and a New Year's Eve party. Also, visit the Taste of Minnesota, the Minneapolis Aquatennial, the St. Paul Winter Carnival, and La Fete de Saint Jean-Baptiste. From Red Wing to Winona, stop and visit the Red Wing Shoe Museum.

Historical: When Henry Rowe School-craft identified the true source of the Mississippi as the crystal-clear waters that flow from Lake Itasca, the final boundaries of the Louisiana Purchase

were set. The Mississippi River, however, was important to Native Americans centuries before the Europeans arrived. In fact, the name Mississippi was an Algonquin name that, when applied to rivers, meant Great River (hence the name Great River Road). During the 1820s and 1830s, Fort Snelling and Grand Portage (on Lake Superior) were the focal points of Euro-American activity in the region. Strategically located at the confluence of the Mississippi and Minnesota Rivers, Fort Snelling served as the first U.S. military outpost in the area.

The Great River Road traces the river through the Chippewa National Forest, created by Congress in 1902. Although originally only small areas of pines were preserved, now more than 600,000 acres of land are managed by the National Forest Service. In this forest is historic Sugar Point on Leech Lake, another of the Mississippi River reservoirs.

You can also visit Battleground State Forest, the site of the last recorded American Indian battle with the U.S. government, and Federal Dam, one of six dams constructed in the area between 1884 and 1912 to stabilize water levels on the Mississippi downstream. The legacies of the great pine forests along the Mississippi live in the majestic trees that remain. In Bemidji, the most recognizable landmark is the 1937 colossal statues of Paul Bunyan and Babe the Blue Ox, located on the shore of Lake Bemidji. The legend of the giant

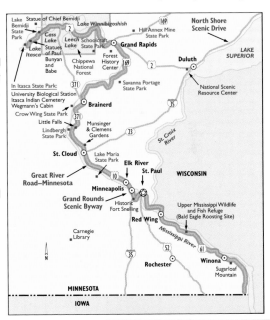

lumberjack illustrates the importance of the lumber industry for many northern Minnesota towns.

Due to its closeness to the river, St. Paul became a transportation hub, opening up the upper Midwest. It also became Minnesota's state capital, and Minneapolis became the nation's main flour-milling district. St. Anthony Falls in Minneapolis and the city's locks and dams provide testimony to people's success at harnessing the power of the river to create a thriving urban center. Flour, beer, textiles, and lumber were produced and successfully transported to the nation and the world through the lock-and-dam system that begins here. In the early 1900s through the 1930s, the Cuyuna Iron Range produced more than 100 million tons of ore that was used to build the U.S. military machines of the great world wars. In Crosby, travelers visit the Croft Mine Historical Park; this mine operated between 1916 and 1934 and produced the richest ore found on the Cuyuna Range, with a composition of 55 percent iron. Portsmouth Lake in Crosby, once the largest open pit mine on the Cuyuna Range, is now one of the deepest lakes in Minnesota at 480 feet.

Camp Ripley, a Minnesota National Guard facility, tells two stories: the history of Minnesota soldiers from the Civil War to the present and the development of the weapons of war.

In Little Falls, the Great River Road follows Lindbergh Drive to the boyhood home of Charles Lindbergh, pilot of the first solo flight across the Atlantic Ocean. The evolution of the United States can be traced along the Great River Road on the Ox Cart Trail, still visible though Schoolcraft and Crow Wing State Parks. Across the river from the Great River Road, Elk River's most noted resident, Oliver H. Kelley, founded the Patrons of Husbandry (popularly known as the Grange), a group that evolved into the Democratic Farmer Laborer, or DFL, party. Today, the Oliver H. Kelley Farm is a 189-acre living-history farm operated by the Minnesota Historical Society. This historic site explores the life and lifestyle of the Kelleys, who lived here in the late 1800s. Byway travelers also learn through excellent interpreta-

Humble Lake Itasca in the pine forest of Minnesota is the source of the Mighty Mississippi River.

tion about the historic importance of the Great River Road and the river as transportation routes and vital links among Mississippi River communities.

Recreational: From the headwaters to the Iowa border, Minnesota's portion of the Great River Road allows visitors to partake in a vast variety of recreational opportunities. No matter what the itinerary or expectation, there is something to suit every taste on the Great River Road. And the fun and adventure continues throughout all four of Minnesota's very distinct seasons.

The water itself creates a large amount of the recreational draw to the Great

River Road. A taste of the recreational possibilities that are available on the water include swimming, sunning, fishing, boating, sailing, canoeing, kayaking, and waterskiing—just to name a few. Strung along the edge of the river are plenty of things to do as well—particularly for outdoor enthusiasts. One of six state parks may be the perfect stop after a drive on the byway. At places like Itasca State Park, visitors can enjoy hiking or biking the trails, picnicking, or even bird-watching. The northern part of the byway provides a haven for hunters and anglers. The wilderness in this area is home to a great deal of wildlife.

Nine thousand years of human history and archaeological importance have made Mille Lacs Kathio State Park a National Historic Landmark.

Winter weather is no excuse to stay indoors in Minnesota. Several places along the byway offer miles of cross-country skiing and snowmobiling. Visitors also find places for downhill skiing. But if moving through the snow doesn't sound appealing, perhaps drilling through the ice does. Ice fishing is a popular pastime for visitors to the Great River Road; ice-fishing resorts, services, and house rentals can be found from one end of the Great River Road to the other. And large catches from the icy waters of Minnesota's many lakes are not uncommon and are a well-known secret among residents of the state.

Highlights:

The following must-see tour of the Great River Road's northern section gives you a sample itinerary to follow, if you so choose.

Itasca State Park:
Covering about 32,000 acres, Itasca State Park embraces the headwaters of the Mississippi River and 157 lakes, the foremost of which is Lake Itasca, the source of the great river. Site of the University Biological

Station, the park has stands of virgin Norway pine. Camping and hiking, as well as historic sites, are abundant here. Itasca Indian Cemetery and Wegmann's Cabin are important landmarks in the area.

Lake Bemidji State Park:
Leaving Itasca State Park, the Great River Road heads northeast toward the Chippewa National Forest and Lake Bemidji State Park. Just 31 miles north of Itasca State Park along Highway 371, the Bemidji area is rich in diverse activities. Stopping at Lake Bemidji State Park provides a lot of fun, including the two-mile Bog Walk, a self-guided nature trail. A small fee per car (per day) applies when visiting Lake Bemidji State Park.

Paul Bunyan, Babe, and Carnegie Library Building:
Outside the park, along the shores of Lake Bemidji, lie several historic sites, including the famous statues of Paul Bunyan and Babe the Blue Ox, and of Chief Bemidji. The Carnegie Library Building, on the National Register of Historic Places, is also located here. You'll find many campgrounds and resorts in the area for staying the night.

Cass Lake:
Cass Lake is the next stop along the tour of the Great River Road. It's a popular spot for fishing and camping. This lake is unique: Star Island, in Cass Lake, is an attractive recreation

Itasca State Park has specimens of nearly every kind of wild animal, tree, and plant native to the state.

area because it contains an entire lake within itself. Other fabulous lakes in the area are worth visiting as well.

Grand Rapids: Enjoy the scenery of northern Minnesota as you follow the signs into the city of Grand Rapids. The city offers many activities, including the Forest History Center, a logging camp that highlights the logging culture of Minnesota.

Savanna Portage State Park: Heading south out of Grand Rapids, follow the signs toward Brainerd. On the way to Brainerd, be sure to stop at Savanna

Portage State Park, with its 15,818 acres of hills, lakes, and bogs. The Continental Divide marks the great division of water—where water to the west flows into the Mississippi River and water to the east runs into Lake Superior. Be sure to walk along the Savanna Portage Trail, too, a historic trail traveled by fur traders, Dakota and Chippewa Indians, and explorers more than 200 years ago.

Brainerd and Lindbergh State Park: The town of Brainerd is a great place to stop for lunch. Many lake resorts nearby offer camping, hiking, and fishing. After Brainerd and south

of Little Falls, just off of Highway 371, is Lindbergh State Park. Look for bald eagles here when visiting in the spring or fall. During your visit, stop in at the historic boyhood home of Charles Lindbergh, the famous aviator. The home is operated by the Minnesota Historical Society and is adjacent to the park.

Munsinger and Clemens Gardens: Once in the city of St. Cloud, the Munsinger and Clemens Gardens offer a relaxing end to this portion of the Great River Road. The nationally known gardens are located near Riverside Drive and Michigan Avenue, right in town. One treat of the gardens is the display of antique horse troughs filled with unique flowers. The gardens are popular but spacious, so they're hardly ever noticeably crowded. The southern tour continues from this point all the way through Minneapolis and St. Paul and along the Mississippi River and Wisconsin border, down to the border of Minnesota and Iowa.

Historic Bluff Country Scenic Byway

The geology of the Historic Bluff Country Scenic Byway yields unique habitats including caves, underground streams, and the Sinkhole Capital of the United States.

Follow the panoramic Root River Valley to the Mississippi River. The scenery along the western end of the byway showcases Minnesota's rich and rolling farmland, while the eastern part of the route winds toward the Great River Road along a beautiful trout stream and canoe route through spectacular tree-covered bluffs featuring limestone palisades and rich hardwoods.

Traditional Midwestern farms punctuate the landscape and provide nostalgic scenery along the byway.

This valley was untouched by the glaciers, and has weathered gradually over time to create a magnificent pastoral setting dotted with small towns, quaint and historic lodgings, and a recreational bike and hiking trail.

Cultural: Among the small Minnesota communities of the Historic Bluff area, a trail to the past defines today's cultures. Some of these cultures, such as the Old Order Amish population, have changed little since first settling here. Others have evolved and yet keep a firm hold on their heritage. The descendants of Norwegians and Germans still celebrate many of the same events that their ancestors did 150 years ago.

Little is left, however, of the Native American culture that once dominated the lands along the byway. At one time, the Winnebago and the Dakota developed celebrations and rituals around the Root River. The nations that survive appreciate cultural sites and sacred places in Bluff Country, and archaeological sites provide a look at places that were important to these cultures.

Quick Facts

Length: 88 miles

Time to Allow: Three hours

Consideration: An extremely scenic route through the Yucatan Valley, the segment between Houston and Caledonia to the south curves frequently and climbs many steep grades in response to the area's topography. When traveling the Bluff Country, be careful of the wildlife inhabiting the area. Rattlesnakes are occasionally found on rock outcrops and on river bottoms.

The settlers who built the towns in Bluff Country were industrious. Towns flourished, and their downtown sections contained splendid architecture that can be observed today. The attitude of growth amid small-town life is still present in byway towns. Meanwhile, the past is alive in Amish communities, where people live without electricity, automobiles, and many of the cultural ideals that most Americans hold. Amish buggies can be seen near Harmony,

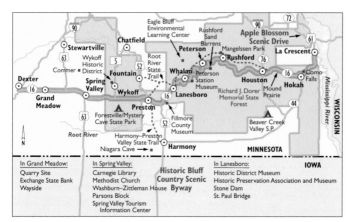

Preston, and Lanesboro. Furniture created by Amish craftspeople can be found at shops in byway towns.

Historical: When southeastern Minnesota was settled, little towns sprang up as the centers of agricultural trade and social activity. Farmers congregated to sell their crops and buy supplies, while grain was stored in silos or grain elevators such as the one in Preston, which once belonged to the Milwaukee Elevator Company. This grain elevator is now a rest stop for travelers along the Root River Trail. The towns profited from agricultural success, and now many of them display historic districts and buildings with elaborate architecture. Many of the buildings, including churches, libraries, and banks, are available to travelers as they explore history on the byway.

As a result of the successful farming industry, mills began to appear in Bluff Country. In Lanesboro, a dam on the river provided power for three flour mills. The commercial district thrived there from the 1860s through the 1920s, and visitors today can tour these brick buildings and the shops and restaurants inside them. Towns along the byway also benefited from the coming of the railroad. The entire town of Wykoff was platted and settled when the railroad passed through. The old Southern Minnesota Depot in Rushford now serves as a trail center. When the railroad left, the tracks lay in disrepair for many years until they were converted to the Root River Trail.

Recreational: The forests, the trails, and the river are the central places for recreation on the byway. And because most of the byway goes through these places, recreation is never far away. State parks and natural areas provide places for hiking, camping, and exploring. With two caves within the byway vicinity, spelunking is a skill that every traveler will want to develop.

Most travelers like to explore places with unique names and histories. The Forestville/Mystery Cave State Park has both. Not only do visitors have the opportunity to go spelunking in the Mystery Cave, but they also are able to explore the site of one of Minnesota's oldest communities, Forestville.

Two state trails on the byway are the perfect place for bikers, hikers, and, in wintertime, cross-country skiers. The Root River State Trail and the Harmony–Preston Valley State Trail connect to provide miles of scenic trail for visitors to enjoy. Along the way, signs give information about the surrounding area.

Perhaps the most inviting trail on the byway is one made of water. The Root River is perfect for an afternoon or a day in a canoe. The Root River is not just a waterway, but also home to a population of trout. Anglers enjoy the wooded atmosphere of the Root River as they try to tempt a prizewinning fish. The Root River is central to many of the activities along the byway, but even if you stray from the riverside, you'll be sure to find something to do.

Highlights:

Use this itinerary to enjoy some of the distinctive geologic attractions on and near the byway.

Mystery Cave: Mystery Cave is the longest cave in Minnesota, with more than 12 miles of passageways in two rock layers, and is the state's best example of karst features. In dry years the entire South Branch of the Root River sinks into the cave through gravel crevices in the river bottom. Mystery Cave is a constant 48 degrees Fahrenheit, so be sure to bring a jacket.

The Root River Trail follows along the Root River, providing hikers and bicyclists an opportunity to view the Bluff country from a different vantage point.

Forestville: While at the Forestville/Mystery Cave State Park, be sure to also tour the vestiges of historic Forestville. All eight of the remaining buildings are listed on the National Register of Historic Places, and historians will guide you through the experience, explaining what life was like for the original settlers of the area.

Niagara Cave: Well worth the detour off the byway, is Niagara Cave. From Fountain follow Highway 52 south (it will join the byway road of Highway 16 briefly) beyond the byway about four miles to the town of Harmony. At Harmony take county Highway 139 south 2.5 miles to Highway 30. Turn west on Highway 30 for approximately 21.5 miles, and follow signs for Niagara Cave. It is one of the largest caves in the Midwest.

Harmony: On your way back to the byway, be sure to stop in Harmony. At the Visitor Information Center near the picturesque Village Green in downtown Harmony you can learn about Historic Bluff Country.

Mangelssen Park: Just before entering Rushford on the north side of Highway 16 is Mangelssen Park, which sits atop a bluff, offering a sweeping panorama of the city of Rushford and the Root River Valley. Mature trees, including a bur oak estimated to be 175 to 200 years old, outline scenic views.

Rushford: After returning to the byway on Highway 16, enjoy the southeastern Minnesota scenery as you head east toward Rushford. About 21.5 miles before you arrive in Rushford, within the Richard J. Dorer Memorial State Forest, is the Rushford Sand Barrens, a distinctive Scientific Natural Area.

Como Falls: Inspired by the bluffs and steep sides of the Root River Valley, continue east to the last of this sampling of geologic formations of southeastern Minnesota. Como Falls is a peaceful part of the quiet village of Hokah near the eastern edge of the byway. Located in Como Falls Park at the east end of Falls Street just off of Main Street, Como Falls is on Thompson Creek. Signage explains the history of the falls, Thompson Creek, and Edward Thompson, the town founder who established a dam and a mill there.

Minnesota River Valley Scenic Byway

The Green Giant Company began in the village of Le Sueur along the Minnesota River Valley Scenic Byway where agriculture from both the past and the present wait to be explored.

The Minnesota River flows gently between ribbons of oak, elm, maple, and cottonwood trees. The Minnesota River Valley Scenic Byway, which follows the river, wanders past rich farmland and through towns steeped in Minnesota history. Passing through rolling farmland and woodlands bordering the river between Belle Plaine and Browns Valley—300 miles of highways and gravel roads—is a scenic, historical, and cultural experience.

The Minnesota River offers an impressive visual treasure for visitors as it meanders across the state before joining the waters of the Mississippi River.

Quick Facts

Length: 287 miles

Time to Allow: Seven days

Consideration: The best time to drive this route is in the fall, due to changing leaf colors.

Cultural: The Minnesota River Valley is a productive land, and as a result, people have been living here for hundreds of years. They thrive on the land and develop rich cultures to complement their successful lifestyle along the Minnesota River. In every town and stop along the byway, travelers have the opportunity to discover the industrious society that has made this land thrive.

The Dakota people share their regional history and thriving modern-day culture through festivals, museums, restaurants, hotels, casinos, and trading posts. European pioneers left their mark as well, and their strong ties to their European heritage remain and are celebrated today. Residents of New Ulm welcome visitors to numerous celebrations, shops, restaurants, and lodging, all of which focus on their

German heritage. Milan residents are likewise proud of their Norwegian heritage, and their community festivals focus on the food, crafts, and traditions of their ancestors. Many other communities on or near the byway demonstrate their proud heritage through festivals, events, and museums.

Historical: Once a wild and untamed river valley, the land of the Minnesota River Valley Scenic Byway used to belong solely to the Dakotas. The land was rich and fertile and seemed ripe for the picking, yet struggles erupted during the same years that the Civil War was raging. In 1862, the largest and bloodiest Native American war in the history of the United States occurred. For ten years, the land was divided between the Dakota people and new settlers. The first reservations were hunting, camping, boating, snowmobiling, cross-country skiing, and golfing. State parks and recreation areas combine outdoor recreation with opportunities to discover history.

All of these activities can be found along the byway at the six state parks, at scientific and natural areas, at wildlife management areas, or at the local parks or waysides. Camping along the byway is one of the best ways to experience the nature of the river valley. Spending time near the river, you can better enjoy the beautiful scenery at one of the byway's lakes or take a stroll along the Minnesota River itself.

developed, but the Dakotas eventually wanted their land and their way of life back. The result was a six-week war in which many settlers and Dakotas were killed. When the war was over, Abraham Lincoln pardoned many of the more than 300 Dakota men who were going to be hanged. The remaining 38 men became part of the largest mass execution in U.S. history.

Recreational: The Minnesota River is one of the great tributaries of the Mississippi River. It provides some of the best recreational opportunities in the upper Midwest. Outdoor recreation abounds, including bird-watching, canoeing, hiking, trail riding, fishing,

Highlights:

The following itinerary is suggested to explore some of the offerings of New Ulm. It is a unique city with a distinctly German–American heritage and much to offer the visitor.

Schell's Brewery: Coming into town from Mankato, turn west on 18th South. Your first stop will be the Schell Brewery, New Ulm's oldest industry and the second-oldest family-owned and managed brewery in the country.

Brown County Historical Society and Museum: The Brown County Historical Society and Museum is located at the corner of Center and Broadway Streets. Giving an excellent overview of the area, this German Renaissance building was built in 1910 for use as the New Ulm Post Office.

Hermann Monument: At Center and Monument Streets is the Hermann Monument, giving a nod to local German heritage by paying homage to a Teutonic hero, Hermann. Designed by architect Julius Berndt and dedicated in 1897, the 102-foot-tall monument can be climbed for a commanding view of New Ulm and the Minnesota River Valley.

Way of the Cross: About halfway up the 5th North Street hill is the Way of the Cross, behind the New Ulm Medical Center. This unique outdoor Catholic shrine was built into the hillside in 1903 and 1904. The Sisters of the Order of the Poor Handmaids of Jesus Christ pushed wheelbarrows up the hill, hauling cobblestones to build the Stations of the Cross, rock walls, and paths.

North Shore Scenic Drive

The North Shore Scenic Drive is home to the Superior Hiking Trail, a 200-mile recreation trail connecting all eight of Minnesota's state parks.

The North Shore of Lake Superior, the world's largest freshwater lake, is 154 miles of scenic beauty and natural wonders. It has what no other place in the Midwest can offer—an inland sea, a mountain backdrop, and an unspoiled wilderness.

Historical: It is believed that the first people to settle the North Shore region arrived about 10,000 years ago. These Native Americans entered the region during the final retreat of the Wisconsin glaciation.

The first Europeans, French explorers, and fur traders reached Lake Superior country around A.D. 1620. By 1780, the Europeans had established fur-trading posts at the mouth of the St. Louis River and at Grand Portage.

The late 1800s saw a rise in commercial fishing along the North Shore. Some of the small towns along the North Shore, such as Grand Marais and Little Marais, were first settled during this period. Many of the small towns still have fish smokehouses.

Lumber barons moved into the region between 1890 and 1910, and millions of feet of red and white pine were cut from the hills along the North Shore. Temporary railroads transported the logs to the shore, where they were shipped to sawmills in Duluth, Minnesota, and Superior, Bayfield, and Ashland, Wisconsin. Today, many of those old railroad grades are still visible, and some of the trails still follow these grades.

Miners digging for high-grade ore from the Iron Ranges in northeastern Minnesota established shipping ports such as Two Harbors in 1884. With the rise of taconite in the 1950s, they developed shipping ports at Silver Bay and Taconite Harbors along Superior's shores. These harbors are still in use, and visitors driving the route may see large 1,000-foot-long ore carriers being loaded or resting close to shore. The shipping history and Lake Superior's unpredictable storms

The Gooseberry River tumbles over five falls on its way to Lake Superior. Gooseberry Falls State Park is considered to be a gateway to the North Shore.

have left the lake bottom dotted with shipwrecks, which now provide popular scuba diving destinations.

Recreational: The North Shore is one of the primary destinations for recreational activities in the Midwest, with facilities for outdoor activities including camping, hiking, biking, skiing, snowmobiling, fishing, and canoeing. The impressive natural beauty of the North Shore has been an attraction since the completion of Highway 61 in the early 1900s.

When you're ready for a break from outdoor excitement, try touring some of the classic historical sites in the area. The Minnesota Historical Society takes care of the Split Rock Lighthouse and provides interpretive programs. The Lake County Historical Museum, which is housed in the old Duluth & Iron Range Railway Depot, contains excellent exhibits on the region's history.

Highlights:

Here are some highlights of the North Shore Scenic Drive.

Canal Park: Begin your experience in Canal Park in Duluth. Follow Canal Park Drive over Interstate 35 to Superior Street.

Fitger's Brewery Complex: Located in historic downtown Duluth, the refurbished Fitger's Brewery Complex offers many fine shops and restaurants.

Rose Garden: To continue along the byway, take a right onto London Road. Follow London Road for the next 5.5 miles, to Leif Erikson Park, which contains the Rose Garden, a popular attraction for visitors.

Two Harbors: Connect with the byway loop in downtown Two Harbors by turning right onto Highway 61 west of town. You can see steam-powered boats and other attractions in Two Harbors. Follow Highway 61 to 6th Street (Waterfront Drive), where you take a right and pick up the byway once again.

Burlington Bay: Continue on the route by taking a left onto 1st Street (Park Road) and following it to Highway 61. Here, hiking trails line the shore of Burlington Bay. Taking a right on Highway 61 and continuing on that route

will lead you along the remainder of the drive, which ends about 122 miles later at the Canadian border.

3M Museum: Follow 6th Street to South Avenue, where you will take a left. Prior to taking a left, be sure to stop at the 3M Museum. The 3M Museum is the only museum in the world dedicated to sandpaper. As you drive down South Avenue, you can begin to see the massive ore docks that extend from the waterfront.

Great River Road

The Wisconsin Great River Road corridor incorporates four nationally recognized, naturally significant areas and more than a dozen state-recognized scientific areas.

Wisconsin's Great River Road flanks the majestic and magnificent Mississippi River as it winds its way along 250 miles of Wisconsin's western border. The road is nestled between the river on one side and towering bluffs on the other. Most of the time, the road parallels the river, but when the road does meander a short way from the river, it treats its guests to vistas of rolling farmland, as well as beautiful forested valleys and coulees.

Cultural: The varied past and present cultures of the corridor are recorded and revealed in the 33 river towns, the many state historical markers, and the archaeological sites found along the byway. The residents of the corridor take pride in preserving their heritage, as evidenced by the many festivals. Some of these festivals include La Crosse's Riverfest and Octoberfest, Villa Louis's Carriage Classic, Prairie du Chien's Fur Trade Rendezvous, Alma's Mark Twain Days, and Pepin's Laura Ingalls Wilder Days.

Well-maintained early homes and storefronts are evident throughout the corridor as well. Architecture from the 19th and 20th centuries is scattered throughout the towns and cities of the byway; many of them reflect the varied architectural trends of the early days of settlement. As you watch for unique architecture, you will also want to notice the mail-order houses that were constructed in a matter of days after arriving by train. Today, unique buildings and art forms continue to surface on the Great River Road. At Prairie Moon Sculpture Garden in Cochrane, for example, a unique form of art typical of the Midwest is displayed.

Historical: American Indians were the first people to live in this region, as evidenced by artifacts from archaeological sites and the presence of burial mounds. Thousands of mounds can be found throughout the area that display the culture of the Hopewell Indians who once lived here. The culture of this people evolved over the years, and they began to establish large, permanent villages. Known as the Oneota people, they were able to farm the river valley using hoes made from bison shoulder blades. By the time the first Europeans arrived, this culture had disappeared, replaced by a group of Sioux.

The bluffs above the unique village of Alma offer sweeping views of the Mississippi River.

French missionary Jacques Marquette and explorer Louis Jolliet were the first Europeans to come through the area. They were searching for a waterway that would connect the Atlantic Ocean and the Gulf of Mexico. Later, French forts were established, and commerce and trade between the European and native cultures ensued. The area changed hands from the American Indians to the French to the British and finally to the Americans, but not without struggle. From the beginning, Native Americans fought to retain their ancestral lands, but to no avail. Settlement began in Wisconsin soon after the Black Hawk War between the Sauk Indians and American troops. In 1848, Wisconsin became a state.

Recreational: Every season offers spectacular recreational opportunities on the Upper Mississippi River along the Wisconsin Great River Road. The Upper Mississippi provides excellent boating and sailing, and there are more than 50 local parks, beaches, recreational areas, and water access sites along the route. On Lake Pepin, a huge lake in the Mississippi River, boaters have access to numerous boat landings, marinas, and docking sites. Fishing is a favorite activity because of the variety of fish species, ranging from catfish to walleye. The sandbars along the river provide places for public camping, picnicking, or just getting off the road.

Bird-watchers enjoy seeing bald eagles as the magnificent birds catch their dinners. Berry-picking and mushroom-hunting are also popular activities, and many travelers choose to experience a farm vacation by milking a cow. Shopping and antique hunting in quaint river towns may be of interest to shoppers, while golfers will find enticing, scenic golf courses.

The Wisconsin Great River Road provides safe accommodations for bikers—with alternate choices of separate bike trails and local roads or streets. Depending on the cyclist's preference and skills, the rider has a choice of touring the Great River Road on-road or off-road. Canoe and bike rentals are available so that every visitor may enjoy these forms of recreation.

Winter in Wisconsin provides ice fishing and wind sailing on the river. Many travelers prefer cross-country or downhill skiing, snow-shoeing, and snowmobiling through deep valleys and scenic bluffs. Summertime is excellent for dinner cruises on the river, or you can rent a houseboat and explore on your own. The river valley features hiking and biking trails, picnic areas, and camping opportunities in the numerous parks and campgrounds along the byway.

Highlights:

The following is an itinerary for the Victory to Bridgeport section—which is only one portion of Wisconsin's Great River Road.

Victory: Begin your tour in Victory. This small settlement along the Great

River Road has a picturesque setting: snuggled next to the river on one side, with bluffs acting as a backdrop on the other. Five settlers laid out this village in 1852 and named it Victory to commemorate the final battle of the Black Hawk War fought south of the village 20 years earlier. Victory prospered during the wheat boom of the 1850s, but today, it is only a remnant of its past.

De Soto: The village of De Soto is four miles south of Victory. This river town has the distinction of being named after the famous Spanish explorer Fernando de Soto, the first European to see the Mississippi River. It was platted in 1854 on the site of a small outpost of the American Fur Company. Today, this community is a shadow of its past, when it peaked with sawmills, grain dealers, blacksmiths, dressmakers, breweries, and hotels. Learn from the locals how the wing dams constructed in the Mississippi diverted the river closer to their community.

Ferryville: Eight miles south of De Soto lies Ferryville. This little town clings to the bluffs along the river and is the longest one-street village in the world. It was first called Humble Bush but was renamed Ferryville when platted in 1858. The name reflects the founder's intentions to establish ferry service across the Mississippi to Iowa. Ferryville still clings to the bluffs and portrays a true river town experience.

Lynxville: Your next stop, Lynxville, is eight miles past Ferryville. Because of the stable depth of the river at Lynxville, it was a reliable and popular landing during the steamboat era of the mid- to late-1800s. Although the steamboats are gone, this quaint little river town remains as the host community to Lock and Dam 9 as well as some apple orchards.

Prairie du Chien: With about 6,000 residents, Prairie du Chien is the largest town on your tour. Stop at the Wisconsin Tourist Information Center to find out about the many area attractions of this second oldest settlement in Wisconsin. It became a trade center as early as the 1670s with the arrival of Marquette and Jolliet. Hercules Dousman built Villa Louis, now owned and operated by the State Historical Society, an opulent 1870s estate with one of the nation's finest collections of Victorian decorative arts. The Villa Louis Historical Marker at this site provides an overview of the origin

The Wisconsin River meets the waters of the Mississippi near Prairie du Chien.

and history of this luxurious mansion. Artifacts of medical history from the 1800s and an exhibit of medical quackery are displayed at the Fort Crawford Medical Museum. Some warehouses built in the early 19th century by the American Fur Company survive on historic St. Feriole Island, as do remnants of the old American Fort built to protect this outpost.

Bridgeport: Driving seven miles southeast of Prairie du Chien, you arrive in Bridgeport. The name of this village is most fitting. In the late 1800s, a ferry carried grain and other farm products across the Mississippi River to a railroad in Minnesota. Today, Bridgeport is near the highway bridge crossing the Wisconsin National Scenic River and the gateway to Wyalusing State Park and Sentinel Ridge.

Woodward Avenue (M-1)

In Motor City, activities and history focus on the automobile, but downtown Detroit is also home to the International Freedom Festival in July, the largest fireworks display in America.

The Motor City put the world on wheels, so welcome to Detroit's main drag: Woodward Avenue. Stretching out from the base of Detroit at the Detroit River, Woodward follows the pathway of growth from the heart of the city. Lined with history, cultural institutions, and beautiful architecture, Woodward Avenue travels through downtown Detroit and the Boston Edison neighborhood; past Highland Park, the Detroit Zoo, the delightful city of Birmingham, and the Cranbrook Educational Community in Bloomfield Hills; and into the city of Pontiac. Nearly every mile has historical sites that have shaped the industrial life of our nation.

Woodward Avenue includes both landmarks of the past and monuments to the future. You can find one of the largest public libraries in the nation as well as one of the five largest art museums. From the Freedom Fireworks Display on the Detroit River to the annual Thanksgiving Day Parade to the phenomenal Woodward Dream Cruise, it's as if this street were meant to blend memories with the future.

Cultural: Much of the culture in southeast Michigan stems from the development of the automobile. When visiting museums such as the Detroit Institute of Arts (DIA) and the Detroit Historical Museum, the impact of the automobile is evident. Your first steps into the DIA will take you to huge two-story murals painted by Diego Rivera that depict life on the assembly line.

Quick Facts

Length: 27 miles

Time to Allow: Five hours

Consideration: The busiest months are August because of the Woodward Dream Cruise and November because of America's Thanksgiving Day Parade. Because this byway passes through downtown Detroit, avoid driving it during rush hour.

The heart of Detroit's vibrant downtown can be viewed from the Detroit River. The river is the most traveled border between Canada and the United States.

The Woodward corridor is one of six areas comprising the Automobile National Heritage Area (under the jurisdiction of the National Park Service). Woodward Avenue is home to other major cultural institutions as well, including the Cranbrook Educational Community, Orchestra Hall, and the Detroit Public Library, which is among the ten largest libraries in the nation.

The region's culture can also be defined by its faith. Traveling from Detroit to Pontiac, you pass by more than 50 churches, many of which are on national or state historic registers. Prominent among these is the National Shrine of the Little Flower in Royal Oak.

Historical: Detroit is known internationally as the Motor City because of its role in the development of the automobile. This is the birthplace of the assembly line (Ford's 1913 Model T Plant on Woodward), a major technological innovation that made the automobile affordable to most families. The assembly line had a major impact on American society and in the development of urban areas.

The first people who may come to mind when talking about the automobile industry are the Fords, Chryslers, and Durants. But you should also remember the thousands of auto workers who established the industry and carry on to this day—the United Automobile Workers (UAW). Henry Ford's five-dollar-a-day wage attracted thousands to his factories, but the working conditions were brutal—this was true of all auto plants. In the late 1930s, the UAW was born and, with fair wages and better working conditions, auto workers and their families now enjoy a decent quality of life. Some of the former homes of early auto barons are located in Detroit's historic neighborhoods, such as the Boston Edison Historic District.

Recreational: The city of Detroit and neighboring communities have worked hard and invested a lot of energy to develop safe, fun activities that the whole family can enjoy. Some of the highlights found along this byway include watching animals at the world-class Detroit Zoo, attending the Woodward Dream Cruise (where thousands from around the world gather to view classic cars from around the country), touring historic homes and mansions, making maple syrup at the festival in Cranbrook, standing on the sidewalk during the famous America's Thanksgiving Day Parade, or watching the largest fireworks display in the nation explode over the shimmering Detroit River.

Highlights:

This byway begins in Pontiac and ends in Detroit, where you can take the following downtown Detroit historical tour.

Detroit River: The tour begins just south of Woodward Avenue at the Detroit River, a designated American Heritage River. It is the most frequently traveled major boundary between Canada and the United States. It is also a major national and international waterway for the movement of freight and other commodities from the United States to foreign markets. In 1701, French explorer Antoine De la Mothe Cadillac founded Detroit at the foot of the present-day Woodward Avenue at the Detroit River.

Campus Martius: Located at the intersection of Michigan, Monroe, Cadillac Square, and Fort Street on Woodward Avenue, Campus Martius was part of the historic 1807 plan of Detroit by Judge Woodward. This site includes the Michigan Soldiers' and Sailors' Monument of 1872.

Lower Woodward Historic District: The Lower Woodward Historic District is on Woodward north of State Street and south of Clifford. This district contains many former retail and office buildings constructed from 1886 to 1936. Significant loft development activity is underway in these buildings.

Woodward East Historic District: Woodward East Historic District (Brush Park) is located east of Woodward, bounded by Watson and Alfred Streets within the Brush Park neighborhood. Known for its high-Victorian-style residences constructed for Detroit's elite in the late 1800s, it is the location of a major urban town-home development.

Peterboro–Charlotte Historic District: The Peterboro–Charlotte Historic District is located on Peterboro at Woodward Avenue. The architecture represents a study in late 19th-century middle-class single-family dwellings and early 20th-century apartment buildings.

Charles H. Wright Museum of African American History: The Charles H. Wright Museum of African American History is located in Detroit's Cultural Center on Warren.

Detroit Historical Museum: The final stop, the Detroit Historical Museum, is located on Woodward in Detroit's Cultural Center. The museum specializes in telling the history of the Detroit area from its founding in 1701 to the present, and includes permanent exhibits, temporary exhibitions, programs, and events.

The Charles H. Wright Museum of African American History offers one of the nation's largest collections of African American history and culture.

Native American Scenic Byway

Watch for excellent interpretive signage and natural wonders as you travel through Sioux tribal lands. Buffalo and other native animals truly do roam free here.

Along this byway, the lakes and streams of the Great Plains tell the story of the Sioux's connection with the land. Journey through the Crow Creek and Lower Brule Indian Reservations, and view their unique cultures firsthand. Buffalo roam on the high plains that sharply contrast the nearby bottomlands and the bluffs along the river. The Big Bend of the Missouri River features prominently in the geography of the area. Dams created Lake Francis Case and Lake Sharpe, which are excellent recreational areas as well as places of beauty.

Cultural: Travel through the grounds of one of the most significant Native American nations in the country. You encounter two Sioux reservations as you drive the byway: the Crow Creek Indian Reservation and the Lower Brule Indian Reservation.

When Lewis and Clark made their journey through this part of the country, they came with the intention of forming a peaceful relationship with the people there. Remnants of that journey remain today, as travelers explore a new landscape and a new culture.

The Native American Scenic Byway is a journey through the heart of the Sioux nation. Excellent cultural interpretive sites give you an in-depth, educational, and entertaining experience with Native American culture.

Historical: The history of the Sioux and other indigenous peoples who preceded them is an important part of Native American culture. A major change in the Sioux culture was initiated by their contact with Lewis and Clark, who went up the river in 1804 and returned in 1806. Their voyage of discovery is one of the major interpretive themes of this byway. In this area, Lewis and Clark first observed mule deer, coyotes, antelopes, jackrabbits, magpies, and several other animals, plants, and birds. Lewis and Clark were followed by fur traders, who in turn were followed by steamboats, which were followed by settlers. Fur-trading posts were converted into military posts, and the great Sioux Reservation was reduced to its present size. Communities were built, and the river was dammed. Through it all, the land remains, giving evidence of the past.

Recreational: The damming of the river along this byway created Lake Francis Case and Lake Sharpe. These impounded waters provide excellent recreational opportunities. All types of water sports are available, and the fishing is among the best in the country. The recreational

The Oahe Dam provides flood control for the powerful Missouri River.

today the dam is a popular site for water recreation activities of all sorts.

Pierre: Six miles southeast is the north terminus, at South Dakota's capital, Pierre. While in Pierre, tour the Cultural Heritage Center, which showcases South Dakota history. Also in Pierre is the state capitol, one of the most fully restored U.S. capitols.

Missouri River:

The Missouri River runs parallel to the byway. You can enjoy numerous water recreational activities, including swimming, camping, boating, and fishing, at many points along the byway.

Farm Island Recreation Area:

Located four miles southeast of Pierre is the Farm Island Recreation Area. The park is nestled along the shores of the Missouri River and provides a great place for a variety of outdoor recreation activities. Camping, boating, and fishing are popular here. Swimmers enjoy the beach of the Missouri River.

Fort Pierre National Grassland:

Traveling south of Pierre, you pass through the Fort Pierre National Grassland. The land is publicly owned and administered by the U.S. Forest Service. The grassland is noted for crop fields of sorghum, wheat, and sunflowers.

Lower Brule Indian Reservation:

Only 30 miles southeast of Pierre begins the Lower Brule Indian Reservation. Visitors to the reservation enjoy the tribal casino, as well as visits to Lake Sharpe and the Big Bend Dam.

Crow Creek Indian Reservation:

The Crow Creek Indian Reservation begins near Big Bend and continues until the southern terminus of the Native American Scenic Byway. Casinos, water sports, fishing, entertainment, and hunting are available on the reservation.

Lake Sharpe: Lake Sharpe stretches some 80 miles from the Oahe Dam in the north to the Big Bend Dam in Fort Thompson. It is easily accessed at the West Bend State Recreation area 50 miles east of Pierre on the byway.

Big Bend Dam: Big Bend Dam is located approximately 50 miles southeast of Pierre. Built to control flooding of the Missouri River and to provide hydroelectric power, the dam has created vast reservoirs that today provide ample opportunity for fishing and water recreation.

facilities along the lakes are managed by the U.S. Army Corps of Engineers, and nice camping facilities are also available. The communities at either end of the byway offer biking, hiking, and nature trails.

Highlights:

This itinerary takes you the entire length of the byway, from north to south. If you're traveling in the other direction, read this list from the bottom and work your way up.

Oahe Dam: You can begin traveling the Native American Scenic Byway at the Oahe Dam, the world's second-largest earth-filled dam. Originally built to control flooding from the Missouri River,

Peter Norbeck Scenic Byway

Not only home to beloved American landmark Mount Rushmore, the Peter Norbeck Scenic Byway also fascinates visitors with ghost tours from 1800s gold rush days, amazing geological formations, and the occasional mountain goat.

This 68-mile scenic route honors a South Dakota conservationist, governor, and U.S. senator. Peter Norbeck first saw the Black Hills in 1905 after crossing the prairie on rugged, unimproved roads. His first visit began a lifelong love affair with the hills. Norbeck Overlook, Norbeck Wildlife Preserve, and now this byway all bear his name and memorialize his conservation achievements.

Sylvan Lake, located in Custer State Park, is the oldest reservoir in the Black Hills of South Dakota.

Cultural: The earliest modern inhabitants of the Black Hills were the Crow Indians. Not much is known about these residents, except that they were forced to move west by the Cheyenne Indians. Ironically, the Cheyenne held the Black Hills for only a few decades. Westward-expanding Sioux Indians reached the hills around 1775 and quickly defeated the Cheyenne nation.

The Sioux reigned over the High Plains for nearly a century.

In 1876, following the discovery of gold in the Black Hills, the Sioux War broke out. After several defeats by the U.S. Cavalry, the Sioux, with neighboring nations in Wyoming and Montana, united to battle General George Custer's troops. Custer and his troops were massacred in the Battle of Little Bighorn, and the Sioux emerged victorious. However, as more U.S. troops arrived on the plains, most American Indians were disarmed and forced onto reservations. The government bought the Black Hills from the Sioux. Tension between the Sioux and the settlers remained high. The government built Fort Meade to permanently house soldiers who would protect the settlers. Hundreds of Sioux people died at Wounded Knee Creek when a minor melee triggered nervous troops to open fire.

Historical: In 1905, Peter Norbeck traveled to the Black Hills from his home on the eastern Dakota prairies. He soon became the unlikely steward of the Black Hills and a nationally prominent conservationist and legislator.

One of Norbeck's greatest concerns was creating a great state park befitting the extraordinary beauty and diversity of the Black Hills. He envisioned a pre-serve that would encompass features such as the Needles, Harney Peak, and the Sylvan Lake area. His tireless efforts led to the establishment of Custer State Park in 1919 and the Norbeck Wildlife Preserve in 1920.

In 1919, work began on the Needles Highway, following a route through rugged terrain that was often impassable on horseback. Norbeck supplied 150,000 pounds of dynamite to one of the engineers who said he would need it to build the road. By 1921, the Needles Highway was completed.

Recreational: One of the best ways to see the Peter Norbeck Scenic Byway is to see it as Peter Norbeck did—on foot. Trails wind throughout Custer State Park and the Black Hills National Forest. For cyclists and hikers, Centennial Trail runs into backcountry areas.

Many visitors travel the byway for the sole purpose of seeing a national landmark. Roads with names like the Needles Highway are just waiting to be explored. The Needles Highway is a natural attraction for scenic drivers, and rock climbers find the granite spires of the area irresistible.

Highlights:

Please be aware that portions of the Peter Norbeck Scenic Byway have steep grades, sharp curves, tunnels, and bridges.

General Custer Expedition Campsite: General Custer Expedition Campsite was the base camp for the 1874 Custer Expedition that explored and mapped the Black Hills and discovered gold here.

Gordon Stockade and Stockade Lake: The Gordon Stockade is a replica of the 1874 structure built by the first settlers in the hills. Also in the area is Stockade Lake, where you can camp.

Sylvan Lake: Sylvan Lake is the oldest reservoir in the Black Hills, constructed in 1898. Take time to swim, fish, hike, camp, or rock climb in the area.

Forest Ecology Wayside: Next up is the Forest Ecology Wayside, which conveys the natural history of the Black Hills forests and fire.

Norbeck Wildlife Preserve: This preserve is home to deer, elk, mountain goats, bighorn sheep, and many bird species.

Horsethief Lake: Horsethief Lake is a favorite spot for camping and for hiking into the backcountry.

Mount Rushmore: Mount Rushmore was carved by Gutzon Borglum between 1927 and 1941 and stands as a memorial to significant figures of America's government.

Great River Road

Prehistoric Native American mounds are common from the prairies of the Midwest to the Eastern Seaboard, but the Effigy Mounds National Monument along Iowa's section of the Great River Road is the only place in America where the large mounds are shaped in the lifelike outlines of mammals, birds, and reptiles.

Join travelers from around the world to discover dramatic vistas of Old Man River during all seasons. View soaring eagles and 100,000 migrating geese and ducks. Experience Midwest hospitality on the main streets of river towns and cities, or visit sacred sites and landscape effigies of Native Americans. You can also experience the Mississippi River on steamboats, commercial barges, and recreational crafts.

The byway's story begins with the landscape: Abrupt and dramatic limestone bluffs cut by glacial meltwater in the north contrast with broad sandy floodplains in the south. For thousands of years, Native Americans knew the importance of the continent's largest river. Later, its meandering course marked the political boundaries of territories, towns, cities, states, and counties of the advancing society. Today, the Upper Mississippi River and the Great River Road are national repositories of geological wonders, unparalleled scenic beauty, wildlife, native vegetation, and the miracles of hydrology. The river and road are also milestones to the expansion and development of the United States and the Midwest.

Historical: Although most of Iowa was settled in the mid-1800s, the Mississippi River made it an accessible territory long before the United States became a nation. Native Americans and explorers alike saw the raw, unharnessed power of this beautiful passageway. One of the first outposts was Fort Madison, where history is recreated today. Like much of the United States, the Great River Road was under Spanish and French rule until the time of the Louisiana Purchase in 1803.

Soon after, settlers and industry came to Iowa. Bustling river towns created cultural landmarks such as Snake Alley—the curviest road in the United States. Little towns along the road grew and became the cities they are today. During the booming days of river trade, writer Samuel Langhorne Clemens (better known as Mark Twain) captured the atmosphere and the time period in his novels.

When the Civil War came to Iowa, most of the people living there fought for the Union. Civil War memorials are now found in several of the towns on the byway.

Effigy Mounds National Monument contains 195 prehistoric mounds. Eastern Woodland Indians built the mounds with 31 being in the shape of effigies.

Recreational: Recreational opportunities abound along the Iowa Great River Road. Water activities include boating, sailing, fishing, waterfowl hunting, and swimming. For decades, the Iowa Great River Road and its side roads have been popular pleasure routes for sightseeing. Numerous multipurpose trails and support facilities are available along the road.

Highlights:

Not sure where to begin? Consider taking this Lansing-to-Guttenberg tour of Iowa's Great River Road.

Lansing: The tour begins in Lansing, home of Mount Hosmer Park. Also of interest is the Fish Farm Mound (an Indian burial site) and the nearby Our Lady of the Wayside Shrine.

Harpers Ferry: The next stop, Harpers Ferry, is 15 miles past Lansing. The town is built on a concentrated area of Native American mounds and was an important river town after the introduction of the steamboat.

Yellow River Forest State Recreation Area: Just south of Harpers Ferry lies the Yellow River Forest State Recreation Area. This 8,000-acre forest contains some of Iowa's greatest terrain, with high scenic bluffs and cold streams. The Iowa Department of Natural Resources harvests the Yellow River Forest timber for use all over the state. The Paint Creek section of the forest houses most recreational opportunities, including camping, canoeing, snowmobiling, hunting and fishing, and hiking trails.

Effigy Mounds National Monument: Effigy Mounds National Monument, the next stop, is just two miles south of Yellow River Forest. Prehistoric mounds are common from the plains of the Midwest to the Atlantic seaboard, but only in this area were some of them constructed in an effigy outline of mammals, birds, or reptiles. Eastern Woodland Indian cultures built these mounds from about 500 B.C. to A.D. 1300. Natural features in the monument include forests, tallgrass prairies, wetlands, and rivers.

Pikes Peak State Park: Pikes Peak State Park is five miles south of Marquette. This park boasts one of Iowa's most scenic views across the Mississippi. It was named for Zebulon Pike, who was sent in 1805 to scout placement of military posts along the river. A fort was never built on this land, and it went into private ownership. Because settlers were not able to build on this property, the peak remains as Zebulon Pike saw it 200 years ago.

Guttenberg: The tour terminates in Guttenberg, 15 miles south of Pikes Peak State Park. Guttenberg boasts two scenic overlooks and a mile-long landscaped park along the river. A copy of the Gutenberg Bible is on display at the local newspaper. The city offers blocks and blocks of historic buildings.

Loess Hills Scenic Byway

The Lewis and Clark Trail, Oregon Trail, Mormon Trail, and California Trail all traverse the Loess Hills Scenic Byway. Some of the natural features on the byway are only found here and one other place on the planet— on the opposite side of the world, in China.

Quick Facts

Length: 220 miles

Time to Allow: Seven hours

Consideration: Occasionally, winter weather may necessitate a slower rate of travel. Also, the gravel roads on some of the excursion loops may also become somewhat degraded during periods of high rainfall.

The Loess Hills Scenic Byway weaves through a landform of windblown silt deposits along the eastern edge of the Missouri River Valley. This unique American treasure possesses natural features that are found in only two places in the world: western Iowa and the Yellow River Valley of China. Travelers are intrigued by the extraordinary landscape of prairies and forest-covered bluffs.

The loess (pronounced LUSS) soil deposits were initially left by glacial melt waters on the flood-plain of the Missouri River. These deposits were then blown upward by strong winds. The steep, sharply ridged topography of this area was formed over thousands of years by the deposition and erosion of the windblown silt. The rugged landscape and strong local contrasts in weather and soil conditions provide refuge for a number of rare plants and animals.

As you drive the western edge of Iowa, you pass through dozens of prairie towns. Larger cities such as Council Bluffs and Sioux City offer venues of recreation, culture, and history.

You will want to enjoy the many nature areas along the way as well. The Dorothy Pecaut Nature Center, the Hitchcock Nature Area, and the Loess Hills State Forest are just a few of the many places on the byway that are dedicated to preserving and restoring the native prairies of western Iowa.

Cultural: Many of the first European settlers of the Loess Hills of Iowa came from Danish, German, or Swedish cultures that settled in the United States nearly 200 years ago to create a unique heritage. These people learned to live among each other, creating a diverse culture characteristic of the United States.

The byway culture today is a blend of the old and new living side-by-side. Urban centers such as Sioux City and Council Bluffs give way to hidden corners of agricultural hamlets.

From cities to villages, cultural events occur regularly on the byway. While some

Soil deposits left by glacial melt waters in the floodplain of the Missouri River, wind-blown and eroded over thousands of years, formed the unique Loess Hills.

visitors may choose to attend theatrical events and tour museums, others may want to taste some of the local flavor at a farmer's market, county fair, or heritage celebration. When travelers come to the Loess Hills Scenic Byway, many of them take part in activities such as the rodeo or apple harvest festivals. To learn more about the people of the Loess Hills, visit the Moorhead Cultural Center, which has displays and activities that tell the story of people and culture on the byway.

Historical: The history of human settlement in the Loess Hills has left many stories behind in old buildings and sacred places. A home and hunting ground to some of the continent's earliest people, human habitation in the Loess Hills has been developing for many years. The people native to this land had a great respect for the Loess Hills. The land was greatly honored until the early 1800s; when explorers began to wind their way through this land in the 1700s, it was the end of an old way of life around the Loess Hills. Historical treasures remain within the Loess Hills from the period of European settlement as well. To see pieces of this history, follow the Lewis and Clark Trail north and south along the hills or prepare for a trip along one of the many trails that traveled to the West. The Oregon Trail, Mormon Trail, and California Trail all traversed the Loess Hills in their route westward. In fact, the Mormon Trail had a stopover point in the hills called the Great Encampment that was used during the winter months. At this point, permanent settlement in the Loess Hills became an option for pioneers crossing the plains.

The places left behind are protected as designated historic sites. You will find National Historic Landmarks, places on the National Register of Historic Places, and National Historic Trails. Museums and information centers along the byway allow visitors to study the history that surrounds the hills. Buildings such as the General Dodge House and the Woodbury County Courthouse display styles of architecture from another time. Many sites in the Loess Hills were also used on the Underground Railroad to transport escaped slaves to the north. And you will find monuments to the first explorers, including Sergeant Floyd of the Lewis and Clark expedition, who was the only explorer to die during the journey. Museums cover everything from Civil War history to prehistoric life in this part of Iowa.

Recreational: During a drive on the Loess Hills Scenic Byway, you will want to get out of the car and stretch. And there are several places along the byway that are perfect for more than just stretching. Opportunities for outdoor recreation are around every corner.

Between preserves and state parks, you will have an excellent chance to view unique wildlife. DeSoto National Wildlife Refuge is a home and hotel to many waterfowl and migratory birds. Wildlife watching is a popular activity on the byway's four preserves. At Stone State Park, try camping or tour the trails in your own way. Whether you love hiking, biking, or horseback riding, all these modes of transportation are welcomed. Even snowmobilers ride through these wooded trails onto the white prairie in the wintertime. Stop at an orchard or farm to pick your own apples.

If outdoor recreation isn't a priority, try touring historical sites and monuments. Historical museums are located throughout the byway, along with many unusual buildings and historic districts. Gaming is also a popular activity on the byway at the casinos in the byway communities. Visitors will find slot machines, table games, and nightlife. In addition, the best antique shopping in Iowa is rumored to be found in the communities along the byway. Cross the river from Council Bluffs to Omaha, Nebraska, to explore this busy city full of distractions. Or simply settle down at a quiet restaurant for a bite to eat and time to look at the map.

Highlights:

When driving this byway, consider using this Loess Hills prairie tour as your itinerary.

Broken Kettle Grasslands: The tour starts in the Broken Kettle Grasslands, just south of Akron. The preserve constitutes the largest remaining section of the vast prairie that once covered most of Iowa. It contains some flora and fauna not found in any other part of the Loess Hills to the south or the state of Iowa, including the prairie rattlesnake and the ten-petal blazing star.

Five Ridge Prairie Preserve: Five Ridge Prairie Preserve, located on the Ridge Road Loop, about five miles south of Broken Kettle Grasslands, is a combination of prairie and woodlands. This is one of the best sites of unbroken prairie remnants in Iowa. You'll notice the climate changes between open grasslands, which are warmed by the sun and dry prairie breezes, and the shadowy woods, which remain cooler and more humid. Expect to find more than a few rugged hiking trails at this site.

DeSoto National Wildlife Refuge preserves habitat for migratory waterfowl, and presents interpretive displays on the historic development of the Missouri River basin.

Dorothy Pecaut Nature Center: The Dorothy Pecaut Nature Center is on the Stone Park Loop just south of the Highway 12 entrance to Stone State Park. The center is devoted wholly to Iowa's Loess Hills.

Stone State Park: Your final stop, Stone State Park, is located on Sioux City's interpretive northwest side. It has 1,069 acres of prairie-topped ridges and dense woodlands. Dakota Point and Elk Point provide scenic overlooks of Nebraska, South Dakota, and Iowa. The multiuse trails handle hikers, bicyclists, horseback riders, and snowmobilers. Campsites with showers are available. This park is a site on the Lewis and Clark National Historic Trail.

Great River Road

The Illinois section of the Great River Road gives an overview of the complete timeline of American history. From the Underground Railroad to the westward movement of the Mormons, this section of the byway tells it all.

Quick Facts

Length: 557 miles

Time to Allow: Four or five days

Consideration: Generally, the entire route of Illinois' portion of the Great River Road is within the 100-year flood plain. While flooding does not occur regularly, roads are closed and detours are marked when flooded.

Experiencing the Mississippi River for the first time is a memory few can forget. The awe that many people feel toward this river may come from the power of a flood or the beauty of a golden sunset that reflects off the still winter waters, turning graceful steel bridges into shimmering lines of color.

Looking out over the river, it is almost impossible to comprehend the complex layers of history that have been acted out along its banks. From the large communities of the Hopewell Indian culture (the most complex society in North America that existed from approximately A.D. 700 to 1400) and early French colonial settlements and fortifications to the frightened, cautious, and optimistic slaves who sought freedom on the Underground Railroad, this corridor has played a role in many of this continent's most dramatic hours. Today 15 percent of the nation's shipping passes through the river's complex system of locks and dams, yet such commercial activity occurs under the spreading wings of the newly thriving American bald eagle.

It is from the Great River Road that most visitors and residents understand and define their relationship with the Mississippi. It is from this road that the historic sites and cultural artifacts of the area can be accessed, from Native American mounds to the Mormon (Church of Jesus Christ of Latter-Day Saints) temple. The beautiful Mississippi bluffs tower over the byway as permanent sentinels for the great river. Whether directly along the banks of the river or winding through the vast flood plain miles from the water, the Great River Road links resources, people, and history.

Cultural: Some of the first people to settle along the banks of the Mississippi River were Native Americans. These nations were embedded in a culture that held the utmost respect for nature and

This Italianate home was a gift to the Ulysses S. Grant family by a group of Galena citizens upon the General's triumphant return from the Civil War.

ranged from gold rushes to religious freedom. The people who live in these communities maintain a distinct place on the byway, with their styles of architecture and inventiveness. Today, the culture of the Great River Road embodies the relaxed hometown pace. The towns and villages along the byway offer you a change of scenery and a chance to slow down. These towns are often small and full of rich historical detail that influences cultures even today.

You can find historic architecture in several of the towns along the road: Nauvoo, Quincy, Alton, Belleville, and Cairo allow you to experience the Great River Road as the settlers of nearly 200 years ago did. These cities all have their share of historic places and buildings that are full of pioneer stories and Civil War tales. As a passage on the Underground Railroad, the river represents a piece of African American history as well. The river itself holds a story of steamboats chugging up the river. It represents the ingenuity of inventors and engineers in the earliest days of travel. The river is the lifeblood of the area that has drawn so many people to its shores.

Recreational: On and around the river, you have places to go and different ways to get there. Hikers and bikers find riverside trails attractive, while other travelers may prefer to enjoy a pleasant afternoon on a riverboat. Ferries, canoes, and even old-fashioned steamboats give you a closer view of the greatest river in the nation. To see more of the communities on the byway, you may enjoy a trolley tour or a park area, as well as museums and historical buildings. Museums and monuments to the past are sprinkled along the road to give you a sense of what came before on the Great River Road.

the resources of the land. Their inextricable connection to the land can be seen in the burial mounds they left behind, as well as in museums and monuments.

Since the habitation of the first cultures in the area, several other cultures have passed through the Illinois Great River Road area, and some have stayed permanently. During the 1800s, the now-historic communities along the Great River Road were settled for reasons that

Historical: As an area that has enraptured American Indians, explorers, and settlers, the Illinois Great River Road holds pieces of the past that are intriguing to today's visitors. Since 1938, the road has been protected and enhanced in order to preserve its scenic and historical qualities. The heritage of the native nations of the Sauk and Fox Indians remains prevalent in many places along the byway.

Other forms of fun can be found on the byway as well. More than 75 golf courses help you track your progress along the byway by greens. Travelers who would like to test their luck can try a riverboat casino. Communities all along the byway offer numerous stops for antique shoppers who are looking for a piece of Illinois' past to take home with them, and if antiques aren't enough, plenty of novelty shops and gift shops abound. For the hungry traveler, many restaurants along the byway are sure to suit your fancy. Entertainment is an element of the byway's recreational offerings, too. Many towns host musicals, dinner shows, and old-fashioned theater experiences.

Chances to enjoy the outdoors along the Great River Road come often. In addition to the Shawnee National Forest, 29 state recreation and/or conservation areas are available along the route of the Great River Road. The Mississippi Palisades State Park and National Landmark offers phenomenal views to and from the bluffs (palisades) along the Mississippi River. The facilities for tent and trailer camping, fishing, cross-country skiing, and ice fishing are top notch.

The Big River State Forest is a 2,900-acre facility dedicated to demonstrating sound forestry practices. Firebreaks and a fire tower afford breathtaking views and hikes. Nearby, camping, hiking, and river and lake fishing are available at Delabar State Park. In the south, Horseshoe Lake Conservation Area is one of the loveliest places to hike, camp, hunt, and boat. Horseshoe Lake is a quiet, shallow lake lined with cypress and tupelo gum and wild lotus. You can find places for bird-watching and exploring wetlands, and canoeing along the river is a popular recreational pursuit all along the byway.

Highlights:

When traveling the Moline-to-Nauvoo

section of the Illinois Great River Road, consider using the following itinerary.

Moline: Both the past and present of the world-famous John Deere & Company operations are centered in Moline, where you begin your tour. At the John Deere & Company Commons, catch historic trolleys to other Deere sites, tour the John Deere Pavilion with interactive displays of historic and modern farm equipment, and visit the John Deere Store. The Deere Administrative Center, Deere corporate headquarters, lies on the outskirts of Moline. This building, designed by Eero Saarinen, and grounds are widely regarded as masterworks of architecture and landscape architecture. The Deere-Wiman House and Butterworth Center are mansions built in the late 1800s by Charles Deere. Guided tours of the homes and gardens are available.

Rock Island Arsenal: Rock Island Arsenal lies on spectacular Rock Island in the Mississippi River directly in front of the John Deere & Company Commons. Visitors to the island can visit Historic Fort Armstrong (1816–1817), the Rock Island Arsenal Museum (with exhibits of military equipment and small firearms), and other historic structures. The Rock Island Arsenal is the largest weapons manufacturing arsenal in the country. Located next to Lock and Dam 15, the

The 4,500-foot-cable Clark Bridge connects Alton, Illinois, with St. Louis, Missouri.

largest roller dam in the world, the U.S. Army Corps of Engineers Mississippi River Visitors Center features an observation deck for towboats and birds. The visitors center has displays about Upper Mississippi geography, ecology, and the lock-and-dam system. It is also a designated Great River Road interpretive center.

Black Hawk State Historic Site:
Two miles south of Rock Island lies the next stop on the tour, Black Hawk State Historic Site—a wooded, steeply rolling 208-acre tract. American Indians and 19th-century settlers made their homes here, but the area is most closely identified with the Sauk nation and the warrior-leader whose name it bears—Black Hawk. The site, which is also noted for its many natural features, is managed by the Illinois Historic Preservation Agency. The Hauberg Indian Museum, located in the lodge constructed by the Civilian Conservation Corps, interprets the culture of the Sauk and the Mesquackie. Nearly 175 species of birds and 30 species of wildflowers, as well as a prairie restoration, can be observed here. Dickson Pioneer Cemetery is where many early settlers are buried. Picnicking and hiking are also available.

Big River State Forest: Following the byway along the Mississippi River for another 50 miles, you arrive at the

2,900-acre Big River State Forest. The forest lies in Henderson County, six miles north of Oquawka, where gas and food are available. The area's oldest pine plantation, the Milroy Plantation, with towering red, white, and jack pines lies within. The forest is a remnant of a vast prairie woodland border area that once covered much of Illinois. Two endangered plants, penstemon and Patterson's bindweed, are found here. A prominent landmark in the forest is its fire tower, located at the headquarters area and accessible to the public at nonemergency times. Sixty miles of firebreaks interlace Big River State Forest, which are used by hikers, horseback riders, and snowmobilers. Tent, trailer, and equestrian camping sites, boat launch, picnic areas, hunting, stables, and scenic drives are available.

Delabar State Park: Located on the Mississippi River about 4.5 miles south of Big River State Forest and 11.5 miles north of Oquawka, the 89-acre Delabar State Park offers quality outdoor

Tower Rock, blanketed by stands of upland forest, is a small limestone island carved by the powerful forces of the Mississippi River.

experiences for anglers, hikers, campers, and picnickers. More than 50 species of birds have been sighted in the park, making it a destination for bird-watching, too. Picnic areas, playground facilities, tent and trailer camping, trailer dumping, hiking trails, river and lake fishing, boat launching, ice fishing, and ice skating are available in the area.

Nauvoo: This tour of a short section of the byway terminates about 45 miles south of Delabar State Park in Nauvoo. The town is located at a picturesque bend in the river at Hancock County. Nauvoo was settled by Joseph Smith and members of the Church of Jesus Christ of Latter-Day Saints (LDS).

Historic National Road

Along the Historic National Road visitors will have a chance to view bridges that are engineering marvels. But be sure to also look for Monk's Mound, a Native American engineering marvel. It took 300 years to build and is now a United Nations World Heritage Site.

The route of the Historic National Road is a road of history. Nineteenth century river transportation and commerce, ralong with historic cemeteries, tell of the struggles of the early settlers on the western frontier. County fairs and main street storefronts speak of small towns where you can still find soda fountains, one-room schools, and old hotels.

Small and large museums, a National Register Historic District, and National Register Historic Sites are found all along the byway. Prehistoric Native American life is evident here as well, along with giant earthwork mounds that took 300 years to build. The atmosphere of old-fashioned travel is stored in the little shops and lodgings in towns along the way. The western end of the byway takes you to Eads Bridge and the gateway to the West.

Historical: In 1806, Congress appropriated funds to construct a National Road that would run westward from Cumberland, Maryland, to the Mississippi River. The Illinois section was surveyed in 1828 by Joseph Schriver, and construction was started in 1831. The section to Vandalia was completed in 1836. However, the western section was never funded due to

Monk's Mound at Cahokia Mounds State Historic Site is the largest earthen mound built by Native Americans in the North American continent.

high costs and waning interest in road building. With the coming of the Terre Haute–Vandalia–St. Louis Railroad that paralleled the road, the National Road fell into disrepair, only to be resurrected in the early 1920s when it was hard surfaced and designated U.S. 40. Today, most of the original alignment of the 1828 surveyed road is still in place and is in public hands.

On the eastern end of the byway is Marshall, home to Illinois' oldest continuously operating hotel. Also on the eastern end is the village of Greenup, with its unique business section decorated with original overhanging porches. This village was designated as a Historic Business District on the National Register of Historic Places. In the central section is Vandalia, the second capital of Illinois. The Capitol, in which Abraham Lincoln passed his test to practice law, is now a State Historic Site and sits on the Historic National Road.

Recreational: The byway offers many recreational opportunities. You can bike or hike on the various trails along the way. Numerous state parks allow you to enjoy the natural characteristics of the byway; many of the towns have parks and recreational facilities.

At Lincoln Trail State Park, you can travel the route Abraham Lincoln took from Kentucky to Illinois. This park is on part of that route, and today, it is a place where you can enjoy hiking, fishing, boating, or camping. Summer is not the only time to enjoy this area, however; wintertime sports include ice fishing, ice skating, and cross-country skiing.

Many lakes, rivers, and streams provide recreational opportunities. Carlyle Lake is a 26,000-acre multipurpose lake known for its great fishing and waterfowl hunting. At Eldon Hazlet State Park, controlled pheasant hunting is available, and bird-watching is also a popular activity. Carlyle Lake is well known among sailors, and you can rent a houseboat at the park. Camping and golf courses are available here as well.

Highlights:

The Illinois section of the Historic National Road begins in Martinsville and goes to Collinsville.

Lincoln School Museum: This quality museum is located near Martinsville. The building itself was built in 1888, and the school is open to groups for an interpretation of early pioneer days.

Franciscan Monastery Museum: Dating to 1858, this historic monastery has a wonderful museum that displays artifacts from early settlers as well as the Franciscan Fathers. Visitors can view pioneer items such as toys and kitchen utensils, and religious items such as Bibles and vestments. There are also antique legal documents on display, such as marriage licenses. The

monastery is located about five miles east of Effingham in Teutopolis.

My Garage Corvette Museum: This museum, located in Effingham, about 30 miles west of Martinsville, is a must for automobile lovers. On display are vintage Corvettes from the 1950s and 1960s.

Collinsville Historical Museum: Located about 90 miles west of Effingham in Collinsville, this museum offers visitors a unique glance into the region's residents all the way back to John Cook, the first settler in 1810. Many interesting artifacts are on display, including a variety of Civil War objects and miners' tools.

Lincoln Highway

Transportation might not be the same today without the Lincoln Highway. It was here where they had the idea of paving several one-mile stretches of the formerly dirt roads to create "seedling miles" in an effort to foster a public desire for good roads, thus changing transportation history.

This historic byway follows the original alignment of the Lincoln Highway, the first paved transcontinental highway in the United States. The 179-mile route crosses the width of northern Illinois, starting in Lynwood on the Indiana border. The route ends in Fulton at the Iowa border. The Illinois portion of the highway, located near the center of the 3,389-mile transcontinental route, was the site of the first seedling mile of paved roadway constructed to demonstrate the superiority of pavement over dirt roads. The Lincoln Highway was also the first instance in which directional signs and urban bypasses were used.

Cultural: The culture of the Lincoln Highway centers around its communities, which share a pride in being part of the history and future of transportation. In most of the Lincoln Highway communities, you find at least one defining characteristic. In Dixon, it is the Victory Arch that spans the highway; in Chicago Heights, it is the Arche Fountain commemorating Abraham Lincoln; in Batavia, it is the unique architecture.

Historical: In 1912, a core group of automobile industrialists and enthusiasts established an organization to promote the development of "good roads" and conceived a route for a paved, transcontinental road. This group sought to secure private funding to build a road that would serve the needs of industry, particularly the automobile industry. The first seedling mile was completed in Malta, Illinois, just west of DeKalb, in October 1914. Four more seedling miles were constructed in 1915. The stark contrast between these smooth patches of pavement and the bumpy or muddy roads leading up to them created a groundswell of public opinion in favor of good roads.

This clamor for action was directed at local, state, and federal officials and resulted in the passage of the Federal Aid Road Act of 1916, which authorized

Quick Facts

Length: 179 miles

Time to Allow: Five to six hours

Consideration: The best time to drive this route is early summer. This byway is long and may be difficult to follow as it winds its way through and around the Illinois interstate system and countryside. To experience all that the Lincoln Highway has to offer, you may want to spend two days driving the route.

An arched footbridge adds to the ambience at the Fabyan Japanese Tea Garden, one of the attractions of Fabyan Forest Preserve.

and appropriated 75 million dollars for the construction of what were called post roads. This amount was to be matched by the states seeking to build the roads, thus starting the practice of federal-state grant matching for road construction. Many segments were constructed by volunteer labor, such as the Mooseheart segment, which was built by area businesspeople, manual laborers, and others to demonstrate their support of their community and of local businesses.

Shortly thereafter, America became involved in World War I, shifting national attention onto the war effort and away from the roadbuilding effort. However, interest in good roads resumed in earnest shortly after the war ended in November 1918. In 1919, Lincoln Highway Association leader Harry Ostermann persuaded the War Department to conduct a transcontinental motor convoy trip from the East Coast to San

Francisco on the marked route of the Lincoln Highway. A 69-vehicle convoy combining public and private vehicles took off from the White House on July 7, 1919. The convoy, primarily following the Lincoln Highway route, finally arrived in San Francisco, but not after considerable difficulty on the dirt roads traveled en route. The seedling miles of concrete made a strong impression. Among those participating in the convoy was Lt. Colonel Dwight D. Eisenhower, who much later applied his experiences on the Lincoln Highway, along with his experiences with World War II and the German Autobahn system, to conceive of an interstate road system to aid the movement of troops, goods, and people across the country.

Various aspects of the Lincoln Highway's early development predated and predicted some of the technical and fundamental elements of current U.S. transportation policy. They included di-

rectional signage, a system of concrete markers designed to assist travelers determining their location along a given roadway. Never before had a consistent road signage system been employed. Another new concept was the urban bypass: The Lincoln Highway was purposely routed 25–30 miles south and west of Chicago to avoid congestion and time delays.

Since 1935, much of the original Lincoln Highway has been paved over, bypassed, or converted to numbered U.S., state, and county highways or municipal streets. Very few of the 1928 cement markers still exist. However, the name Lincoln is still attached to much of the route in the form of roadway and street names, local Lincoln businesses and brochures, articles, and artifacts preserved in museums and historical societies along the route.

Recreational: From the rolling hills of western Illinois and the Mississippi River Valley to the sights and sounds of the Chicago metropolitan area, the Lincoln Highway includes an impressive collection of diverse recreational opportunities. Near Franklin Grove, stop at Franklin Creek State Natural Area to enjoy a picnic by the edge of Franklin Creek. Hiking, skiing, horseback riding, and snowmobiling trails are available there. As you near Chicago, you'll find

The Fox River separates the famous Dutch windmill and lighthouse at the Fabyan Forest Preserve.

increased shopping opportunities in places such as Chicago Heights and Joliet. In Geneva, tour the Japanese Gardens or go biking on the Riverwalk. While touring each community, you are sure to come across several enticing activities.

Highlights:

This tour begins north of Aurora and travels west across the state. If you wish to take the tour traveling east, read this list from the bottom and work your way up.

Mooseheart: Just north of Aurora on Illinois Route 31, you'll find Mooseheart. This lodge is an important piece of history for the Lincoln Highway because members of the Moose Lodge raised 12,000 dollars to fund the initial paving of the Lincoln Highway. Members of the lodge from all over the country then traveled to Illinois and helped grade the road using picks and shovels. In appreciation for the efforts of the lodge, the state later paved an extra ten-foot strip, which is still visible today, in front of Mooseheart.

DeKalb Memorial Park: Traveling west from Mooseheart on State Route 60, you come to the city of DeKalb. The Memorial Park in DeKalb is famous for its memorial clock called Soldiers and Sailors, which was originally dedicated in 1921. The clock was restored completely in 1996, and in 1999, a community mural was painted on the side of the old Chronicle building, located behind the park.

First Seedling Mile: Cement companies donated the cement to pave seedling miles on the highway. The first seedling mile in the country is located west of Malta on State Route 38.

Railroad Park: Located in Rochelle, west of Malta, is Railroad Park, one of two X rail crossings in the country. People come from all over the world to watch the rail traffic of the Union Pacific and the Burlington Northern Santa Fe Railroads, the two major rail carriers in the eastern United States.

Meeting of the Great Rivers Scenic Route

With the confluence of three major rivers, there is an abundance of activity. Visitors sample peaceful solitude amidst sublime natural features, abundant water recreation, and historical and cultural attractions in genuine river towns that have been gateways for pioneers of all kinds.

Within a 25-mile expanse, the Mississippi, Missouri, and Illinois Rivers meet to form a 35,000-acre flood-plain. This confluence is the backdrop for the Meeting of the Great Rivers Scenic Route. The river systems have been vital transportation routes as long as there has been human habitation, moving people and goods to world markets.

The Meeting of the Great Rivers Scenic Route offers a dramatic composite of the Mississippi River. Beneath white cliffs, the byway runs next to the Mississippi, beginning in an industrial, urban setting and changing to a scenic, natural area. As though moving back through time, expanses of pastoral countryside and stone houses are reminders of a time long ago. Artifacts of the earliest aboriginal people in America reside here, and the byway's rich historical and archaeological qualities unfold. Little towns along the byway seem almost forgotten by time, giving travelers a look at historic architecture and small-town life along the Mississippi River.

The Pere Marquette Lodge was built in the 1930s and expanded in recent years.

Cultural: Visitors discover real river towns along this byway. To celebrate each unique aspect of their culture, many of the communities on the byway have established their own museums. In addition, the region displays an appreciation of high culture through orchestras, theaters, galleries, institutions of higher learning, and many diverse festivals

that celebrate the arts. Throughout the year, more than 50 festivals and fairs celebrate the history, art, music, and crafts of this region.

Historical: The Mississippi River is internationally famous. Father Jacques Marquette and Louis Jolliet first made their expedition down the Mississippi in 1673. Later, when the Illinois Territory was formed, the Missouri River was the gateway to the unexplored West, and

Quick Facts

Length: 57 miles

Time to Allow: Two hours

Consideration: One of the only gas stations along the entire byway is located in Grafton. Roads can be closed during the spring due to flooding and during the winter due to ice. When this happens, alternate routes are provided. Also, ferries cannot operate when the river freezes. During these times, use the Joe Paige Bridge at Hardin to connect with Kampsville in Calhoun County.

the Illinois River led to the Great Lakes and was also a connection to the East. Early American explorers began in the confluence area. Lewis and Clark, for example, embarked from Fort Dubois near the mouth of the Missouri. Eventually, towns were settled on the shores of the rivers, providing a secure way for travel and commerce using the rivers. The buildings that composed these towns still stand, many of them dating to the early 1800s.

As the nation grew and developed, many of the towns along the byway were growing and developing as well. Although many of the towns that stand today seem to be nestled somewhere in history, some of the byway's commu-

nities have been at the edge of new ideas. During pre-Civil War times, the Underground Railroad ran through this area, bringing escaped slaves to the safety of the north. Confederate prison ruins found on the byway are another testament to this corner of Illinois' involvement in the Civil War.

By the late 19th century, Mark Twain's Mississippi River stories had inspired an ideal of Mississippi legends, history, and culture in the minds of Americans. Meanwhile, as the river and its uses were also evolving, paddleboats gave way to barges and tows. River traffic increased as industries grew, and Lock and Dam 26 was built. Today, historic 18th-century river towns, islands, bars, points, and bends create beautiful scenery beneath limestone bluffs, which are covered by forests that extend nearly 20,000 acres. Historical and cultural features in the 50-mile corridor have received national recognition, with seven sites presently registered on the National Register of Historic Places.

Recreational: After you have seen the sights on the Meeting of the Great Rivers Scenic Route, you may decide to enjoy the surroundings on a closer level. Trails and paths along the byway offer excitement for hikers and bikers. Also, forests that line the roadsides are perfect places for camping, picnicking, or simply enjoying the peaceful solitude that nature affords. Be sure to tour the historic districts of the byway communities and stop at the museums and visitor centers that provide a closer look at the byway and its characteristics.

There is always fun to be found on the Mississippi River. Visitors enjoy the water in every way, from parasailing to jet skiing. Sailboats and riverboats keep the river alive with movement year-round. During the summer, families stop at one of the two water parks along the byway or travel on one of the four free river ferries located in the area. The Meeting of the Great Rivers Scenic Route is one of the most accommodating to bikers, with a bicycle path that goes directly along the byway.

Shopping for crafts and antiques in the historic riverside towns along the byway is a pleasant pastime, and golfers enjoy the ten courses in the region. In addition to the attractions along the byway, festivals, fairs, and events are always occurring in its communities.

Highlights:

This must-see tour of the Meeting of the Great Rivers Scenic Route begins at the northernmost point (Kampsville) and concludes at the southernmost point (Alton).

Kampsville: Kampsville is in Calhoun County on the Illinois River. Take the free ferry ride (drive east on Highway 108 approximately five miles to Eldred), and go to the home of the American Center for Archaeology, which is the site of Old Settlers Days with Lewis and Clark, and Civil War and other reenactments.

Eldred: Eldred is a wonderful village in Greene County at Highway 108 and Blacktop Road. The Eldred Home shows a glimpse of life in the 1800–1900s. Turn south onto Blacktop Road. Drive approximately 15 miles to the intersection of Blacktop Road, Highway 100, and Highway 16; continue straight ahead and onto Highway 100 southbound. Drive approximately ten miles south to Pere Marquette State Park.

Pere Marquette State Park: This park is in Jersey County on Route 100. This 7,895-acre preserve overlooks the Mississippi and Illinois Rivers. Outdoor enthusiasts will enjoy the park's nature trails, prehistoric sites, horseback riding, camping, fishing, boating, and hiking. The park also has a wonderful lodge built in the 1930s by the Civilian Conservation Corps. The fireplace alone soars 50 feet into the grand hall, and the great room is rich with massive timber beams and stone. Continue southward out of Pere Marquette State Park onto Highway 100. Drive approximately three miles to Brussells Ferry.

Brussells Ferry: Take a free ride on the Brussells Ferry across the Illinois River, and get a feel of the river under the wheels of your vehicle. Nearby is the Mark Twain Wildlife Refuge, the seasonal home for hundreds of thousands of migratory birds including American bald eagles, herons, owls, pelicans, geese, ducks, and many rare species.

Grafton: Grafton is on Highway 100 in Jersey County. All but wiped out by the Great Flood of 1993, this amazing river town bounced back and is now considered one of the most important stops on the byway. Bed-and-breakfasts, inns, antiques and specialty shops, casual family dining, riverside entertainment, summer outdoor family amphitheater, a small museum, a visitor center, parasailing, jet skiing, pontoon boats, fishing, hunting, hiking, bike trails, cottages, horseback riding, a mystery dinner theater, and more can be found in Grafton. Festivals abound throughout the spring, summer, and fall. Continue southbound approximately 1/2 mile to the bluffs running along the Mississippi River.

Scenic Bluffs: Without question, the most spectacular view along this route is from just outside Grafton, approximately 15 miles northwest of Alton. The bluffs tower above the river with the byway road between the peaks and the riverbank. The Mississippi is alive with commercial traffic, sailboats, and

Sights such as this one of the Mississippi River can be seen while driving the Meeting of the Great Rivers Scenic Route.

wildlife, in contrast to the majestic bluffs overhead. Any time is good viewing, but late afternoon and sunset are very rewarding. Be careful: Many people stop along the highway to take pictures of the bluffs and river. Try to remain in your car to photograph the scenery. Also exercise caution because of many bicyclists and fast-moving traffic at all times. Continue eastbound on Highway 100 about five miles from Grafton to Elsah. Be prepared to make an abrupt northward turn.

Elsah: Elsah is considered by many national travel writers as the river town that time forgot. This adorable village contains more than two dozen homes built in the 1800s, when Elsah was an important riverboat stop. Because the town has almost no contemporary structures, you immediately feel as if you have been transported back into the mid-1800s. Bed-and-breakfasts and small shops abound. Continue eastbound onto Highway 100 about ten miles to the Cliffton Terrace Park.

Cliffton Terrace Park: This roadside park features picnic facilities, seasonal wildlife viewing, and a playground. Continue eastbound onto Highway 100 about five miles to the legendary Piasa Bird. Be alert for an abrupt turn northward as you begin seeing riverside barges along the banks.

Piasa Bird: This mythical creature was seen by American Indian nations and early European explorers. Today, a gigantic bluff painting depicts the half-dragon, half-cat creature. Restored from early sketches and photography of the 1800s, the site is being developed into an interpretive park and wetlands area. Continue southeasterly about one mile on Highway 100, and enter Alton.

Alton: The community dates to the early 1800s as a major river port just north of St. Louis and can best be summed up by the word historic. Continue eastbound on Highway 100, going approximately three miles. Turn north into the Melvin Price Locks and Dam Complex and National Great Rivers Museum site.

Melvin Price Locks and Dam Complex, National Great Rivers Museum:
About two miles past the Clark Bridge, on Highway 100, is the Melvin Price Locks and Dam Complex and the site of the National Great Rivers Museum. This colossal structure tames the mighty river and aids in flood control and navigation. A wonderful riverfront walkway surrounds the dam and museum. Watch long strings of barges full of fuel and grain pass through the locks to be lowered or raised as the river winds down to the delta. It offers a wonderful view of the Alton skyline and Clark Bridge.

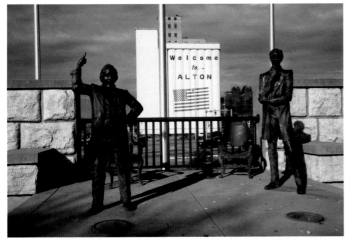

Life-size bronze statues of Abraham Lincoln and Steven Douglas in Alton, Illinois, pay homage to their famous 1858 Senatorial debate.

Ohio River Scenic Byway

Along the Ohio River Scenic Byway interesting spurs offer must-see natural highlights. For instance, the Cache River Spur takes visitors to an ecosystem designated by the United Nations as a Wetlands of International Importance.

This byway's history is closely tied to the Ohio River, which it follows. Many forts from the Civil War and the French and Indian War were strategically placed along this route, and the Underground Railroad had many stops along this byway. This is where you can find the Cave in Rock, an enormous cave that was once home to river pirates.

The earliest written record of Cave in Rock is from a French explorer who visited the cave in 1729.

It is now a great vantage point from which to watch today's river traffic.

Cultural: The spirit of those who live along the Ohio River can be seen at Fort Defiance Park in the town of Cairo. The park is a beautiful place to watch the constant meeting of the Ohio and Mississippi Rivers that refuse to merge. The Ohio River waters become a blue ribbon, rippling far down the brown Mississippi currents.

Because all this magnificent scenery is found along the Ohio River, there is much evidence in Cairo of the people's desire for beauty. For example, located in the Halliday Park at Washington and Poplar is "The Hewer," a statue that was made in 1906. Sculpted by George Grey Barnard and exhibited at the St. Louis World's Fair, this original bronze statue was declared by Laredo Taft to be one of the finest nudes in America.

Historical: Many historical sites are situated along the Ohio River Scenic Byway. These sites cover everything from early Native American cultures to Civil War sites. Kinkaid Mounds, a designated byway site, is a monument to the Native American people who once inhabited this region.

The cities of Old Shawneetown and Golconda have numerous historic structures from the 1820s and 1830s. Cairo, positioned at the confluence of the Ohio and Mississippi Rivers, was a thriving port city and an important strategic site during the Civil War, a history that's alive today in Cairo's many old houses and buildings. Fort Massac State Park in Metropolis is a reconstructed fort from the French and Indian War.

The Ohio River has been a river of both opportunity and tragedy. While the state of Illinois possesses many Underground Railroad sites, the byway also passes near the Slave House, where captured fugitive slaves and even freed blacks were incarcerated before being returned to the South. This constituted the little-known Reverse Underground Railroad.

Recreational: You can enjoy camping in both the Fort Massac State Park and in the Shawnee National Forest. The Shawnee National Forest in Illinois has 338 miles of equestrian/hiking trails, 454 campsites, 16 designated campgrounds, and 27 designated picnic areas. Seven wilderness areas in the Shawnee National Forest are available for wilderness study.

In the tradition of the Mississippi steamships that featured gambling, drinking, and Old West living, a casino steamship still leaves the port of Metropolis. Along the Metropolis riverfront is the Merv Griffin Theater, which presents a range of entertainers on special dates throughout the year.

Highlights:

The Ohio River Scenic Byway must-see tour begins in Cairo and runs to the Indiana border.

Fort Defiance Park: Fort Defiance Park is right on the byway. Stop and view the confluence of the Ohio and Mississippi Rivers, where you can see tugs working.

The Hewer, Safford Memorial Library, and U.S. Custom House Museum: Taking Highway 51 right through Cairo (on Washington Avenue), travel 1.5 miles to The Hewer statue in Halliday Park on the corner of Washington and Poplar Avenues.

About 1/2 mile later, you can see the Safford Memorial Library, where you can pick up a 50-cent book out of the "treasure bin."

Mound City National Cemetery: Heading north out of Cairo is the Mound City National Cemetery. Confederate and Union soldiers are buried side by side here. From Mound City, the byway route goes onto Highway 37.

Olmstead Lock and Dam: Traveling north on Highway 37, about five miles later is the Olmstead Lock and Dam project, which offers a lookout pavilion

and restrooms. The route then goes up Highway 37 about five miles to the Grand Chain Joppa Blacktop, and then it runs into Highway 45.

Superman Square: Highway 45 goes south into Metropolis, where you can see Superman Square in the center of town.

Fort Massac State Park: Fort Massac State Park is the next stop (two miles south of Superman Square), located on Highway 45, with picnic tables, a museum, and a variety of events that occur throughout the year.

Historic National Road

Traversing the entire width of the state, the Historic National Road in Indiana gives visitors a relaxing journey through small-town America, pastoral farmland, natural features formed by ancient glaciers, and the high-octane urban offerings of Indianapolis.

One of America's earliest roads, the National Road was built between 1828 and 1834 and established a settlement pattern and infrastructure that is still visible today. Nine National Register Districts are found along the route, as are 32 individually designated National Register Sites offering education and entertainment. As you travel Indiana's Historic National Road, you find a landscape that changed little since the route's heyday in the 1940s.

Historic villages with traditional main streets and leafy residential districts still give way to the productive fields and tranquil pastures that brought Indiana prosperity. From the Federal-style architecture of an early pike town (a town that offered traveling accommodations and little else) to the drive-ins and stainless-steel diners of the 1940s, you can track the westward migration of the nation in the buildings and landscapes that previous generations have left behind.

Along the way, you will find many of the same buildings and towns that were here during the earliest days of westward expansion. A visit to Antique Alley gives you a chance to

To maximize exposure to the National Road, owners built onto the front of their buildings. Archways between rowhouses gave access to backyards.

do some antique shopping and exploring along this historic road. The Indiana Historic National Road is a unique way to experience the preserved pike towns along the route, such as Centerville and Knightstown.

Cultural: The National Road brought the nation to Indiana. The lure of limitless opportunities and the romance of the West drew tens of thousands of pioneers through Indiana between 1834 and 1848. Many stayed and settled in the Hoosier State, thus creating a new culture—the foundation for our national culture. This is because religious and economic groups left the distinctive colonial societies of the eastern seaboard and merged in the Midwest. Settlers to

Indiana brought with them their own particular mix of customs, religions, languages, building styles, and farming practices. Quakers, European immigrants, and African Americans looking for new opportunities all traveled the National Road.

As the region matured, the culture continued to evolve under the influence of the nation's primary east-west route. Richmond was home of the Starr Piano Company, and later the Starr-Gennet recording studios, where jazz greats such as Hoagy Carmichael and Louis Armstrong made recordings in an early jazz center. The Overbeck sisters, noted for their Arts and Crafts pottery, lived and worked in Cambridge City. The poet James Whitcomb Riley, author of "Little Orphan Annie" and "Raggedy Man," lived in Greenfield. Also, Indianapolis, the largest city on the entire Historic National Road, became an early center for automobile manufacturing.

Historical: The National Road was the first federally funded highway in the United States. Authorized by Thomas Jefferson in 1803, the road ran from Cumberland, Maryland, west to Vandalia, Illinois. Designed to connect with the terminus of the C&O Canal in Cumberland, the National Road gave agricultural goods and raw materials from

the interior direct access to the eastern seaboard. It also encouraged Americans to settle in the fertile plains west of the Appalachians. For the first time in the United States, a coordinated interstate effort was organized and financed to survey and construct a road for both transportation purposes and economic development.

Built in Indiana between 1828 and 1834, the National Road established a settlement pattern and infrastructure that is still visible today. The historic structures along the National Road illustrate the transference of ideas and culture from the east as the road brought settlement and commerce to Indiana. The National Road passes through well-preserved, Federal-style pike towns and Victorian streetcar

neighborhoods, and it is lined with early automobile-era structures, such as gas stations, diners, and motels.

Recreational: You can find many opportunities for recreation along the Historic National Road in Indiana, as well as in nearby cities. Golf is a popular sport along the highway, as evidenced by the many golf courses. Biking and hiking are other extremely popular sports along the byway. Local park and recreation facilities are often directly accessible from the byway or can be found nearby.

Highlights:

The following are just some of the points of interest available to you when traveling west across the Indiana portion of this byway from the western border of Ohio. If you're traveling east, read this list from the bottom up.

Historic Richmond: As one of Indiana's oldest historic towns (founded in 1806), Richmond has one of the Hoosier State's largest intact collections of 19th-century architecture. You can visit four National Register Historic Districts; Hayes Regional Arboretum; a bustling historic downtown full of unique shops and restaurants; and a fascinating collection of local museums, including the Wayne County Museum, the Richmond Art Museum, the Gaar Mansion, the Indiana Football Hall of Fame, the Joseph Moore Museum at Earlham College, and the Rose Gardens located along the road on the city's east side.

Centerville: One of the historic highway's most intact and quaint National Road-era pike towns is listed in the National Register of Historic Places for its fine collection of architecture. Historic brick houses connected by brick archways characterize the town. Centerville also has a noteworthy collection of small antique and specialty shops and is home to the world's largest antique mall, just several blocks north of the National Road.

Pike towns and Antique Alley (Richmond to Knightstown): You can meander along the National Road

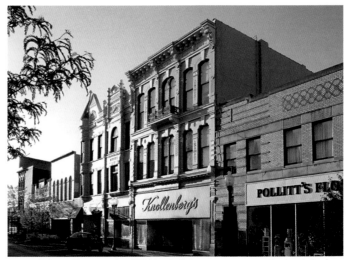

Historic Richmond has more than 200 historically important structures. See late Federal, Greek Revival, Victorian, and early 20th-century buildings here.

and enjoy the tranquil agricultural landscape interspersed with pike towns that recall the early years, when travelers needed a place to rest every five miles or so. This route is also heralded as Antique Alley, with more than 900 antique dealers plying their trade in and between every community along the route.

Huddleston Farmhouse Inn Museum and Cambridge City: A restored National Road-era inn and farm tells the story of the historic highway and the people who formed communities along its length. The museum is owned and operated by the Historic Landmarks Foundation of Indiana and is the home office of the Indiana National Road Association, the National Scenic Byway management nonprofit group. The museum displays the way of life of an early Hoosier farm family and the experience of westward travelers who stopped for food and shelter. Cambridge City is also listed in the National Register of Historic Places and has unique historic buildings that are home to diverse shops and local eateries.

Greenfield: The James Whitcomb Riley Old Home and Museum on the National

Road in Greenfield tells the story of the Hoosier poet and allows you to experience his life and community with guided tours. The small town also is rich in local flavor, with many shops and restaurants to satisfy you.

Irvington: A classic 1870s Indianapolis suburb was developed as a getaway on the city's east side. Irvington has since been swallowed by the city but retains its stately architecture and peaceful winding cul-de-sacs. Listed in the National Register of Historic Places, Irvington recalls turn-of-the-century progressive design principles and allows the modern visitor a glimpse into the city's 19th-century development.

Indianapolis: The center of Indiana's National Road is also its state capital. Downtown Indianapolis offers a growing array of activities and amenities. Along Washington Street just east of downtown, you can visit the Indiana Statehouse, the Indianapolis Zoo, the Eiteljorg Museum of American Indians and Western Art, and White River State Park.

Plainfield: Twentieth-century automobile culture dominates this area. Motels and gas stations remain from the early days and are interspersed with the sprawl and development of the modern city.

Brazil: The western extension of the National Road was surveyed through

what is now Brazil in 1825; today, its National Register-listed Meridian Street remains a classic example of how the historic highway promoted the growth of communities along its length. The village is also full of curios and collectibles.

Terre Haute: The western edge of Indiana's National Road is anchored by Terre Haute, a community offering historic points of interest and cultural experiences of various kinds. Rose–Hulman Institute of Technology on the city's east side was founded in 1874 and is an exceptionally beautiful college campus; just west of the city on State Road 150, the St. Mary-of-the-Woods College campus offers a touch of European elegance in the Indiana forest. Its campus is in a beautiful wooded setting and has several buildings dating to its 1841 founding. You can choose National Road restaurants along the city's Wabash Avenue, located in historic buildings. Dobb's Park, 1/2 mile south of the highway at the intersection of Highways 46 and 42, is home to a nature center and Native American Museum. The Swope Art Museum features 19th- and 20th-century artworks in a 1901 Renaissance Revival-style building with an Art Deco interior. The Children's Science and Technology Museum houses rooms full of hands-on learning displays and special exhibits.

The town of Greenfield has worked to preserve its historic buildings and build new ones.

Ohio River Scenic Byway

Travelers on the Ohio River Scenic Byway in Indiana have the unique opportunity to follow in Abraham Lincoln's boyhood steps, trod the path of freedom seekers on the Underground Railroad, and experience the fascinating history of quaint river towns.

This winding, hilly route follows the Ohio River. The route offers a pleasant escape from suburban concerns as it passes villages, well-kept barns, vineyards, and orchards. Historic architecture along the way retains a charm that is often missing from modern development.

Here, tucked away in the very toe of southwestern Indiana, are swamps full of water lilies and rare birds. The most rugged part of this byway features rock outcroppings, forested hills, caves, and scenic waterways. The limestone bluffs (dotted with cave entrances) are abundant with wildlife.

Historical: In the early days, the Ohio River was the primary way west for early settlers of the frontier. Later, with the coming of the steamboat, the Ohio River became the center of the transportation and industrial revolution. Prior to the Civil War, the river had great significance as the boundary between slave and free states. The river is used today for recreation and to transport coal to generating plants.

Abraham Lincoln's family built a farmstead along Little Pigeon Creek, not far from the Ohio River. At the Lincoln Boyhood National Memorial, you can see and help with the daily chores the Lincoln family performed on the Indiana frontier.

Corydon was the place where the Indiana State Constitution was drafted in 1816. The Corydon Capitol State Historic Site preserves the state's first capitol, constructed of Indiana limestone.

The Culbertson Mansion State Historic Site in New Albany preserves a 22-room French Second Empire home built in 1869. It was built by a wealthy local merchant.

The Levi Coffin House in Fountain City (which is north of the byway and was

The Lincoln Living Historical Farm is a re-created 1820s homestead with a cabin, outbuildings, split rail fences, animals, and field crops.

back then called Newport) was the place where more than 2,000 freedom seekers found refuge. Levi Coffin, known to many as the President of the Underground Railroad, opened the doors to his home to offer food, shelter, and clothing to runaway slaves on their journey to freedom.

Recreational: The Hoosier National Forest has plenty of opportunities for enjoyment. Falls of the Ohio State Park in Clarksville offers many nature hikes where you can look at fossil beds and various aquatic habitats. There are also picnic areas and a museum.

Highlights:

Heading east to west on the byway, consider using the following itinerary.

Hillforest Mansion: Begin at Hillforest Mansion in Aurora and sightsee. Travel along Highway 62, and continue on Highway 56 to Madison. This stretch is approximately 60 miles, but it's on very curvy roads and will take longer than you may expect.

J. F. D. Lanier State Historic Site and Clifty Falls State Park: The J. F. D. Lanier State Historic Site is located in Madison, and Clifty Falls State Park, with its many trails (some of them rugged), is located just outside the town on Highway 56. The town of Madison also has several historic sites open to the public.

Howard Steamboat Museum and Falls of the Ohio State Park: Follow Highway 56 out of Madison, and head south on Highway 62, just past the town

of Hanover. Highway 62 will take you into Jeffersonville, Clarksville, and New Albany. These are also known as the Falls Cities and are directly across the Ohio River from Louisville, Kentucky.

Corydon Capitol State Historic Site: Continue on Highway 62 out of New Albany to Corydon. This is where the Corydon Capitol State Historic Site is located—Indiana's first state capital. Other historic sites and a Civil War battle memorial are also located in Corydon.

Wyandotte Caves and Woods: About ten miles west of Corydon on Highway 62, you come to the Wyandotte Caves and Wyandotte Woods. A variety of cave tours are available, and Wyandotte Woods offers hiking, camping, and picnic areas. Just past the town of Leavenworth, about eight miles from the Wyandotte area, take Highway 66. Around this area, you'll enter the Hoosier National Forest.

Lincoln Boyhood National Memorial: Stay on Highway 66 through the Ohio River towns of Cannelton, site of the Cannelton Cotton Mill (a National Register site), Tell City, and Grandview. As a side trip, take U.S. 231 north just past Grandview to Lincoln Boyhood National Memorial. This national park celebrates the life of Abraham Lincoln.

Western Trails Scenic and Historic Byway

Whether ruffians of the Old West capturing their ill-gotten gains or hopeful pioneers on the way to capturing their version of the American dream, their story and more is told on the Western Trails Scenic and Historic Byway.

Quick Facts

Length: 144 miles

Time to Allow: 2.5 hours

Consideration: Roads are occasionally closed in the winter due to blizzard conditions.

Sometimes it was a destination, as in the case of the cattle drives to the railroad town of Ogallala. Other times the towns along the Western Trails Scenic and Historic Byway were simply campsites on the way to the Rocky Mountains and beyond. The natural features of the landscape provided the signposts marking the way along the path, the terrain as rugged as those who traveled it. Today the Western Trails Scenic and Historic Byway in the panhandle of Nebraska greets visitors with a feast, inviting them to drink in the stark beauty of the Plains, devour the history of the Old West, and consume the wonders of the geology, archaeology, and paleontology that await all who venture here.

Plenty of western trails cut through Ogallala on the eastern edge of the Western Trails Scenic and Historic Byway—including the Oregon Trail, Mormon Trail, Pony Express, Union Pacific, and Texas Trail—providing a wealth of frontier history. Gamblers, cattlemen, and fur traders gathered in the romping, rollicking town of Ogallala

in the late 1800s where liquor flowed freely across the bar. Originally an outpost for fur trappers from St. Louis who were able to get along with the nearby Pawnee Indians, pioneers followed as the western trails came through. But it was the coming of the Union Pacific Railroad that dramatically changed the destiny of Ogallala. Massive cattle drives from Texas drove the economy during the summer months in the latter part of the 19th century, with ten to twelve herds, each with 2,500 head of cattle, locating south of town. Various "service" industries came in each summer also, bringing a temporary population of floaters, gamblers, tradespeople, and dance hall hostesses.

As the Western Trails Scenic and Historic Byway travels west, it follows the Oregon and Mormon Trails. More than simply pathways to the state of Oregon, they were

the only practical routes to the western United States. In a 25-year period more than a half million people went West via this corridor. The wagon ruts of these intrepid voyagers are still visible at Ash Hollow. Natural features of the western Nebraska landscape provided landmarks for Native Americans and pioneers as they traveled these trails. Chimney Rock

Chimney Rock was the most recognized and noted landmark along the Oregon Trail. The unique formation now rises 325 feet above the prairie floor.

is the landmark most often noted by the pioneers on the trails and one of the most famous features of the American West. Courthouse and Jail Rocks were landmarks for the pioneers but were also used by Native Americans for sending smoke signals and camping. The story of the people and the places of the past is told at the Oregon Trail Museum at Scotts Bluff National Monument.

Highlights:

The Western Trails Scenic and Historic Byway has many attractions to share with visitors. The following itinerary is suggested as a sampling of some of the many things to see and do.

Ogallala: On the eastern edge of the byway is the town of Ogallala. Since cowboys generally were buried with their boots on, the first cemetery in the area was aptly named Boot Hill. Another must-see in Ogallala is Front Street, a replica of some typical businesses from Ogallala's heyday. Visitor attractions include a museum, saloon, and evening entertainment.

Ash Hollow State Historical Park:

Just beyond Big Mac is Ash Hollow State Historical Park, a haven for weary travelers for centuries. Prehistoric Native Americans used the area for encampments, and pioneer wagon trains would rest here for a day or two. Wagon wheel

ruts are still visible on the bluffs of Windlass Hill overlooking Ash Hollow. A visitor center and abundant exhibits help visitors learn about the geology, prehistoric animals, ancient Native American nations, and the pioneer trek west.

Courthouse and Jail Rocks: In the absence of modern road signs to guide their way, early travelers used the natural terrain as guideposts. Courthouse and Jail Rocks, located five miles south of Bridgeport on Highway 88, are two remarkable geological formations, which became landmarks along the Oregon and Mormon Trails.

Chimney Rock National Historic Site: Outside of the town of Bayard, 1.5

miles south of Highway 92 on Chimney Rock Road is Chimney Rock National Historic Site. Once the most recognized landmark on the Oregon Trail, today the visitor center features original maps made from Captain John C. Frémont's exploration of the Oregon Trail in 1842–43.

Gering: Gering has several sites and activities for travelers. North Platte Valley Museum has an authentic sod house, log house, and military exhibits. Robidoux Trading Post has been faithfully reconstructed using historical information and 100-year-old handhewn logs.

Amish Country Byway

Reportedly the largest concentration of Amish in the world is in this part of Ohio. This fascinating people hold true to their rich traditions and heritage, making the Amish Country Byway a trip to their ongoing yesteryear.

The Amish people in Holmes County, Ohio, make up the largest concentration of Amish communities in the world, and they provide a unique look at living and adapting traditional culture.

The Amish community is a living reminder of the principles of reli-

An Amish horse and buggy travels down a peaceful road in Ohio. Holmes County has the largest concentration of Amish communities in the world.

gious freedom that helped shape America. With a devout sense of community and adherence to beliefs, the Amish Country Byway gives a rare opportunity to witness a different way of life.

Cultural: The Amish have established themselves in the Holmes County area, and it is estimated that one in every six Amish in the world live in this area. The Amish choose to live a simple way of life, which is clearly evident by the presence of horses and buggies, handmade

quilts, and lack of electricity in Amish homes. Entrepreneurial businesses owned by the Amish add to the friendly atmosphere along the byway while creating a welcome distance from the superstores of commercial America. In the 21st century, the Amish Country Byway is an important example of a multicultural community, as both the Amish and non-Amish traditions are strong in the region. These two cultures have built on similarities while still respecting differences. By working

together, they have created a thriving, productive community.

The Amish, as a branch of the Anabaptist people, are traditionally devout and religious. Like so many other immigrants, they came to America in search of religious freedom. In Europe, the Anabaptists had been persecuted for their beliefs, but today Amish beliefs are more accepted and laws have been passed protecting their rights in regard to education, Social Security, and military service. Horses and buggies, plain dress, independence from electricity, homemade quilts, spinning tops, and lots of reading materials are some of the things you might find in an Amish home. A community event, such as a barn raising, helps build relations among neighbors and is an efficient way to get work done.

Another important aspect of the byway is the influence of early Native Americans and Appalachian folklore. Coalfields and stone quarries drew settlers from the east, and today this influence is manifested in the strong mining and manufacturing industries in the area.

Agriculture is the economic heart of Amish Country, and visitors to the area are likely to see rows of haystacks or fields being plowed. Holmes County boasts the second largest dairy production in the state, the largest local produce auction during the growing season, and weekly livestock auctions in the communities along the byway. The Swiss and German heritage of the early settlers in the county is evident in the many specialty cheese and meat products and delicious Swiss/Amish restaurants. A variety of festivals and local produce stands along the byway allow visitors to taste a part of Amish Country.

Historical: The story of the Amish Country Byway is the story of the movement and settlement of people. The byway serves as a reminder of why people came to America and the struggles that many had in settling new and uncharted lands. Today, roads forged by the early settlers in the area have been upgraded to highways, and while Amish farmers still use horses and buggies as transportation, the roads have improved their journey. The historic nature of the byway is felt from these roads to the numerous buildings that stand on the National Historic Register.

Long before the Amish came to call Holmes County home, bison herds crisscrossed the state, led by instinct down the valleys and along the terminal moraine. American Indians later used the trails left by the bison. Eventually, these trails became the main paths of the Amish. Today, those paths make up State Route 39, one of the main arteries of the Amish Country Byway.

Recreational: From leisurely drives to hiking and biking, recreational opportunities exist for everyone traveling the Amish Country Byway. Every season can be enjoyed, with hiking, biking, rodeos, horseback riding, tennis, golfing, and hunting in the summer months. You can also enjoy numerous water activities, such as canoeing, swimming, fishing, and boating. Winter can be a memorable experience, with activities such as cross-country skiing and snowmobiling.

The Amish Country Byway is not one for speed demons. By slowing down, you get to experience the many recreational opportunities that are unique to this byway. There are carriage rides, hay rides, and sleigh rides that reflect the agricultural traditions of the area, while unique activities, such as hot air balloon rides and airplane rides, may also be enjoyed. One of the most popular activities is visiting Amish homesteads and farms, antique shops, and museums. In addition, you can find many places to stop and enjoy some good cooking or shopping.

The Holmes County Trail goes through Millersburg and links the byway with the northern part of the county and state. This trail is open to bicycles, hikers, and buggies. The local Amish citizens who sit on the Rails to Trails board provide valuable insight into how to make this a success for the Amish, their non-Amish neighbors, and visitors. This trail travels through beautiful Amish

Killbuck Marsh Wildlife Area is noted for being Ohio's largest marshland outside of the Lake Erie region.

Country and is a good way to get off of the main byway route.

Highlights:

The following itinerary gives you an idea for spending a day on the eastern half of U.S. 62.

Killbuck Marsh Wildlife Area: Enjoy the peace of the early morning at the Killbuck Marsh Wildlife Area. Fish or hike while the sun rises. Have a picnic breakfast while enjoying the birds and scenery.

Millersburg: Downtown Jackson, Clay, and Washington Streets are a Historic

District. There are plenty of National Register of Historic Places homes to see, such as the G. Adams House, the G. W. Carey House, and the Victorian House Museum. There are also a lot of shops downtown. Take time to look around and see what else you can discover. You can find plenty of places to eat in Millersburg.

Amish & Mennonite Heritage Center: This is an essential next stop because you can learn about the Amish and Mennonites and why they live the way they do. See the historical mural. This is interesting, free education.

CanalWay Ohio Scenic Byway

The story of the immigrant life, industrialization, and American innovation can be told along with that of enduring historic farms still operating along the CanalWay Ohio Scenic Byway.

Quick Facts

Length: 110 miles

Time to Allow: 4.5 hours

Consideration: Riverview Road in south Cuyahoga County is occasionally closed due to flooding. This happens only during major storms and does not last for very long. Fort Laurens, Towpath, and Dover Zoar Roads also lie in the flood path.

The construction of the Ohio and Erie Canal in 1825 drastically changed the people and pace of this region. Many byway visitors travel this route to learn about the development of the pre-and post-canal eras. The route also offers an impressive display of historical sites, along with many opportunities for hiking, biking, and water sports.

Cultural: The influences on area culture can be classified into four elements: the resilience of farming communities, life during the canal period, the gumption of immigrants, and the accomplishments of wealthy industrialists.

Farming is still important to area culture, and the strength of past and present farmers is reflected in the sturdiness of the farms themselves: Many farms from the mid-19th century are still standing and working. The village of Zoar, which was founded in 1817 by a German religious sect, the Zoarites, is still working according to many of its old agricultural practices.

The sway of the canal era on area culture is apparent because its flavor is still potent in the historic cities of Clinton, Canal Fulton, Boston, and Peninsula.

The neighborhoods that immigrants developed retain their special foreign flavor, creating small pockets of spice along the byway. These National Register historic neighborhoods near Cleveland are based on Archwood–Dennison Avenue, Broadway Avenue, Ohio City, and Warszawa.

Replete with continuous high-culture events, the larger cities on the route (Cleveland, Akron, Barberton, and Strongsville) retain several historic and well-known venues. The area's culture is manifested in locally produced festivals and entertainment.

Historical: People have lived in the CanalWay Ohio area for nearly 12,000 years. The area was an important transportation route for American Indians, and it was deemed neutral territory so that all might travel safely from the cold waters of the Great Lakes to warmer southern waters. European explorers

Covered bridges are a reminder of earlier days and rural travel in the Cuyahoga Valley.

and trappers arrived in the 17th century, and immigrants slowly moved in to farm over the centuries. The modern catalyst for area development was the Ohio and Erie Canal, which gave way to the area's industrial era. The CanalWay Ohio Scenic Byway takes you through places that still show evidence of the early inhabitants and the effects of industrial development.

Towns such as Dover, Bolivar, Navarre, Barberton, Canal Fulton, and Clinton show the influence of the canal with their early 19th-century architecture, original canal-oriented street patterns, locks and spillways, and towpath trails along the historic canal route. Waters from the area's lakes provided the cooling needed for the industrial rubber boom, which created the prosperous Akron of the 1920s. Brick factories illustrate life in industrial-era Akron.

Recreational: There is plenty to do along the CanalWay Ohio Scenic Byway. Towpath Trail near the Ohio and Erie Canal is extremely popular; more than three million users enjoy the trail in a typical year. Other recreation includes skiing, golfing, picnicking, hiking, fishing, and boating, and water excursions are available along the rivers as well.

Highlights:

This itinerary takes you through Cuyahoga Valley National Park and into Akron.

Cuyahoga Valley National Park: Start with a dawn picnic breakfast at the Cuyahoga Valley National Park (CVNP). The CVNP is on the byway, and its entrance is about eight miles south of Cleveland.

Hale Farm & Village: For another two (or three) hours before lunch, stop at Hale Farm & Village, which is at the southern end of the CVNP. You can wander the grounds and talk to the artisans who make the impressive wares for sale there. The glass blowers, candlemakers, potters, and blacksmiths demonstrate the industries of the mid-1800s.

Akron: Akron is a buzzing city with much to do. One possibility is to stop at the Akron Art Museum. The museum always has engaging exhibits.

Cascade Locks Park: After your visit at the museum, go to the Cascade Locks Park (also in Akron). This park has 15 canal locks in a one-mile stretch (all necessary to climb over the

Continental Divide), and you can follow them along on a trail; signs along the trail explain the locks and the history of the canal.

Historic National Road

Time and topography determined the development of the Historic National Road in Ohio as pioneers' wagons gave way to railroads and then to autos, and as travelers will see, steep climbs and deep valleys gave way to gently rolling hills.

The Ohio Historic National Road paved the way west through the newly formed states of Ohio, Indiana, and Illinois and provided a direct connection to the mercantile and political centers of the East Coast, helping to secure the influence and viability of these new settlements. As much as the road's boom times during the early and mid-19th century signified its importance to national expansion, its decline during the late 19th and early 20th centuries reveals the rise of the railroad as the primary means of transport and trade across the nation. Likewise, the renaissance of the National Road in the mid-20th century reflects the growing popularity of the automobile.

Today, the byway is a scenic journey across Ohio. The steep, wooded hills and valleys of the eastern edge of the byway give way to the gently rolling farmland of the western part of the byway. Picturesque farms, hiking trails, craft industries, and historic sites and museums await you along this portion of the Historic National Road.

Cultural: The Historic National Road in Ohio hosts a rich tradition of culture. Museums, festivals, and other cultural facilities offer a chance to both explore more of the National Road's history and seek diversions from it. Outstanding performing arts venues are represented along the byway. In addition to these cultural features, the eastern section of the byway is known for its selection of traditional and modern crafts.

Historical: The history of the Historic National Road in Ohio highlights the importance of this road in terms of development and settlement that it brought to the Ohio area. The history of the construction of the National Road is significant because it serves as an example of larger events that were transpiring in America simultaneously. Early pioneer settlement gave way to

Brick Road, a stretch of the path of the original National Road, gives visitors a glimpse into early 1900s travel.

Norwich: Approximately three miles beyond New Concord turn right onto Norwich Drive. This road, the old route into the burg of Norwich, becomes Main Street. At the end of the street, veer

railroads, and finally the automobile became the most frequent traveler along the National Road.

Recreational: A tremendous network of large state parks, regional metropolitan parks, local parks, and privately run facilities provide a bountiful array of outdoor recreational facilities. For the most part, the state parks are located on the eastern half of the byway, and more than 50,000 acres of state parks, forests, and wildlife areas are easily accessible from the byway. Along portions of the byway, you can hike, camp, fish, hunt, and picnic while relishing the various species of local flora and fauna.

Highlights:

The Historic National Road is sometimes known as "Main Street of America." While the Historic National Road in Ohio crosses the entire state, this itinerary suggests travelers linger a bit along a

few of the quaint main streets and their towns that helped make the Historic National Road legendary.

Cambridge: Although Cambridge brand of glass ceased production in 1958, the name remains synonymous with quality glass, and collectors are drawn to this town to visit the National Museum of Cambridge Glass.

New Concord: Following U.S. 40 west from downtown Cambridge for about nine miles, tourists come to the village of New Concord. Former U.S. Senator John Glenn, the first U.S. citizen to orbit planet Earth and the oldest human ever to venture into space, grew up in New Concord. The John & Annie Glenn Museum includes Senator Glenn's fully restored boyhood home as well as plans to expand the site to include additional buildings and educational opportunities in coming years.

right onto Brick Road. This is a one-mile stretch of the former path of the National Road and is entirely paved with bricks, a popular way to pave during the early part of the 20th century. The road is open to automobiles so visitors can get the feeling of what it was really like to motor along the National Road in the early 1900s.

National Road & Zane Grey Museum: The final stop is the National Road & Zane Grey Museum, located outside of Norwich just before I-70. Mile markers, a 136-foot diorama, vehicles, and films come together to tell the tale of the Historic National Road. Additionally the museum has a collection of memorabilia interpreting the life of area native and western novelist, Zane Grey. This particular part of Ohio is known especially for its production of art pottery, and this museum also does a notable job of telling this part of the area's history.

Ohio River Scenic Byway

Including the birthplaces of three U.S. Presidents, the Ohio River Scenic Byway is ripe with history and culture, sharing the story of centuries of human activity in the area.

This scenic route follows the Ohio River, so you can enjoy majestic river views for the entire drive. The Ohio River is a historical American icon. Native Americans and early European settlers used it heavily, especially to access the West. It marked the boundary between the North and South during the slavery era and was later the gateway to freedom for many slaves. The river was also the means of progress for industrialists and merchants.

Cultural: The Ohio River has been a center of human activity for centuries and, therefore, is a cultural hotbed.

Academic and historical organizations recognize this fact and have made the river and the immediate area the focus of their cultural studies. One such organization is the University of Kentucky's Ohio River Valley Series. This intercollegiate project specifically studies how the state's history has been affected by the social use of the Ohio River.

Historical: The region's rich history includes the migration of people along the river into the states that border it, as well as those states that are located within the river's basin. The industry and technology of the area were important to the river as well. They changed the river's influence on the region through the development of steamboat travel and shipping, the creation of locks and dams, the establishment of

The John Rankin house sits near the Ohio River. Reverend Rankin was one of the most active "conductors" on the Underground Railroad.

industries such as steel and coal plants and their associated landing docks, and the development of large chemical and electrical power generating facilities.

Recreational: Several state forests and parks along this byway offer opportunities for outdoor recreation. Camping is available at the Barkcamp State Park, in the Forked Run State Park near Belpre, and in the Shawnee State Forest near Portsmouth. The Wayne National Forest begins near the town of Gallipolis and ends near Hanging Rock along the byway. You can camp at the Vesuvius Recreation Area in the forest as well.

Highlights:

Starting from North Bend, you can travel alongside the Ohio River without flood walls obstructing your view.

North Bend: Your first stop is at the nation's great monument, the Harrison Tomb, located off Cliff Road, west of U.S. 50, North Bend. The 60-foot marble obelisk in this 14-acre park pays tribute to William Henry Harrison, the ninth U.S. president.

Cincinnati: Continue to Cincinnati, and visit the historic Harriet Beecher Stowe House. It was here that Stowe learned of the injustices of slavery and wrote her famous novel, *Uncle Tom's Cabin*.

Point Pleasant: Point Pleasant is the birthplace of the 18th U.S. president, Ulysses S. Grant (U.S. 52 and State Route 232): a one-story, three-room cottage.

Georgetown: Follow Grant's life back on U.S. 52, heading north, taking State Route 231 to historic Georgetown, where you can visit Grant's boyhood home on Grant Avenue. From Georgetown, head south again on State Route 68 to State Route 62, back to U.S. 52.

Ripley: Stop in the town of Ripley, and visit the John Rankin House. Aboli-

tionists John and Jean Rankin hid some 2,000 escaped slaves in this way station on the Underground Railroad.

Portsmouth: Continue on U.S. 52 to the town of Portsmouth, a traveler's delight. Here you'll see artistic floodwall murals that beautify the byway and protect the city from the rising waters of the Ohio River.

Gallipolis: Continue to the French Art Colony of Gallipolis. Here, you can learn about the rich history of the local area and state. While traveling through, note the French-style homes along the riverbanks.

Marietta: The early days of Marietta are remembered at the Campus Martius Museum, which offers displays of riv-

erboats and other antiquities. You can also stop at the Ohio River Museum next to the Campus Martius Museum.

Steubenville: Heading north up the river, you run into the town of Steubenville, where you witness the Old Fort Steuben reconstruction. Demonstrations, land office tours, and food are available here. In downtown Steubenville, you'll see murals depicting the 1850s and 1920s city life of the town.

Wellsville: Continuing on State Route 7, you come to Wellsville and the River Museum Wellsville, a three-story building constructed in 1870. Period furniture and paddlewheel displays are featured in the various rooms.

Flint Hills Scenic Byway

Rare virgin prairie and cowpokes who still wrangle bovines in the spirit of generations past join with Native American and pioneer history to make this an enthralling experience.

The Flint Hills Scenic Byway is a modern road easily reached from the Kansas Turnpike, I-70, U.S. 50, and U.S. 56, but it is a scenic trip back in time. Panoramic views of now-rare tallgrass prairie, Native American historic sites, the still visible wagon ruts left by the countless thousands who traversed the Santa Fe Trail, and of course, the stark beauty of the Flint Hills all greet the visitors to this area.

The area, as with so much of the Great Plains, became the site of friction between the indigenous people and the European pioneers. Treaties were needed as far back as 1825. Meaningful historic sites all along the Flint Hills Scenic Byway tell the tales of the native people groups, the pioneers who came to homestead in these hills, and those who merely passed through on their way to seek their fortune elsewhere in the Old West.

The geologic time period in the Flint Hills represents the Permian Period, with the area being covered by the shallow Permian Sea some 250 to 290 million years ago. The marine fossils, time, and the effects of nature worked together to create the unique topography of the Flint Hills: flat-topped hills of limestone and flint and verdant valleys, all accented by the pre-served tall-grass prairie and cattle ranches that have been operating for generations.

A precious remnant of prairie, a fraction of the once vast expanse that greeted pioneers, can be found at Tallgrass Prairie National Preserve.

The Tallgrass Prairie National Preserve has nearly 11,000 acres of virgin, never-plowed prairie safeguarded. The preserve protects a nationally significant example of the once vast tallgrass prairie ecosystem. It is one of the rarest and most endangered ecosystems in the world. It is a treat to stop and listen, perhaps hearing as the pioneers did from their Prairie Schooners, the wafting waves of this grassland ocean as the wind whistles through the bluestem and other native grasses.

Highlights:

The Flint Hills Scenic Byway stretches between Council Grove on the northern end at the intersection of U.S. 57 and U.S. 56, and Cassoday on the southern named for the treaty council held here in 1825 with the Osage natives allowing safe passage of Americans and Mexicans along the Santa Fe Trail. The Kaw Mission State Historic Site on Mission Street was where 30 Kaw (or Kansa) Indian boys lived and studied from 1851–1854. The Kaws, known as "The People of the South Wind," gave the state its name.

Council Grove:

Council Grove's early day calaboose is a friendlier place to visit today. Built in 1849 and believed to be the lone jail on the Santa Fe Trail at the time, it used to house desperados, ruffians, robbers, and horse thieves. Other "must-sees" in and around Council Grove include the old bell that was erected in 1866 to warn townsfolk of impending American Indian raids, the still-visible ruts from the Santa Fe Trail, and the Last Chance Store, built in 1857 and truly the "last chance" for trail travelers to buy supplies for their trip to Santa Fe, New Mexico.

Tallgrass Prairie National Preserve:

Farther south the byway passes one of America's newest national parks, Tallgrass Prairie National Preserve. Ranger-guided and self-guided tours are available as well as hiking and wheelchair-accessible trails with interpretive kiosks. The preserve is also home to Spring Hill Ranch. Original owner, Stephen F. Jones, named his ranch the Spring Hill Ranch in 1881 for the abundant springs on the property. Living history interpreters enhance the visit and invite guests to participate in activities.

Cottonwood Falls:

After visiting Tallgrass Prairie National Preserve and Spring Hill Ranch, the Flint Hills Scenic Byway then through Strong City and a mile later, Cottonwood Falls, site of the Chase County Courthouse, in operation since 1873 (the oldest courthouse in Kansas and the oldest operating courthouse west of the Mississippi). The Roniger Native American Museum is also in Cottonwood Falls.

Prairie Overlook:

South of Cottonwood Falls, the picturesque highway travels among the hills for grand vistas of the ranches in the area, then eases down to the stream to follow splendid stone walls around farms still in operation.

end of the byway at K-177 and I-35. It is a beautiful drive year-round showing off the unique views of the prairie. The following itinerary is suggested to experience some of the highlights along the byway.

Kaw Mission State Historic Site:

At the northern end of the byway historic sites are abundant in Council Grove,

Crowley's Ridge Parkway

Pure ocean sand in this landlocked state and the earliest recorded cemetery in the New World are but two of the wonders awaiting visitors to Missouri's section of Crowley's Ridge Parkway.

Quick Facts

Length: 14.25 miles

Time to Allow: One hour

Consideration: Plenty of services are available along the route for any special needs; however, watch your engine temperature so that you notice if it begins to increase.

Crowley's Ridge, characterized by sand, gravel, and deep gullies, has formed a primary route of transport and commerce for the people of this region for centuries. Various peoples have used the ridge to escape the swamps and wetlands. A combination of land travel on the ridge and connecting rivers provided a means of subsistence over a vast corridor.

Morris State Park has 27 types of trees and more than 300 different kinds of plants.

Historical: Crowley's Ridge, with its heavy clay and gravel, proved to be a focal point for the historical and cultural events that shaped the region around it. From the unique plant life of the ridge to the low-land swamps, this region is a story waiting to be told.

The first known Native Americans were known as the Mound Builders. They date from A.D. 900 to 1500 and were agriculturists who lived in permanent villages. They made ceramic pots and various utensils, some of which remain on and below the surface today. Sizable collections of these artifacts can be found in the small museums throughout this region. However, these mounds are being challenged by the migration of a rice-planting culture and the disastrous raids of illegal collectors and artifact thieves.

The early European immigrants to this region were German, Scots-Irish, and English. Many of them came from Virginia, Tennessee, Kentucky, and Mississippi, and they brought African-American slaves with them. The byway intersects many of these ethnic islands that have shaped the history and culture of the region. The migration of the cotton culture brought a lifestyle that continues to influence local food, architecture, family values, and religion.

There continues to exist in this region what the residents call the Chalk Bluff Trail. This trail extends from Cape Girardeau, Missouri, to Helena, Arkansas, and runs along the high ground of the ridge. The trail was originally used by Native Americans as they moved through the region on hunting expeditions. European settlers used the trail as they migrated to the West: it was the only safe way to travel through the swamps in order to capitalize on the 19th-century opportunities that existed in what is now the great American Southwest. Crowley's Ridge was the only

In Malden:
Malden Historical Museum
Bootheel Youth Museum
Billy DeMitt Gravesite
Gunnels Hill Civil War Cemetery
Beachwell Gullies
Jim Morris S.P.
Peach orchards
Military Road
Four Mile House
Sharecopper Homes
Cotton Gin

Bernie
Qulin
St. Francis River
Malden Speedway
Malden
Crowley's Ridge Parkway–Missouri
Campbell
Chalk Bluff Conservation Area and Battlefield Park
Clarkton
Holcomb
Crowley's Ridge Parkway–Arkansas

region's transformation. In 1933, Congress passed the Agricultural Adjustment Act, which sought to stabilize agriculture. Soil conservation acts also impacted the region and reflected the changing nature of the times. Those benefits that came into the area generally went to the large planters, while little went to the growing number of sharecroppers and tenant farmers.

all-weather access for settlers to transport trade items. The ridge became a vital highway during the Civil War, used by both Union and Confederate troops.

Following the Civil War, many changes occurred in this area, including a restructuring of agriculture and technology that provided for increased farm size. New plows, threshers, seeders, and shellers allowed farmers to work more acres and increase yields per acre. This put more pressure on transportation and further changed the region. The importation of cotton added to the

The land on and around Crowley's Ridge was generally worked well into the 20th century by sharecroppers who lived at the poverty level. The Southern way of life that existed in this area meant that there was little in the way of a middle class. African Americans in the region were almost entirely in the sharecropper class. This system was widespread across the South in the aftermath of the Civil War, but was especially rigid in the new cotton lands of southeast Missouri. This situation led to one of the greatest stories to come out of Missouri

in the 20th century, the story of the sharecropper strike of 1939.

Highlights:

The following is a suggested itinerary for traveling Crowley's Ridge Parkway in Missouri.

Malden: Visit the Malden Historical Museum, and enjoy the exhibits. Or spend some time at Malden's Bootheel Youth Museum, where adults and kids can both enjoy activities that explore the worlds of math, science, the arts, and more. When you are ready to continue your drive, leave Malden on County Route J to the west.

Billy DeMitt Gravesite: About three miles from the junction of Routes J and WW is the famous site where 10-year-old Billy DeMitt was killed during the Civil War for refusing to tell a group of guerrillas where his father was. A marker at the spot commemorates this tragic story, a true legend in southeast Missouri.

Jim Morris State Park and the Military Road: Shortly after you turn south on County Route WW, you find Jim Morris State Park. In addition to showcasing many varieties of trees and other vegetation unique to the ridge, the park is the most practical way to see the Military Road. Access the road by the bicycle or pedestrian paths here. This road was used by military troops in the Civil War and by settlers as they moved across the Missouri bootheel. The entire road runs from the intersection of Routes J and WW to one mile north of Campbell, with a total length of approximately six miles, and can be reached at various points along the route.

Beachwell Gullies: Near County Route WW are the visible remnants of erosional forces that scoured the ridge about 200 feet deep from the top of the ridge to the bottom of the gully. The sand here is pure ocean sand (in a landlocked state!), and saltwater shells have been found in this area, evidence that this area was once part of a vast ocean. The gullies can be accessed by a pedestrian trail that is approximately one mile long.

Campbell: Next, visit the historic city of Campbell, which has roots dating back to before the Civil War. Several buildings in the Historic District, many of which are on the National Historic Register, are open to visitors. Dine in the quaint local restaurants, and visit the antique shops in the Historic District.

Chalk Bluff Conservation Area: As you leave Campbell, turn southeast onto U.S. Highway 62. Shortly before the St. Francis River and the Arkansas border, stop and visit the Chalk Bluff Conservation Area. This area is full of Civil War history. The Military Road and trenches from the Civil War can still be seen today, especially along the river. Continue on across into the tip of Arkansas to see a related Civil War historical site, Chalk Bluff Battlefield Park.

Chalk Bluff Battlefield Park: This park will be of interest if you are seeking Civil War history. It is located at a Civil War battlefield site where several skirmishes were fought. The history of the area is interpreted on plaques along a walking trail. Picnic tables are available as well.

The St. Francis River is the lowest point in the state of Missouri.

Little Dixie Highway of the Great River Road

River's edge experiences as well as bird's-eye views from the bluffs of the Mississippi River give travelers a glimpse of what has inspired others for centuries. The area is a habitat for eagles, including the stately bald eagle.

The Little Dixie Highway (also called the Mississippi Flyway Byway) is home to a culture expressing a unique Southern flair. Accents of the South are revealed in the area's Victorian-era streetscapes and plantation-era mansions. This touch of the South has earned the region its nickname, Little Dixie.

Cultural: As you may expect from a region with such a diverse history, the Little Dixie Highway can boast equally varied and rich cultural qualities. Although the issue of slavery and the Civil War divided the nation, the cultural heritage of the United States proved remarkably resilient. The same can be said about Pike County, where churches and fraternal organizations helped to create a close-knit society that rebuilt itself after the war.

Clarksville's crafters have taken an active role in preserving this town's cultural heritage by restoring its historic commercial district, which is listed on the National Register of Historic Places. Artisans have performed the work necessary for the historically accurate restoration of this Victorian-era commercial district.

Historical: Perhaps more than anything else, the Mississippi River has provided this entire nation with stories. Mark Twain probably would have agreed that no single geological feature in the country could claim to be the father of a historical and cultural offspring as rich and colorful as the Mississippi River. During the early 1800s, the river served as the edge of the West, the barrier dividing civilization from the wild frontier. As the young nation continued its growth and expansion, clashes continued between new settlers and the native peoples. Eventually, the river proved no longer to be a barrier to the frontier, but a starting line for settlers' hopes and dreams.

Missouri was a state whose role in the slavery debate proved pivotal. The plantation homes and Southern-style

Near the town of Hannibal, the Mississippi River is as inspiring to those who gaze upon it as it was to young local writer Mark Twain.

architecture that marks the landscape throughout the length of the byway stands as a testament to that time. As travelers look out over the Mississippi River and see the shores of Illinois just across the mighty river, they are also reminded of the fact that freedom for the slaves always lay tantalizingly close.

The stories of the struggle for justice and freedom soon turned into tales of triumph and renewal. New struggles for a new kind of justice and freedom accompanied the hope ushered in by the Emancipation Proclamation. As the nation attempted to rebuild, so, too, did the residents of Pike County work to repair the damage caused by slavery and the Civil War. The county's buildings provide evidence of the prosperous society that overcame the ravages of division.

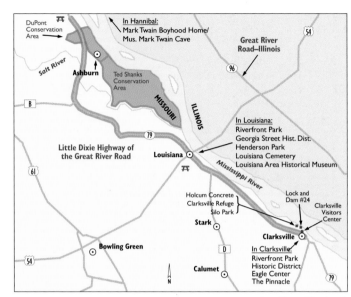

Recreational: The Little Dixie Highway runs parallel to the area's major source of recreation, the Mississippi River. Recreational opportunities related to the river include some river islands open to the public; great opportunities for fishing, hiking, and cycling; a few wildlife reserves; two boat launches; the Eagle Center in Clarksville; a pair of riverfront municipal parks; and a variety of other scenic overlooks.

The Mississippi River has long been a prominent source of fish; catfish and crappie are the most common types found in the river. The parks and other points along the byway offer great opportunities to land that 20-pound Mississippi River catfish. The reserves along the byway also offer exceptional fishing.

Highlights:

Beginning at the southern end of the Little Dixie Highway, this itinerary offers some historic and scenic highlights along the route.

Clarksville Historic District: The Clarksville Historic District is noteworthy for the historical accuracy in the extensive restoration efforts. The detail work on the buildings of this quaint riverfront district is evident not only on the edifices themselves but also in the businesses that occupy them.

Clarksville Eagle Center: Operated by the World Bird Sanctuary of St. Louis, Missouri, the Eagle Center prepares visitors for the eagle-viewing opportunities along the byway. Overlooking the Mississippi River, the Clarksville Eagle Center provides maps and brochures.

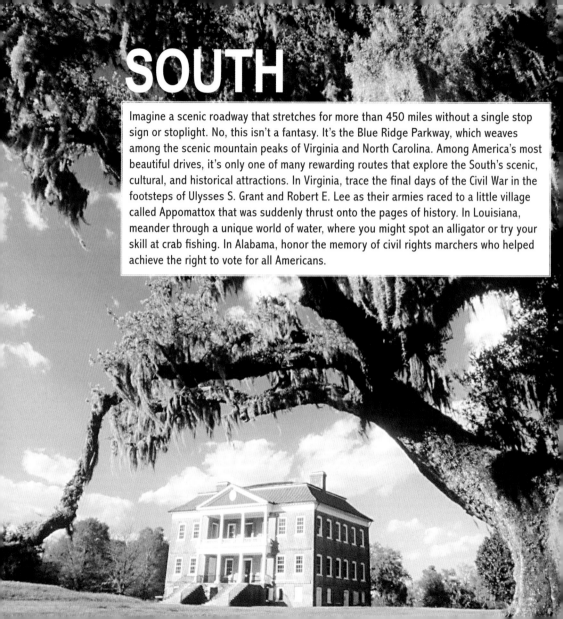

SOUTH

Imagine a scenic roadway that stretches for more than 450 miles without a single stop sign or stoplight. No, this isn't a fantasy. It's the Blue Ridge Parkway, which weaves among the scenic mountain peaks of Virginia and North Carolina. Among America's most beautiful drives, it's only one of many rewarding routes that explore the South's scenic, cultural, and historical attractions. In Virginia, trace the final days of the Civil War in the footsteps of Ulysses S. Grant and Robert E. Lee as their armies raced to a little village called Appomattox that was suddenly thrust onto the pages of history. In Louisiana, meander through a unique world of water, where you might spot an alligator or try your skill at crab fishing. In Alabama, honor the memory of civil rights marchers who helped achieve the right to vote for all Americans.

Country Music Highway

Tracing the length of eastern Kentucky, the highway unveils the rich musical heritage of a region that produced such country music stars as Loretta Lynn, Wynonna Judd, and Dwight Yoakam.

Quick Facts

Length: 144 miles

Time to Allow: Two days

Consideration: Summer and fall are the best seasons to drive this route. Summer is especially popular for travelers because there are many festivals and entertainment venues open during the summer months.

Running almost the entire length of eastern Kentucky, the Country Music Highway is a byway devoted to the rich heritage and history of the region. You will be immersed in the traditions of eastern Kentucky mountain music since this byway has been home to over a dozen well-known country music stars, including Naomi Judd, Billy Ray Cyrus, Ricky Skaggs, Keith Whitley, Dwight Yoakam, and Patty Loveless.

Cultural: The quality of the musical heritage of the byway is exhibited by its famous musicians; however, it is also exhibited through the continued commitment to the arts by current residents. The best evidence of this is at the Mountain Arts Center (MAC) in Prestonsburg. This seven-million-dollar facility houses the Kentucky Opry, a group of local musicians who perform regularly and work to preserve the tradition of eastern Kentucky mountain music. In addition to the Opry, the MAC also sponsors a wide variety of country music performances.

And, of course, music can be heard in a variety of venues along the route including the historic and beautiful Paramount Theater in Ashland and the Mountain Arts Center. Appalshop is an award-winning film and music documentary and preservation organization in Whitesburg. In addition to these sites, music can be heard at numerous small venues such as the coal camps of Seco and Carcassone and at a long list of festivals such as the Seedtime Festival in Whitesburg.

Historical: Before settlers called eastern Kentucky home, Native Americans lived and hunted in the region. The history of these early American Indians is depicted in the Highlands Museum & Discovery Center in Ashland.

The American Indians' lands were soon encroached upon by early settlers. The life of early pioneers is documented in Paintsville at Mountain HomePlace. This facility consists of a reconstructed 19th-century pioneer farm, complete with oxen and an award-winning film on the settlement of eastern Kentucky narrated by local native Richard Thomas (best known for the role of John Boy in *The Waltons*).

Within Jenny Wiley State Resort Park is Dewey Lake, shown here on a misty morning. The lake is a great place to boat and fish.

The discovery and mining of coal in this region has been influential on the history of eastern Kentucky. The Van Lear Historical Society explains the importance and history of this resource. Coal also affected the community by creating rich coal barons. John C. C. Mayo was one such person. The elegant Mayo Mansion in Paintsville provide visitors with details about Mayo's rags-to-riches story.

A more well-known story from the region exemplifies the influence of these industrial barons who exploited the resources in small areas such as eastern Kentucky. The Hatfield–McCoy feud has become a well-known story about feuding families. The legendary feud from the mid-1800s has no singular cause, rather it developed over several years with real and imagined grievances and very real and tragic events. The Hatfield–McCoy feud is an example of how the Appalachian people sought to deal with outside barons who purchased much of the land in the region and then mined it for coal and lumber for generations without allowing the locals to gain much profit from the enterprise.

Highlights:

Music is everywhere along the byway, but there are definitely other must-see attractions. Here are a few of the sites you will want to visit.

Ashland: Begin at Ashland, birthplace of country music legends the Judds and Billy Ray Cyrus. Visit the Paramount Arts Center, housed in the historic Paramount Theater in downtown Ashland. The Ashland Paramount Theater was built in 1930 using the design of a model theater created by Paramount Pictures for construction at the Chicago World's Fair of 1932.

Highlands Museum and Discovery Center: Also in Ashland is the Highlands Museum & Discovery Center. The Country Music Heritage exhibit and other displays give a wonderful overview of the Country Music Highway.

Prestonsburg: The best way to get oriented in Prestonsburg is to first stop by the tourism office for maps and information about not only the town of Prestonsburg but also the surrounding area and attractions, including Loretta Lynn's childhood home in Butcher Hollow between Prestonsburg and Paintsville, the Kentucky Appalachian Artisan Center, and the Samuel May House.

The cantilever Ben Williamson Memorial Bridge crosses the Ohio River and connects Coal Grove, Ohio, to Ashland, Kentucky.

Middle Creek National Battlefield: This area was impacted by the Civil War, and Middle Creek National Battlefield outside Prestonsburg tells the story. At the Battle of Middle Creek, an obscure Ohio professor and newly minted colonel in the Union army attacked and defeated the Confederate forces. James Garfield's victory on the battlefield led to a military career that eventually propelled him to the presidency.

Pikeville Cut-Through: Pikeville Cut-Through is an engineering feat second only to the Panama Canal as the most extensive landmoving project in the Western Hemisphere. The cut is more than 1,300 feet long and 523 feet deep and required the moving of a mountain, major highway, railroad, and river.

Breaks Interstate Park: Comprising 4,500 acres of lush mountain scenery and 13 miles of hiking trails, this park is also home to the deepest gorge east of the Mississippi River. The chasm is named for the break in Pine Mountain caused by the rushing waters of the Russell Fork of the Big Sandy River. Visitor activities and services include a restaurant, museum, gristmill, guided tours, spelunking, horseback riding, and driving and biking trails.

Elkhorn City: Elkhorn City was the girlhood hometown of Patty Loveless and home of the Elkhorn City Railroad Museum. More than 1,000 pieces of railroad memorabilia are on display.

Red River Gorge Scenic Byway

Following the scenic Red River, the byway through Daniel Boone National Forest enters a rugged landscape of tumbling waterfalls, steep cliffs, rocky crags, and countless natural stone arches.

Take a journey through magnificent natural wonders on the Red River Gorge Scenic Byway. From the historic Nada Tunnel to the end of the byway in Zachariah, discover more than 100 stone arches, waterfalls, and plenty of natural beauty. Carved over eons by the Red River, today's gorge is now the site for outdoor adventures.

Cultural: The culture along the byway has been one focused on nature. American Indians resided in this area for thousands of years, living off the land and using the naturally occurring rock shelters as homes. Today, these shelters can be seen along the byway.

The logging industry brought another culture to the area. The land was used as a profitmaking resource, and the remnants of that culture survive today at the Gladie Historic Site and the Nada Tunnel.

Historical: The most important historical aspect of the Red River Gorge area is the impact and development of the logging industry from 1880 to

Sky Bridge Arch is accessible from a trail that passes over and beneath this interesting rock formation.

1920. Once Kentucky was opened up to settlement, people began building in the area. This development created the need for building supplies, such as timber, and as a result, the forest in the Red River Gorge area became a rich resource.

The logging industry enjoyed many prosperous years in the Red River Gorge area, and evidence of that era of history remains today. The Gladie Historic Site celebrates the settlement that evolved around the logging business. Only the cabin exists today, but more than a hundred years ago the area would have been alive with the busy sounds of a thriving logging camp. The Nada Band Mill is another example of the importance of the logging industry in the area.

As the area developed into a rich logging region, the need arose for a means of transporting the timber out of the area. Logs were floated down streams and shipped to distant markets by railroad. The railroad was most readily available after 1912 with the opening of the Nada Tunnel. Construction of that tunnel had begun in 1910 and 1911.

Recreational: The Red River Gorge Scenic Byway can be a recreational destination unto itself. The Red River provides you with some stunning views of water tumbling over boulders and through steep cliffs. However, the river is also a prime spot to go canoeing and kayaking. The abundance of rock formations and cliffs make this byway a first-class spot for rock climbing.

The byway travels through a national forest and also Natural Bridge State Resort Park. An extensive trail system,

known as the Sheltowee Trace National Recreation Trail, runs through the Daniel Boone National Forest. Trails in the Red River Gorge Geological Area also visit more than 100 stone arches. In addition to this extensive system, within Natural Bridge State Resort Park, there are nine trails. Camping, miniature golf, swimming, and square dancing can also be enjoyed at the resort.

Highlights:

Use this itinerary as a guideline to catch the highlights of the Red River Gorge Scenic Byway.

Sky Bridge: One of the best known and most accessible arches of this area is Sky Bridge, 75 feet long and 23 feet high. Sky Bridge's arch features a magnificent view of Clifty Wilderness.

Nada Tunnel: Enter the Red River Gorge Geological Area through the 900-foot Nada Tunnel. Open to one-lane traffic only, the tunnel

was hand-carved without any modern technology for use by a logging railroad during the early 1900s. The tunnel is listed on the National Register of Historic Places.

Clifty Wilderness: Within the gorge is Clifty Wilderness, a hardy and untamed area designated as wilderness by Congress in 1985. This 12,646-acre area features arches, rock shelters, and towering cliffs encircling steep, forested slopes and narrow stream valleys.

Gladie Historic Site: Gladie Cabin, a reconstructed log house, is the only structure in the gorge that dates back to the late 19th century.

Raven's Rock and Angel Windows: Raven's Rock offers some of the best views of the Red River Gorge. Angel Windows is another of the most easily reached of the arches.

Natural Bridge State Resort Park: Standing 65 feet high and 78 feet long, the great natural sandstone arch known as Natural Bridge is located in the Natural Bridge State Resort Park.

Torrent Falls and Via Ferrata: Near the southern end of the byway are Torrent Falls and Via Ferrata. Torrent Falls is actually three waterfalls, the highest being 165 feet high and the tallest in Kentucky.

Wilderness Road Heritage Highway

Daniel Boone marked this trail through the Appalachian Mountain forest that now bears his name. Following his path, tap your toes to the mountain music that echoes in the high ridges and hidden hollows.

From panoramic views of the Appalachians in Cumberland Gap National Historic Park, to a community culture centered on folk art and mountain music, this byway is packed with reasons to immerse yourself in the woodland culture of the Southeast.

Cultural: From music to crafts, this byway is a celebration of the early influence of pioneers. Today, traditional country music and entertainment is alive in Renfro Valley, which hosts performances throughout the year.

In addition to the preservation of traditional music, many communities along the byway promote the making and selling of crafts.

Historical: The Wilderness Road Heritage Highway begins at perhaps one of the most historically significant sites in regard to the settlement of the United States. Cumberland Gap National Historic Park celebrates an important corridor, the Cumberland Gap. Native Americans crossed the Appalachians on what they called the Warriors Path, and they relied on this naturally occurring route to provide access to the country across the Appalachian Mountains. Kentucky was seen as a great wilderness for more than 150 years after the initial pilgrims set foot on the eastern seaboard, but soon explorers such as Daniel Boone scouted out the area.

One of the most important pioneers to come through the Cumberland Gap was Dr. Thomas Walker. The Dr. Thomas Walker State Historic Site celebrates the life of this first pioneer to discover the Cumberland Gap and then explore Kentucky. Exploration of the new Kentucky lands opened the area up for settlement, and scores of pioneers followed in Dr. Walker's footsteps.

As America grew, debate turned to war in 1861. Many of the American Civil War battles were fought in Kentucky. The Cumberland Gap was a key transportation route throughout the war. A battle of the Civil War was fought at Camp Wildcat, located along the Wilderness Road Heritage Highway.

Cumberland Gap is the second largest historical park in the nation and features numerous historical and natural sites of interest.

Recreational: Whether you are in the mood for hiking, camping, wildlife viewing, biking, fishing, or boating, the Wilderness Road Heritage Highway offers travelers a variety of opportunities. There are numerous rivers, and the byway is near Laurel River Lake, where visitors can boat and fish. The byway travels over some of these rivers, making it a prime spot to view wildlife, both waterfowl and other species of critters. Near the byway you can even spot some elk, which make up the largest herd in the eastern United States.

Cumberland Gap National Historic Park and Pine Mountain State Resort Park offer the majority of the byway's opportunities to find hiking, biking, and horseback riding trails. There is an extensive system of trails in Cumberland Gap National Historic Park, for anything from easy nature hikes to overnight trails. In Daniel Boone National Forest, the Sheltowee Trace National Recreation Trail covers 269 miles.

There is golfing at Pine Mountain State Resort Park and dramatic views in both Cumberland Gap and Pine Mountain. At Pine Mountain State Resort Park, a swimming pool and an amphitheater set in a natural forest cove offer relaxing entertainment and fun.

Highlights:

This itinerary gives a few of the highlights moving along the Wilderness Road Heritage Highway from north to south.

Kentucky Music Hall of Fame & Museum:
In Renfro Valley is the Kentucky Music Hall of Fame and Museum, honoring all genres of music and musical artists.

Levi Jackson Wilderness Road State Park:
Near London is the Levi Jackson Wilderness Road State Park. In the 20 years after 1774 more than 200,000 pioneers traveled over the Wilderness Road and Boone's Trace during the settlement of Kentucky.

Harland Sanders and Museum:
Just a bit off the scenic byway but well worth the brief detour is the town of Corbin, home of the Harland Sanders Cafe and Museum. First opened in 1940, this is the location of Harland Sanders's first restaurant where he developed his famous chicken recipe.

Dr. Thomas Walker State Historic Site:
Just five miles southwest of Barbourville is Dr. Thomas Walker State Historic Site. Preceding Daniel Boone into Kentucky by 17 years, Dr. Walker led the first exploration into the Cumberland Gap, and a reconstruction of the log cabin he built can be toured.

Cumberland Gap National Historical Park:
The climax of the trip is this park, featuring several historic and natural points of interest. Rangers guide visitors on an adventure through majestic cathedral-like Gap Cave. A shuttle transports visitors to the remote Hensley Settlement. A trek to Cumberland Gap itself is a must.

Coal Heritage Trail

Winding mountain roads search out remnants of a one-time coal-mining boom. Step into a coal miner's home and a company store, view a railroad yard, and brave a visit deep inside a former coal mine.

Quick Facts

Length: 97.5 miles

Time to Allow: Three hours

Consideration: Slower speeds are recommended because the road is narrow and has numerous curves. Drivers may also encounter large coal trucks using the road in some areas. There are no seasonal accessibility limitations. However, be sure to allow extra driving time during inclement weather.

Experience life in the coal camps on the Coal Heritage Trail in West Virginia. As you wind through the mountains and valleys of the byway, you will see many physical remnants of the coal boom that furthered the industrialization of America.

Cultural: Experience the culture of the coalfields that developed from different racial and ethnic groups working and living together. As coal became a primary resource for fuel after the Civil War, southern West Virginia and its coalfields grew quickly. Immigrants from Europe and from the southern states of the nation gathered along the Coal Heritage Trail. Although the byway is a representation of cultural harmony, distinctive ethnic communities, old-world traditions, and festivals are kept alive to enjoy today.

Historical: The story of southern West Virginia's coalfields is one of working-class culture, industrial might, and racial and ethnic diversity. The coal mines along the Coal Heritage Trail produced abundant economical fuel

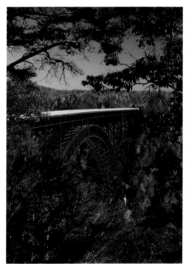
The New River Gorge Bridge is the longest single-span steel arch bridge in the Western Hemisphere.

that transformed rural America into an industrial land, providing jobs and homes for thousands of people fleeing persecution and oppression. Immense fortunes were made by those who invested in the industry, and a society was produced with a peculiar and fascinating legacy.

What makes the Coal Heritage Trail significant are the physical remnants of the coal boom that remain scattered in the deep valleys of the region. These artifacts provide a wonderful opportunity for understanding the role of the West Virginia coalfields in the industrialization of America.

As mining jobs were lost to mechanization, the people of the coalfields left in search of employment in the cities of the industrial Midwest and beyond. The descendants of these people and other visitors interested in the many facets of heritage and culture represented on the byway are visiting the area. Visitors will see historic structures, including coal mines and railroad structures.

Recreational: Visitors to the Coal Heritage Trail enjoy outstanding recreational and natural features. The rugged and beautiful mountains of the coalfields are the physical signature of the region and were instrumental in the development of isolated coal camps that were connected to the outside world only by the railroad that also hauled out coal. Numerous state parks and wilderness areas provide access to recreational areas offering hiking, skiing, canoeing, mountain biking, white water rafting, and other activities.

Highlights:

Not only rich in scenery, this area is rich in heritage, a place where coal reigned supreme. This itinerary gives you a few of the must-see highlights along the way.

Princeton–Mercer County Chamber of Commerce: Before entering the Coal Heritage Trail, a stop in Princeton at the Princeton–Mercer County Chamber of Commerce is a good way to begin your trip. Located just off U.S. 460 on Oakvale Road, the Chamber of Commerce not only has plenty of maps and information about the region, but also is home to the Wiley Cabin & Museum.

Bluefield: From Princeton take U.S. 460 to Bluefield to begin traveling along the Coal Heritage Trail. On Commerce Street is the Eastern Regional Coal Archives. The facility collects, preserves, and makes available coal-related heritage through photographs, memorabilia, and other artifacts.

Bramwell: The historic village of

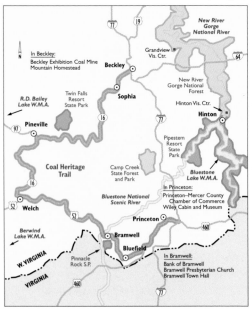

Bramwell was once the wealthiest town per capita in America, home to 14 millionaires who made their fortunes here. A brochure with a walking tour and map of the historic highlights of the luxurious heydays of Bramwell is available at the Bramwell Town Hall and at several of the bed-and-breakfasts.

Bank of Bramwell: The Bank of Bramwell was once so prosperous that the janitor would take heaping mounds of moneybags in a wheelbarrow to the train station each day. Bust by 1933 as a result of the Great Depression, the historic bank building, still oozing with opulence and elegance, was home to the local paper by the turn of the 20th century.

Bramwell Presbyterian Church: The Bramwell Presbyterian Church was patterned after a Welsh cathedral and contains such lavish extra touches as local bluestone tiles cut and laid by Italian masons who also came to seek their fortune.

Beckley Exhibition Coal Mine: This mine gives visitors a realistic glimpse into the world of coal mining as it was in the early 1900s. Tours travel underground through nearly 1,500 feet of passageways in an authentic coal mine.

Highland Scenic Highway

Nonstop panoramas unfold as you ascend forested mountain slopes in the state's wild Allegheny Highlands. Four scenic overlooks invite you to reflect on the views.

Travel through a wild and undeveloped portion of the Monongahela National Forest on the Highland Scenic Highway in West Virginia. See rolling, mountainous terrain covered by hardwood forests and capped by dark spruce at higher elevations from one of four overlooks. This view is one you won't want to miss. Hidden within this panoramic view, you'll find plenty of places to visit and things to do.

Cultural: As an isolated area with abundant natural resources, the wilderness of the Highland Scenic Highway was an early haven for Americans seeking to avoid the horrors of the Civil War. Families who moved to the area at this time maintained their seclusion for decades.

In the 1960s, the descendants of these families experienced a visit from people researching for the Smithsonian Institution. As the researchers studied and recorded the oral histories of the families in this area, they discovered that the language spoken was still the Elizabethan English of the early U.S. settlers. Tradition and folk tales of the area

have been recorded and are a remnant of the mountain cultures of the East.

Historical: There are many historical events associated with the Highland Scenic Highway. As intensive logging developed along this road, so did the habitation of the area. In the early 1900s, logging of almost all the timber in the area was done. Due to the lack of transportation possibilities into the area, the land surrounding the Highland Scenic Highway remained relatively unsettled for decades. However, once the area was trld War II Mill Point Prison Camp. This camp housed federal prisoners of the time, conscientious objectors, and moonshiners.

Recreational: The Highland Scenic Highway area offers recreational opportunities for travelers who enjoy hunting, fishing, hiking, or camping. For example, along the Cherry, Cranberry, and Williams Rivers, you'll find anglers casting for trout. The West Virginia Division of Natural Resources stocks the streams with rainbow, brook, brown, and golden trout.

Quick Facts

Length: 43 miles

Time to Allow: Two to four hours

Consideration: There are no services along the route, and there is no snow removal during the winter. Also, be aware that some of the road is used by large coal trucks.

The Falls of Hills Creek includes three falls, with Hells Creek descending a total of 220 feet between the upper and lower falls.

Summit Lake, a beautiful 42-acre reservoir, contains trout, bass, and panfish.

More than 150 miles of trails are located in the area of the Highland Scenic Highway. The Falls of Hills Creek Scenic Area, the Cranberry Glades, and the Big Spruce Overlook offer three barrier-free trails. For those interested in a backpacking experience, Cranberry Wilderness and the Tea Creek area offer places for camping. Visitors should camp away from trails and streams. Many trails in the area also offer opportunities for horseback riding and are suitable for cross-country skiing in the winter.

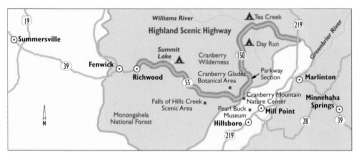

Three campgrounds are included in the Highland Scenic Highway area. If a stay by the lake sounds appealing, Summit Lake Campground is two miles from State Route 39/55. For campsites by the Williams River, Tea Creek Campground is one mile from the parkway portion of the byway, and Day Run Campground is only four miles away.

Highlights:

"Scenic" is the key word when traveling along this route. A natural wonder, the highlights of the trip are listed here.

Richwood: Begin your journey in the town of Richwood. Originally known as Cherry Tree Bottoms, it was a "company town" of the Cherry River Boom and Lumber Company. Today this is the place to find local outfitters and guides to prepare for a rigorous adventure in the Monongahela National Forest.

Falls of Hills Creek Scenic Area:

The Falls of Hills Creek Scenic Area, a 114-acre area, contains three waterfalls. The first 1,700 feet of trail is a paved, wheelchair-accessible path to the upper falls viewing platform. The rest of the trail is more demanding with stairways and boardwalks leading to the lower falls.

Cranberry Mountain Nature Center:

This nature center offers information about the Monongahela National Forest and other nearby attractions. An exhibit hall and audiovisual programs provide interpretation of forest ecosystems and local history.

Cranberry Glades Botanical Area:

Cranberry Glades Botanical Area is an ecological anomaly. The four glades, or bogs, contain plant life normally found 500 miles north. Many of the distinctive plant species found here are descendants of plants that were forced south by the glaciers that covered Canada and the northern United States about 10,000 years ago.

Cranberry Wilderness: Not suitable for homesteading but quite appealing to the Cherry River Boom and Lumber Company, the area now known as Cranberry Wilderness was completely logged out by 1930. The U.S. Forest Service purchased the land in 1934. Cranberry Wilderness is 35,864 acres and has approximately 60 miles of trails, many of which follow old railroad grades, logging roads, or Forest Service roads.

Historic National Road

West Virginia's share of this historic corridor crosses the state's slender northern panhandle, edging past Oglebay Resort Park, a beautifully landscaped preserve with many recreational attractions.

Quick Facts

Length: 16 miles

Time to Allow: One hour

Consideration: The byway is open all year, but many feel it is best to drive during the summer, the high season, when more cultural activities are taking place.

West Virginia's Historic National Road takes you on a trip through history. In 1863, West Virginia developed into a new state. The building where the Restored Government of Virginia was established is located along the byway; many important decisions and debates regarding the Civil War took place in this building. You can tour this historic site that has been painstakingly preserved and beautifully restored.

The Historic National Road boasts many impressive museums and art galleries. One of the most popular museums along the byway is the Kruger Street Toy and Train Museum in Wheeling. The byway also features restored mansions, such as the Oglebay Institute Mansion Museum. This 16-mile attraction offers a high level of historic aesthetics and cleanliness. To make this route even more accommodating, you can find bike paths and paved trails through most of the byway's highlights.

Cultural: The cultural qualities of the Historic National Road are many in number and offer diverse experiences. Two of perhaps the most meaningful include music (particularly Jamboree U.S.A.) and religion.

The Capitol Theatre, located next to the famous Wheeling Suspension Bridge, is home to both Jamboree U.S.A. and the Wheeling Symphony Orchestra. The Jamboree is the second-longest-running live radio program in America's history. Since 1933, famous artists from all over the nation have their show aired live over the radio each Saturday night. It was founded with the idea of promoting the regional country music that is dear to the South. When the Jamboree first

The Bissonnette Gardens at Oglebay Resort Park are enticing. Visitors can walk on the red brick paths and view the seasonal flower displays.

In Oglebay Resort Park:
Bissonnette Gardens
Oglebay Institute Mansion Museum
Oglebay Institute Glass Museum
Oglebay's Good Zoo

OHIO
WEST VIRGINIA

Historic National
Road–Pennsylvania

40

Historic National
Road–Ohio

Wheeling Suspension
Bridge

Long Run

Oglebay Resort
Park

Waddles
Run

Mount Echo

Capitol Music Hall

Wheeling Downs

40

Wheeling
Park

40

40

70

Historic National
Road–West
Virginia

Wheeling

470

Kruger Street Toy & Train Museum
W.V. Independence Hall

Bethlehem

In Wheeling:
Wheeling Custom
House

Ohio River

Jakes Run

Wheeling Run

WEST VIRGINIA
PENNSYLVANIA

250

88

The Historic
National Road

Glen Dale

80

N

Moundsville

Pleasant
Valley

In Moundsville:
Grave Creek Archaeology
Complex

began, fans drove hundreds of miles for this weekly event.

Religion has played a powerful role in shaping the communities along the byway. Places of worship dot this area, some with beautiful aesthetics and architecture. Churches along the route tell the story of the great diversity of those who traveled and settled here.

Historical: Without question, the historic qualities are the richest attribute this byway has to offer. With two national historic landmarks, numerous designated historic districts, and National Register structures, the Historic National Road had a great impact on not only West Virginia's past, but on America's, too.

The National Road Corridor Historic District consists of a variety of homes built by Wheeling's wealthy industrial class. It also includes Wheeling Park, Greenwood Cemetery, and Mount Cavalry Cemetery. In 1888, farms outside the city began to be developed as "suburbia." The Woodsdale–Edgewood Neighborhood Historic District is a result of this type of development. The district contains many high-style houses, such as Queen Anne, Colonial Revival, and Shingle styles. As the route descends Wheeling Hill into the city of Wheeling, you enter the North Wheeling Historic District. Ebenezer Zane, the founder of Wheeling, laid out the Victorian district in 1792. The houses include a variety of simple Federal townhouses offset with the high styles of Italianate, Queen Anne, Second Empire, and Classical Revival architecture.

The Wheeling Suspension Bridge crosses the Ohio River to Wheeling Island. The engineering marvel spans 1,010 feet and was the first bridge to cross the Ohio River. You cross the bridge to get to Wheeling Island, one of the largest inhabited river islands in the country.

Recreational: The city of Wheeling has some of the world's fastest canines in the races. This popular event is usually open every day.

Visitors go to Wheeling Downs to watch the races in person. These sleek thoroughbreds give quite a show as they thunder along at speeds of up to 40 miles per hour. At Wheeling Downs, people can enjoy the luxury of attending the races while eating at a fine diner that overlooks the track.

Highlights:

Look to these points of interest for a great tour of West Virginia's Historic National Road.

Oglebay Resort Park: Covering 1,650 rolling green acres, Oglebay Resort Park is a major regional recreation center. It features the 30-acre Good Zoo, displaying 80 species of animals; the Benedum Science Theater, offering laser shows; a 1.5-mile miniature train ride; 16-acre Bissonnette Gardens, a recreation of 19th-century gardens; two championship golf courses; two swimming pools; tennis courts; horse stables; and lodging, restaurants, and specialty shops.

Oglebay Institute Mansion Museum: Built in 1846 as an eight-room farmhouse, the Greek Revival-style home later was expanded to become a private summer estate. Willed to the city of Wheeling, in 1930 it became a museum, and it displays period antiques.

Oglebay Institute Glass Museum: Adjacent to the mansion, the Glass

Designed by Charles Ellet, Jr., the Wheeling Suspension Bridge was the longest single span in the United States at the time of its completion in 1849.

Museum features 3,000 examples of Wheeling glass made from 1829 to 1939. Displays include cut lead crystal, Victorian art glass, carnival glass, and other Ohio Valley glass designs. Of note is the 225-pound Sweeney Punch Bowl, the largest piece of cut lead crystal ever made. It is regarded as a masterpiece of Victorian glass.

Grave Creek Archaeology Complex: The Adena, a mound-building people who lived in the region from 1000 B.C. to A.D. 700, are represented by the 2,000-year-old Grave Creek Mound. It is the largest of the Adena burial mounds. In the adjacent Delf Norona Museum,

exhibits detail the life of the Adena people. The mound was built by hauling 60,000 tons of dirt in basket loads.

Midland Trail

Peer into the deep New River Gorge from high above, or sign onto a white water rafting trip that splashes beneath the soaring cliffs. Beyond the gorge, small towns are reminiscent of a bygone day.

Travel the Midland Trail, and enter a land of world-class white water rafting, Civil War remnants, African-American history, and small towns full of country charm. The byway will carry you through areas rich in industrial culture, over hills and through valleys arrayed in scenic beauty, and finally out into rolling farmland settled during the colonial era.

Cultural: Part of the cultural heritage of today comes from the history of yesterday. The Midland Trail holds many historical sites significant to the life of Booker T. Washington who played an influential role in African American education and equality. He is memorialized today at historic buildings and information centers on the byway. People remember the first developments of industry along the byway when Elisha Brooks used 24 kettles to extract salt from the area's brine in 1797.

Although West Virginians have found a significant role in the industry of natural resources, an appreciation for the arts and outdoors has also been cultivated here. Nothing is more revered in today's West Virginia culture than outdoor recreation and adventure. White water rafting is second to none. The skill and craft of byway residents can be found in the many stores along the way. Quilts are a specialty, and visitors will be able to find quilt shops in Malden, Lookout, Ansted, and several other byway communities.

Historical: There are many historical events associated with the Midland Trail. As the new country struggled to move westward over the Appalachian Mountains, the Midland Trail was the most direct but most difficult passage from the mideastern colonies. Following buffalo and Native American trails, Daniel Boone explored the route. Eventually a combination of land and water routes opened up the land and the natural resources to the nation. Buffalo, American Indians, settlers, and later industrialists sought out the rich

At Oakhurst Links, the first organized golf club in the United States, the "mowing" flock of sheep adds to the authenticity of the 19th-century experience.

salt brines of the Kanawha Valley. The river provided transportation for coal and timber. The battles fought over this route started before the Revolutionary War and continued through the Civil War.

Claudius Crozet was responsible for planning Virginia's road system. He designed and constructed many roads, including the Midland Trail.

For a time, the Midland Trail was nearly forgotten as people used the railways. Meanwhile, the 20th century began, and the area's resources fueled the industrial development. The slaves who toiled in the salt works and the immigrants who cut the Hawks Nest Hydroelectric Tunnel through silica rock left behind a history of the nation's growing pains. In the mid-20th century America's love affair with the automobile was heightening, and the trail became U.S. 60, the preferred truck route over the mountains. Today, its roadside parks, turnouts, and mom-and-pop businesses still resemble the traveling conditions present after World War II. Yet the road leads to a place of change and history in Charleston, the state's capital.

Recreational: World-class rafting and outdoor sports are found along the Midland Trail. The best white water east of the Mississippi annually draws more than 160,000 people to raft the New

River, and more than 60,000 people raft the Gauley River during its 22-day fall season. Outdoor adventurers also participate in kayaking, canoeing, fishing, hunting, rock climbing, hiking, and mountain biking. One of the most adrenalizing activities happens once a year on the third Saturday in October. For a thrilling spectacle, watch trained jumpers as they leap from the 876-foot-high New River Gorge Bridge.

Local communities also offer recreational activities. Ansted has an annual street luge competition. The Greenbrier Hotel Resort, a National Historic Landmark, has 54 holes of championship golf, including the golf course called Oakhurst Links. At the 1884 course, golfers must still use 19th-century wooden clubs and equipment, and play by 19th-century rules.

Highlights:

Before the interstate system criss-crossed the country, the Midland Trail was a major thoroughfare in West Virginia. Here are some of the highlights.

Charleston: Begin your journey at Charleston, the capital of West Virginia. The town is filled to the brim with historic landmarks.

West Virginia State Capitol Complex: The complex includes the capitol

with its marble rotunda containing a splendid two-ton chandelier. The complex also has several statues and fountains, a veterans' memorial, a museum, the Governor's Mansion, and the antebellum Holly Grove home.

Hawks Nest State Park: At Hawks Nest State Park visitors can ride the tram 876 feet to the base of the New River Gorge. The park also features a museum, lodging, scenic dining, and four trails.

Ansted: Continuing east on U.S. 60 visitors come to the town of Ansted. Attractions include the gravesite of Julia Neale Jackson, mother of Thomas "Stonewall" Jackson; Halfway House, a former tavern on the Kanawha Turnpike and headquarters of the Chicago Dragoons during the Civil War; and African American Heritage Family Tree Museum.

Sam Black United Methodist Church: Farther east near the junction with I-64 is this church, built in 1901. Reverend Sam Black was a Methodist circuit rider for nearly 50 years.

Lost World Caverns: North of Lewisburg are the Lost World Caverns, featuring the nation's largest compound stalactite, the 30-ton "Snowy Chandelier." The Lost World Caverns Visitors Center and Natural History Museum features the largest collection of dinosaur and fossil replicas in West Virginia.

Lewisburg: The historic town of Lewisburg has enough attractions, including a 235-acre historic down-town district, to keep visitors busy for several days.

White Sulphur Springs: The climax of the trip is the resort town of White Sulphur Springs. Among many highlights is the Oakhurst Links. Duffers at Oakhurst play the course just as golfers did in 1884.

The Greenbrier: The Greenbrier housed a secret until 1992. Buried 720 feet into the hillside specifically to accommodate the U.S. Senate and House of Representatives in case of a nuclear attack is a bunker. Visitors are encouraged to tour the facility. Guided tours of the elegant interior design and architecture are offered year round; the Presidents' Cottage Museum details the

memorable moments from the visits of 27 U.S. presidents; tours give a glimpse into the history as well as the natural beauty that surrounds the resort.

Washington Heritage Trail

George Washington crisscrossed the state's eastern panhandle, and you can follow in his path. Soak in the mineral waters of the little spa town of Berkeley Springs, as he once did.

Follow the footsteps of America's first president and founding father when you travel the Washington Heritage Trail. So much of George Washington's history is preserved and relived along the byway that you can almost feel his presence. The byway offers a retreat from the hustle and bustle of metropolitan life. Travel through farms and apple orchards and enjoy the scenic beauty of the area as you explore the history of the people and places that shaped this great nation.

Cultural: Cultural qualities along the Washington Heritage Trail reflect the rich history and diverse culture of West Virginia's heritage, which blends Virginia gentility with mountain hospitality and charm. The panhandle's pioneers are recognized by annual events. Berkeley Springs honors the nation's first president each March with the George Washington's Bathtub Celebration.

In addition, the Belle Boyd House retains extensive historical and genea-logical archives. Civil War scholars can immerse themselves in the archives at

Shepherdstown's George Tyler Moore Civil War Center.

Far from being confined to history, celebrations along the byway focus on other facets of the eastern panhandle's unique cultural legacy, such as arts and crafts, apples, and drinking water.

Historical: Beginning in the days of George Washington, the eastern panhandle of West Virginia has been a

pocket of history. It has seen troops of three wars, the growth of a population,

Lined with more than six million bricks, the Paw Paw Tunnel in the C&O Canal National Historic Park is the largest made-by-hand structure on the C&O Canal.

the industrialization of a society, and the developments that have allowed the area to achieve national recognition. For example, the eastern panhandle was an important source of quality enlisted officers during the Revolutionary War.

Many of the region's settlements were established during the late 18th century, including Shepherdstown and Martinsburg. Much of the panhandle's early activity occurred around these settlements, and historic structures line the roads of the Washington Heritage Trail.

By urging the establishment of a federal armory at Harper's Ferry, George Washington inadvertently played a role in the tensions that sparked the Civil War. The armory was seized by abolitionist John Brown during his famed 1859 raid, an event that focused the nation's attention on the issue of slavery. The Potomac Valley was the stage for a number of critical Civil War campaigns, one of which culminated in the battle at Antietam, the bloodiest of all Civil War battles.

Also, George Washington's interest in making the Potomac River navigable sowed the seed for what became the Chesapeake and Ohio Canal, which was critical to the movement of goods and people through the Potomac Valley for more than 70 years.

Confederate forces traveled portions of the Washington Heritage Trail in Morgan County during Thomas Jonathan "Stonewall" Jackson's 1861–1862 winter campaign. In Morgan County, nearly 16,000 Union forces camped at Camp Hill Cemetery east of Paw Paw—the same location used by General Edward Braddock's forces during the French and Indian War. Panhandle railroads like the Baltimore and Ohio were strategically important during the war as well, and Martinsburg's B&O Roundhouse Complex National Register of Historic Places District preserves some of the resources that were targeted by Confederate raiders.

Recreational: Recreational activities are abundant on the Washington Heritage Trail. Sightseeing is one of the most popular activities. In addition to visiting historical sights and passing scenic overlooks, fishing, hunting, boating, golf, and racing are all activities that are offered.

Resources for walkers and hikers abound in the eastern panhandle, including everything from historic walking tours of Shepherdstown and Charles Town to many wonderful hiking trails. Shorter hiking trails can be found in the Cacapon Resort State Park and at the Coolfont Resort, and longer hikes exist along the Tuscarora Trail that runs the length of Sleepy Creek Mountain. The 2,100-mile-long Appalachian Trail has its headquarters in Harper's Ferry and can be accessed there. Another great hiking trail, the C&O Canal Trail, is probably the least strenuous and one of the most scenic trails. It can be accessed at Harper's Ferry and Paw Paw.

The network of mountain streams and rivers in the panhandle provides ample opportunities for both fishers and boaters to enjoy the water. River rafting, canoeing, and kayaking trips on the Shenandoah and Potomac Rivers can be arranged through outfitters in Harper's Ferry.

Not surprisingly, the Sleepy Creek Public Hunting and Fishing Area remains the largest public area open to hunters. Golfers can enjoy a round or two at public and private courses such as those at the Woods Resort, Locust Hill, and Cacapon Resort State Park. Fans of thoroughbred racing can try their luck on a trifecta wager at the Charles Town Race Track. Auto racing enthusiasts can also get their fill at the Summit Point Raceway.

Highlights:

Meandering through the stunning scenery of the West Virginia panhandle, this itinerary highlights some of the fascinating things to see and do along the way.

Paw Paw Tunnel: Just a mile north of the town of Paw Paw is the Paw Paw Tunnel in the C&O National Park. Built by the C&O Canal Company in the 1800s, the structure is a 3,118-foot passage through Sorrell Ridge lined with six million bricks.

Berkeley Springs: George Washington visited the colonial spa town of Berkeley Springs nearly a dozen times. Several Washington Heritage Trail sites are here as well as full-service spas, award-winning eateries, antique malls, museums, and more.

Berkeley Springs State Park: Berkeley Springs State Park is in the center of town and features the original 74-degree warm mineral springs, including a public tap for free spring water. Two facilities operated by the State of West Virginia offer treatments to the public, including the historic Roman Bath House. Also at the park is George Washington's Bathtub, the only outdoor monument to presidential bathing.

Belle Boyd House: The Belle Boyd House in the historic town of Martinsburg houses several noteworthy Civil War history displays. Ms. Boyd was quite a successful Confederate spy during the war.

Shepherdstown: Shepherdstown began as a gristmill in 1739 and is the oldest incorporated town in West Virginia. Many 18th- and 19th-century buildings still exist, including the former Entler Hotel.

Harper's Ferry: In addition to George Washington, other famous fellows who had key roles in the history of this town include Thomas Jefferson, Meriwether Lewis, and Frederick Douglass. Harper's Ferry National Historic Park interprets the history of this fascinating town with tours, several museums, park exhibits, interpretive signage, special events, and activities.

Charles Town: John Brown was tried for treason, convicted, and hanged in the nearby village of Charles Town. Of the three treason trials in U.S. history, two of them have been tried here. The courthouse is open for guided tours.

The picturesque village of Harper's Ferry is at the confluence of the Shenandoah and Potomac Rivers and at the crossroads of major episodes of American history.

Lee's Retreat: On the Road to Appomattox, The Civil War's Final Days

Lee's Retreat, an official Virginia Civil War trail, traces the historic route through lush farm country only lightly changed in the decades since.

Quick Facts

Length: 110 miles

Time to Allow: Three hours

Consideration: A brochure detailing the route of Lee's Retreat is available at Virginia tourism information offices and at the Petersburg Battlefield visitor center. The route can be driven year-round, although snow-covered roads are an occasional possibility from December into March.

In the waning days of the Civil War, Union and Confederate armies raced across the Virginia countryside to the village of Appomattox, where Robert E. Lee ultimately surrendered to Ulysses S. Grant.

Civil War armies traveled mostly by foot, horse, and wagon. Today, motorists with an interest in American history can follow their path in a series of drives recalling the major campaigns in Virginia. You follow the course of action, often on the same roads used by the combatants. Directional signs guide you, and waysides along the route explain what happened.

The most poignant of the Civil War drives (because it culminated in the war's end), and the most scenic is Lee's Retreat, a 110-mile driving tour that follows the day-to-day, and sometimes hour-to-hour, progress of

Small and rustic, General Grant's cabin was meant to simply protect the Union commander from the elements during the long siege of Petersburg.

the armies west from Petersburg to Appomattox. Perched atop a broad, grass-covered hill, the village where the two armies converged has been preserved as a national historical park. Surrounded by acres of rolling green farmland and pastures, it looks much as it did on the day of Lee's surrender, April 9, 1865.

Essentially a history lesson, the drive provides plenty of opportunities for fun-filled recess. At Farmville, where Lee hoped to find food for his hungry troops, you can lunch in an outdoor café alongside the racing Appomattox River.

Highlights:

Consider using the following itinerary as you travel Lee's Retreat.

Petersburg National Battlefield:
Site of the nearly ten-month siege, the park's most notable sight is the Crater, symbol both of Union ingenuity and bungled opportunities. Early in the siege, military mining experts devised a plan to dig a nearly 500-foot tunnel under a Confederate fort to blow it up. The blast succeeded, digging a

huge hole and leveling 500 yards of Confederate lines. But the Union attack force, stunned by the violent spectacle, delayed its advance, giving defenders a chance to rally.

Pamplin Historical Park and the National Museum of the Civil War Soldier: Seven galleries recreate the life of the common soldier in camp, on the march, and in battle. The museum is located on the site of a Union attack that breached Lee's defenses shortly before his flight to Appomattox. A one-mile trail explores the battlefield.

Sailor's Creek Battlefield Historic State Park: Fought here on April 6, 1865, dubbed "Black Thursday," the battle resulted in a harsh Confederate defeat. It proved a key in Lee's decision to surrender. His already shrunken army lost 7,700 men, including eight generals.

Farmville: A central Virginia commercial hub, Farmville boasts an attractive downtown center, where visitors can browse for antiques and enjoy a lunch alongside the Appomattox River. Lee hoped to feed his army here, but the federal cavalry intruded. Just to the south, Twin Lakes State Park operates a swimming beach on Goodwin Lake.

Appomattox Court House National Historical Park: Other Civil War parks

commemorate the violent clash of armies. Appomattox is a place of peace, a beautiful and quiet memorial to the end of four long years of war. As such, it honors the remarkable dignity and the generosity of the combatants in the final hours of the conflict.

Holliday Lake State Park: Ringed by public forest, the park is a recreational antidote to the somber story told on Lee's Retreat. Swimming, fishing, canoeing, rowboats, and paddleboats can be found here.

The tiny village of Appomattox includes not only the house where General Lee surrendered his Confederate troops to Union General Grant, but also several other buildings such as Meek's Store.

Virginia's Skyline Drive

Virginia's Skyline Drive flows like a stream among the high rocky peaks of the Blue Ridge Mountains in Shenandoah National Park, allowing majestic views of green farm valleys and a famous river far below.

One of the wonders of America's national parks, the 105-mile-long Skyline Drive was built to show off the Blue Ridge scenery. On both sides of the winding road, tree-covered slopes drop sharply to the valley floor. To the east is the Piedmont, Virginia's rolling foothill country, where green pastures and golden fields form a patchwork quilt. To the west sprawls the broad Shenandoah Valley, where the Shenandoah River, fabled in song and story, makes repeated silvery loops.

From beginning to end, the drive tempts motorists to stop at nearly 80 overlooks, although only the most dedicated of sightseers would try to take in them all. Running north to south, the route parallels a 101-mile segment of the Georgia-to-Maine Appalachian Trail, which it crosses some 32 times. Almost any of these intersections is a good place to stretch the legs on a short stroll on the trail. During fall foliage season, the mountains are ablaze in color.

Deer are plentiful along the drive, so much so that it is wise to keep alert at the wheel. And it is not unusual to spot a startled mama bear and her cubs dashing into the woods to get out of your way. Shenandoah National Park is home to an estimated 300 to 500 bears. Learn along the way of the hard-scrabble life of the Appalachian folk who once farmed these lush Blue Ridge slopes and hollows.

Highlights:

Start this beautiful tour in Front Royal, and end in Rockfish Gap.

Numerous overlooks along Virginia's Skyline Drive offer motorists an opportunity to stop and absorb the dramatic views.

Quick Facts

Length: 105 miles

Time to Allow: Three to six hours

Consideration: Shenandoah and Skyline Drive are open year-round, but most facilities (lodging, dining, service stations, and campgrounds) are closed from late fall to early spring. Snow, ice, and blinding fog can shut down the road temporarily in winter. The fall foliage show is spectacular, but weekend motorists in October often create near gridlock conditions on Skyline Drive.

Front Royal: A small city, Front Royal is both a gateway to Shenandoah National Park and Shenandoah Valley. Nearby visit Linden Vineyards; Cedar Creek Battlefield; and Belle Grove with its garden and orchard, maintained by the National Trust for Historic Preservation.

Dickey Ridge Visitor Center: This rustically appealing old structure straddles the narrow crest of the Blue Ridge, presenting views east and west. You can stroll the Fox Hollow Trail to the Fox Family homestead.

Hogback Overlook: When a haze doesn't intrude, you can see the South Fork of the Shenandoah River and its many bends.

Elkwallow: The camp store and service station here are open May through October. The picnic ground is open year-round.

Thornton Gap: Panorama Restaurant, a park facility, is open from May through October. From this park entrance, descend west to the town of Luray and Luray Caverns, one of the East's largest commercial caves. It is noted for its "stalacpipe" organ, which produces symphonic serenades from a rock formation.

Pinnacles Overlook: Skyline Drive intersects the Appalachian Trail here. Stretch your legs on a short hike north or south. You might run across hikers en route from Georgia to Maine with interesting tales to tell.

Skyland: The 177-room lodge with a restaurant is the oldest and largest of Shenandoah's two main lodges. Occupying motel-like wings, the rooms are plain but comfortable. Many have outstanding valley views. You will find the horse stables here.

Big Meadows: The park's other major lodge and restaurant, Big Meadows offers 25 rooms in the main building and 72 more rooms in rustic cabins. Built in 1939 of stone cut from nearby Massanutten Mountain, its interior is paneled with native chestnut, a tree now nearly extinct because of the chestnut blight. Learn more about the history of Shenandoah and Skyline Drive at the Byrd Visitor Center.

Rockytop Overlook: Take in a good view of the Big Run watershed and its wild canyon country.

Calf Mountain Overlook: Before this drive ends, enjoy a stunning 360-degree view.

Rockfish Gap: Skyline Drive ends (or begins) here on the outskirts of Waynesboro. Straight ahead is the beginning of the 469-mile Blue Ridge Parkway, another scenic national park route tracing the Blue Ridge south through western Virginia and North Carolina to the entrance to Great Smoky Mountain National Park.

Luray Caverns are ancient in their origins yet familiar in the names of their formations. Here are the famous "fried eggs."

Oklahoma's Little Smokies

This drive meanders through southeastern Oklahoma, a mountainous landscape of rivers, lakes, and forests that offer plenty of outdoor recreational choices. Along the way, it explores the state's rich Native American heritage.

Quick Facts

Length: 130 miles

Time to Allow: Six to eight hours

Consideration: The most comfortable seasons for touring are spring, when the dogwoods and other flowering trees and shrubs are in bloom, and in fall for the foliage show. Winter can be damp; summers are hot and humid.

Oklahomans call southeastern Oklahoma's rumpled terrain the "Little Smokies." Not so lofty as the Great Smoky Mountains, these rugged green mountains boast an abundance of tall timber, splashing streams, and crystal-clear lakes. This is a drive both for outdoor lovers who simply want to savor the views and for those more active travelers eager to tackle a hiking trail, paddle a canoe, or test their skill at fly-fishing. Swimming beaches at several lakes provide an inviting break from touring.

For much of the way, the north-to-south route traverses sprawling 1.8-million-acre Ouachita National Forest, which drapes across the Ouachita Mountains on the border of Oklahoma and Arkansas. Deer and black bear are abundant—this part of Oklahoma claims to be the "deer capital of the world." Ouachita is the French version of an American Indian word that means "good hunting grounds." Colorful wildflowers carpet the meadows along the road. The fall foliage is renowned as some of the finest.

A part of the forest, called the Winding Stair Mountain National Recreation Area, has been designated primarily for outdoor fun. Trails range in difficulty from the

rigorous—for example, the 192-mile Ouachita National Recreation Trail, which intersects this drive—to the comfortably easy. Almost anyone can manage a trio of short, gentle nature trails at the Robert S. Kerr Memorial Arboretum.

Unless you are a resident of the Sooner State, signs that declare this corner of the state Kiamichi Country may puzzle you. The official Oklahoma Travel Guide also uses the phrase. Kiamichi, tourism officials explain, is a French word for a "water bird." French explorers, fur trappers, and traders were early visitors here.

The drive begins among the farmlands and orchards of Spiro, where a dozen ancient mounds display evidence of the people who lived here from A.D. 850

The Victor Area of Lake Wister State Park offers visitors not only superb scenery, but also such amenities as a boat ramp, picnic area, and playground.

In Poteau:
Robert S. Kerr
Museum/Robert S.
Kerr Memorial
Arboretum and
Botanical Area

Oklahoma's
Little Smokies

Cavanal
Hill

Lake Wister
State Park

In Heavener:
Heavener Runestone S.P.
Peter Conser House

Ouachita National
Recreation Trail

Ouachita Mountains
Winding Stair Mountain
National Recreation Area

Talimena
Scenic Drive

OKLAHOMA

Near Broken Bow:
Gardner Mansion

Little River National
Wildlife Refuge

Red River

In Idabel:
Museum of the
Red River

TEXAS

Fort Smith

Spiro

In Spiro:
Spiro Mounds
Archaeological
Park

Poteau

Heavener

Ouachita Nat'l.
Forest

Beavers
Bend State
Resort Park

Broken
Bow

Idabel

ARKANSAS

271

59

259

259A

N

to 1450. And it ends in the state's far southeast corner at Idabel, the state's "dogwood capital" and home to the Museum of the Red River. The museum houses what is considered some of the finest art and artifacts from the earliest residents here.

Highlights:

Begin in the prehistoric Spiro Mounds Archaeological Park. Travel through his-

tory to the Museum of the Red River.

Spiro Mounds Archaeological Park:

An important prehistoric American Indian site, the park harbors 11 grass-topped mounds. They formed a complex that began as a small farming village and grew to become an important trading, religious, and political center flourishing between A.D. 850 and 1450. Workers hauling basket loads of dirt constructed the mounds in layers. Initially there were 12 mounds, but a burial mound was excavated haphazardly in the 1930s for its numerous artifacts of stone, copper, shell, basketry, and fabric.

Robert S. Kerr Memorial Arboretum and Botanical Area:

An 8,000-acre preserve, the arboretum shelters special plant communities. At the Kerr Nature Center, three short interpretive trails introduce the region's natural heritage.

Cavanal Hill: Dubbed "the world's highest hill," this pine-draped knob rises to 1,999 feet, just 12 inches short of being officially designated a mountain. It stands within the city limits of Poteau, a onetime pioneer outpost—Poteau comes from the French word for "post." Cavanal is visible from almost anywhere in town. A 41/2-mile paved road climbs past beautiful new homes edging up its slopes. At the summit, a grand panoramic view of the Poteau River Valley is spread before you.

Lake Wister State Park: Wrapped by mountain slopes cloaked in dogwood, spruce, and ponderosa pine, the park takes full advantage of 7,300-acre Lake Wister. Park officials claim the fishing is among the best in the state. A beach invites swimming, and concessionaires provide bike rentals and water skiing options.

Heavener Runestone State Park: A historical curiosity, the Heavener runestone is a 12-foot-tall slab of stone onto which eight letters have been carved. Research suggests the stone is a Norse land claim dating back to the 8th century. The theory is that Norse explorers entered the Gulf of Mexico, found the Mississippi River, and sailed up two tributaries, the Arkansas and Poteau Rivers, about A.D. 750.

Peter Conser House: Built in 1894, the two-story, white-frame house was the home of Peter Conser, a Choctaw statesman, wealthy landowner, and leading member of the Choctaw Lighthorsemen. A law enforcement group, the Lighthorsemen are considered the Choctaw equivalent of the Texas Rangers; they patrolled the Choctaw region of the old American Indian Territory. The house, restored to pre-statehood condition, displays antiques and photographs of Oklahoma history.

Talimena Scenic Drive: This 54-mile drive (Oklahoma Route 1/Arkansas Route 88) winds along mountain ridge tops through the Ouachita National Forest. Cross this scenic drive as it dips between Winding Stair and Rich Mountains—about 18 miles south of Heavener. Make a detour west here to enjoy some of the panoramic vistas.

Winding Stair Mountain National Recreation Area: A part of Ouachita National Forest, the 26,445 acres of the Winding Stair Mountain National Recreation Area were set aside in 1988 for recreational purposes by the late President Ronald Reagan. A place of forest-clad mountains and majestic vistas, it is also noted for odd geologic formations, an abundance of lakes and streams, a rich natural and cultural history, and plentiful wildlife. The Ouachita is the South's oldest national forest.

Beavers Bend State Resort Park: Overlooking huge Broken Bow Lake, which boasts a 180-mile shoreline, the park is a popular vacation destination. A 40-room lodge and 47 cabins provide overnight lodging, and there's a wide choice of recreational activities, including paddleboating, horseback riding, hayrides, miniature golf, and trout fishing. The Forest Heritage Center Museum features dioramas describing the evolution of local forests.

Gardner Mansion: The antebellum-style mansion south of Broken Bow, completed in 1884, was the home of Jefferson Gardner, principal chief of the Choctaw Nation from 1894 to 1896. Choctaw artifacts and pioneer relics are displayed in the mansion.

Little River National Wildlife Refuge: A wet bottomland, this 15,000-acre refuge is habitat for waterfowl, principally mallard and wood duck. Ancient American Indian mounds exist on the refuge, but they have been disturbed by early forestry practices. A three-mile graded road leads though a forest to the hardwood bottom-land and Little River.

Museum of the Red River: The museum houses a collection of more than 20,000 Native American objects. They focus both on the local mound-building groups and the Choctaw Indians. The Choctaws were moved into Oklahoma from their Mississippi homelands in the 1830s. The collection also includes contemporary native arts and crafts from throughout the Americas.

This roadway is one of the Oklahoma drive's many winding paths.

Crowley's Ridge Parkway

An odd geological formation duplicated only in Siberia, Crowley's Ridge rises and runs for miles. A forested region, it harbors five state parks and a national forest offering varied outdoor recreation.

Imagine a geological wonder that took wind, water, and ice together 50 million years to create. Now imagine yourself enjoying the dramatic views and rolling topography you'll experience as you drive along on top of it! Named for the earliest settler in the area, Crowley's Ridge is one of only two such formations in the world, and the Crowley's Ridge Parkway allows you to experience it firsthand. This unique, crescent-shaped ridge rises 100 to 250 feet above the flat delta lands that surround it and boasts plants found nowhere else, along with many beautiful native wildflowers and cacti.

Along with its natural qualities, the ridge and surrounding areas are rich in Southern history and culture. Take the time to stop at one of the many fresh fruit and vegetable stands or browse the shelves at an old-fashioned country store. As you travel the byway, you will also find numerous museums, Civil War battlefields, African-American heritage sites, culture centers, and festivals. If you prefer the great outdoors, be sure to visit one of five nearby state parks or the St. Francis National Forest. Along the way, you'll discover opportunities for world-class waterfowl hunting, fishing, boating, picnicking, hunting, camping, golf, birdwatching, and more. With all of these recreational opportunities at your fingertips, you're sure to have a good time.

Cultural: Culturally, the most notable part of this byway is the historic development of the Delta Blues at Helena. The Delta Cultural Center and the annual King Biscuit Blues Festival keep the legacy alive.

Historical: The Civil War battlefield at Chalk Bluff plays a key role in understanding the historical importance of Crowley's Ridge. A site of significant battles, this area has remained largely undisturbed since Civil War times.

The railroad also played a significant role in the history of Crowley's Ridge. The arrival of the railroads to remove

The Hemingway barn studio in Piggott is on the National Historic Register. Part of Hemingway's A Farewell to Arms *was written here.*

Ernest Hemingway's time in Piggott.

Highlights:

Though Crowley's Ridge Parkway has a variety of stories to tell, ranging from geologic to human, ancient to modern, this itinerary gives a taste of how the Civil War affected the Confederate state of Arkansas, bordering the Union-aligned Missouri, as both sides used the road on Crowley's Ridge.

Chalk Bluff Battlefield Park and Natural Area: At

the northernmost edge of the Arkansas section of Crowley's Ridge Parkway, begin the journey at Chalk Bluff Battlefield Park and Natural Area. A prosperous town before the railroad bypassed it in the 1880s, the village of Chalk Bluff saw many skirmishes during the Civil War. Interpretive signage along a walking trail explains the battles and history of Chalk Bluff.

Crowley's Ridge State Park: Crowley's Ridge State Park, though not having any particular Civil War sites, does give the visitor some spectacular bird's-eye views of the surrounding delta and an understanding of why this parkway was so important to travelers navigating the eastern edge of Arkansas.

Forrest City: Farther south on the byway is the town of Forrest City, named for Confederate General Nathan Bedford Forrest. During the Civil War, soldiers stopped here near Stuart Springs, and those who were injured were treated in the spring's healing waters.

Helena: The town of Helena, a picturesque town situated strategically along the Mississippi River, is at the southernmost part of the Crowley's Ridge Parkway and has several Civil War sites to visit.

Civil War Batteries: Helena was a Union stronghold coveted by the Confederates, and four Civil War batteries can be viewed by visitors.

Helena Confederate Cemetery: Helena Confederate Cemetery was created in 1869 in the southwest corner of Maple Hill Cemetery. More than half of those interred here were victims of the unsuccessful Confederate raid on the Union stronghold at Helena on July 4, 1863.

harvested timber from the ridge and delta led to the beginning and end of many towns. After the railroads traversed the ridge, numerous towns were established along the tracks. Several county seats were abandoned and relocated near the railroads as well.

Also significant is that one of the world's most-famous American authors had great connections with this area; the Hemingway-Pfeiffer Museum shares the story of

Great River Road

The road navigates the state's delta, a region of rivers, lakes, and swamps. This is a cultural drive, glimpsing a southern culture in transition from agricultural to modern industrial.

Quick Facts

Length: 159 miles

Time to Allow: Three hours

Consideration: During the winter, there may be some icy patches in rural parts of the roadway. There is one 11.5-mile segment through the St. Francis National Forest that is gravel, but it is accessible for all vehicles.

Look out over the river, and try to comprehend the complex layers of history that have been acted out along its banks. Imagine the large communities of the Hopewell Indian culture—the most complex society in North America—and early French colonial settlements and fortifications. Or reflect on the frightened, cautious, and optimistic eyes of slaves seeking freedom on the Underground Railroad.

Chamber of Commerce, and pick up a map of the walking tour of the historic downtown district. Around 45 of the buildings here are listed on the National Register of Historic Places. Also in Marianna is the Missouri–Pacific railroad depot, built in 1915.

Highlights:

The Arkansas section of the Great River Road has some varied architectural highlights. You will want to be sure to see them as you travel from north to south on the southern part of the byway.

Marianna: Begin in Marianna at the

This house in Helena was built in 1826 and is on the Historic National Register.

from California during World War II. The Rohwer Memorial Cemetery is a National Historic Landmark.

Arkansas City: Arkansas City is one of the few remaining examples of an old Mississippi River town in eastern Arkansas. A walking tour of the historic downtown area yields a variety of building styles.

Eudora: Eudora has some interesting sites. The Dr. A. G. Anderson House is a restored 1901 home. The Rubye and Henry Connerly Museum offers a quaint bit of local history in a historic grocery store. And the American Legion Post is a 1934 rustic-style structure.

Helena: Helena is a fascinating port town with a mixture of Mississippi River charm, blues music, Civil War history, and a generous blend of building styles. Helena's Delta Cultural Center tells the story of this area.

Rohwer War Relocation Center: Though only a few scattered building foundations and the cemetery remain, the Rohwer War Relocation Center had a very basic functional style of architecture. The camp was opened in 1942 to intern Japanese American evacuees

Cherohala Skyway

Opened in 1996, the skyway yields mile-high mountain and woodland vistas as it winds into the heartland of the Cherokee Indian ancestral territories. Hiking, fishing, and wildlife spotting tempt you from behind the wheel.

Experience first-hand amazingly towering trees by traveling the Cherohala Skyway in North Carolina and Tennessee, and you will agree that nothing could be lovelier. Visit in the fall when vibrant vermilion, golden, and orange leaves drape the trees surrounding the skyway. Or plan a leisurely summer road trip, leaving plenty of time for picnics, hikes, fishing, or many of the other activities available on the Cherohala Skyway.

The Tellico River parallels part of the skyway, delighting canoeists and kayakers from all over. Follow the river with paddle in hand, and bask in the sunlight and beauty of the surrounding forests. With hundreds of miles of hiking trails traversing the national forests, you're bound to find a favorite. Botany lovers will want to whip out their sketchbooks to capture in ink some of the 2,000 native plant species that thrive around the Cherohala Skyway. Catch your breath by pausing to admire the wildflowers sprinkled throughout the landscape in the spring, or make camp at one of the many campgrounds and spend several days exploring the backwoods.

Just a quarter of a mile from Bald River Falls, the smaller Baby Falls is known as a "playpen" for kayakers and swimmers.

Highlights:

With spectacular views it is hard to leave the heights of the Cherohala Skyway, but some of the most interesting natural and Native American sites are just beyond the byway. A few of those venues are highlighted here.

Quick Facts

Length: 43 miles

Time to Allow: Two hours

Consideration: There are no services available on the skyway. However, there are services available in Tellico Plains and Robbinsville in North Carolina. Byway visitors should be aware that there are some grades as steep as 9 percent. Use caution on the skyway, but take particular care during winter storms. Roads may close during heavy snows.

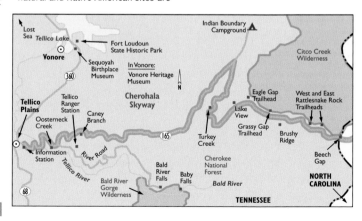

Fort Loudoun State Historic Park:
Nearby is Fort Loudoun State Historic Park. Operating from 1756 to 1760, Fort Loudoun was built by the British to protect the Cherokee during the French and Indian War. Though the original buildings are long gone, the current replica is historically accurate.

Sequoyah Birthplace Museum: Learn about the lifestyle of the Overhill Cherokee at the Sequoyah Birthplace Museum. Born near where the museum stands and roaming the area as a boy, Sequoyah was born in 1776 and was the man who gave the Cherokee nation, formerly illiterate, its unique writing system.

Vonore Heritage Museum: Before leaving the Tellico Lake area, be sure to stop at the Vonore Heritage Museum on Church Street. The museum features farm implements and tools, household items,

and lovingly created miniature replicas of local historic venues. Also exhibited are many items donated by local citizens to help in the telling of the Vonore story.

Lost Sea: Descending even farther from the heights of the Cherohala Skyway at the town of Sweetwater is the Lost Sea, America's largest underground lake. Part of the larger Craighead Cavern system known and used by the Cherokee, the lake is extensive, its depths never having been completely mapped.

Bald River Falls and Baby Falls:
Viewable from the car or via hiking paths, Bald River Falls in the Cherokee National Forest is a stunning sight as the plunge over rock outcroppings makes for an 80-foot white water falls.

Stratton Ridge: Be on the lookout on the left side of the road for the next noteworthy overlook. At 4,420 feet,

Stratton Ridge looks over lower portions of the Cherohala Skyway and provides information about the byway and surrounding area on informational kiosks.

Spirit Ridge Overlook: From the roadway take a gentle walk less than a mile through the hardwood forest to the Spirit Ridge overlook. Here visitors get seemingly unending panoramas of splendid mountaintops. The trail leading to the overlook is wheelchair accessible and is appropriate for people of all ages.

Hooper Cove: Hooper Cove is an open area to get out and enjoy the view from this 3,100-foot high vantage point. Four picnic tables give visitors an opportunity to eat a bit while drinking in the beautiful vistas. This is a great location for fabulous photos of the Santeetlah Creek rushing below.

Joyce Kilmer Memorial Forest:
Just north of the Cherohala Skyway is the Joyce Kilmer Memorial Forest. Once the uncharted hunting ground of the Cherokee, the best way to see the Memorial Forest is on foot using the Joyce Kilmer National Recreation Trail. A tribute to World War I soldier and author of the poem "Trees," the forest is a rare and outstanding gathering of virgin Appalachian hardwood trees, some as old as 400 years and as large as 20 feet in circumference at their base.

Blue Ridge Parkway

Unhampered by stop signs and stoplights, the parkway glides along mountain ridge tops, offering nonstop views right and left of quilted fields and towns far below.

The Blue Ridge Parkway is a scenic drive that crests the southern Appalachian Mountains and takes you through a myriad of natural, cultural, and recreational places. Many people drive the Blue Ridge Parkway for its natural botanical qualities. And where there is lush vegetation, there is also abundant wildlife.

The diverse history and culture of the southern Appalachians are described at many overlooks and facilities along the parkway.

Cultural: Along the Blue Ridge Parkway, evidence of the local cultures is found in communities, museums, and shops.

Mountain handicrafts are one of the most popular attractions along the byway, and traditional and contemporary crafts and music thrive in the Blue Ridge Mountains. Along the parkway in North Carolina are several places to view and purchase locally made items. The Folk Art Center in Asheville offers an impressive collection of crafts.

Historical: The parkway was conceived as a link between the Shenandoah

Many of the trees of Mount Mitchell are being destroyed by pests, including Balsam Woolly Adegid.

National Park in Virginia and the Great Smoky Mountains National Park in North Carolina and Tennessee. The vision came to fruition in 1935. The idea to build the parkway resulted from a combination of many factors, the primary one being the need to create jobs for those people suffering from the Great Depression and for poor mountain families.

World War II halted construction, but roadbuilding resumed soon after the war ended. By 1968, the only task left was

the completion of a seven-mile stretch around North Carolina's Grandfather Mountain. In order to preserve the fragile environment on the steep slopes of the mountain, the Linn Cove Viaduct, a 1,200-foot suspended section of the parkway, was designed and built. Considered an engineering marvel, it represents one of the most successful fusions of road and landscape on the parkway.

Recreational: The very nature of the Blue Ridge Parkway allows for outstanding recreational opportunities, such as camping, hiking, cycling, swimming, and kayaking. Festivals and events are often occurring in local towns and communities.

Highlights:

The following points of interest are excellent sights along or just off of the byway.

Cumberland Knob: Cumberland Knob, at 2,885 feet, is a great spot to walk through fields and woodlands.

Brinegar Cabin: Brinegar Cabin was built by Martin Brinegar about 1880 and lived in until the 1930s; it is still standing.

Northwest Trading Post: Northwest Trading Post keeps alive the old crafts within North Carolina's 11 northwestern counties.

Moses H. Cone Memorial Park: This park has 25 miles of carriage roads, ideal for hiking and horseback riding.

E. B. Jeffress Park: E. B. Jeffress Park has a self-guided trail to the Cascades and another trail to the old cabin and church.

Linn Cove Viaduct: Linn Cove Viaduct, a highlight of the parkway and a design and engineering marvel, skirts the side of Grandfather Mountain.

Linville Falls: Linville Falls roars through a dramatic, rugged gorge. Take trails to overlooks.

Museum of North Carolina Minerals: This museum has a display of the state's mineral wealth.

Mount Mitchell State Park: This park has a picnic area and a lookout tower. It is the highest point east of the Mississippi River.

Folk Art Center: This center offers sales and exhibits of traditional and contemporary crafts of the Appalachian Region.

Biltmore Estate: This is George Vanderbilt's impressive 250-room mansion and grounds landscaped by Frederick Law Olmstead, designer of Central Park.

Mount Pisgah: Part of the Biltmore Estate became home of the first U.S. forestry school. That tract of land is the nucleus of the Pisgah National Forest.

Devil's Courthouse: Devil's Courthouse is a rugged exposed mountaintop rich in Cherokee legends. A walk to the bare rock summit yields a spectacular view.

Richland Balsam Trail: This trail takes you through a remnant spruce-fir forest. It's the highest point on the parkway at 6,047 feet.

Waterrock Knob: Waterrock Knob provides a panorama of the Great Smokies, as well as a trail, exhibits, and comfort station.

San Antonio Missions Trail

The Alamo is famous, but a chain of four other lovely Spanish frontier missions along the San Antonio River form the Missions Trail, a pleasant drive into an often-overlooked aspect of America's past.

It must be noted up front that the San Antonio Missions Trail, a 25-mile loop south of San Antonio, is an urban drive that weaves its way at times through city traffic before reaching more open countryside dotted with farms. But the five missions—the Alamo, Concepcion, San Jose, San Juan, and Espada—and other historic structures, set in parklike grounds, provide scenic beauty enough. And each is a cool and relaxing oasis of quiet. Scattered along the San Antonio River, which the drive follows south from the city, the missions form San Antonio Missions National Historical Park.

Mission San Antonio de Valero, better known as The Alamo, represents nearly 300 years of human activity from early pre-colonial days to the modern landscape that surrounds it.

The Alamo, established as a dusty outpost of the Spanish Empire in 1718, was the first of San Antonio's missions to be founded. It assumed legendary status in March 1836 when a small garrison of Texas independence fighters, including Davy Crockett and Jim Bowie, fought to the death rather than surrender to a Mexican army. Texans enter its cool ado-be walls as if paying homage at a shrine.

The other four missions are less political but no less interesting. Each is different, but they all served the goal of introducing the local Tejas Indians (after whom Texas is named) to Spanish society and Christianity. Franciscan friars founded the four between 1718 and 1731, gathering scattered tribes into church-oriented communities near the river. These and Spain's many other New World missions went into decline during the Napoleonic wars in Europe, and their lands were redistributed in the 1820s when Mexico gained its independence from Spain. In Texas, preservation efforts began in the 1930s.

Highlights:

Begin your tour at The Alamo.

The Alamo: In the heart of San Antonio on Alamo Plaza, the sunbaked Alamo is the most historic spot in Texas, known as "The Cradle of Texas Liberty." Founded as the city's first mission in 1718, it served as a fortress in 1836 when Mexican General Santa Anna's army attacked. A total of 189 defenders died here. Today, only the chapel and the barracks remain, encircled by beautifully landscaped gardens. A hallowed site, The Alamo houses mementos of Texas history, including Davy Crockett's beaded buckskin vest with onyx buttons.

Paseo del Rio (River Walk): The Paseo del Rio is an urban treasure, a masterful use of the city's river frontage. Cloistered 20 feet below street level in the midst of the busy commercial district, it winds for 2.5 flower draped miles along both sides of the San Antonio River. Lovely arched bridges vault the slender river, and brightly painted motor barges pass beneath, carrying visitors. Milky green in color, the river is barely the width of a two-lane city street. Throngs stroll the cobblestone walks day and night.

El Mercado: A few blocks east of the river, El Mercado, San Antonio's historic Market Square, claims to be the largest Mexican market outside of Mexico. Inside a barnlike building, numerous individual stalls crammed along narrow aisles sell the typical tourist wares of Mexico—ceramics, serapes, sombreros, baskets of all sizes, pottery, leather goods, hand-worked silver, giant piñatas, and Mexican sugar cookies and other treats. Covering two city blocks, Market Square has been the site of a public market for more than a century.

Institute of Texan Cultures: A museum of Texas history, the Institute of Texan Cultures in HemisFair Park explores the culture of 27 ethnic groups who helped settle the state with exhibits, photos, and multimedia presentations.

San Antonio Museum of Art: Of interest on the Missions Trail is the San Antonio Museum of Art's collection of Spanish colonial artworks and its Mexican and other Latin American folk art. The museum occupies a former Lone Star Beer brewery.

Mission Concepción: This mission, the first on the Missions Trail, preserves a lovely stone church built in 1755 with typical Spanish-colonial features: thick walls, Moorish windows, a pair of tall bell towers, and a solid stone staircase. It is the least restored of San Antonio's missions, looking much as it did more than two centuries ago.

Mission San Jose: Down the trail, San Jose, founded in 1720, is the largest and best preserved of the missions. Known as the Queen of Missions, it houses a visitor's center for the Missions Trail.

Mission San Juan Capistrano: Much simpler than the first two missions on

the trail, San Juan Capistrano, established on its present site in 1731, offers its own rewards. A Romanesque arch marks the entrance to the courtyard, which is a quiet place to relax.

Mission Espada: Seemingly as remote as it was in 1731 when it was established, Mission Espada preserves segments of the historic acequias, the irrigation system built to provide water for crops. A marvel of Spanish colonial engineering, the Espada Aqueduct, was built to carry water from the San Antonio River across a small creek.

Creole Nature Trail

In this unique world of water, encompassing thousands of acres of wetlands, explore three wildlife refuges and a bird sanctuary. Along the way, try your hand at crabbing, and keep an eye open for alligators.

The Creole Nature Trail travels through thousands of acres of untouched wetlands that reflect an area blessed with some of the most beautiful scenery imaginable. If you like to photograph or hunt wildlife, the trail takes you to three different wildlife refuges and a bird sanctuary. If you aren't a duck hunter, you may like to try your hand at a little Louisiana fishing. The combination of fresh and saltwater areas provides a unique habitat for many of the plants and creatures that live along the byway.

Traveling the edge of the Gulf of Mexico, you will be enchanted by the entwining ecosystems of the coastland and the marshland. So drive the trail through Louisiana's very own outback and discover the culture, nature, and history awaiting you there.

Cultural: The culture along the Creole Nature Trail is one that has been mixing and evolving for hundreds of years. Spanish, French, and African influences have all collided here in this coastal outback where alligators roam and hurricanes are known to swallow entire

Sabine Pass Lighthouse was built in 1856 and served as a beacon for mariners for more than 90 years.

villages. The people of southwest Louisiana understand the place they live in and they revel in it. Throughout the year more than 75 festivals celebrate living on the Creole Nature Trail. Visitors might learn how to skin an alligator or enjoy some real Cajun cooking.

Shrimp boats and ships in the Cameron Ship Channel reflect the importance of the Gulf in the area. Shrimp, crabs, oysters, and a host of fresh and salt-

water fish are harvested daily. Visitors can sample these delicacies at area restaurants or purchase fresh seafood for their own recipes.

Historical: An infamous history prevails throughout much of the early 1800s on the byway. The pirate Jean Lafitte made a huge profit from capturing Spanish slave ships and selling the slaves to Louisiana cotton and sugar

Quick Facts

Length: 180 miles

Time to Allow: A self-guided tour could take a day or two.

Consideration: It is a good idea to bring insect repellent. Also, some wildlife in the refuges may be dangerous. For example, do not try to feed, tease, or prod an American alligator; it is perfectly capable of defending itself. The best months for alligator watching are April through October. Wildlife refuges are closed on federal holidays. Some hunting and fishing grounds require permits. Also, it is advised not to take dogs along at Marsh Trail because alligators may consume them.

cane planters. His exploits involved everything from the African slave trade to liaisons with French spies. It is rumored that Lafitte buried riches and treasure chests all along the Calcasieu River.

When the Civil War came to Louisiana, battles were fought over Sabine Pass and Calcasieu Pass where the Confederates were successful. Standing today as a stalwart landmark, the Sabine Pass Lighthouse was built in 1856 and became a point of conflict during the Civil War.

Recreational: One of the most popular activities for locals and visitors alike is the excellent fishing on Louisiana's coastline. Here, visitors will catch more than just fish. Crabs, shrimp, and oysters are also popular items to pull from the sea. Freshwater, saltwater, and brackish fishing are all available to travelers.

Even on the Creole Nature Trail, you may want a taste of civilization every now and then. Visitors love to stop in places such as Lake Charles or Cameron Parish just to take a look at the historic sites that make each town memorable.

Highlights:

This tour of the Creole Nature Trail begins in Sulphur, Louisiana.

Sulphur: At Sulphur, the area is characterized by rolling pastureland that gradually turns to wetland.

Cameron Parish: Cameron Parish is the largest parish in the state. The vegetation in the area is mostly of the salt marsh variety. Additionally, the landscape is dotted with oil wells and oilfield pumping stations.

Hackberry: In Hackberry, you find an abundance of shrimp and crab houses along Kelso Bayou.

Sabine National Wildlife Refuge: At Sabine National Wildlife Refuge, you see views of birds and other marsh animals. The refuge includes the 1.5-mile self-guided Marsh Trail with interpretation stations, an observation tower, and panoramic view of marsh terrain.

Holly Beach: Also known as the Cajun Riviera, Holly Beach provides 25 miles of year-round beaches, campsites, accommodations, and a variety of outdoor recreation.

Rockefeller Wildlife Refuge: The Rockefeller Wildlife Refuge is home to a variety of wintering waterfowl and resident mammals. The refuge is also an important area for research studies on a number of marsh-management strategies. While you can enjoy recreational fishing in this area, hunting is prohibited.

Natchez Trace Parkway

Part of a 445-mile, three-state route, the scenic parkway follows the historic late 18th- and early 19th-century footpath north from Natchez to the Ohio River Valley. Rock-studded hills line this segment.

Quick Facts

Length: 312 miles

Time to Allow: Two days

Consideration: Be alert for animals on the parkway. The parkway is a designated bike route, so please watch for bicyclists. Commercial trucking is not allowed, and tent and trailer camping is allowed at designated campgrounds only.

At first, the Natchez Trace Parkway was probably a series of hunters' paths that slowly came together to form a trail that led from the Mississippi River over the low hills into the Tennessee Valley. By 1785, Ohio River Valley farmers searching for markets had begun floating their crops and products down the rivers to Natchez or New Orleans. Since the late 1930s, the National Park Service has been constructing a modern parkway that closely follows the course of the original trail.

Cultural: The people who live along this parkway embody its rich culture. Southern traditions and hospitality are apparent as you meander through the heart of Dixie. From Natchez to Memphis, you'll enjoy the people you meet along the Natchez Trace Parkway.

Historical: The Natchez Trace Parkway was established to commemorate the historical significance of the Old Natchez Trace as a primitive trail that stretched some 500 miles through the wilderness from Natchez, Mississippi, to Nashville, Tennessee. Although generally thought of as one trail, the Old Natchez Trace was actually a number of closely parallel routes. It probably evolved from the repeated use of meandering game trails by the earliest human inhabitants.

Recreational: Take in one of the many museums located throughout the byway or take a walk among the dogwoods. The byway has many historic battlefields, allowing you the chance to reminisce about the past. Pack a picnic and see the many Southern mansions along the route or hunt for souvenirs in one of the many quaint shops along the way.

Highlights:

Start in Natchez, Mississippi, and end in Nashville, Tennessee.

Natchez: The historic Mississippi River port of Natchez boasts as many as 14 palatial homes open to the public. One of the finest is Melrose, a national park site.

Emerald Mound: Dating to A.D. 1250, 35-foot-high Emerald Mound is the second-largest American Indian temple. It covers eight acres.

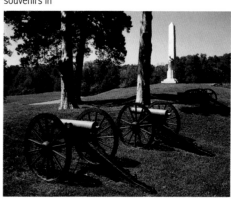

Monuments and artillery are reminders of the personal and tactical resources required by both Union and Confederate troops during the Battle of Vicksburg.

Mount Locust: Take a quick tour of Mount Locust. It is a rustic inn, or "stand," one of the first that provided food and shelter along this trail.

Sunken Trace: Here are three sections of the original road that show how the route was relocated to avoid mudholes.

Rocky Springs Site: A church and cemetery mark the site of the once prosperous town of Rocky Springs. In the 1790s, the rural community grew to more than 2,600 residents. But by 1920, the Civil War, yellow fever, the boll weevil, and erosion had devastated the town.

Vicksburg National Military Park: Vicksburg's major attraction is the national military park, where on July 4, 1863, Union General Ulysses S. Grant's army dealt a mortal blow to the local planter population.

Jackson: Mississippi's state capital is an attractive river city with fine museums and parks. Of particular note is the Old Capitol.

Jeff Busby Site: The campground at Jeff Busby Site is named for Thomas Jefferson Busby, who introduced a bill in Congress that led to the creation of the Natchez Trace Parkway.

Tupelo National Battlefield: Fought on July 13–15, 1864, the battle resulted in a Union victory.

Freedom Hills Overlook: A steep quarter-mile trail climbs to the highest point on the parkway—an altitude of 800 feet.

Coon Dog Memorial Graveyard: An Alabama curiosity, more than 100 coon dogs have been buried here since 1937.

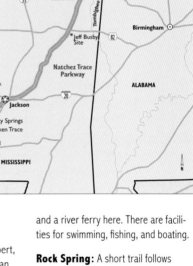

Buzzard Roost Spring: Levi Colbert, a Chickasaw Indian chief, operated an inn, or "stand," nearby. His story is told in exhibits.

Colbert Ferry Park: In the trace's heyday, George Colbert operated an inn and a river ferry here. There are facilities for swimming, fishing, and boating.

Rock Spring: A short trail follows Colbert Creek. It is one of numerous easy trails along the trace that offer motorists a chance to climb from behind the wheel.

Within the Parkway, approximately 900 species of plants help to support dozens of species of mammals and more than 200 species of birds.

Meriwether Lewis Monument: A campground, picnic area, ranger station, and Meriwether Lewis's grave are here.

Old Trace: Here the Trace marked the boundaries of the Chickasaw lands ceded to the United States in 1805 and 1816.

Tobacco Farm: Exhibits at the farm and barn explain tobacco growing.

Sheboss Place: This is the site of one of the stands that once served travelers on the trace.

Jackson Falls: Named for Andrew Jackson, the falls are on the intermittent Jackson Branch that empties into Duck River.

Tennessee Valley Divide: When Tennessee was admitted to the Union in 1796, this watershed was the boundary between the United States and the Chickasaw nation.

Garrison Creek: Named for a nearby 1801–1802 U.S. Army post, this area is a trailhead for horseback riders and hikers.

McGlamery Stand: The nearby village still bears the name of this old stand.

Sweetwater Branch Nature Trail: A clear, fast-flowing stream parallels the route of this 20-minute walk.

Napier Mine: This open pit was worked during the 19th century.

Metal Ford: Travelers crossed the Buffalo River here; an ironworks and McLish's Stand were nearby.

Selma to Montgomery March Byway

This historical route, rich in poignant stories, honors the memory of civil rights marchers whose efforts helped Southern African Americans gain access to the ballot box with passage of the 1965 Voting Rights Act.

Designated as a National Historic Trail, this byway has known many facets of history in its years of existence. However, it wasn't until Dr. Martin Luther King, Jr., began leading voting rights demonstrations in Selma early in 1965, culminating with the historic Selma to Montgomery March, that the route became internationally known.

After a failed attempt just three weeks earlier, Dr. King marshaled a group of protesters who made their way 43 miles from the Edmund Pettus Bridge in Selma to Montgomery, giving birth to the most important piece of social legislation of the 20th century. This march helped bring access to the ballot box for many African Americans in Southern states.

Cultural: Dr. Martin Luther King, Jr., stood on the platform in front of the stark-white state capitol in Montgomery, Alabama, and gazed out at the crowd of 30,000 people on March 25, 1965. The largest civil rights march ever to take

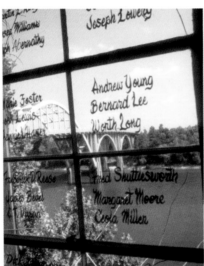

Overlooking the infamous Edmund Pettus Bridge, the Window of Fame in the National Voting Rights Museum and Institute memorializes those who participated in the Selma to Montgomery March.

place in the South had finally reached its destination after weeks of uncertainty and danger. Two blocks down the street, at the edge of the vast assemblage, was Dexter Avenue Baptist Church, from whose pulpit King had inspired black bus boycotters a decade earlier. Their year-long display of nonviolence and courage had not only earned blacks the right to sit where they wanted on the buses; it had also started a fire in the hearts of many Americans.

King did not refer directly to the brutal attack by state and local law officers just 18 days earlier. However, that attack, seen on national television, drew the attention of the world to this moment.

Less than five months later, the 1965 Voting Rights Act was signed, and African Americans throughout the South streamed into courthouses to register as voters. They were at last exercising a fundamental promise of democracy, a promise that took our nation 178 years to fulfill.

Historical: African Americans in Selma formed the Dallas County Voters League (DCVL) under the leadership of Samuel W. Boynton, a local agricultural extension agent and former president of the local chapter of the National Association for the Advancement of Colored People (NAACP).

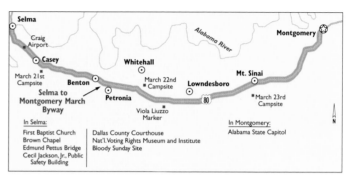

Despite stiff resistance from white officials, local activists persisted. Their courage attracted the attention of other African-American leaders. In early 1963, Bernard and Colia Lafayette of the Student Nonviolent Coordinating Committee (SNCC) went to Selma to help the DCVL register African American voters.

The Selma activists quickly found themselves battling not only bureaucratic resistance, but also the intimidation tactics of Sheriff Jim Clark and his deputized posse. In 1961, the U.S. Justice Department filed a voter discrimination lawsuit against the County Board of Registrars and, two years later, sued Clark directly for the harassment of African Americans attempting to register.

Fearful that more "outside agitators" would target Selma, State Circuit Judge James Hare on July 9, 1964, enjoined any group of more than three people from meeting in Dallas County.

As protests and meetings came to a virtual halt, local activists Amelia Platts Boynton and J. L. Chestnut asked Southern Christian Leadership Conference (SCLC) officials for help. SCLC leaders, following their hard-won victory in Birmingham, had already declared that their next push would be for a strong national voting rights law. Selma offered the perfect opportunity.

On January 2, 1965, Dr. King defied Judge Hare's injunction and led a rally at Brown Chapel African Methodist Episcopal (AME) Church, promising demonstrations and even another march on Washington if voting rights were not guaranteed for African Americans in the South. Immediately, a series of mass meetings and protest marches began with renewed momentum in Selma and nearby Marion, the seat of Perry County.

Then, on February 18, a nighttime march in Marion ended in violence and death. Alabama State Troopers attacked African Americans leaving a mass meeting at Zion Methodist Church. Several people, including Viola Jackson and her son Jimmie Lee, sought refuge in a small café, but troopers soon found them.

An officer moved to strike Viola Jackson, then turned on Jimmie Lee when he tried to protect her. Two troopers assaulted Jimmie Lee, shooting him at point blank range. On February 26, Jimmie Lee Jackson died in Selma from an infection caused by the shooting.

His death angered activists. Lucy Foster, a leader in Marion, bitterly proposed that residents take his body to the Alabama Capitol to gain the attention of Governor George Wallace—a proposal repeated later by SCLC's James Bevel. Bevel and others realized that some mass nonviolent action was necessary, not only to win the attention of political leaders, but also to vent the anger and frustration of the activists.

Even as Jimmie Lee was buried, the idea for a Selma to Montgomery march was growing. By March 2, plans were confirmed that Dr. King would lead a march from Selma to Montgomery beginning on Sunday, March 7, 1965.

Highlights:

The following tour encompasses the first section of the byway beginning

Brown Chapel is commemorated as the starting point for the historic 1965 march for voting rights.

on the corner of Martin Luther King, Jr., Street and Jeff Davis Avenue and passes the George Washington Carver Home, historic landmark Brown AME Church, and the Martin Luther King, Jr., monument. Through the written word and vivid historic photographs, each of the 20 memorials along the route tells the story of the individuals who came together for a common cause.

Cecil B. Jackson Public Safety Building: On the byway, the first point of interest is the Cecil B. Jackson Public Safety Building, which was once the old Selma city hall. This building served as the city and county jail in which Dr. King and other protesters were imprisoned in 1965.

Dallas County Courthouse: The Dallas County Courthouse was the destination of most protest marches in an effort to register to vote.

National Voting Rights Museum and Institute: Just before the Alabama River is the National Voting Rights Museum and Institute dedicated to honoring the attainment of voting rights.

Edmund Pettus Bridge: Crossing the Alabama River is the Edmund Pettus Bridge, the famous landmark where "Bloody Sunday" took place on March 7, 1965.

Montgomery: From here, the byway travels along Highway 80 to Montgomery, passing numerous campsites that were used by marchers during the historic event. Between the cities of Petronia and Lowndesboro stands the memorial to Viola Liuzzo, who was murdered while supporting the civil rights movement.

Alabama State Capitol: The final destination of the Selma to Montgomery march is the Alabama State Capitol in Montgomery. On the steps of this great building, Dr. Martin Luther King, Jr., told marchers that even though the journey was through, the struggle for civil rights was far from over. But it would be won, he said, and it wouldn't be long.

Talladega Scenic Drive

Wild turkeys, quail, and bald eagles are among the wildlife to be spotted on this drive through Talladega National Forest. At Cheaha State Park, the road climbs to 2,407 feet, the state's highest point.

Catch a bird's-eye view of Alabama when you drive the Talladega Scenic Drive. At its highest point, you will find yourself on Cheaha Mountain, 2,407 feet above sea level, the highest point in Alabama. You will be awestruck by the view of the Appalachian Mountains, rock outcroppings, and small rural settlements nestled among the trees.

In addition to simply enjoying the scenic beauty of the Talladega National Forest, be sure to take advantage of its abundant recreational opportunities. You will find many developed areas where you can camp, picnic, fish, and hike. If you're up to an all-day adventure, spend some time in the Cheaha Wilderness or on the Pinhoti National Recreation Trail.

No trip is complete without a fine meal and a souvenir, so be sure to visit the restaurants and shops at the top of Cheaha Mountain in Cheaha State Park. While you're at the top, keep a close eye out for wildlife such as white-tailed deer, quail, turkeys, rabbits, opossum, and even bald eagles. A glimpse of one of these natural inhabitants could be one of the highlights of your trip on the Talladega Scenic Drive.

Recreational: The Talladega Scenic Drive provides one of the primary recreational driving routes in Alabama, as well as the access route to Cheaha State Park. Running through the heart of Cheaha State Park, which is located on the highest mountain in the state of Alabama, the byway provides numerous recreational opportunities.

Most mileage of the Talladega Scenic Drive is located in the Talladega National Forest. The Talladega National Forest offers numerous recreational experiences, including the Pinhoti National Recreational Trail, which intersects with the scenic drive in several locations. Other National Forest recreational experiences available near the scenic drive include hunting, fishing, nature study, photography, and numer-ous other activities. Lake Chinabee offers camping, fishing, picnicking, hiking, and boating opportunities as well.

The calm, cool waters beneath Devils Den Falls make this spot a popular swimming hole.

Talladega: Begin in the city of Talladega, known for its NASCAR raceway. The Davey Allison Memorial/Walk of Fame is a beautiful landscaped park that covers an entire block in downtown. Honoring NASCAR driver Davey Allison and other heroes of the track, the park is shaped like Talladega Superspeedway and includes a brick walkway and bronze plaques honoring drivers.

Talladega Superspeedway: Records for both speed and competition have been established at Talladega Superspeedway, north of the city of Talladega. With track speeds in excess of 200 mph, it is the largest and fastest closed track in the world. The racing facility can accommodate more than 143,000 seated guests and thousands more in the 212-acre infield.

Anniston: From the Talladega Superspeedway, travel east on Interstate 20 to the Oxford exit. Moments north on U.S. Highway 431, the city of Anniston includes such sites as the Anniston Museum of Natural History, located in Lagarde Park in Anniston. The historic downtown area has intriguing architecture as well as superb dining opportunities.

Talladega National Forest: For a more serene version of this part of Alabama, head south on U.S. Highway 431 south, where you will enter the Talladega National Forest. Turn south on State Road 281 to begin your trek on the Talladega Scenic Drive. The magnificent scenery visible from your car, scenic overlooks, and hiking trails give vistas of the southern backbone of the Appalachian Mountains.

Cheaha State Park: Within the quiet appeal of the Talladega National Forest, one of the highlights is Cheaha State Park, named for Cheaha Mountain, the highest point in the state. Overlooks give panoramic vistas and trails give hikers an opportunity for up-close observation of the profusion of native flora and fauna. More than just a wilderness area with breathtaking views, you will also find 73 campsites, and at the top of the mountain an old-fashioned stone lodge, stone cabins, and comfortable hotel rooms.

The Talladega Scenic Drive does not provide lanes designated for bicycle use, but it is not uncommon to find road bicyclists challenging the steep slopes found on the drive. To avoid heavy automobile traffic, most of these bicyclists use the scenic drive on weekdays.

Highlights:

While the Talladega Scenic Drive has some splendid natural areas to explore, this itinerary offers travelers a mix of urban and rustic, modern speed and slower tempos.

Russell–Brasstown Scenic Byway

A mountainous loop, the byway passes numerous sparkling waterfalls, climbing to Brasstown Bald. It's the state's highest point, yielding a 360-degree view of rumpled green highlands.

Quick Facts

Length: 40.5 miles

Time to Allow: At least three hours.

Consideration: The only regular seasonal limitations are imposed on recreational facilities.

Cool in the summer, mild in the winter, this byway beckons you to lose yourself in its luscious timberland. Linger atop Brasstown Bald to absorb all 360 degrees of rolling highlands. Escape the crowds and retire to the cooling mists of the byway's numerous waterfalls. Got a hanker for a hike, but the Appalachian Trail isn't what you had in mind? Sparkling waterfalls and secluded valley views are just a short stroll from the main road. The average weekend hiker could spend years exploring these trails and never retrace a step. Share a meal at a cozy picnic site or break bread in a real Bavarian hamlet enveloped in the Georgian mountains. Whether you're looking to hike the hinterland or lounge in a lazy village, the Russell–Brasstown Scenic Byway is an ideal getaway.

Recreational: Hiking trails that lead visitors to tumbling waterfalls or breathtaking mountain overlooks abound in the Chattahoochee National Forest of North Georgia. The most prominent of these is the Appalachian National Scenic Trail. Extending more than 2,000 miles from Georgia's Springer Mountain to Maine, traveling the entire Appalachian Trail is a goal for many hikers. The Russell–Brasstown Scenic Byway provides access to the trail, which covers nearly 80 miles in Georgia. Atop Brasstown Bald, hikers can explore the Jacks Knob, Arkaquah, and Wagon Train Trails. These trails, ranging from 4.5 to 6 miles in length, radiate from the visitor center parking area. Numerous smaller trails snake their way around the area and can be accessed from Andrews Cove, Chattahoochee Campground, Dukes Creek Falls, Raven Cliff Falls, and the other state parks and scenic areas.

Highlights:

The following itinerary offers a sampling of what the byway has to offer.

Helen: To begin your journey fully equipped with maps, brochures, and food and drink, stop at the charming town of Helen, just two miles before officially reaching the byway. Originally this area was a vibrant center of the indigenous Cherokee culture. When gold was discovered in the area in 1828,

Meandering creeks and both large and small waterfalls are highlights of a visit to the Russell–Brasstown Scenic Byway.

thousands of Europeans flooded the region. Gold mining and then the timber industry flourished until the mid-20th century. In the 1960s the village once again reinvented itself, this time as a quaint Bavarian hamlet.

Smithgall Woods–Dukes Creek Conservation Area:
Formerly a private estate, this conservation area has been described as being home to one of North Georgia's best trout streams as well as nature trails and wildlife viewing stands.

Dukes Creek Falls:
Leaving the Smithgall Woods–Dukes Creek Conservation Area, turn north on State Route 348 for 1/2 mile to Dukes Hollow Road and follow the signs to Dukes Creek Falls. The falls are actually on Davis Creek before it joins Dukes Creek. Dropping 250 feet down a steep granite canyon, Dukes Creek Falls is a spectacular sight. A wheelchair-accessible trail from the parking lot to observation platforms gives an overview of the falls. Hikers can continue down Dukes Creek Gorge to the base of the falls for an up-close experience.

Raven Cliff Falls:
Returning to State Route 348, continue another 2.5 miles north. Parking is available along the left side of the road. Follow the signs marking the trail to Raven Cliff Falls. Tumbling a total of 100 feet down Dodd Creek, Raven Cliff Falls is actually a series of three splendid waterfalls. The middle section flows through a split in a solid rock outcropping. Other waterfalls are found on the creek with the largest having a drop of 70 feet. The surrounding wilderness, measuring more than 9,100 acres, is federally protected.

Brasstown Bald:
Brasstown Bald is Georgia's highest mountain. At 4,784 feet above sea level, this vantage point offers a commanding 360-degree view.

High Shoals Creek Falls Scenic Area:
Near the intersection of State Routes 17/75 and 180, Forest Service Road 283 leads visitors through the Swallow Creek Wildlife Management Area to the High Shoals Creek Falls Scenic Area. A 1.25-mile trail takes visitors down to the High Shoals Creek Falls and Blue Hole Falls. It is highly recommended that the falls be viewed only from the established trails and observation platforms.

Smith Creek:
From State Route 17/75, turn left on State Route 356 for 1.5 miles, and then left at the sign for Anna Ruby Falls. Follow this road for 3.5 miles to the parking area. Fed by underground springs, rain, and snow, Curtis Creek and York Creek thunder down Tray Mountain to form Smith Creek. Paths and trails traverse the area. Lion's Eye Trail gives people with visual impairments the opportunity to experience the Smith Creek environment with Braille signs.

Ashley River Road

A short excursion from Charleston, the road tunnels beneath towering live oaks dripping in Spanish moss en route to a wealth of historic low-country gardens and mansions open to the public.

Quick Facts

Length: 11 miles

Time to Allow: 25 minutes without stopping, or as much as two days to experience all the National Historic Landmarks.

Consideration: There are no fees on this byway.

Covering a distance of only 11 miles, the Ashley River Road is a journey into the history, culture, and beauty of the South Carolina low country. Ancient live oaks, Spanish moss stirring in a warm summer breeze, and elegant brick gates hinting at the architecture within hearken back to days gone by. The Ashley River Road itself reflects the history and culture that has been at home along this great river.

Cultural: In addition to the grand architecture of the mansions and gardens of the area, the African-American churches that chronicle their religion from slavery to emancipation are no less remarkable. As the first non-native culture to live in the area, the early slave and subsequent emancipated African cultures contributed to the shaping of the Ashley River Road and the surrounding area.

The Springfield Baptist Church along the byway is an example of community efforts of the African-American culture of the area. Coming together in the mid 1860s, African Americans established the first freely organized Baptist congregation. The Ashley River Road connected these congregations with rural African-American communities such as Red Top, Marysville, Sanders, Drayton, Bullfield, and Cherokee.

The plantation mansions and magnificent gardens are witnesses of the influence of English architecture for both mansion and garden. Drayton Hall is an example of the Georgian-Palladian architectural style, which meant that these homes were often rectangular in shape and that the rooms were arranged symmetrically around a spacious hall. The Middleton Place Gardens also illustrate order, geometry, and balance, with a variety of sweeping vistas and blooming flowers, shrubs, and trees.

Historical: An extraordinary blending of plantation, slave, religious, war, and mining history along the Ashley River Road

secures this 11-mile stretch of road as an important snapshot of the history of South Carolina. The grand architecture of the plantation mansions, the road itself, and local historic churches speak of a time rich in tradition.

During the colonial period of U.S. history, the low country of South Carolina

Stately oaks form a scenic canopy over the road leading in to the grounds of the Magnolia Plantation.

was ideal for rice plantations, and the nearby Ashley River was used to cultivate these rice fields.

In addition to work on the plantations, slave labor was an integral part of the construction and development of the Ashley River Road itself. Plantation owners were required to send their slaves to work on the road; consequently, while the funds generally came from the white landowners, the labor for the road is due to the work of the slave population.

The Ashley River Road saw dramatic changes when action at Fort Bull during the Civil War resulted in the abandonment of the fort to Union troops and the burning and looting of many of the great manor houses along the road. With the slave labor era waning, the search for new ways to make money resulted in the mining of nearby phosphate rock.

Highlights:

The following itinerary takes you from the beginning of the Ashley River right on in to the city of Charleston.

Colonial Dorchester State Historic Site:

Not officially on the byway, but a significant site in the telling of the Ashley River history, and just six miles outside of Summerville on State Road 642 south is the 325-acre Colonial Dorchester State Historic Site. This historic park is the former location of a village founded in 1697 by a group of Congregationalists from Massachusetts who abandoned the community after the American Revolution. Attractions here include the site of the tabby fort, ruins of the once thriving village, ongoing archaeological excavations, the tower of the St. George's Parish Church, and signage explaining the history of the town and the upper Ashley River area.

Middleton Place:

Originally constructed in the mid-1700s, this plantation

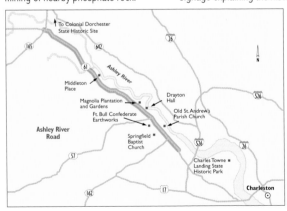

survived the American Revolution, hurricanes, and an earthquake, but the manor house nearly didn't survive the Yankee troops intent on burning it to the ground in the Civil War.

Magnolia Plantation and Gardens:

Adjoining Drayton Hall and still in the possession of the original owners, the Drayton family, is Magnolia Plantation and Gardens. Dating back to 1676, the plantation offers tours of the manor house and the world-famous gardens, including the Barbados Tropical Garden and a horticultural maze.

Drayton Hall:

Drayton Hall, a National Historic Landmark, is the oldest preserved plantation house in America that is open to the public and has remained in nearly original condition. Jointly owned by the National Trust for Historic Preservation and the State of South Carolina, Drayton Hall is considered one of the finest examples of Georgian Palladian architecture in the nation.

Old Saint Andrew's Parish Church:

The oldest surviving church in South Carolina, Old Saint Andrew's Parish Church still retains many of its historic features, including original flooring and the original baptismal font.

Cherokee Foothills Scenic Highway

The state's lofty green mountains, drawing flatland vacationers for generations, offer cooling breezes, cascading streams, and a brief history lesson at Cowpens, a Revolutionary War battlefield.

Looming majestically beyond the low, soft hills of the Piedmont, the Blue Ridge escarpment thrills the soul of the mountain lover. The Cherokees called these heights the "Great Blue Hills of God." The stream-laced foothills and rugged mountains of the Blue Ridge have helped shape the development of South Carolina's Upcountry. The Blue Ridge Mountains are forested and steep, and in some places they are penetrable only along narrow passes cut by roaring, cliff walled rivers. From the mountain heights, some of these rivers plunge hundreds of feet in breathtaking falls.

The Robert Scruggs cabin, built about 50 years after the Battle of Cowpens, gives a glimpse into rustic early American life.

While today's travelers may hear echoes of the area's Cherokee heritage in place and river names such as Seneca, Keowee, Jocassee, Tamassee, Tokeena, Toxaway, and Eastatoe, the first strains of the Cherokee recessional were truly heard in 1776. As the new American nation was forming, the region's first white settler, Richard Pearis, married a Cherokee woman and built the area's first business—a trading station and gristmill—on the falls of the Reedy River in what is now downtown Greenville. Following the Revolutionary War, treaties with the Native Americans opened up what was called the Pendleton District (now Anderson, Pickens, and Oconee counties) and land-hungry settlers flowed in.

Cultural: This scenic roadway serves as a home address for many families descended from early settlers whom William Bartram (author of the 1791 book of Travels) called "friendly and hospitable" but with manners and customs different from his other experiences. A great deal of the area still seems remote and undeveloped, particularly in Greenville and Pickens Counties. Most of the development is located in Spartanburg and Cherokee counties, where the terrain is conducive to development and the roadway has existed the longest.

Historical: Cowpens National Battlefield commemorates a decisive battle that helped turn the tide of war in the South. On this field on January 17, 1781, Daniel Morgan led his army of tough Continentals, militia, and cavalry to a brilliant victory over Banastre Tarleton's force of British regulars.

Because he had sciatica so bad that it was too painful for him to sit on a horse, Morgan retired to his home in Virginia after the Battle of Cowpens. On March

25, 1790, he received a gold medal that Congress had struck to honor him for his victory at Cowpens. Following the Revolution, Morgan organized and led a group of militia against the protesters during the Whiskey Rebellion. In 1797 he was elected and served one term in the House of Representatives. He died on July 6, 1802.

Recreational: Located just 45 miles from Greenville, South Carolina, Lake Keowee provides a majestic view, beautiful freshwater lakes, and mountain views. The lake is located close to the small town of Seneca in the northwest corner of South Carolina. Lake Keowee consists of about 18,000 acres and approximately 300 miles of shoreline. Only a small percentage of the shoreline has been developed, resulting in an uncrowded lake. Boating, sailing, fishing, and a variety of outdoor activities are popular in this region.

Highlights:

This itinerary begins with a sampling of outdoor adventures in a variety of settings, and climaxes in two of the most historically significant national battlefield parks in America.

Stumphouse Tunnel Park: Just six miles north of Walhalla on SC Highway 28 is the Stumphouse Tunnel Park. The park is home to the Stumphouse Tunnel and Issaqueena Falls. The tunnel, a failed effort from days gone by to complete a railroad system from Charleston to Cincinnati, is now used as a recreation site. The Issaqueena Falls is a 100-foot majestic waterfall. One trail goes under the falls, and another trail leads to the bottom of the falls.

Oconee State Park: Twelve miles northwest of Walhalla off SC Highway 28

onto SC Highway 107 is Oconee State Park. A popular mountain park with several cascading waterfalls, Oconee sits on a plateau in the foothills of this beautiful mountain area. Rustic cabins and ample opportunities for swimming and fishing in the park's mountain lakes are part of the charm. Hiking on the Foothills Trail and rafting on the nearby Chattooga River are also popular pastimes.

Table Rock State Park: Only twelve miles north of the town of Pickens on SC Highway 11 is Table Rock State Park, home of Table Rock Mountain. Some of the most challenging hiking trails in the state are here, and a nature center and interpretive programs offer outdoor delights to visitors.

Cowpens National Battlefield: Cowpens National Battlefield is 11 miles west of Interstate 85 near the SC Highway 11/Highway 10 intersection. The crucial Battle of Cowpens contributed to the defeat of the British forces during the Revolutionary War.

King's Mountain National Military Park: Just east of Cherokee Foothills Scenic Byway is the King's Mountain National Military Park, commemorating a significant Patriot victory during the American Revolution.

Savannah River Scenic Byway

Skirting J. Strom Thurmond Lake, where you can swim, the byway continues north through a varied region of dense woods, rolling farmland, and historic villages, where antique shopping is popular.

Quick Facts

Length: 110 miles

Time to Allow: One could easily spend three hours to all day exploring this byway.

Consideration: Lane widths and highway designs do not present problems for motor vehicles with standard clearances.

Outdoor excitement and historic adventures await you on the Savannah River Scenic Byway. Running along the western edge of South Carolina, the byway is a beautiful country drive through the dense wooded Hickory Knob State Resort Park and Sumter National Forest, quaint towns such as McCormick and Willington, and past rolling farmland dotted with historic churches. The J. Strom Thurmond Dam and Lake and the Savannah River are both only seconds off the byway, providing camping, fishing, and other recreational opportunities that you will be able to enjoy with the whole family.

For antique hounds and history buffs, a small side trip off the byway will be well worth your time. Head to the town of Abbeville, just a few miles off the byway, to experience some great shopping, dining, and historic architecture.

Cultural: The Savannah River Scenic Byway is the primary touring route within the upper regions of the South Carolina Heritage Corridor. As a key segment of the Heritage Corridor's "Nature Route," the scenic highway serves both as a touring route and as the major north/south pathway for visitors to the area.

Examples of this region's unique cultural traditions include basket making and shape-note singing. Numerous places along the route also offer cuisine that is unique to the region.

The visual character of the present-day landscape was shaped by many different cultural and economic influences. These influences include the early cotton-dependent economy, the introduction of the railroads, the creation of the lakes, and the completion of I-85 and the development of Savannah Lakes Village.

This corridor tells the vibrant story of South Carolina's (and the South's) evolution and culture. Visitors will learn of rice and indigo, pirates and patriots, slaves and freemen, cotton fields and mill villages, swamps and waterfalls, railroads and back roads, soul food and "pig-pickin's," and spirituals and bluegrass. Locations of natural beauty, recreational

Calhoun Falls State Park is located on Russell Lake, one of South Carolina's most popular fishing lakes.

opportunities, military history, local arts and crafts, agricultural traditions, and the state's rich African-American heritage are identified and interpreted along the way.

Historical: The Savannah River Scenic Highway winds more than 100 miles along the shores of three major lakes and through four counties. In the 18th century, this was the western frontier, and it was bustling with soldiers, American Indian traders, and adventurers when South Carolina's first battle of the Revolution erupted here.

Abbeville is a historically significant town along the byway. This town was so actively involved in events relating to the Civil War that it claims the title "Birthplace and Deathbed of the Confederacy." On November 22, 1860, Secession Hill was the site of the first public meeting organized to consider seceding from the Union. On May 2, 1865, at the Burt–Stark Mansion, Jefferson Davis met for the last time with his Council of War and agreed to disband his Confederate troops.

Edgefield is home to the Old Edgefield Pottery where a resident potter still makes alkaline-glazed stoneware in the Old Edgefield tradition. Antebellum homes, such as Oakley Park and Magnolia Dale, are open for tours. Nearby Johnston, with its Victorian architecture and antique shops, has designated itself "the Peach Capital of the World."

Recreational: The Savannah River Scenic Highway serves as a major recreational gateway to the freshwater coast. It includes more than 2,700 miles of shoreline along lakes Hartwell, Russell, and Thurmond. The scenic highway provides access to 59 recreation areas, including the developed recreational sites operated by the Corps of Engineers, SCPRT, and the U.S. Forest Service, as well as a few sites that are operated by local government.

In addition, the route connects to 104 recreational access sites that have boat ramps, campgrounds, welcome centers, or shoreline access points and other points of interest.

Some of the recreation areas accessible from the scenic highway include the five state parks associated with the freshwater coast. These parks are Sadlers Creek State Recreation Area, Calhoun Falls State Park, Hickory Knob State Resort Park, Baker Creek State Park, and Hamilton–Branch State Park.

Highlights:

With the Savannah River Scenic Byway offering a mix of natural wonders, historic treasures, and southern hospitality, this itinerary gives just a sampling of what there is to see and do on and near the byway.

J. Strom Thurmond Dam and Lake:

West of the byway is the J. Strom Thurmond Dam and Lake, one of the ten most visited Corps of Engineers lakes in the nation. It is the largest Corps project east of the Mississippi River and offers camping, boating, fishing, hunting, and a variety of trails for up-close views of wildlife in their stunning natural habitats.

McCormick's Historic District:

Directly on the byway, the former gold mining town of McCormick has several interesting and noteworthy buildings in its historic downtown district. Strom's Drug Store on Main Street still offers old-fashioned fountain sodas, ice cream, and shakes. And the McCormick Visitor's Center was the first service station in the county. Maps and information about the region can be picked up here.

McCormick Hotels:

Along with the historic depot, hotels from the turn of the 20th century have been preserved and restored and function now as an integral part of the business life of McCormick. The McCormick Hotel now serves hungry diners as a locally popular eatery.

Ninety Six National Historic Site:

Northeast of McCormick is the Ninety Six National Historic Site, a frontier settlement and battlefield from the Revolutionary War. The park site covers more than 989 acres and includes a visitors center, self-guided tours, special events, interpretive trails, archaeological digs, and insightful restorations.

Abbeville:

With more than 300 homes and buildings in the National Register Historic District, a stop at the Welcome Center is essential for maps and information about walking tours, attractions, and events.

Trinity Episcopal Church and Burt–Stark Mansion:

The Trinity Episcopal Church features a massive tracker organ, stunning stained-glass windows, original handmade pews, and a soaring 125-foot spire. The Burt–Stark Mansion, a National Historic Landmark, is where the secession papers for the state of

The Abbeville Opera House emulates the atmosphere of an early 20th century theater.

South Carolina were read and where Jefferson Davis, former President of the Confederacy, held his final cabinet meeting and formally disbanded the Confederate armies.

Calhoun Falls State Park:

The town of Calhoun Falls is the gateway to the Calhoun Falls State Park on the shores of popular Lake Russell. With 438 acres of woodlands, the park facilities include 100 campsites, a lighted marina, boat ramps, fishing pier, park store, seasonal swimming beach, bathhouses, restrooms, nature trails, picnic shelters, playgrounds, and tennis courts.

A1A Scenic and Historic Coastal Highway

Miles of white sand beaches invite splashing in the surf. Keep watch offshore for migrating whales and schools of dolphins. The highway also visits St. Augustine, a fascinating lesson in the Spanish exploration of the coast.

Dip your toes in the ocean off the Florida coast during your journey along A1A Scenic and Historic Coastal Highway. With miles and miles of white sand beaches, you will have plenty of space to spread out with buckets and blankets. You can charter a fishing boat and dangle a line for flounder, snook, whiting, snapper, or blues, just to name a few varieties. Or swing your feet over the pier while fishing from land.

If you don't want to get your feet wet but still enjoy watching the ocean, try jogging, biking, roller blading, or strolling along the 19-mile path from Marineland to the Volusia County line. Or stash your binoculars in your beach bag for views of wildlife and birds.

Cultural: The A1A Scenic and Historic Coastal Highway stretches through an area whose culture is heavily influenced by its natural surroundings. The scenic ocean landscape certainly plays a part in this influence, as do the scents and sounds of the coast, giving shape to the art, architecture, and even livelihood of the inhabitants along the byway. This maritime culture is expressed in the byway's attractions, architecture, art, and festivals.

Historical: The byway traverses an area full of colorful history. Glorious hotels still stand as memorials to Henry Flagler's influence on tourism. Remnants of vast plantations allow

The Castillo de San Marcos guarded the Spanish colonial interests in the settlement of St. Augustine against onslaughts of pirates and other nations.

Quick Facts

Length: 72 miles

Time to Allow: Two hours

Consideration: There are no seasonal limitations, except during the hurricane season (June–November) when a hurricane or tropical storm is within the vicinity.

views into the life of General Joseph Hernandez, Florida's first delegate to the U.S. Congress.

In 1565, Spanish Admiral Don Pedro Menendez de Aviles arrived with 600 soldiers and settlers, founding the city of St. Augustine at the site of the Timucuan Indian village of Seloy. He and the settlers successfully colonized Florida, 42 years before the English colony at Jamestown, Virginia, and 55 years before the arrival of the Pilgrims at Plymouth Rock, Massachusetts. St. Augustine today contains more than 2,500 historic structures.

Recreational: There are miles of beaches along the byway. Recreationalists can participate in beachcombing, sunning, beach strolling, and even beach driving; Crescent Beach allows motor vehicles on its expansive beaches.

With the ocean on one side and a river on the other along much of the byway, there is plenty of room for aquatic activities, including surfing, swimming, fishing, and boating, with free public boat launches such as the one found at Bing's Landing. Kayaking and canoeing are also popular activities, whether in the river or in shallow lakes and canals in the area. Other popular aquatic activities include sailing, taking a scenic cruise, and scuba diving. The traveler can even observe or interact with dolphins and sea turtles near the town of Marineland.

Highlights:

Since being first explored by Ponce de Leon in 1513, this area has had a distinctly Spanish flair. With that in mind, here are a few of the highlights exploring that heritage.

St. Augustine: Start with a visit to the St. Augustine and St. Johns County Visitor Information Center. St. Augustine can be experienced by horse and buggy, tram/trolley, and on foot. Visitors may want to stop at the St. Augustine Historical Society, located in the "Oldest House in the United States" (the Gonza-lez-Alvarez House).

Ponce de Leon's Fountain of Youth National Archaeological Park:

Seeking the Fountain of Youth and believing he had found it, Ponce de Leon landed here in 1513 and planted a stone cross into the ground. Ponce de Leon's Fountain of Youth National Archaeological Park exhibits foundations and artifacts of the first St. Augustine mission and colony.

Mission de Nombre de Dios: In 1565, Pedro Menendez de Aviles landed at what became the Mission de Nombre de Dios and claimed this site for Spain and the Church. It was on these grounds that Father Lopez would celebrate the first parish mass in the New World.

Castillo de San Marcos National Monument: The Castillo de San Marcos National Monument represents the oldest remaining European fortification in the continental United States.

The masonry fort and its surrounding land comprise 25 acres in historic downtown St. Augustine. There is no visitor center in the park, but extensive museum exhibits are maintained within the casemates.

Fort Matanzas National Monument: Fort Matanzas National Monument, a former Spanish outpost fort, was built from 1740 to 1742 to guard Matanzas Inlet and to warn St. Augustine of enemies approaching from the south. Fort Matanzas now serves as a reminder of the early Spanish empire in the New World.

Indian River Lagoon Scenic Highway

This coastal loop explores Atlantic beaches and a diverse estuary, where you can take your pick of water sports. Then step into the Kennedy Space Center Visitors Complex for an update on America's space program.

For a truly diverse adventure, travel the Indian River Lagoon Scenic Highway. Explore wildlife refuges, seashores, historic districts, and even the intricacies of the NASA Space Program. While traveling the highway, you will meander through three national wildlife refuges and several state and local parks and sanctuaries. And, speaking of diversity, while visiting the Indian River Lagoon, you will find yourself in the most biologically diverse estuary in North America.

The lagoon is home to more than 4,000 species of plants and animals.

Cultural: The Indian River Lagoon Scenic Highway is just as rich in cultural diversity as it is in natural diversity. From porch swings to surfboards, Florida's central coast is home to a wide variety of people. With a casual beach lifestyle, many have found Florida's space coast to be a refreshing getaway. Many communities along the byway have refurbished their historic districts into quaint shopping areas. The area is rich with theaters for the performing arts, and museums of art, history, natural science, and technology.

Historical: History comes alive on the Indian River Lagoon Scenic Highway. From the history of the space race to the preservation of the ecosystem,

In the Rocket Garden at Kennedy Space Center visitors can experience the same rockets that first put NASA astronauts into space.

> ## Quick Facts
>
> **Length:** 150 miles
>
> **Time to Allow:** Ten hours for a quick tour or two days for an exceptional adventure.
>
> **Consideration:** Patrick Air Force Base (Cape Canaveral Air Station) does not allow through traffic. Visitors can take a bus onto the base and see the Space and Missile Museum. Florida has some of the greatest beaches in the world, with opportunities for contact with wildlife such as manatees, dolphins, and sea turtles. These are wild animals and may behave unpredictably. They may also be protected by law. For your safety and theirs, please do not approach them.

this byway is filled with museums that dynamically illustrate the lessons of the past. Each museum tells a vibrant story about Florida's rich heritage and biodiversity. Many communities also have restored historic districts that preserve the exceptional architectures of Florida.

Recreational: In addition to showcasing shuttle launches, the byway is host to practically every recreational activity imaginable.

Surfing and scuba diving are enjoyed all along the coast, and those who enjoy fishing will be amazed at the excellent fishing on Florida's central shore. The ocean also provides opportunities for sailing and other boating.

The lagoon, on the other hand, offers its own activities. Travelers can rent an airboat or take a jungle cruise to see the wonders of Florida's unspoiled natural habitats. One of the best ways to experience the peaceful appeal of Florida is to rent a canoe or kayak on the Indian River Lagoon and try your hand at paddling your way to pleasant adventures.

Highlights:

Working from south to north, travelers on the Indian River Lagoon Scenic Highway have a variety of opportunities for things to see and do. This itinerary highlights just a few.

Wabasso Island: Beginning at Wabasso Island, visit the Environmental Learning Center. Here there are hands-on learning opportunities, various nature trails with interpretive signage, wet and dry labs, and a butterfly garden.

Sebastian: Treasure hunters have two museums in Sebastian dedicated to adventure. At the Mel Fisher Treasure Museum visitors observe the preservation techniques used to save the recovered treasure that is currently being salvaged from the ocean floor.

McLarty Treasure Museum: This museum sits on the site of a salvaging camp created by the 1715 Spanish Plate Fleet. The museum exhibits include artifacts and displays re-creating the camps.

Sebastian Inlet State Park: Sebastian Inlet State Park is home to a fishing museum and beaches, as well as wildlife-viewing opportunities, nature trails, camping, and scuba diving. It also has the largest nesting assemblage of sea turtles in the United States.

Kennedy Space Center: Tours of the complex include IMAX Theater, the launch facilities, the Vehicle Assembly Building, and a full-size Space Shuttle mock-up.

Merritt Island National Wildlife Refuge: Stop first at

the Visitor Information Center for details about hiking trails, the manatee observation deck, the seven-mile auto tour route, educational programs, boating, canoeing, fishing, and more.

Canaveral National Seashore: Canaveral National Seashore is on a barrier island that includes ocean, beach, dune, hammock, lagoon, salt marsh, and pine flatland habitats. Opportunities for recreational activities include lagoon fishing, boating, canoeing, surfing, sunbathing, swimming, hiking, horseback riding, and backcountry camping.

Tamiami Trail Scenic Highway

A plunge into the subtropical climes of southern Florida, the highway edges Everglades National Park and bisects Big Cypress National Preserve. Huge cypress trees, 130 feet tall, line the horizon.

Quick Facts

Length: 49.5 miles.

Time to Allow: Just three to four hours will allow you ample time to capture the charm of this byway.

Consideration: Portions of the trail are relatively isolated, so travelers should make sure they have plenty of gasoline.

Travel under a canopy of hardwood hammocks with bright splashes of tropical flowers and watch for kelly green tree frogs leaping across your trail. The Tamiami Trail Scenic Highway on the southern tip of Florida will lead the adventurous through a tropical landscape unlike any other in the United States. Venturing straight through the

The subtropical Everglades is a low-lying floodplain with cypress trees, mangrove thickets, and palms.

Big Cypress National Preserve, the Tamiami Trail offers visitors an opportunity to escape into the wilds of Florida where you can search for endangered Florida panthers or cigar orchids. While in Big Cypress National Preserve, take advantage of opportunities to bike, hike, canoe, and picnic.

Historical: The completion of the Tamiami Trail in 1928 led to the construction of first buildings along the route, called way stations. These way stations, similar to gas or filling stations, were built along the trail specifically to assist stranded motorists. The stations were located at ten-mile intervals, and each one was operated by a husband and wife team. Five of the way station sites are found within the corridor limits, and include Royal Palm, Weavers, Monroe, Turner River, and Paolita Stations.

Settlements and businesses began to develop soon after the road was completed. Three sawmills were located along the trail to harvest cypress and pine trees. Lumbering activities became an important activity in Collier County in

the 1930s. Other business opportunities developed around agriculture.

Recreational: Recreational opportunities are abundant along the Tamiami Trail. The unique Everglades region, coupled with the 800,000 acres of public land located around the byway, give visitors and recreational enthusiasts a variety of chances to enjoy themselves. Picnic areas, wildlife viewing, photographic opportunities, and a visitor center area are all available for casual visitors.

Fishers can try their hand at salt- or freshwater fishing via canoe or along the canal edges. The Florida National Scenic Trail crosses the byway and provides 31 miles of hiking for day hikers and overnight backpackers. There are primitive campgrounds that offer a few facilities, as well as many campgrounds with full facilities. Hunting and off-road vehicle exploration of the Big Cypress National Preserve is allowed.

Highlights:

Here are some of the natural and historical highlights along Florida's Tamiami Trail Scenic Highway.

Smallwood Trading Post: Smallwood Trading Post was built in 1906, located on Chokoloskee Island on the western edge of the Everglades. One of the oldest standing buildings in southwest Florida and listed on the National Register of Historic Places, it is a time capsule of Florida pioneer history. When the business closed in 1982, 90 percent of the original goods remained in the store. Ted Smallwood's granddaughter reopened the store in recent years as a museum.

Big Cypress National Preserve: The Big Cypress National Preserve covers more than 729,000 acres of open prairie dotted with cypress trees, pinelands, and dark forested swamps. The most common tree species are bald cypress, which grow to heights of 130 feet with broad canopies. Visitors will want to start with the orientation video at the visitor center. Other opportunities include wildlife viewing and birdwatching; hiking, biking, and driving trails; and special ranger-guided programs.

Big Cypress Swamp: Experience this swamp on a swamp buggy or airboat. Swamp buggies provide a mechanical mode of transportation into the swamp, and airboats enable visitors to cruise atop grasses and marshes, covering great distances in little time. Also, canoeing and kayaking provide fun water exploration.

Museum of the Everglades: This museum showcases the history of the southwestern Everglades. Artifacts and displays in the recently restored laundry building tell the story of two millennia of human occupation. The building is the only remaining, unaltered structure original to the town. A company town built during the 1920s by Barron Gift Collier, the laundry served the workers who completed the Tamiami Trail to Miami.

Everglades National Park: The Gulf Coast entrance to the Everglades National Park is located just a short distance from the Tamiami Trail. Everglades National Park has been designated a World Heritage Site, an International

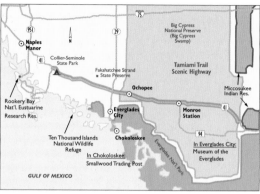

Biosphere Reserve, and a Wetland of International Importance. It is the only subtropical preserve in North America. Ranger-led boat trips, walks, and canoe programs allow you to learn more about this park's history.

Ten Thousand Islands National Wildlife Refuge: Though best accessed by boat, the Ten Thousand Islands National Wildlife Refuge is worth the trip. This 35,000-acre refuge protects important mangrove habitats and a rich diversity of native wildlife, including several endangered species.

MOUNTAIN

From Idaho's green forests south to Arizona's high deserts, the vast mountain region spans the Old West of America's history and imagination. The area's landscapes range from rugged to serene, but for drivers along its most scenic byways, one theme unites them all: the allure of wide-open spaces, punctuated by snowcapped mountain peaks and adorned by sparkling rivers, amazing rock formations, and a frontier spirit mirrored in the small towns and cities. Colorado's San Juan Skyway journeys to the top of the world. New Mexico's Billy the Kid Trail rides through outlaw country. And Idaho's Pend Oreille Scenic Byway is a water lover's dream. Enjoy the drives, but don't forget to stop and savor the views and diversions along the way.

Beartooth Highway

With the rugged peaks of the glacier-flanked Beartooth Range as a backdrop, this stunning highway travels through three national forests to Yellowstone National Park, luring vacationers year-round.

From its beginning at the border of the Custer National Forest to its terminus near the northeast entrance to Yellowstone National Park, the Beartooth Highway (U.S. 212) offers travelers the ultimate high country experience. It travels through the Custer, Shoshone, and Gallatin National Forests.

Since its completion in 1936, the highway has provided millions of visitors with a rare opportunity to see the transition from a lush forest ecosystem to alpine tundra in the space of a few miles. The Beartooth range is one of the highest and most rugged areas in the lower 48 states, with 20 peaks higher than 12,000 feet in elevation. Glaciers are found on the north flank of nearly every mountain peak higher than 11,500 feet in these mountains.

Cultural: The Beartooth Highway's most important cultural value is the chance to appreciate some of the activities that flourish in natural environments. After understanding the people's occupations and interests in this part of Montana and Wyoming, visitors often leave with

Brooks Lake in Wyoming's Shoshone National Forest has fishing, campgrounds, trailheads, and commanding views of the Absaroka Range.

a longing to return to the simple yet strenuous life found in this area.

Some of the locals' occupations include ranchers, lumberjacks, sports enthusiasts, and anglers. These and other similar activities thrive today along the Beartooth Highway, continuing a long tradition of using the natural resources of these public lands.

Historical: The first recorded travel across the Beartooth Pass area occurred in 1882, when General Sheridan with a force of 129 soldiers and scouts (and 104 horses and 157 mules) pioneered and marked a route across the mountains from Cooke City to Billings. A year later, Van Dyke, a packer, modified the trail and located a route off the Beartooth Plateau into Rock Creek and Red Lodge. Van Dyke's trail was the only direct route between Red Lodge and Cooke City until the Beartooth Highway was constructed in 1934 and 1935. Remnants of Van Dyke's trail are visible from the Rock Creek Overlook parking lot, appearing as a Z on the mountain.

Doctor Siegfriet and other visionaries from the Bearcreek and Red Lodge communities foresaw, in the early 1900s, the value of a scenic route over the mountains to connect to Yellowstone Park. These men spent many years promoting the construction of a road over the mountains and even began the construction of a road with hand tools and horse-drawn implements.

Other routes were surveyed from 1920 to 1925, and in 1931 President Herbert Hoover signed the Park Approach Act, which was the forerunner to the funding of the road now known as the Beartooth Highway.

Recreational: Recreational opportunities are abundant in the area traversed by the Beartooth Highway. You can cross-country ski on the snowfields in June and July or hike across the broad plateaus and Red on Forest Service trails (some of which are National Recreation Trails). Camp, picnic, or fish for trout in the streams and lakes adjacent to the highway. View and photograph nature at its finest, including wildflowers and wildlife (moose, Rocky Mountain goats, mule deer, black bears, grizzly bears, marmots, and pikas). You can even visit a guest ranch, take a guided horseback trip from Cooke City, bicycle, and downhill ski on the headwalls.

If you enjoy skiing, each summer in June and July, the Red Lodge International Ski Race Camp is conducted on the north side of the East Summit on the Twin Lakes Headwall. This camp is for aspiring Olympic-caliber skiers.

Highlights:

Consider seeking out these sites as you travel the Beartooth Scenic Byway.

Red Lodge: Red Lodge is an 1880s coal-mining and ranching town lined with turn-of-the-19th-century red brick storefronts and hotels that cater mainly to skiers and visitors to Yellowstone. Visit the Beartooth Nature Center, at the north end of Red Lodge, which exhibits native wildlife. The road follows Rock Creek into the mountains, winding through grassy hills that soon give way to heavily forested mountains. Rocky outcrops interrupt evergreen forests, and an occasional spire juts over the trees. About 13 miles from Red Lodge, the road climbs away from the creek, and suddenly the vista opens up toward the 1,800-foot cliffs that bend around the head of the valley in a semicircle.

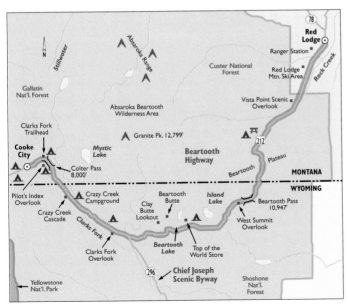

Vista Point Scenic Overlook: After five miles of dramatic switchbacks, stop at the Vista Point Scenic Overlook. Here, at 9,200 feet, a short path leads to the tip of a promontory with phenomenal views across Rock Creek Canyon to the high rolling country of the Beartooth Plateau. As you continue on U.S. 212, the trees give out entirely, and you begin crossing a landscape of low, rounded hills covered with grasses, sedges, and lavish wildflowers in summer. Soon, the road cuts back to the rim of the canyon, and from the narrow turnouts, you can see a chain of glacial lakes 1,000 feet below.

Beartooth Plateau: As you travel farther on the byway from the north on U.S. 212, the Beartooth Plateau looms over the surrounding prairie foothills as a hulking mass of black, rounded mountains.

Absaroka Range: As you pass the ski lift, the Absaroka Range breaks over the western horizon in a row of jagged volcanic peaks. Wildflower meadows lead to the west summit of Beartooth Pass, at an exalted 10,947 feet. From the pass, you descend to a forest of lodge-pole and whitebark pines toward 10,514-foot Beartooth Butte. Soon, you pass Beartooth Lake.

Clay Butte Lookout: In another mile, follow the gravel road to Clay Butte Lookout, a fire tower with a smashing view of some of Montana's highest mountains.

Crazy Creek Campground: Continue 5.5 miles to an unmarked bridge over Lake Creek, and take the short path back to a powerful waterfall thundering though a narrow chasm. A completely different sort of cascade fans out over a broad ram of granite in the trees above Crazy Creek Campground, 2.5 miles farther.

Pilot and Index Overlook: At the Pilot and Index Overlook, you're looking at the northern edge of the Absaroka Range, an eroded mass of lava, ash, and mudflows that began forming 50 million years ago.

Cooke City: From here, the road follows the Clarks Fork River through what is left of a centuries-old forest, much of which fell victim to the great Yellowstone fires of 1988. Soon, the road passes through the tiny tourist crossroads of Cooke City, begun as a 19th-century mining camp. Four miles beyond, the drive ends at the northeast entrance to Yellowstone National Park.

Overlooks give interpretive information as well as awe-inspiring views of the valley below in this beautiful mountainous area of Montana.

Northwest Passage Scenic Byway

In the spirit of Lewis, Clark, and Sacagawea, this modern-day Northwest Passage follows the historic route of the Nez Perce Indians through canyons, valleys, and evergreen forests, past wild rivers and Native American cultural sites.

Quick Facts

Length: 90 miles

Time to Allow: Three hours to three days.

Consideration: U.S. 12 above Kooskia is a winding, two-lane road with occasional passing lanes and slow vehicle turnouts.

Follow the footsteps of Meriwether Lewis and William Clark as they searched for the Northwest Passage—a link between the Missouri River and the Columbia River through the unexplored Rocky Mountains. Lewis and Clark's arduous journey proved that no easy route existed; however, they were led by Sacagawea to the trail through the mountains that had been used by generations of Nez Perce Indians. Along this byway, you will see numerous Nez Perce cultural sites and Lewis and Clark campsites.

Cultural: Although a conglomeration of cultures and people make up the Northwest Passage, none of the cultures has preserved its heritage like the Nez Perce. Agriculture and industry fostered by the coming of homesteaders and gold miners exist side by side with the customs of the Nez Perce. Experience one of their powwows, or see the Nez Perce National Historic Park, where local arts and crafts are displayed.

Historical: Before the Northwest Passage became a nationally recognized corridor, the route was home to the Nez Perce, and it remains their home even today. For thousands of years, this native culture built villages and camps along the Clearwater River. The Northwest Passage was a main route for the Nez Perce as they traveled through the mountains and forests of what is now northern Idaho. The society of the Nez Perce met the society of European culture when Lewis and Clark traveled through the area in 1805 and 1806.

After the coming of the Lewis and Clark Expedition, new visitors wanted to do more than explore. Trappers, missionaries, and miners soon followed, and they interacted with the Nez Perce. For a time, people gathered in the area in hopes of discovering gold. The mining districts from this period in history eventually became the towns that are now on the byway.

In the 1870s, conflict mounted between the Nez Perce and the U.S. government. The battle ended with many of the Nez Perce dead; the rest were moved to reservations. Today, the byway travels

The first battle of the Nez Perce War was fought at White Bird Battlefield in the summer of 1877. The historic site is about 15 miles south of Grangeville.

along the Nez Perce Indian Reservation and passes Nez Perce National Historic Park in Spalding and Kamiah.

Recreational: The road is surrounded by rivers. Along the byway, travelers can hardly escape the allure of the Clearwater River and its forks. Nearby, you will also find the Snake and Salmon Rivers. And whether you choose to enjoy what's in the water or the water itself, you won't be disappointed. Chinook salmon swim in the waters, and fly-fishing for steelhead trout is one reason people return to the Northwest Passage. White water rafting on one of the byway rivers is also irresistible.

If you get enough of the water, a walk in the woods may entice you. Travelers take trails through mountains for the sweeping vistas they can enjoy along the way. National forests, wilderness areas, and even state parks give you the opportunity to find trails and go exploring.

Highlights:

Begin at the byway's western end at the town of Spalding.

Nez Perce National Historic Park: The Nez Perce National Historic Park in Spalding is located on U.S. 95, the best place to get an overview of the park. The Nez Perce National Historic Park is spread across 38 separate sites in four

states; several of the sites lie along this byway. Learn the history of the Nez Perce people at one of the sites.

Nez Perce Village: The highway rest stop at Lenore contains interpretive signs about a Nez Perce village that used to stand here. The site was believed to have been occupied for some 8,000 years.

Canoe Camp: Four miles west of Orofino comes Canoe Camp, where Lewis and Clark built five dugout canoes in 1805 so they could continue their expedition down the rivers. It's a good spot for fishing or bird-watching.

Big Eddy: Northeast of there, on the Dworshak Reservoir, is Big Eddy, where you can picnic, swim, canoe, fish, hike, or camp.

Long Camp: One mile west of the town of Kamiah is the site of the Lewis and Clark Long Camp, part of the Nez Perce

National Historic Park in Kamiah.

Heart of the Monster: In East Kamiah, two miles upstream from the Clearwater River bridge in Kamiah and the point at which the Nez Perce forded the river in 1877, is the Heart of the Monster, a rock formation and source of one of the Nez Perce nation's oldest legends. (The legend has it that a coyote saved the Nez Perce, as well as all animal life, from being swallowed by the monster.)

Clearwater Battlefield: Two miles south of Stites, watch for a pull-off on the west side of the road that marks the Clearwater Battlefield; the Nez Perce were pursued here in 1877.

Payette River Scenic Byway

As the pulsating white water of the Payette River rushes alongside, this byway cuts through pine forests and a picturesque valley dotted with resort towns and is framed by jagged mountain peaks.

A drive along the Payette River Scenic Byway can be distracting for motorists. Rather than watching the road, you may be more inclined to watch the river as it crashes and tumbles its way over rocks and through the narrow river valley. Be sure to take advantage of the occasional pull-offs that allow you to view wilder parts of the river and treat your senses to the sights, sounds, smells, and rhythms of Idaho's famous white water.

Enjoy the scenic drive along the river through the Boise and Payette National Forests before arriving in the high, picturesque mountain valley dotted with the resort towns of Cascade, McCall, and New Meadows. Between the thunderous roll of the white water and the quiet serenity of the valley landscapes, you will find a thrilling adventure as you travel this mountain byway.

Historical: The people and events associated with this river stretch thousands of years back in time, creating generational ties between the past and present and between old-timers and new arrivals in Idaho. But most of the

Although serene in some places, the Payette River is known for its challenging and exhilarating white water.

recorded history of this area started only a couple hundred years ago. Fur trappers of the early 1800s, working for Hudson's Bay Company, named the Payette River in honor of their comrade, Francois Payette, a French-Canadian who explored much of southwestern Idaho. After explorers mapped the territory, pioneers began to settle the area.

Later, people began the construction of a bridge now called the North Fork Bridge, although locals refer to it as the Rainbow Bridge because of its arch. It crosses the North Fork of the Payette River north of Smiths Ferry. Built in 1938, it displays an open-spandrel design introduced to Idaho in the 1920s. Unlike other bridges of this type, the North Fork Bridge has not been altered over the years and is listed on the National Register of Historic Places.

Recreational: Of all the activities available here, white water rafting ranks perhaps as the most popular. People find braving the rapids on the Payette River especially enjoyable. There is an abundance of white water along the byway, and rafters rarely experience a boring moment. The rapids range in size, so rafters with less adventuresome spirits can usually avoid the more commanding waves. As you raft in the

Payette River, you'll witness sparkling clean water and gorgeous, jagged peaks looming high above the canyon.

Other than rafting, you can find numerous places to settle down for a relaxing picnic, enjoy world-class trout fishing, and hike or bike the plentiful mountain trails. Many enjoy viewing wildlife in the wetlands around this area, which attract bald eagles, ospreys, and Canada geese. During the cold winter months, snowmobiling replaces rafting as the most popular activity, although skiing and snowshoeing follow close behind.

Highlights:

The byway's southern end begins in Boise, the Idaho state capital. Start here, and end in Ponderosa State Park.

Boise: Boise is the home of the Basque Museum and Cultural Center, with exhibits about the local Basque community, the largest in the United States; the Idaho Botanical Gardens; the Idaho State Museum (with exhibits on fur trading, ranching, mining, and other historical aspects of Idaho and the Pacific Northwest); and nearby 1,100-foot-high Table Rock.

Payette River: Take Route 55 north to the old mining town of Horseshoe Bend on the Payette River. Between Horseshoe Bend and the town of Banks to the north, the Payette River offers white water rapids of moderate difficulty, with several easy access points. There are also good swimming beaches south of Banks.

Rainbow Bridge: North of the town of Smiths Ferry is the Rainbow Bridge, built in 1938. Also called the North Fork Bridge, it forms a 410-foot span across the North Fork of the Payette.

Cascade State Park: Continue north to Cascade State Park on Cascade Reservoir, which is popular for fishing, boating, swimming, camping, and wildlife viewing.

McCall: Farther north is the old timber town of McCall, settled in the 1820s and now a resort town on the shore of Payette Lake. You can find good boating, sandy beaches, and mountain scenery here.

Ponderosa State Park: Near McCall, Ponderosa State Park occupies a peninsula that juts into Payette Lake. Besides scenic overlooks of the lake, the park has boating, swimming, hiking, biking, camping, and winter skiing amid ponderosa pines and Douglas firs.

Pend Oreille Scenic Byway

A water-lover's dream, this byway hugs the northern shores of Idaho's largest lake and follows a sparkling, splashing river to the Montana border—with fishing, hiking, bird-watching, and even moose-spotting along the way.

Quick Facts

Length: 33 miles

Time to Allow: Two hours

Consideration: Idaho 200 is a two-lane road with no passing lanes. It can be icy during winter months, so drive with caution. Also remember that the Pend Oreille Scenic Byway and most of northern Idaho is in the Pacific time zone.

Visit the Pend Oreille Scenic Byway, and discover a water-lover's paradise! The byway follows the shore of Lake Pend Oreille (pronounced OH-ray) for the majority of the length of the byway and then winds alongside the Clark Fork River to the Montana state line. You'll find yourself beneath towering mountains that are reflected in the many miles of water along the byway.

The area is largely undeveloped, ensuring that you will be treated to the serene outdoors of Idaho by viewing waterfowl, other species of wildlife, and a variety of plants. Be sure to take advantage of the many pull-offs along the road to experience an uninhibited view of this majestic area.

These days, there's never a dull moment with Lake Pend Oreille and the Clark Fork River nearby. You can go boating, fishing, sailing, canoeing, kayaking, and swimming in the lake, rivers, and streams that line the byway. If water sports aren't your thing, go camping, hiking, biking, horseback riding, or golfing. In the wintertime, hit the slopes at Schweitzer Mountain Ski Resort.

Historical: Lake Pend Oreille and the Clark Fork River have been important in the development of the area that is now the Pend Oreille Scenic Byway. Before humans had an impact on the environment, however, glacial Lake Missoula had a significant effect on the land. Subsequent glacial cycles caused cataclysmic flooding, which began in the area of Cabinet Gorge, near the Idaho–Montana border, and then spread across Oregon and Washington before reaching the Pacific Ocean. This tremendous phenomenon created many of the geological formations seen in the area today.

After the glacial ice abated, the land became habitable, and the native Kalispel people lived in the area. The Clark Fork River was an important aspect of their existence, and the Kalispels hosted an annual regional gathering at the mouth of the river. There, they hunted, fished,

Clark Fork River offers many opportunities to view wildlife, enjoy canoeing or kayaking, and simply rest and relax in this natural setting.

picked berries, and traded. The importance of this event and the key location at the mouth of the river continued as traders and trappers moved through the area, exploring the West. One British explorer, David Thompson, established a trading post on the banks of Lake Pend Oreille while he was searching for the headwaters of the Columbia River, and he was instrumental in the settlement of the Pend Oreille region.

As traffic through the West and Northwest continued to grow, new routes of transportation were needed. With the creation of the steamboat, the waterways in the area of the Pend Oreille Scenic Byway became connected, enabling people to travel efficiently from one place to another. When the Northern Pacific Railroad was being built in the Pend Oreille section, many structures, such as bridges, were built to span the many areas of water. The wooden bridge built to cross the Pack River was the longest structure in the entire transcontinental system.

Recreational: With unspoiled landscapes and clean country air, it is no wonder that Idaho is known for its many outdoor activities. Pend Oreille Scenic Byway is no exception, and with more than 100 miles of shoreline along Lake Pend Oreille, water recreational opportunities are never far away. Boating, fishing, sailing, and other water sports are all available along the byway. The water is clean and pure, and it draws visitors from around the world. In addition to the scenic and recreational Lake Pend Oreille, two rivers are accessible along the byway. The Clark Fork River stretches across two miles of delta and wetland; the river itself is a popular place to go fishing. The Pack River does not create such a vast delta, but it provides wonderful opportunities for canoeing and kayaking. The byway is located in Bonner County, which accounts for 20 percent of the total surface water in Idaho's 44 counties, and follows either a lake or river for its entire length.

Water sports may dominate the recreational scene, but a look toward the forests to the sides of the lake reveals an area rich in other recreational opportunities. A number of trails are accessible through the Kaniksu National Forest, affording you the chance to go hiking, biking, or horseback riding. Hunting, berry picking, and snowmobiling are additional activities that you can enjoy.

The abundance of water along the byway makes this an ideal route to travel for bird-watching. The delta area at the confluence of the Clark Fork River provides prime opportunity to see different waterfowl up close in the marshes and wetlands. A variety of fish can also be found in the lake and rivers of the byway, and 20-plus-pound rainbow or Mackinaw trout can be caught during week-long fishing derbies that begin in May and end in November. You may also spot deer and moose all along the byway and near the water.

Highlights:

Start at the resort town of Sandpoint, and end at the Cabinet Gorge Dam.

Sandpoint: Sandpoint has a public beach with swimming and boat access to Lake Pend Oreille, as well as plenty of places to shop, eat, and stay.

Schweitzer Mountain Ski Resort:

If it's winter, skiers can detour a short distance north from Sandpoint on Routes 2/95 to Schweitzer Mountain Ski Resort, Idaho's second largest, with six chairlifts. In summer, the chairlifts operate for scenic rides and to ferry hikers and mountain bikers up to the top.

Lake Pend Oreille: Head south and then go east on the Pend Oreille Scenic Byway, as the road hugs the northern shores of Lake Pend Oreille, Idaho's largest lake with more than 100 miles of shoreline.

Pack River Wildlife Area: Next, go to the Pack River Wildlife Area, a river delta system that's a haven for waterfowl and other wildlife. (Watch for moose along the shores.) There's primitive access for canoes and kayaks here.

Trestle Creek Recreation Area:

When the Trestle Creek Bridge crosses the Pack River, watch for the Trestle Creek Recreation Area, which provides open access to the lake as well as hiking trails. You might spot eagles in winter.

Pend Oreille Geologic Site: A turnout along the roadside marks the Pend Oreille Geologic Site, where there are panoramic views of the lake and its major islands.

Hope: The tiny town of Hope was the site of a settlement in 1809 by British explorer David Thompson, who built the first fur trading post in the Pacific Northwest. Hope is also a boating and swimming access area, with boat ramps and docks on Lake Pend Oreille.

Clark Fork River: As soon as Lake Pend Oreille ends, the Clark Fork River begins. Consider doing some fishing, or bird-watch for blue herons, ospreys, swans, and grebes. The Johnson Creek Recreation Area, close to the Clark Fork River, and the Denton Slough Waterfowl Area, a bay near the river, are good spots.

Clark Fork River Recreation Area:

The Clark Fork River Recreation Area offers river access for those who want to float down the peaceful Clark Fork River, as well as primitive campsites.

Cabinet Gorge Dam: The byway ends at the Idaho–Montana state line. Watch for the privately owned Cabinet Gorge Dam. Cabinet Gorge is the historic location of the face of the ice dam that created ancient glacial Lake Missoula. When the dam burst some 15,000 years ago, the rushing waters formed Lake Pend Oreille.

Lake Pend Oreille features plenty of opportunities for boating, kayaking, fishing, swumming, camping, and picnicking.

Wyoming Centennial Scenic Byway

Quick Facts

Length: 28 miles

Time to Allow: One hour

Consideration: The busiest season is July through September and the last week of December. There are occasional brief road closures during snowstorms.

Crossing the Continental Divide and a high mountain pass, the Wyoming Centennial Scenic Byway offers stunning mountain views, access to several national parks and forests, and chances to spot wildlife along the way.

Wyoming Centennial Scenic Byway is one of the most beautiful drives in the West, passing through some of the continent's most wild and spectacular country. The landscape changes dramatically along the way, from high desert badlands to alpine conifer forests and sage-covered hills. The byway begins nearly 7,000 feet above sea level, then climbs even higher, crossing the Continental Divide at the 9,658-foot Togwotee Pass. Before it reaches the pass, the byway offers a series of stunning views, including the Upper Wind River Valley, two mountain ranges, and strikingly shaped cliffs and rock formations. The descent into Grand Teton National Park is equally dramatic, with wonderful views of the jagged-peaked Grand Teton range as the road plunges down into Jackson Hole Valley.

The route provides access not just to Grand Teton, but to Yellowstone National Park to the north and the Jackson resort area to the south. Recreational opportunities are available all along the way, including two national forests with campgrounds and hiking trails, rivers and lakes popular for fishing and boating, and, in winter, venues for skiing and snowmobiling. Chances to spot wildlife—including elk (which spend their winters in the National Elk Refuge near Jackson and their summers in Grand Teton and Yellowstone National Parks)—are abundant.

Highlights:

You are encouraged to take this enjoyable tour of the Wyoming Centennial Scenic Byway.

Dubois: The southern tip of the byway begins at the rustic town of Dubois, elevation 6,917 feet, a center for trout fishing on the Upper Wind River. In Dubois, the National Bighorn Sheep Interpretive Center has educational exhibits and information on bighorn sheep habitat and conservation. Dubois is also home to the Wind River Historical Center, which features displays on the settlement and history of the Upper Wind River Valley as well as the geology and natural history of the region.

Shoshone National Forest: Take U.S. 26/287 northwest, which parallels

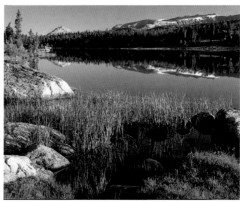

The varied landscape of the Shoshone National Forest includes breathtaking rivers, meadows, and mountains.

the Wind River as it travels past the Wind River Range and the volcanic Absaroka Range; watch for the nearly 12,000-foot Ramshorn Peak. The 2.4-million-acre Shoshone National Forest, which blankets the land both to the east and west of the road, is thick with aspens, evergreens, spruce, and willows and is home to 236 peaks and 156 glaciers.

Tie Hack Memorial: About 17 miles from Dubois, the byway passes the Tie Hack Memorial, dedicated to the early 20th-century lumberjacks (mostly from Sweden and other Scandinavian countries) who cut and shaped railroad ties by hand from local forests, for use in building the transcontinental railroad. Each man could hack about 30 ties per day, earning 10 cents per tie.

Breccia Cliffs, Pinnacle Buttes, and Falls Campground: Next, watch for the castlelike rock formations known as the Breccia Cliffs and the Pinnacle Buttes in the Teton Wilderness. Stop at Falls Campground to follow the short trail to Brooks Falls, or hike farther to Wind River Lake. In the meadows, watch for wildlife such as elk, moose, deer, and even grizzlies.

Togwotee Pass: The road rises to Togwotee Pass, elevation 9,658 feet, which marks the Continental Divide. Snow can be heavy in winter and often lingers by the roadside into July. Stop at the overlook for a great view.

Grand Tetons: The road then descends, steeply at points. Soon coming into view are the Grand Tetons, the jagged, glacially carved string of snowcapped peaks that rise like skyscrapers out of the valley and are the most recognizable mountains in Wyoming. Be sure to stop at the overlook, which provides one of the best views of the range, including 13,770-foot Grand Teton and seven other peaks topping 12,000 feet. There are also campgrounds and picnic areas as the road levels off into a valley.

Grand Teton National Park: When the byway reaches beautiful Grand Teton National Park, there are continuing views of the Tetons, framed by sagebrush, forests, lakes, and the Snake River. Float trips are offered on the Snake River. Hiking, camping, mountain climbing, boating, and kayaking are all popular in the park, which is also a favorite of photographers.

Yellowstone National Park or Jackson: At Moran Junction, the end of the byway, drivers face a tough choice. The largest park in the lower 48, Yellowstone National Park lies 27 miles to the north via the Rockefeller Parkway. Route 26, meanwhile, turns south toward the resort area of Jackson, passing the 25,000-acre National Elk Refuge en route. The refuge is home to some 7,500 elk each winter. In summer, watch for elk in Grand Teton National Park or in Yellowstone.

Lake Tahoe–Eastshore Drive

The eastern shore of America's highest alpine lake is the scenic centerpiece of this resort-lined roadway. Four-season recreation abounds, from swimming in crystalline waters to skiing down snowcapped peaks or even rolling the dice.

Called the most beautiful drive in America, the 28-mile Lake Tahoe–Eastshore Drive affords breathtaking views of spectacularly clear Lake Tahoe. The pristine alpine lake is surrounded by the snowcapped mountains of the Sierras. The byway is mostly undeveloped, except for the excellent recreational opportunities afforded by the lake, including the Zephyr Cove Resort, stables, campgrounds, the Tahoe Rim Trail, ski resorts, hotels, casinos, and fabulous golf courses. As part of the Pony Express Trail and home to the historic sacred grounds of the Washoe Indians, Lake Tahoe's eastern shore offers a wide variety of activities during every season. The Lake Tahoe–Eastshore Drive is one of the most beautiful winter byways in the country, with the draw of an alpine climate and the ever-crystalline lake. Throughout the year, visitors come from miles around to enjoy Lake Tahoe.

Cultural: Lake Tahoe is well known for its diverse and interesting culture of both recreation and arts. Events take place through the year that attract visitors for reasons ranging from high drama to downhill ski relays. During the summer months, artists gather at Lake Tahoe for exhibitions and workshops, making the area one of the best places to find cutting-edge and classic artwork. While Tahoe's art is a sight to behold, don't miss out on any of the many festivals that take place throughout the year. The festivals themselves are works of art.

Perhaps Lake Tahoe's best-known summer festival is the Lake Tahoe Shakespeare Festival at Sand Harbor, which takes place every summer. Imagine relaxing on a beautiful sand beach while enjoying your favorite Shakespearean drama. Enjoy the first-class performance near crystal blue waters, set against the stately backdrop of the Sierra Nevada, under a thousand glittering stars.

Lake Tahoe offers a variety of winter festivals as well. Winter begins early here with the Native American Festival and Snow Dance. During the Snow Dance, a two-day event held the first weekend in October, Native Americans

Crystal-clear Lake Tahoe provides a variety of recreational choices including sailing, fishing, and swimming, all with the snowcapped Sierras as a backdrop.

dance in full regalia and pray for snow to ensure an abundantly snowy winter.

Historical: Lake Tahoe was originally a peaceful, earthy place, connected to the rest of the world by narrow trails over high mountain passes. Native Americans would gather in the summer to fish, hunt, and harvest nuts and berries for the long winter spent in Nevada's high desert. The American Indians called their special place Da ow aga, meaning "the edge of the lake." It is believed that Tahoe got its name from the European settlers' mispronunciation of the first two syllables. Tahoe remains a gathering place for people hoping to enjoy the outdoors.

While on an expedition in search of the mythical Buenaventura River in 1844, explorers Kit Carson and John C. Frémont instead stumbled on Lake Tahoe, letting out the secret that had long been kept from the outside world. Frémont's accurate accounts of his High Sierra travels led other curious explorers to the mountain lake. Soon after, gold and silver prospectors flocked to Lake Tahoe, but their explorations were in vain. However, in 1859, rich silver deposits in nearby Virginia City began a logging boom. While the Comstock Lode opened the area to big business, it nearly stripped the Lake Basin of its first growth of trees because its lumber was used for timber supports in the underground mines.

As more people laid eyes on the natural treasure, word of the wondrous lake spread through the land. Among these proclaimers was humorist Mark Twain, who described the area as wholesome and pure. Stagecoach stops over the Sierra exposed visitors to Tahoe's scenic beauty and tranquility. Many were lured to stay because they felt that they had found paradise.

Westerners began to develop Lake Tahoe's shore in the early 1900s as a summer retreat for San Francisco's elite. Plush hotels sprang up, and guests amused themselves at Lucky Baldwin's Tallac House and Casino, known today as the Tallac Historic Site at South Shore. Gambling was illegal on the California side of the lake, but enforcement was sporadic, and arrangements with cooperative authorities were routine. Raiding law enforcers often found patrons playing nothing more objectionable than pinochle and canasta. By 1941, the Tahoe Tattler was reporting that Tahoe's number two industry was nightlife, a close second to the resorts. Each weekend, an estimated 3,000 people would flock to the bars, casinos, and dance halls and spend anywhere from 25 cents for a glass of beer to $50,000 for an expensive game of chance.

A boom of another kind was soon occurring at Lake Tahoe. Using Nevada's advantageous tax laws as bait, an enterprising businessman named Norman Blitz convinced more than 80 of the nation's most rich and famous to make Lake Tahoe their home. This effort sparked the development of thriving real estate and construction industries at the lake.

Recreational: When it comes to winter activities, Lake Tahoe has it covered (literally). Tahoe has more snow (averaging about 400 inches per season), more variety, and more ways to play than just about any other place. Lake Tahoe has the largest concentration of ski resorts in North America, including six world-class resorts you won't want to miss. The terrain ranges from leisurely bowls to steep hills that make your heart thump. However, excellent skiing and snowboarding are not all that Lake Tahoe has to offer. Snowmobiling, snowshoe excursions, snow tubing, and cross-country treks open up the millions of acres of national forest land waiting to be explored. Ice skating, sleigh rides, and sledding are fun activities close to the byway. Lake Tahoe also hosts numerous special events all winter long, including SnowFest!

If you prefer warmer weather, Lake Tahoe's links are second to none. Extra altitude makes even the worst golfer feel like a pro, and the breathtaking backdrops and outstanding course architecture will make bogeys seem a little less burdensome. The Lake Tahoe region boasts more than a dozen courses at all levels of play.

Surrounded by national forest lands, wilderness, and state parks, Lake Tahoe possesses some of the country's most spectacular scenery. With almost 300 miles of trails, hikers have plenty of room to roam. Backcountry buffs can trek up waterfall trails, hike along wildflower-carpeted meadows, or visit serene alpine lakes and stunning overlooks of Lake Tahoe. There are flat, moderate, and steep trails to suit every ability. Looping its way around the lake, the Tahoe Rim Trail, with

Abundant hiking trails in the Lake Tahoe area afford ample opportunity for scenic vistas.

paths for hiking and horseback riding, offers 165 miles of trail, with elevations ranging from 6,300 feet to 9,400 feet. This trail is generally moderate in difficulty, with a 10 percent average grade, and provides views of Lake Tahoe, the high desert, and snowcapped peaks of the Sierra Nevada. Trailheads accessible along the byway include Tahoe Meadows Trailhead to Tunnel Creek Road (Highway 431), Spooner Summit Trailhead (Highway 50), and Spooner Summit South to Kingsbury Grade. The Tunnel Creek Station Road Trail starts at Highway 28 across from Hidden Beach about one mile past Ponderosa Ranch (there's no sign, so look for the gate). This is a steep trail road located

at the ruins of the western portal of the old log flume tunnel. There is limited parking along Highway 28. The Marlette Lake Trail starts near the Spooner Lake Picnic Area at the junction of Highway 28 and 50 at the green metal gate on the east side of Highway 28. This trail is about five miles each way to the lake and passes through mostly mild terrain.

A combination of one of the world's top single-track trails, spectacular views, and miles of open backcountry beckons bikers from around the world to the Lake Tahoe basin. The best-known Tahoe bike trail is the spectacular Flume Trail, carved out of the edge of a mountain some 2,000 feet above the lake's stunning east shore. The Flume Trail follows a precarious route dug out of the granite cliffs more than a century ago by laborers developing a water supply and lumber transport for the mines of the Comstock Lode.

Today, the 14-mile Flume Trail offers a challenging ride with a 1,000-foot elevation gain and sweeping views, all within Nevada's Lake Tahoe State Park. The common starting point for this trail is Spooner Lake, which features parking and trail information. Located at the junction of Highways 28 and 50, Spooner Lake is a 15-minute drive south from Incline Village. Groves of aspen trees, towering peaks, old-growth pine, and high mountain lakes greet bikers along the Flume Trail. After a quick turn onto a small outlet creek, the trail suddenly clings to a slope overlooking the azure Lake Tahoe. The northern terminus of the trail can take the rider to either Sand Harbor or the Ponderosa Ranch. For the ambitious rider, a loop via Tunnel Creek Road, Red House, and Hobart Lake creates a 25-mile loop back to Marlette Lake, as well as a stunning downhill ride to Spooner.

Highlights:

To hit the highlights of the Lake Tahoe–Eastshore Drive, consider following this itinerary.

Crystal Bay: You may want to begin traveling the byway at the northern terminus at Crystal Bay along the California–Nevada border. There are several casinos in this area to enjoy.

Incline Village: The highway winds toward Incline Village, one of Tahoe's finest communities. A side trip up Mount Rose Highway, approximately four miles, leads to a lookout over the entire Tahoe Basin.

Ponderosa Ranch: Back on Highway 28, the Ponderosa Ranch is the location of TV's legendary Bonanza series that made Lake Tahoe famous worldwide. The Ponderosa offers Cartwright Ranch House tours, an Old West town with shops and memorabilia, summer hay-wagon breakfasts, and more.

Sand Harbor, Spooner Lake, and Glenbrook: The byway continues south down the east shore. One of Tahoe's most beautiful beaches, Sand Harbor is located here in the Lake Tahoe Nevada State Park. Following the bouldered Nevada shore, the highway continues south through forests of pine and fir. Stop at Spooner Lake for wooded picnic areas and a walk along the water. Turn right at the intersection of Highway 50, and head south past historic Glenbrook, once a busy logging town and now an exclusive community and golf course.

Cave Rock and Zephyr Cove: Your next landmark is Cave Rock, where the highway passes through 25 yards of solid stone. This is a holy spot for the native Washoe Indians who put their deceased to rest in the cold waters below the outcropping. Farther along is Zephyr Cove with its beautiful old lodge, beach, and tour boats.

Stateline: The tour now returns you to South Lake Tahoe and the high-rise hotel/casinos in the Stateline area, a perfect place to stop at a restaurant or lounge, take in a show, or try your luck in the casinos.

Recreational opportunities abound at Incline Village. Private beaches with picnic areas and world-renowned golf courses can be enjoyed here.

Las Vegas Strip

The most glittering, neon-lit drive in America explodes with visual delights as it leads past exotic and lavish casino resorts. It's the only byway in the country that's more scenic by night than by day.

Often referred to as the Jewel of the Desert, Las Vegas has long been recognized as the entertainment vacation capital of the country. The Las Vegas Strip—at the heart of this playland—sparkles like no other place on Earth. More than 35 million visitors from around the world are drawn to the lights of the strip each year to experience its unique blend of exciting entertainment, scenic beauty, and lavishly landscaped resorts.

Gambling is only the beginning for many of the resorts along the Las Vegas Strip. These outrageous destinations transport their visitors through time and place, and offer much more than slot machines.

The Las Vegas Strip hosts thousands of motorists a week; after you arrive on the strip, however, you may be surprised to find that it's also a very enjoyable walking environment. The strip is the only byway that is more scenic at night than during the day. In fact, 365 days of the year, 24 hours a day, the Neon Trail offers a fascinating foray past

New York–New York Casino is one of the famous gaming attractions in Las Vegas, Nevada.

spectacular resorts featuring a variety of visual delights. Whether it's pirates plundering, fiery volcanoes spouting, or tropical gardens luring the weary, the Las Vegas Strip offers a variety of fascinating visual experiences that enchant and mesmerize visitors of all ages. The many facets of this corridor make it truly a one-of-a-kind destination.

Cultural: While Las Vegas is perhaps best known for its gaming culture—the popularity and influence of which have spread to cities all over the world—the Las Vegas Strip possesses many other outstanding cultural amenities. The diversity and magnificence of the architecture of the hotels and resorts along the strip are certainly worth noting. Some of the world's most talented architects have created complex fantasylands all along the strip. Just a few of the more recent projects include reproductions of the streets of New York, a bayside

Tuscan village, the canals of Venice, and a replica of the Eiffel Tower and the Arc de Triomphe.

Many of the resorts on the Las Vegas Strip also feature world-class art galleries full of paintings by world-renowned artists, such as Renoir, Monet, and van Gogh. Other resorts hold galleries of unique items, such as antique automobiles or wax figures. The Guinness World of Records Museum offers an interesting array of the unusual, and the World of Coca-Cola Las Vegas features an interactive storytelling theater.

Various hotels on the Las Vegas Strip feature a variety of top-caliber theatrical and dance shows. Several hotels and casinos host world-class sporting events and concerts featuring top-name entertainers. And no matter where you go on the strip, you are bound to run into the dazzling light displays that permeate the area. The magical recreations found along the byway are the symbols of our society's most fantastic dreams of luxury.

The Las Vegas Strip, world-renowned for its neon glitter, possesses an equally colorful historical past. The unique history of Las Vegas is undeniably entwined with the culture of gaming. Gambling was legalized in Nevada in 1931, and the first casino opened downtown that same year. Competition was intense, and casino builders soon were looking at land outside the city limits just south of downtown along Highway 91 (the Old Los Angeles Highway), which is now known as the Las Vegas Strip.

Most of the Las Vegas Strip is not really located within the Las Vegas city limits, but along a corridor of South Las Vegas Boulevard located in unincorporated Clark County. The area was sparsely developed until 1938, when the first resort property was built four miles south of downtown Las Vegas at the corner of San Francisco Avenue (now Sahara) and Highway 91 (South Las Vegas Boulevard). Reportedly, city officials had denied licenses to certain businesspeople with questionable connections who had applied to build a casino downtown. Undaunted, they decided to build outside the city limits, just south of the downtown district.

In 1940, construction began on El Rancho Vegas resort at the corner of San Francisco Avenue and Highway 91. The original El Rancho Vegas introduced a new style of recreation and entertainment to the Nevada desert by combining lodging, gambling, restaurants, entertainment, shops, a travel agency, horse-back riding, and swimming in one resort. El Rancho Vegas was followed a year later by the Last Frontier Resort Hotel and Casino. The well-known Little Church of the West was originally constructed in the resort's Frontier Village. Listed on the National Register of Historic Places, the small chapel has survived four moves on the strip.

Map labels: Bonzana Gift Shop; To Downtown Las Vegas; Guiness World of Records Museum; Sahara; Saharа Avenue; Industrial Road; Paradise Road; Joe W. Brown Drive; Circus Circus; Spring Mountain Road; Visitor Information Center; Las Vegas Convention Center; Desert Inn Road; Treasure Island; Venetian; Las Vegas Strip; Swenson Street; The Mirage; Koval Lane; Caesar's Palace; Bellagio; Paris; Flamingo Road; University of Nevada Las Vegas; Park MGM; Las Vegas Boulevard; Audrie St.; Koval Lane; Harmon Avenue; Paradise Rd.; New York–New York; MGM Grand; Tropicana Avenue; Excalibur; Tropicana; Luxor; Reno Avenue; Swenson Street; Mandalay Bay; Russell Rd.; Little Church of the West; McCarran International Airport; "Welcome to Fabulous Las Vegas" sign

One of the strip's more colorful (and infamous) characters, Ben "Bugsy" Siegel (reputed hit man for New York mobster Lucky Luciano) oversaw the construction of the fabulous Flamingo Hotel, the third major (and most extravagant) resort to be built on the strip. Although Siegel met his unfortunate demise soon after the resort's 1946 opening, his prophecies for the future of Las Vegas came true. This new popular playground of Hollywood stars prospered, with the Flamingo setting the stage for the many luxurious resorts yet to be imagined.

As the 1950s began, only four major resorts stood along the strip, but three more major players were about to hit the scene. The Desert Inn, the Sahara, and the Sands all arrived on the strip in the early 1950s, further enhancing the strip's image as a self-contained playground by featuring elaborate tennis courts, an 18-hole golf course, larger casinos, and fabulous showrooms with Broadway's and Hollywood's brightest stars. Las Vegas has continued to build on this legacy, developing newer and more elaborate resorts often to make certain that Las Vegas retains the image of the most fabulous playground on Earth.

Recreational: The simplest and easiest recreation on the strip is strolling and sightseeing along the boulevard.

Intriguing arrays of fantasylands in lush surroundings welcome you to the strip. But the excitement only begins with sightseeing. From comfortable and plush hotels to exciting displays of lights and fountains, Las Vegas creates a dreamlike environment with color, sound, and light all combined to make the experience on the strip memorable.

The Bellagio Hotel and Casino in Las Vegas is accented by Lake Bellagio and the spectacular Fountains of Bellagio.

For the more adventuresome, roller coasters featured at several hotels provide rides that twist, loop, and turn for your delight. Other resorts provide 3-D ride films appealing to the senses of sight, sound, and motion. Many of these rides feature the latest technologies for extra thrills. Most of the resorts along the strip offer displays of grandeur for every visitor to enjoy. Anyone driving the byway can stop to see erupting volcanoes, dueling ships, dancing fountains, circus acts, and lush tropical gardens.

In addition to a variety of theatrical and dance shows, the resorts have varied spectator sports, such as boxing matches. There isn't a resort on the strip that doesn't offer visitors every amenity imaginable. World-class spas, pools, and exercise rooms are as enticing as the casinos. When you aren't searching for slot machines, you may choose to browse through the many stores and boutiques each resort has to offer. You will find everything from designer fashion to specialty candies to Las Vegas souvenirs. Whatever you choose to do, you can find it in Las Vegas.

Highlights:

The Southern Las Vegas Strip Walking Tour begins at Las Vegas Boulevard and Russell Road, although you can go the opposite way by reading this list from the bottom up.

Little Church of the West: The famous "Welcome to Fabulous Las

Vegas" sign announces that you're on the right track. On the east side of the strip, you see the Little Church of the West, the site of many celebrity weddings and a favorite place today to have a memorable wedding.

Mandalay Bay: Park the car at the free parking garage at Mandalay Bay (most of the large hotels offer plenty of covered free parking). Explore the tropical-themed hotel, including a fun sand and surf beach. Mandalay Bay is one of the newer hotels on the strip (built in 1999), and that makes it a popular attraction.

Luxor: From Mandalay Bay, you can walk north to Luxor, the great black glass pyr-

Caesars operates a half-scale, 540-foot tall replica of the Eiffel Tower.

amid. (If you prefer, hop on the free tram that takes you right to the front doors of Luxor—you may want to save your energy for later in the trip.) While at Luxor, don't miss the King Tut Tomb exhibit, an exact replica of the ancient Egyptian pharaoh's tomb. A rotating IMAX film experience is also a popular attraction here. This unique hotel is amazing and has one of the largest atriums in the world.

Excalibur: After spending time at Luxor, hop on the tram that takes you over to Excalibur. This is the place for an exciting dinner and show. The majestic castle offers adventure at its Fantasy Faire Midway, an arena of games appropriate for everyone in the family.

New York–New York: After spending time at the medieval castle, cross the over-street walkway into 1930s- and '40s-inspired New York–New York. Billed as "the Greatest City in Las Vegas," New York–New York has attractions that are all themed to the New York life. Park Avenue shopping, a fast-paced Manhattan roller coaster, and Greenwich Village eateries help keep the theme intact.

Monte Carlo: It's not time to stop yet. The Monte Carlo, just north of New York–New York, is just as classy, but with a purely European twist.

Bellagio: After a jaunt to Monte Carlo, walk farther north, getting close to the

halfway point. The big lake and fantastic fountains are part of Bellagio, a hotel that strives for utter perfection. Check out the art gallery here; it houses some fantastic pieces. The gallery has original paintings by van Gogh, Monet, Renoir, Cezanne, and other masters.

Paris: Now, at Flamingo Road, cross the street to the east—over to Paris. This is the midpoint of the tour, and this area is full of places to sit and rest or to grab a bite to eat. While at Paris, tour the Eiffel Tower. This is an exact replica, in half scale, of the original in France. The plans for the original were lent to the developers of the hotel so they could be as accurate as possible. There's also a two-thirds-scale replica of the Arc de Triomphe near the hotel entrance—complete with Napoleon's victories inscribed on it.

Tropicana: Just south of the MGM Grand is the famous Tropicana, home to the longest-running show on the strip: Folies Bergere.

Southern Las Vegas Strip: Finish off the tour of the Southern Las Vegas Strip by driving north back past the Tropicana and MGM Grand and beyond. The drive provides amazing views that you may have missed on the walk.

Pyramid Lake Scenic Byway

Shimmering like a blue jewel in the desert north of Reno, ancient Pyramid Lake is a haven for migrating waterfowl and home to striking rock formations. This byway offers enchanting views of its natural treasures.

Pyramid Lake is a bright jewel in the arid Nevada landscape. Fish, animal, and plant life are sustained by its 300-foot-deep waters and by the fresh water flowing in the Truckee River. In addition to the cui-ui fish, an indigenous species found only in Pyramid Lake, the lake is known for the Lahontan cutthroat trout that the Native Americans manage through their fisheries program. The mountains surrounding the lake support deer, antelope, and bighorn sheep. The lake is also a resting place for a variety of migrating waterfowl. Anaho Island, a National Wildlife Refuge, is the breeding ground for a large colony of American white pelicans. It is also home to a variety of other shorebirds. The tufa formations found at this lake are some of the lake's most distinctive natural features. These formations are calcium carbonate deposits formed by precipitation over hot springs. They include the Pyramid (which gives the lake its name) and the Needles.

Cultural: The Pyramid Lake Paiute nation is governed by ten council members who are elected biannually in December

and on staggered two-year terms. The majority of enrolled members, numbering around 1,700 people, reside on the Pyramid Lake Indian Reservation, and approximately 12 percent of this membership live in other areas throughout the western United States.

There are strong cultural ties between the lake and the Kuyuidokado. Unfortunately, the cui-ui fish are endangered. So are the Lahontan cutthroat trout, which are also indigenous to Pyramid Lake and Truckee River. The Kuyuidokado feel it is their duty to save these two fish species because they consider themselves the keepers of the lake.

Historical: Hundreds of years before settlers traveled through Nevada, the Paiute Indians lived near Pyramid Lake, then called Coo-yu-ee Pah. Their traditional culture was centered around the lake. The Paiute depended on

the cui-ui fish to survive. Unfortunately, in 1859, the Paiute Indian Reservation was formed, giving only a fraction of the land to the Paiute people. They continued to live as they had been and create a culture rich in history and family.

The unusual stone pyramid shape rising up out of the water is what gives Pyramid Lake its name. Other interesting rock formations can be found here as well.

The present name of the lake was given by John C. Frémont in January 1844. The first band of explorers stumbled upon the lake after a difficult journey through the harsh desert that lasted several weeks. They pitched their camp near a striking 400-foot-high rock island outcropping. Frémont wrote in his journal on January 14 and suggested a name for the fascinating lake: Pyramid Lake. The explorers were also captivated by the stone needles, pinnacles, and steaming sulfur springs, which the Paiute people still hold sacred today.

Recreational: Pyramid Lake offers all kinds of opportunities to enjoy the surrounding nature. You can hike, rock climb, ride horseback, backpack, and so much more. And, after a full day of activity, hot springs at the north end of the lake among the needle rocks allow you to relax while enjoying Pyramid Lake's famous tufa formations. The lake itself draws the most recreationists; it is a favorite of anglers, who throughout the history of the lake have gone from fishing as a means of survival to fishing as a business venture to fishing for sport.

Fishing at Pyramid Lake is an experience all its own. The water is unlike most lake water and is a startling pastel blue. The surroundings are pure desert, with little vegetation. After some practice, many fishers have discovered that the best way to catch fish in Pyramid Lake is from the top of a five-foot ladder or other tall object. The fish come into the shallows, and the added altitude gives anglers a better view, as well as a longer casting range. Be careful, though. While you can see the fish, the fish can also see you. Fish often roam the edges of the lake near a series of ledges or drop-offs. If you stand on a tall object and wear polarizing lenses, you can actually see the fish take the fly ten feet away. Pyramid Lake has also been known for the size of its fish, especially the cutthroat trout. In 1925, a Paiute named Johnny Skimmerhorn caught the world's record cutthroat—a 41-pounder. Photographs from the '20s and '30s show celebrities such as Clark Gable struggling to hold up a pair of massive cutthroat. Another photograph shows a group of Nevadans peeking out from behind a line of shimmering fish that stretches eight feet long from a day's catch. Unfortunately, the fish are no longer as large due to extensive fishing, but five- to ten-pounders are not uncommon.

Highlights:

On this Pyramid Lake must-see tour, you can start in either Sparks or Wadsworth because the driving directions given here start and end in the Reno/Sparks area.

Numana Hatchery and Visitor Center: Start your trip in Wadsworth, and then drive north along Route 447, following the course of the Truckee River. You can stop at the Numana Hatchery and Visitor Center to learn about the area's natural history and the Native American fisheries program or take a walk along the wetlands nature trail, where you experience the unique habitats of the river valley.

Museum and Visitor Center: As you continue to drive north, you will come over a rise and see the lake spread out before you. Just ahead is the Scenic Byway Visitor Center and Tribal Museum. From here, you can take a side trip north on Route 447 into the town of Nixon, site of the Tribal Headquarters, and beyond to Marble Bluff Fish Facility and Lake Winnemucca.

Pyramid Lake: You can also head west on Route 446 toward Sutcliffe. Route 446 follows the west shore of Pyramid Lake, with plenty of beaches for swimming, fishing, or enjoying a picnic lunch. In Sutcliffe, you'll find the Pyramid Lake Marina, with a visitor center and museum, as well as stores and visitor services. North of Sutcliffe are more beaches, especially at Pelican Point and Warrior Point.

Mullen Pass: Returning south from Sutcliffe, take Route 445 south toward Sparks. As you drive up toward Mullen Pass, you can stop at the pull-off on the left for a scenic vista of the lake. If you get a chance to visit here as the sun sets, the Pyramid, Anaho Island, and the slopes of the Lake Range may be bathed in a red glow, offering a dramatic counterpoint to the urban glitter awaiting you as you return to Reno.

Petroglyphs like this one at Lake Winnemucca can be found on the byway.

Dinosaur Diamond Prehistoric Highway

Following this diamond-shaped byway is like taking a trip to prehistory. Dinosaur bones, Native American rock art, and geological wonders await—along with current-day hiking and biking trails, desert festivals, and wide-open spaces.

Arches National Park preserves more than 2,000 natural sandstone arches, including the world-famous Delicate Arch.

Quick Facts

Length: 512 miles

Time to Allow: 12 hours to several days

Consideration: The mountain passes at Reservation Ridge on U.S. 191 and Douglas Pass on CO 139 can be treacherous during winter storms. These roads are rarely officially closed, but there can be delays of up to a few hours. Cleveland Lloyd Dinosaur Quarry is at the end of 13 miles of gravel road that is accessible to sedans in all weather except deep snow; it is closed during the winter months. The Mill Canyon Dinosaur Trail and Copper Ridge Dinosaur Trackway are reached by a couple of miles of dirt road that is accessible to two-wheel-drive automobiles in good weather but are not advisable in wet conditions. Dinosaur trackways are difficult to see under snow cover.

The Dinosaur Diamond Prehistoric Highway provides a unique and unparalleled opportunity to experience the thrilling story of dinosaurs and the science and history of discovery behind them. The route combines opportunities to witness dinosaur bones still in the ground being excavated and to see dinosaur bones prepared by paleontologists for museums. Museums all along the byway display both reconstructed skeletons and fleshed-out recreations of dinosaurs found in the area. Between and sometimes overlapping the dinosaur sites are areas of major archaeological interest. The prehistoric Native Americans who occupied this area saw its many rock cliffs as ideal surfaces for their petroglyphs and pictographs. Some of the finest examples and densest concentrations of this rock art in North America are located along or near the byway.

Along with unique red, gray, and green rock formations, you can enjoy forested mountain passes, canyons, cliffs, rivers, and plateaus along the Dinosaur Diamond Prehistoric Highway. Wide-open spaces and miles of unobstructed views are the reward for those who travel this byway.

Cultural: Eastern Utah has been and continues to be home to many ranches and cattle. In celebration of this culture, rodeos are held periodically throughout the area. In Vernal, the Dinosaur Round-up Rodeo is one of the largest rodeos in the world. In Price, the Black Diamond Stampede Rodeo is held every year. In Moab, Butch Cassidy Days celebrate the history of the area's most famous outlaws. The San Rafael Swell was a favorite hideout for Butch Cassidy and the Sundance Kid and their gang. The Outlaw Trail went from the wild country of Robber's Roost down by Hanksville, up through the San Rafael Swell and either Nine Mile Canyon or along the canyons of the Green River into the Uinta Basin. It then either continued along the Green or up and over the eastern Uintas to Brown's Park in the tri-state area of Wyoming, Colorado, and Utah. Matt Warner, a former outlaw in the gang, was elected marshal in Price for a number of years.

Moab is known as the mountain bike capital of the world, but it is also home to many different festivals and celebrations. Every year in the early spring, participants from all over gather for the Jeep Safari. The slick red rock and warming temperatures in the desert at that time of the year make it a perfect location for extreme driving. If you have more traditional events in mind, the Moab Film Festival showcases the work of independent filmmakers, and Moab hosts an outdoor music festival as well.

Stroll by Colorado's largest and most diverse outdoor sculpture exhibit, on display along Grand Junction's downtown shopping park. The exhibit, entitled Art on the Corner, highlights a unique variety of work by local artists. The nearly 20-year-old ongoing event introduces visitors to many distinct artistic approaches.

Historical: The first recorded venture of Europeans into the area was the Escalante–Dominguez Expedition in 1776. This expedition began in Santa Fe and attempted to blaze a trail to California in order to access the missions located there; however, their journey was unsuccessful due to the barriers formed by the western Utah deserts. The expedition was led by Father Silvestre Velez de Escalante and Father Francisco Dominguez, accompanied by Captain Bernardo de Miera y Pacheco, a retired military engineer. They explored Canyon Pintado

from Douglas Pass toward what is now Rangely, Colorado; crossed the Green River near Jensen, Utah; and traveled as far west as Spanish Fork before turning back south to return to Santa Fe.

While Escalante and Dominguez came to the area in search of another route west, others have been drawn to eastern Utah because of scientific exploration. Beginning with John C. Frémont in the early 1840s, reports of the majesty of the mountains, the roaring rivers, the expanse and austerity of the deserts, the abundance of game, and the clues to vast mineral resources

Island in the Sky area of Canyonlands National Park rests 1,000 feet above the surrounding terrain. Green River Overlook gives visitors a sweeping view.

have enticed adventurers to the inter-mountain west of the United States. John Wesley Powell, Clarence King, and Ferdinand V. Hayden led extensive geological surveys that helped quantify these resources. Their reports tempted paleontologists with a vast array of un-described fossils, particularly dinosaurs and prehistoric mammals.

Settlement in the area inevitably brought about great changes to the landscape, such as mining. In the Uinta Basin, Gilsonite was the first hydrocar-bon to be mined, bringing a small, nar-row-gauge railroad (the Uinta Railroad) into the southeastern edge of the basin near Dragon. Although several attempts were made to build more railroads into the basin, none was successful. As a re-sult, the Uinta Basin remains one of the largest areas of the United States to be undeveloped by railroads. After World War II, petro-leum devel-opment and phosphate mining be-came integral to the rural economy. The railroad from Grand Junc-tion, Colorado, to Price, Utah, brought the development of the coal resources in Carbon and Emery counties. As a result of this mining industry, an influx of some 18 different ethnic groups from across southern and eastern Europe and Asia came to work in the mines.

Recreational: River rafting is a popular sport to participate in along the byway. Both calm-water and white water trips are available through compa-nies out of Vernal, Moab, and Green River. The white water sections can be frightening even to experienced river runners during the high water levels of spring melt, yet some stretches of both the Green and Colorado Rivers have flat-water that can be enjoyable in canoes. Grand scenery waits around every bend in the river. In fact, the Green River in Desolation Canyon has cliffs higher than the Grand Canyon in Arizona.

Hiking opportunities are everywhere along the byway. The terrain is varied, giving visitors a feel for the many aspects of the landscape along this route. In the mountains, numerous spectacular peaks and lakes are ac-cessible to hikers. The Uintas Mountain Range, the largest east–west mountain range in the 48 contiguous United States, includes the highest point in Utah—Kings Peak—at 13,528 feet. The desert, particularly near Moab, is another popular place to hike and is an entirely different experience from alpine hiking. The red slickrock around Moab provides the perfect surface for hiking while looking for dinosaur trackways or arches. All of the national parks and monuments along the byway are outstanding places for hiking and camping as well. Outfitters are available all along the byway for visitors who want guides, horses, or even llamas to help with the load. Hunting and fishing are also popular recreational activities in the area.

Moab has world-famous mountain biking trails to challenge expert riders and lure beginners. The city has quickly become a mountain bikers' paradise, with trails traveling over many miles,

The Fremont Culture of prehistoric American Indians left petroglyphs and pictographs along the walls of Nine Mile Canyon.

often on slickrock. The Slickrock Bike Trail is located east of Moab in the Sand Flats Recreation Area. The Poison Spider Mesa Trail is another popular trail for both jeeps and bikes and is located on the Potash Road. This trail offers spectacular views of the area surrounding Moab and the Colorado River.

Winter sports are also popular along this byway. Snowshoeing, cross-country skiing, snowmobiling, and ice fishing can be enjoyed in the high country, while hiking (without the summer heat) is a popular activity in the southern desert areas.

Highlights:

You can start anywhere along this circular byway, which loops through northeastern Utah and northwestern Colorado. For purposes of this tour, start in the southeastern Utah portion of the loop.

Hole 'N the Rock: At Cisco, Utah, just off I-70, follow Route 128 south to Moab, home of the Hole 'N the Rock, a 5,000-square-foot dwelling carved into huge sandstone rock. Moab sits at the foot of a mini-loop at the bottom of the larger byway loop.

Arches National Park: From Moab, follow U.S. 191 a short distance north to the visitor center for Arches National Park, a spectacular outdoor museum and site of the greatest concentration of natural stone arches and bridges in the world. Once the bed of an ancient sea, Arches National Park has more than 2,000 giant stone arches as well as pinnacles and spires. Dinosaur tracks and American Indian rock art are also preserved here. You can hike, backpack, camp, or sightsee along 24 miles of paved roads.

Cleveland Lloyd Dinosaur Quarry: Now follow U.S. 191 (which temporarily joins with U.S. 6) as it heads west and then north along the large byway loop. The Cleveland Lloyd Dinosaur Quarry lies south of the town of Price not far from the byway. The quarry contains one of the densest concentrations of Jurassic dinosaur bones ever found (12,000, from 70 different dinosaurs), supplying museums around the world. There are picnic areas and hiking trails here.

Flaming Gorge Recreation Area: Continue on U.S. 191, which now loops northeast toward Vernal. If you'd like to cool off or fish at a lake, the Flaming Gorge Recreation Area lies north of Vernal along U.S. 191, surrounding 91-mile-long Flaming Gorge Reservoir and 500-foot-high Flaming Gorge Dam. The reservoir extends north into Wyoming.

Dinosaur National Monument: From Vernal, the byway follows U.S. 40 east toward Colorado. At the junction of U.S. 40 and State Route 49, 13 miles east of Vernal in Jensen, go north on State Route 49 to an entrance for Dinosaur National Monument. More skeletons, skulls, and bones of Jurassic dinosaurs have been found here than in any other dig in the world.

Dinosaur Quarry: Jensen is the site of the Dinosaur Quarry, a remarkable fossil deposit with an exhibit of 150-million-year-old dinosaur remains. The byway now continues east along U.S. 40 into Colorado.

Douglas Pass and Canyon Pintado: Enter Colorado via U.S. 40, which leads to the town of Dinosaur. Drive south on State Route 64 to Rangely. Continue south on Route 139, which travels through the 8,268-foot Douglas Pass. Along the route is Canyon Pintado, which has significant examples of Fremont Indian rock art.

Museum of Western Colorado and Dinosaur Hill: Grand Junction is home to the Museum of Western Colorado, which has exhibits on dinosaurs and regional nature and history.

Colorado National Monument: Route 139 meets U.S. 6 just north of Fruita. Follow U.S. 6 southeast to the town of Grand Junction. Rim Rock Drive, which may be accessed either from Fruita or Grand Junction, leads 23 miles along canyon rims in Colorado National Monument. Deep canyons, rounded domes, towering monoliths, and other geological features are located within the monument.

Rabbit Valley Trail Through Time: Now double back north on U.S. 6 to I-70, which leads west toward Utah. Just before reaching the Utah state line on I-70, the Rabbit Valley Trail Through Time offers a one-mile walking trail through fossilized flora and fauna from the Jurassic Age.

Colorado Canyons National Conservation Area: A bit off the Dinosaur Diamond Prehistoric Highway southwest of U.S. 191 (via route 131) is Colorado Canyons National Conservation Area, which holds more spectacular rock formations, including arches, spires, and canyons. The huge, largely undeveloped park also has Native American pictographs and Puebloan ruins, desert flora, and portions of the Green and Colorado Rivers, where you can arrange white water trips. Some park roads are safe only for high-clearance four-wheel-drive vehicles. The byway then continues its loop into Utah.

The Colorado River cuts along the southern end of Arches National Park.

The Energy Loop: Huntington and Eccles Canyons Scenic Byways

As this two-byway loop winds through the canyons and valleys of Utah's backyard, the legacies of coal mining, ancient cultures, and prehistoric creatures come alive at every stop.

Situated amid mountainous terrain and pine forests, the Energy Loop runs through Utah's beautiful backyard. Travelers come from miles away to fish the trout-filled waters along the route or to enjoy a picnic in the beautiful forest surroundings. You can also see signs of red rock country.

Deriving its name from the rich coal mining history of the area, the Energy Loop combines two of Utah's byways: the Huntington Canyon Scenic Byway and the Eccles Canyon Scenic Byway. Along the way, you can see early Mormon settlements in Sanpete Valley or visit unique museums in the byway communities. Towns from Scofield to Huntington revere the days when coal mining was the livelihood of so many of their ancestors.

Cultural: The cultural patchwork of the area begins with the Fremont Indians. These people moved into the area sometime between A.D. 300 and 500. Although they were a primitive people, they left behind artifacts of a culture in their rock art, baskets, and figurines. The Fremont Indians usually lived in pit houses made of wood and mud that were entered through an opening in the roof. The weapons and tools of this culture were much different than neighboring American Indian cultures, indicating the unique existence of the Fremonts. By the time European settlers reached the area, the Fremont Indian culture had disappeared.

Settlers who came to the area in the early 1800s found an untamed wilderness with many resources. Ranchers found meadows with grass that was perfect for grazing livestock. Coal was one of the most important resources found in the area, and as a result, coal mining towns sprang up all around. The coal mining culture was a society of hardworking men, women, and children who worked in and around the mines—often at the peril of their own lives. Their story can be found in places like the Scofield Cemetery and several deserted towns. Coal mining, power plants, and hydroelectric power harnessed in the reservoirs are all still present today.

Fairview Canyon, east of the town of Fairview, is a favorite of snowmobilers and those seeking rugged beauty any time of the year.

These all play a direct part in the name of this byway—the Energy Loop.

Historical: Few areas in the United States can boast of undiscovered and diverse historical resources the way the area surrounding the Energy Loop can. Travelers along the route see a variety of important historical landmarks, including Native American historical sites, Spanish exploration routes, and the early Mormon settlements that have grown into towns. You are in for a diverse historical experience not likely to be matched as you visit the historic coal mining and railroad industries that have deep roots in the area, along with the small-town museums in the byway communities.

Recreational: All along the byway, cars are stopped at the sides of the roads, but the drivers are nowhere to be seen unless you check the river. Anglers come from all around to fish for the trout that swim in the waters of Huntington Creek. Fly fishers have their pick of cutthroat, brown, and rainbow trout when fishing the streams and rivers on the byway.

Hiking and biking are activities worth trying along the Energy Loop.

Highlights:

Traveling from Fairview, this tour suggests scenic vistas that will make your visit to the Energy Loop a fulfilling one.

Electric Lake and Burnout Canyon:

Beginning in Fairview, take UT 31 approximately ten miles to its junction with Highway 264. Follow 264 for about another ten miles, and you will come upon a turnout, along with a view of Burnout Canyon and Electric Lake. Electric Lake was constructed to provide power for the Huntington Power Plant.

Scofield: Twelve miles past the Electric Lake Overlook on Highway 264, you will meet State Highway 96. Travel north for five miles to the historic town of Scofield, once the largest town in all of Carbon County. On May 1, 1900, one of the worst mining accidents in U.S. history claimed the lives of hundreds of miners. Visit the old cemetery to see the gravestones of the miners lost on that tragic day. A little farther north, Highway 96 runs beside Scofield State Park and Reservoir, which provides good trout fishing.

Sanpete Valley Overlook: Leave the Scofield area by heading south on Highway 96, following the road you came in on. Drive back to the junction of Highways 264 and UT 31, and follow UT 31 southeast toward the town of Huntington.

Joes Valley Overlook: Continue traveling south for around eight miles on UT 31 to another scenic overlook. This turnout provides a view of Joes Valley below, a popular recreation area for locals.

Flaming Gorge–Uintas Scenic Byway

Utah's highest mountains, its favorite outdoor playground, and the real Jurassic Park lie along this colorful desert byway, where Butch Cassidy once rode with his gang; a reservoir promises cool fun on the water.

As one of the most aptly named landscapes in the country, Flaming Gorge provides the kind of scenic vistas that refuse to fit in the viewfinder of your camera and must be relived in your memory after you return home. Driving this byway, you get to watch Flaming Gorge and the Uintas Mountains unfold from several different perspectives.

Historical: The route along the Flaming Gorge–Uintas Scenic Byway is rich in history and culture. The first European explorers were Fathers Dominguez and Escalante. Wesley Powell explored the Green River and named many of the byway's geographic sites, including Flaming Gorge. General William H. Ashley explored the area and established several trading posts. He organized the first Mountain Man Rendezvous in 1825 near Manila.

The byway parallels the Outlaw Trail that Butch Cassidy and members of the Wild Bunch used. Two turn-of-the-19th-century homesteads on the byway, Swett Ranch and Jarvies Ranch, are presently managed and interpreted by the Forest Service and Bureau of Land Management. The town of Vernal celebrates Outlaw Days with an outdoor theater depicting sagas of the Wild Bunch, a ride along the Outlaw trail, and other community events. The influence of Mormon settlers is also evident in the Manila and Vernal areas.

Recreational: Flaming Gorge Reservoir is the most popular recreation spot in Utah. It offers highly developed facilities for camping, hiking, riding, skiing, snowmobiling, and other activities on a year-round basis. The visitor center, gift shops, restaurants, outfitters, guides, boat rentals, and other retailers work together as partners to make this a quality experience.

Hoodoos and other unique geological structures make Red Canyon especially distinctive. These interesting formations become more common as Red Canyon comes closer to Bryce Canyon National Park.

Flaming Gorge Reservoir is surrounded by 367 shoreline miles, creating an angler's paradise. World-record brown trout exceeding 30 pounds and lake trout over 50 pounds have been caught here. People from all over the world visit the Green River for premier blue-ribbon fly-fishing experiences. The nearby High Uintas Wilderness Area (Utah's largest) offers hundreds of miles of hiking trails and numerous camping sites; it also boasts of hundreds of high-elevation lakes with great fishing opportunities.

Highlights:

While visiting the Flaming Gorge–Uintas Scenic Byway, you can take the following self-guided tour.

Utah Field House of Natural History and Dinosaur Gardens: Driving on the byway from Vernal, you don't want to miss the Utah Field House of Natural History and Dinosaur Gardens on the north side of Main Street near Vernal. See life-size dinosaurs and Fremont and Ute Indian artifacts.

Dinosaur National Monument: If you have the time, take a side trip, following U.S. 40 and traveling 20 miles east of Vernal to visit the Dinosaur National Monument.

Flaming Gorge Dam: If you're making a quick trip, continue on U.S. 191 to the Flaming Gorge Dam, six miles from the Greendale Junction (U.S. 191 and UT 44). There you'll find picnic sites and other visitor facilities. Be sure to take the guided tour through the dam.

Swett Ranch: Make a U-turn back on U.S. 191 to travel west on UT 44. If you have time for a longer visit, you could stop at the Swett Ranch and partake of pioneer history.

Red Canyon Overlook and Visitor's Center: Continue on your way to the Red Canyon Overlook and Visitor's Center in the Flaming Gorge National Recreation Area, about five miles off of UT 44. The caves and ledges of this scenic wonder offer glimpses into the ancient history of this area.

Sheep Creek Loop Drive: If you have some extra time, continue on UT 44 and turn left onto the Sheep Creek Loop Drive to the Ute Tower.

A Journey Through Time Scenic Byway—Highway 12

As it passes through rugged and colorful canyons lying between two national parks, this byway showcases a land of ancient cultures, pioneers, and explorers—with a piece of history beckoning around every turn.

The Escalante, the final river in the continental United States to be named, ambles slowly between towering canyon walls.

As you drive the byway that connects Bryce Canyon National Park and Capitol Reef National Park, you are treated to enticing views and stops, along with a kaleidoscope of color. Byway towns in between offer the flavor of a simple life in the middle of a fantastic wilderness. Historic stops and pull-offs provide stories for curious byway travelers. Ancient ruins and artwork can be found throughout the canyons and rock faces that line this byway.

Cultural: The archaeological remains and artwork of the Fremont Indians and the Anasazi enable modern-day experts and visitors to speculate about what these people must have been like. These cultures had a belief system of legends and histories that explained the landforms that surrounded them. One thing is certain: The cultures of the Anasazi, Fremont, and Paiute revered the land of Highway 12 as a special land.

Mormon pioneers established communities more than a century ago whose presence today has brought a new collection of stories and histories. The communities that visitors will observe display the classical elements of a Mormon settlement. Mormons would gather in a town and spread their farms all around the town.

Historical: The first explorers were Spanish and claimed the land for Spain in 1776. The name of the town Escalante comes from one of the priests who was on the expedition, Silvestre Velez de Escalante. John Wesley Powell more thoroughly explored the land nearly 100 years later in 1869 on a treacherous journey on which he lost several of his company. By the time he explored the area, Mormon pioneers had already begun to inhabit the region.

The town of Panguitch was the first place the pioneers attempted to settle. Because of conflicts with the Native Americans, they abandoned the settlement until 1871. A string of other towns, including Tropic and Boulder, retain a western town appearance with wood storefronts, stone walls, and old-fashioned architecture.

Highlights:

While visiting the Flaming Gorge–Uintas Scenic Byway, you can take the following self-guided tour.

Bryce Canyon National Park: Follow Highway 12 east from the intersection of U.S. 89. At State Route 63, turn south into Bryce Canyon National Park, a 56-square mile area filled with colorful, fantastic cliffs and pinnacles created by millions of years of erosion.

Kodachrome Basin State Park: Highway 12 then leads east to Kodachrome Basin

State Park, which contains strange, vividly colored stone pinnacles, believed to be ancient fossilized geysers.

Escalante State Park: Continuing east on Highway 12, the next stop is Escalante State Park, a petrified forest with mineralized wood and dinosaur bones. The park also has a reservoir for swimming, fishing, and boating (with ramps) as well as hiking trails, picnicking, bird-watching, and camping.

Anasazi Indian Village State Park: Highway 12 now swings north toward the town of Boulder. Near Boulder is the Anasazi Indian Village State Park, including a partially excavated village with museum. Probably occupied by Fremont and Kayenta Anasazi Indians from A.D. 1050 to 1200, it was one of the largest ancient communities west of the Colorado River. Picnic areas are available.

Capitol Reef National Park: Off the northeastern end of the byway is 378-square-mile Capitol Reef National Park (the visitor center is located along State Route 24, which leads east off Highway 12). Here, red sandstone cliffs are capped with domes of white sandstone. A 25-mile round-trip scenic drive leads through the park.

Logan Canyon Scenic Byway

With its mountain peaks, sparkling river, inland lakes, and colorful rock formations, this canyon byway entrances not just sightseers but rock climbers, hikers, cyclists, picnickers, anglers, boaters, and skiers.

Beautiful mountains that tower over the city of Logan and the turquoise waters of Bear Lake captivate visitors and residents year-round. You'll be enchanted by inland seas, a dramatic landscape surrounding this byway formed by great earthquakes and mountains that tower over the road on both sides. Driving the Logan Canyon Scenic Byway is like entering a new world where the mountains, trees, and river together reveal the undying patterns of nature.

Cultural: From mountain men to mountain climbers, Logan Canyon has fostered a variety of cultures from its earliest days. As cultures have shifted and evolved over the last few centuries in this corner of northern Utah, memories of the past are still in place. Cultural influences of mountain men and Native Americans still surface from time to time in the modern cultures of agriculture and industry.

The Shoshone and Bannock nations had been living in the areas near Cache Valley and Bear Lake for many years before their lands were forever

Contrary to the name, Ricks Spring is not a wholesome natural spring, but rather a diversion of Logan River.

changed by the coming of fur trappers and, later, settlers. Local nations still gather to practice beautiful cultural dances and songs; their artwork can be seen in summer fairs and festivals. Mountain men are also honored with festivals and activities.

The coming of the Mormon pioneers made a significant impact on the culture of the area. Settlers from the Church of

Jesus Christ of Latter-day Saints (LDS) developed an agricultural society that still thrives in Cache Valley. The Mormon pioneers also brought with them an appreciation for family and heritage.

Today, because they live so close to a perfect wilderness, most everyone in Cache Valley and Bear Lake has a personal attachment to at least one aspect of Logan Canyon. From exploring nature trails to fishing and canoeing, the skills and pastimes of the first people in Logan Canyon remain with today's residents.

Historical: Although most of the places in Logan Canyon were named in the last 150 years, influences from an earlier past can still be found in places along the byway. Guinavah–Malibu Campground carries the Shoshone word for "bird water," which was the earliest name for the Logan River. A mountain man named Jim Bridger gave his name to the region that encompasses the canyon known as Bridgerland. Cache Valley, at the west end of the canyon, was named for the caches that trappers made in the area to store their furs. As Mormon pioneers entered the area in mid-1800s, they established Temple Fork, where they procured the materials they would need to build their temple and tabernacle.

Stories of highfalutin families at Tony Grove or an 11-foot-tall bear named Ephraim can be found in places all along the way. One of the best places to find out about Logan Canyon history is at the mouth of the canyon in Logan. Lady Bird Overlook is a location that carries history of its own. It was named for President Lyndon Johnson's wife, Lady Bird Johnson, who initiated the highway beautification plan in the 1960s. At the overlook, you can discover the story of a 1,000-year-old tree and find out why one of the most beautiful spots on the byway is called China Row.

Logan Canyon was in the land of the Shoshone and the Bannock. Later, Logan Canyon saw the days of mountain men trapping animals for their fur. When the Mormon pioneers arrived, the wild land of Logan Canyon was forever changed. Civilization came to the byway to explore it and discover the wonders of the canyon in the same way that travelers do today.

Recreational: Logan Canyon recreation is one of the main reasons people come to Cache Valley to visit and to stay. After a short drive into the mountains, you'll find a garden of recreational opportunities—some relaxing and others extreme. From an early morning hike to rock climbing, Logan Canyon is the best place for miles around to unwind.

Logan Canyon's limestone outcroppings are calling for you to climb them. Rock climbers gather from spring through fall to challenge the million-year-old mountainsides. Most of the climbs are bolt-protected sport climbs. In winter, climbers can be found making their way up a frozen waterfall. Another mountainside challenge is offered within the crisp winter air at Beaver Mountain, where skiers and snowboarders gather to test skills of balance and coordination.

Although they might be the most exciting of mountain sports, skiing and climbing aren't the only activities available in Logan Canyon. With 300 miles of hiking trails, Logan Canyon is also a hiker's paradise. Trails lead to every kind of destination, from an ancient juniper tree to a pristine mountain lake. Runners and cyclists especially love the

Logan River Trail starting at Red Bridge. On summer mornings, the air is cool and green leaves hang over the trail, creating a scenic place to exercise.

Roads available at Temple Fork and Right Hand Fork provide opportunities for ATVs and motorcyclists to enjoy the exciting back roads to the canyon. During the winter, trailers carrying snowmobiles can be seen entering Logan Canyon. They might be heading to Franklin Basin or The Sinks, where valleys between the trees offer the perfect places to traverse the snow.

When all the snow melts, water sports reach their heights in Logan Canyon, whether you are boating or fishing. Logan Canyon is home to the Logan River and Bear Lake, where many travelers take boats and jet skis during the summer for an exhilarating run across its mesmerizing waters. Visitors can also fish for the Bonneville Cisco, which is only found in Bear Lake. The Logan River is famous for fly-fishing, but anglers of every kind and age gather at Second and Third Dam to try their luck with a pole. A careful observer will be able to see groups of trout as they gather underneath a bridge nearby, but scuba divers at the east end of Bear Lake have the best view of the local fish. A more secluded setting is found at Tony Grove Lake, where the most

popular activity—besides fishing—is canoeing.

Highlights:

For your own Logan Canyon must-see tour, consider following this itinerary.

Second Dam: From summer to spring, Second Dam is one of the most popular fishing spots on the byway. Just a short drive up the canyon, Second Dam is a wilderness getaway with mountains on all sides and shady picnic areas.

Wind Caves: Years of wind and water have worn a delicate triple arch and natural cave into the limestone outcropping at the top of this two-mile trail. Also known as the Witch's Castle, this fascinating formation provides a clear view of China Row.

Logan Cave: This used to be a popular cave to explore, but because of vandalism in 1998, the Forest Service gated and locked the cave entrance. The upside is that by keeping people out of the cave, the native bat population will likely thrive. Nevertheless, curious travelers still make short hikes to the mouth of the cave to peer into its dark recesses.

There are many trails and many caves in Utah. One of the most memorable trails is the one up to Wind Caves with its spectacular view of the canyon below.

Ricks Springs: Ricks Springs has been a wayside stop for a long time. Early settlers drank the water here and experienced discomfort because the water does not come from a natural spring.

Tony Grove Lake and Mount Naomi Wilderness Area: A seven-mile paved road climbs to a height of 8,050 feet to reach Tony Grove Lake and the Mount Naomi Wilderness Area. The area around this glacial lake explodes into wildflowers in the early summer. The campground features 37 popular sites. A popular 0.8-mile trail takes visitors around part of the lake.

Bear Lake Overlook: On a clear day, Bear Lake sparkles an unusually clear turquoise blue. A display explains the history and geology of the lake and surrounding area.

Nebo Loop Scenic Byway

Lakes, forests, rocky overlooks, wildflowers, and fiery displays of fall color line the popular Nebo Loop as it makes its way into the Wasatch Mountains. Take it slow, and enjoy one of nature's grandest shows.

This byway begins in the quiet community of Payson and ascends back and forth through a canyon of deep, fresh forest that turns to visual fire in the fall. The route continues alongside a cold, rocky creek that drops off into intermittent miniature waterfalls; fishers sit aside this creek in the cool of dusk, listening to a cricket symphony and the birds' sonata.

By degrees, the landscape changes into a high-mountain wilderness. Only fields of crisp, bright wildflowers interrupt the thick stands of aspen. Incredibly high overlooks show the Wasatch Mountains sitting loosely below you like a pile of ribbon. From these overlooks, you can also see the byway's namesake, 11,877-foot Mount Nebo.

This area is so well liked that more than one million people visit annually, and a good percentage of them reserve campsites a year in advance. During the summer, most people like to fish at the glass-smooth lakes, such as Payson, or hike on the many trails, such as Loafer Mountain Trail.

Cultural: Settled by Mormon pioneers in 1850, the area surrounding the byway took on the culture of the farmer and the frontiersman, with pieces of the native cultures mixed in. Although towns such as Payson and Nephi were established nearby, Mount Nebo and its surrounding landscape were preserved even after a road was placed through these backwoods areas. Proud of their pioneer and native heritage and the legacy of the Nebo Loop, today's residents of Payson, Nephi, and

Mount Nebo in the Uinta National Forest is the highest peak in the Wasatch Range, reaching 11,877 feet at its summit.

surrounding communities fully enjoy the rivers, lakes, and forest.

The byway covers two counties, and as you continue south, the communities become smaller. The city now known as Payson was once called Peteetneet, named for Chief Peteetneet of the Ute Tribe. Peteetneet, which means "little waters," is now the name of the academy that exhibits art and museum pieces. Visitors stop at the Peteetneet Academy on their way to the natural wonders of the Nebo Loop. And like any communities with traditions, the byway communities host unique festivals throughout the year.

As you drive the byway, you may want to follow the examples of the local residents and grab your tent and a fishing pole to camp your way along the Nebo Loop. Stop by some of the orchards along the way that have been a main supply of food and income for Nebo's communities for nearly two centuries. By stopping at small communities along the way, you get to see what's in store beyond Mount Nebo.

Historical: The road that became the Nebo Loop had been used for centuries by Native Americans and, later, by explorers and sawmill companies. The road was then built by the Civilian Conservation Corps (CCC) and enhanced

by the addition of recreational facilities.

People have inhabited the byway and its surrounding areas for unrecorded amounts of time. The elusive Fremont Indians made their home here before the Utes, who played a part as settlers arrived in Utah. The Walker War, one of two significant wars between Utah Utes and the Mormon settlers, took place on the northern end of the byway.

Important explorers, such as Father Francisco Dominguez and Father Silvestre Velez de Escalante (1776), Jedediah Smith (1826), and John C. Frémont (1843), investigated the area and found it attractive. Frontiersman Daniel Potts, who came in 1827, said that the Utah Valley was beautiful. The Mormon Battalion also used the road in 1848 on their way back from California and the Mexican War, and the 49ers used it to go west for gold.

Early pioneer settlement is marked by places such as the Winward Reservoir. Payson farmers built the reservoir between 1890 and 1907 with horse teams and drags and named it after the city's first water master. Later in

the mid-1930s, the CCC made great contributions to the development of the byway and its components. For example, the CCC's rockwork allowed both the paved byway road and the stream to occupy the narrow space that it does.

The old Loafer Ski Area and the Maple Dell Scout Camp demonstrate the longtime popularity of this byway for recreation. The Loafer Ski Area was a popular place to relax from 1947 to the mid-1950s. The old slope, whose concrete slab foundations you can still see, had a 930-foot-long towrope and a 284-foot elevation drop. The ski area was rudimentarily furnished: a simple shelter, a toilet, and an outdoor picnic area. The Maple Dell Scout Camp has produced vivid memories for Utah scouts since 1947. Continual improvements have been made at the camp; one of the most notable was the construction of a large lodge in 1960. Later, a dance hall, cottages, and a swimming pool filled with water from a nearby icy spring were added.

By preserving the Nebo Loop as it is today, visitors are able to see this beautiful wilderness as it was 100 or 200 years ago. Its more recent history is preserved in its museums and exhibits and in structures and buildings all along the byway.

Peteetneet Academy, named in honor of a local Ute Indian chief, served as an elementary school until 1988. It is now a cultural arts learning center and museum.

Recreational: All the typical outdoor recreational activities can be done here, and some activities, such as hunting and horseback riding, that are rarely allowed in other urban forests are allowed here. Nebo Loop is also a popular area for watching wildlife; specific viewpoints have been designed for observing deer, elk, moose, and bears.

Because the byway is so popular, reservations must be made at least a year in advance for Blackhawk and Payson Lakes Campground; the typical weekend occupancy rate is 95 percent during the camping season. Payson Lakes Campground is the most popular because it offers swimming, canoeing, hiking, fishing, a fully accessible nature trail, and fishing piers for people with disabilities.

Although the byway attracts more than one million visitors each year, the design of the facilities makes them almost fade into the woods, keeping them fairly invisible to a driver. Payson Lakes Campground illustrates this fact by offering a myriad of recreational activities that remain hidden from the byway, yet the

road is only a few hundred feet away. In the midst of the typical camping experiences is the Mount Nebo Wilderness Area, which offers primitive, roadless recreation for the adventurer.

Highlights:

As you travel the Nebo Loop Scenic Byway from Payson, consider following this itinerary.

Peteetneet Museum: The school was built in 1901 by well-known architect Richard C. Watkins and consists of a three-story building with a bell tower and a red sandstone accent on brick walls.

Camp Maple Dell: Since 1947, this camp has given scouts a chance to take in vivid scenery and participate in outdoor recreation.

Payson Lakes: Payson Lakes has trailer camping and disabled-accessible sites and features, a shoreline nature trail, two beaches, and a universal access pier.

Blackhawk Campground: This popular campground has group and individual campsites as well as a horse camping facility. The area accommodates equestrian users by featuring tie racks, double-wide camping spurs, and easy access to the trails.

Frontier Pathways Scenic and Historic Byway

In a land of high-country homesteads and in the shadow of 14,000-foot peaks, this byway threads mountain passes, valleys, and canyons. Historic walking tours and mountain biking trails are just two of the enticing diversions.

During the winter of 1806, Lieutenant Zebulon Pike nearly froze to death in the Wet Mountain Valley within sight of the peak bearing his name. Nevertheless, this valley and its mountain became a beacon to 19th-century settlers, who came to take advantage of the good soil and climate. Today, the valley boasts one of the state's finest collections of historic ranches and farmsteads (some dating to the 1840s), trading posts, and stagecoach stops. Also, this pastoral paradise contrasts with the severe-looking Hardscrabble Canyon, the white-capped Sangre de Cristos, and the sharp mesas and hogbacks that flank the Arkansas River.

Just four miles north of the little burg of Westcliffe, the DeWeese Reservoir Wilderness Area is a beautiful location for wildlife photography opportunities.

Cultural: This byway chronicles the joys and sorrows that its early residents experienced while breaking in the land. It is a living showcase of the evolution of architecture, transportation, and agriculture that you can experience by visiting the Frontier Pathway's old homesteads, cabins, barns, stagecoach stops, and settlements. This landscape hasn't changed much in the last 100 years, so you can still see how different groups of people used their ingenuity to harness the land. Evidence of their resourcefulness is found in the area's nationally important high-country homesteading.

Historical: The Frontier Pathways Scenic and Historic Byway is seeping with nationally significant history. For example, some of the first high-country homesteads, ranches, and farms were developed here. In 1779, the Spanish Governor De Anza, with the help of the Utes, defeated Comanche Chief Cuerno Verde (Greenhorn) right in this very valley. Also, German and English colonists settled here in the mid-1800s, and their heritage still pervades this area.

Recreational: Year-round opportunities at this recreational mecca include climbing 14,294-foot-high Crestone Peak, shopping and dining in Pueblo's Union Avenue Historic District, and playing in the Wet Mountain Wilderness. You can also fish for trout on the banks of Lake Isabel, backpack on the nationally renowned Rainbow Trail south of Westcliffe, and hike the Sangre de Cristos Mountains or Greenhorn Wilderness.

While the summer sun is out, you may enjoy fishing for trout in streams, mountain biking, and horseback riding. You can also get in some sailing, power boating, or water-skiing at the Lake Pueblo State Park. Consider taking time to discover Pueblo Mountain Park, which is on the National Register of Historic Places. During the winter, be sure to cross-country ski, downhill ski, or ice fish on the Pueblo Reservoir.

Highlights:

To take in the highlights of the Frontier Pathways Scenic and Historic Byway, consider this must-see tour.

El Pueblo Museum: This museum, located in the town of Pueblo, gives you an opportunity to learn about the interaction of several different cultures: American Indian, Mexican, and American.

It is a full-size replica of Old Fort Pueblo, which was used by fur traders and other settlers from 1842 to 1855. Fascinating artifacts, colorful murals, and interesting stories bring the history of the Pueblo area to life.

Wetmore and Early Settlements: More than 150 years ago, buckskin-clad French traders, scrappy American farmers, and fur traders lived in nearby settlements. In the 1830s, three French trappers built a fort on Adobe Creek to facilitate trade with the Ute Indians. It was called Buzzard's Roost, or Maurice's Fort, after Maurice LeDuc. Later settlements in the area included Hardscrabble in 1844 and Wetmore in the late 1870s.

Sangre de Cristos Mountains (west of Silver Cliff): Miners, ranchers, and modern-day motorists have all marveled at this breathtaking view of the Sangre de Cristos. This 50-mile stretch of mountains includes 22 peaks that are more than 13,000 feet in elevation.

Westcliff Schoolhouse: This schoolhouse, located in the town of Westcliffe, was built in 1891. No one knows why the school name, still visible above the front doors as "Westcliff," was spelled without the e.

Gold Belt Tour Scenic and Historic Byway

Following historic railroad and stagecoach routes through the Rockies, the splendid Gold Belt Tour leads to atmospheric mining towns, world-class fossil sites, dramatic Royal Gorge, and memorable views of Pikes Peak.

On the Gold Belt Tour, the roads themselves are part of the personality of the byway. The byway follows historic railroad and stagecoach routes, leading you to North America's greatest gold camp, three world-class fossil sites, and numerous historical sites. The Shelf and Phantom Canyon Roads offer adventurous driving experiences along unpaved routes through winding canyons. Paved roads wind through the gently rolling mountain parklands of the High Park route, where Colorado's highest mountain ranges rise in the distance.

Pikes Peak, the inspiration for the song "America the Beautiful," is one of the sights that visitors travel Colorado's Gold Belt Tour Scenic and Historic Byway to see.

The five byway communities invite you to share in their rich history. In Cripple Creek, the historical hub of the mining district and a National Historic Landmark, visitors enjoy the variety and beauty of the early 1900s architectural styles in the downtown district. The area's mining heritage continues in Victor, the City of Mines. Surrounded by hundreds of historic mines, Victor is the headquarters for a modern gold mine. Victor's downtown district, a National Historic District, includes beautifully restored buildings. To the south, you can enjoy the Royal Gorge as well as restaurants, museums, and historic sites in Cañon City and Florence.

Also located along the byway are the Garden Park Fossil Area, the Florissant Fossil Beds National Monument, and the Indian Springs Trace. These sites form an internationally important area for paleontological discovery and research.

Cultural: The Gold Belt Tour once sported a classic culture of the Wild West. Gold miners, saloons, and the untamed land of the Rocky Mountains are all part of the cultural past of this byway. Although you probably won't experience a gunfight in the streets of a byway town, the towns along the Gold

Belt Tour are fiercely proud of their heritage and bring pieces of the past to the surface for visitors throughout the year.

The mining culture was not the first culture to inhabit the mountains of the Gold Belt Tour. Many native cultures, including the Ute, lived here and developed their own unique way of life. The area was a prime hunting spot and a good place to spend the winter because of its relatively mild climate. The history of these cultures has faded to only a few stories and archaeological artifacts.

In the 1800s, a new culture came to the Gold Belt Tour. Settlers from the east brought with them a new organization of towns, roads, and mines, coupled with all the lawlessness of gunfights and hangings. Respect for the land by the area's predecessors was replaced by a way of life that used up the resources around the people. When the gold boom subsided, however, the communities of the area decreased to smaller sizes, allowing the surrounding regions to continue in their natural beauty.

Historical: The three roads that constitute the Gold Belt Tour are the historic routes that connected the Cripple Creek Mining District to the communities to the north and south. The historic communities of Cripple

Creek, Victor, Cañon City, Florissant, and Florence along with the byway played important roles in what was the most productive gold-mining district in North America.

Cripple Creek was the center of the Gold Boom. Bob Womack discovered gold in 1890, setting off a gold rush that brought people from all over the country and put Cripple Creek on the map. By 1900, three railroads, two electric tram lines, modern water and sewer systems, and many other conveniences separated Cripple Creek from the average western mining camp. Cripple Creek became the financial and commercial center of what is known as the Cripple Creek Mining District. Today, many of the historic buildings that played such a prominent role in the days of gold have been restored, and the entire downtown area of Cripple Creek is a National Historic Landmark.

Victor, which lies just southeast of Cripple Creek, was historically the home of the miners and their families. The downtown area of the city

boasts several buildings that are on the National Register of Historic Places, and Victor's downtown itself is a National Historic District.

Florissant is north of the Cripple Creek Mining District. It stands at the crossroads of two important Ute Indian trails. It was a stopover for American Indians, trappers, traders, and mountain men long before silver and gold were discovered in the mountains to the west. In 1886, the railroad came through Florissant and was the closest rail connection to the mining district in the early years of the gold boom.

South of the Cripple Creek Mining District lies the Arkansas River Valley and two more communities that have historical significance. Cañon City and Florence both sought the overflow of wealth coming out of Cripple Creek during the golden years. Both cities were established in the second half of the 1800s and have a rich historical past. In Cañon City, visitors can enjoy a tour of some early railroad depots that have been restored.

Along with the communities found on the Gold Belt Tour, the routes themselves have historical significance. Phantom Canyon Road follows the abandoned railroad grade of the Florence and Cripple Creek Railroad, the first railroad to reach the gold mines. Today, travelers on Phantom Canyon Road go through tunnels, drive over bridges, and see past remnants of train stations used by the railroad back in the 1890s. Shelf Road was constructed in 1892 and was the first direct route from Cripple Creek to the Arkansas River Valley. Today, travelers experience the shelf—a narrow, winding section of road perched high above Fourmile Creek—much the same way that people experienced it in the 1890s.

After you reach the outskirts of Cripple Creek, you pass several historic mines and mills. High Park Road travels through a high-elevation park that is home to cattle ranchers. This land along High Park Road represents 150 years of ranching history. Historic ranch buildings, such as the Fourmile Community building, lie along the byway route. Other roads such as Skyline Drive near Cañon City provide beautiful views and interesting historical background.

Recreational: Although it is no more the gold-mining district it once was, the Gold Belt Tour is still the road to riches as far as recreation is concerned. Camping is available in several places throughout the area, allowing you to camp your way through the Gold Belt Tour. In addition to outdoor recreation areas, you'll likely be pleased with the historic museums and fossil parks along the route.

The Royal Gorge Park, owned by Cañon City, is one of Colorado's top tourist

A petrified Sequoia tree stump is just one of the wonders visitors will see at Florissant Fossil Beds National Monument.

destinations. The impressive chasm of the Royal Gorge is spanned by the world's highest suspension bridge. At the bridge, a concessionaire operates an incline railway, aerial tram, and other attractions for visitors. Hiking trails and picnic areas can be found throughout the park. Beginning at Cañon City, the Royal Gorge Route leaves on a scenic train ride through the bottom of the gorge. Not only are you treated to a view of the natural wonders in the gorge, but you also catch glimpses of history in ruins from the Royal Gorge War. Cañon City also provides you with opportunities to explore prehistoric creatures at the Garden Park Fossil Area.

A portion of the Arkansas Headwaters Recreation Area is located along the byway. Colorado's Arkansas River between Leadville and Cañon City is among the nation's most popular white water rafting destinations, hosting more than 300,000 boaters annually. The river also offers some of Colorado's best fly-fishing.

Shelf Road Recreation Area attracts rock climbers from around the world. The limestone cliffs offer short but extremely difficult climbs in some places. In other spots, they are more than 100 feet high and are enticing even to expert climbers. An extensive trail network along the cliffs provides hiking opportunities for climbers and nonclimbers alike. On Shelf Road, climbers can picnic at Red Canyon Park. Camping and hiking are also excellent pastimes at Red Canyon Park. Additionally, many travelers enjoy picnicking along Phantom Canyon Road after a drive through the forested areas.

Highlights:

As you travel the Gold Belt Tour, consider following this itinerary.

Royal Gorge Bridge: The first place you'll want to stop is the Royal Gorge Bridge. Travel west out of Cañon City on High Park Road for about eight miles, turn right, and you'll come to the bridge (and the park) in about half a mile.

Garden Park Fossil Area: Garden Park Fossil Area has been the location of the some of the most important discoveries of dinosaur fossils in North America. Tours should be made in advance; self-guided trails and exhibits are also available at the Garden Park Fossil Area.

View of Pikes Peak: As you travel Shelf Road north to Cripple Creek, you will be treated to a beautiful vista of the west slope of Pikes Peak, named for explorer Zebulon Pike. Pikes Peak towers 14,110 feet.

Cripple Creek: Take U.S. 50 west and then Shelf Road north 26 miles to historic Cripple Creek, the center of the Cripple Creek Mining District. Cripple Creek is a National Historic Landmark, and many of the buildings that were built during the early 1900s have been restored.

Florissant Fossil Beds National Monument: From Cripple Creek, travel west on Bennett Avenue to Teller 1. Seventeen miles from the junction on Teller 1, stop at Florissant Fossil Beds National Monument, which offers walking and guided tours. The fossils found here are renowned for their variety of species: More than 80,000 fossilized specimens of tree stumps, insects, seeds, and leaves have been catalogued. The historic Hornbek Homestead is also located here.

The world's highest suspension bridge, the Royal Gorge Bridge spans the chasm, crossing 1,053 feet above the Arkansas River.

Grand Mesa Scenic and Historic Byway

Following historic railroad and stagecoach routes through the Rockies, the splendid Gold Belt Tour leads to atmospheric mining towns, world-class fossil sites, dramatic Royal Gorge, and memorable views of Pikes Peak.

The Utes called the Grand Mesa "Thunder Mountain." This name is fitting because, when standing at the Lands End Observatory, the Grand Valley unfolds more than a mile below, and you can imagine yourself as Zeus, ready to hurl thunderbolts. The 63-mile route is transcendent as it climbs through the dusty canyon of Plateau Creek to the cool evergreen forests of the mesa top.

Many scenic overlooks along the byway allow you to glimpse the extraordinary

landscape below. The Lands End Road follows the rim of the mesa for much of the way. From here, you may be able to see the peaks of the LaSal Mountains 60 miles to the west in Utah and may even see the San Juan Mountains in Colorado 90 miles to the south.

Historical: The first Europeans known to have come to the Grand Mesa were members of the famous Dominguez–Escalante expedition. In 1776, Ute guides led them over Grand Mesa because the expedition couldn't find a good land route to California on their own. More Europeans came as fur traders in the mid-1800s.

Early treaties "gave" this land to the Utes, but as settlers moved to Colorado, the U.S. government made a series of treaties with the Utes that reduced the territory by degrees. In the

early 1880s, the Utes were moved to reservations in Utah and southwestern Colorado, and cattle and sheep ranchers soon dominated the area.

Since 1881, the valley floor has been home to farmers, who rely on water from the Grand Mesa for their crops and orchards. Beginning in the late 1800s, numerous water storage and irrigation projects were initiated to bring the water from the mesa. These

The Grand Mesa is the world's tallest flat-top mountain. From the top, you will see breathtaking views of the vibrant valley and the spectacular mountain ranges.

water conservation systems continue to operate today.

Fishing has been promoted since 1893, when the Mesa Resort Company was established. The company built several lodges and more than 300 summer homes. Skiing on the mesa dates back to 1939, with the construction of the Mesa Creek Ski Area. Relocated in 1964, it is now The Powderhorn Ski Resort.

Touring the scenic Grand Mesa began with horse and buggy trips that lasted several days. Access was improved in 1895 with the completion of the first road through Plateau Canyon. A stage line and freight wagons regularly traveled the route. The road was improved with convict labor in 1911 and later became part of the Pikes Peak Ocean-to-Ocean Highway.

A second access route to the top of the mesa was constructed in 1933 by ex-servicemen on a Civilian Conservation Corps (CCC) crew. The twisting, rocky road was then known as the Veteran Road in their honor. It is now called Lands End Road. With the advent of better roads and automobiles, the popularity of Grand Mesa touring has continued to expand.

Recreational: The Grand Mesa offers excellent outdoor recreational opportunities. More than 300 stream-fed lakes

are scattered across the mesa, teaming with rainbow, cutthroat, and brook trout. Numerous roads and trails offer sightseeing and hiking adventures. In the winter, the Grand Mesa provides premier cross-country skiing, downhill skiing, and snowmobiling. Big game hunting, horseback riding, mountain biking, and boating are also popular activities.

Highlights:

You can begin this Grand Mesa must-see tour in the Lands End Observatory and proceed south.

Lands End Observatory: This spur of the byway ends at the spectacular views around the Lands End Observatory. This structure, which is listed on the Register of Historic Sites, was built in the late 1930s as a public-works project. It is perched on the edge of Grand Mesa and offers views of the valley 6,000 feet below and the LaSal Mountains in Utah.

Land-O-Lakes Overlook: When you return to Highway 65, proceed south to the sign for the Land-O-Lakes Overlook. Due to the area's geology, the Grand Mesa is dotted with more than 300 streams and reservoirs.

Grand Mesa Visitor Center: The Grand Mesa Visitor Center provides information and an interpretive hiking trail.

Pioneer Town and Cedaredge Welcome Center: These facilities are located together in the town of Cedaredge. The facilities provide visitor information, exhibits, and a tour of a reconstructed town that depicts the lives of pioneers in the area.

San Juan Skyway

Mountain passes, cliff dwellings, spring waterfalls, winter skiing, and fall splendor mark this "Million Dollar Highway" as it journeys to the top of the world and back in time.

Discover history and new heights on the San Juan Skyway. This loop trip through the San Juan Mountains of southwest Colorado follows more than 200 miles of state-maintained highways on a journey from towering mountains and alpine forests to the rolling vistas and ancient ruins of Native American country.

Mesa Verde National Park offers visitors an outstanding view into the lives of the ancient Pueblo people who once inhabited these cliff dwellings.

On this byway, you can drive through the heart of five million acres of the San Juan and Uncompahgre National Forests. The skyway takes you over mountain passes and through quaint towns.

Historical: The discovery of precious metals led to the exploration and settlement of areas along the San Juan Skyway during the late 19th century. Narrow-gauge railroads played an important role during the mining era and in the history of southwest Colorado as a whole.

With their rails set three feet apart as opposed to the standard gauge of nearly five feet, the narrow-gauge lines made it possible for trains to operate in mountainous country with tight turns and steep grades. Evidence of these defunct, narrow-gauge lines is manifested by the water tanks, bridges, trestles, and sections of railroad bed found along the byway. One narrow-gauge railroad, the Durango and Silverton, continues to operate as a tourist line. It was constructed from 1881 to 1882 by the Denver and Rio Grande Railroad to haul ore and provisions, and in 1968

Quick Facts

Length: 233 miles

Time to Allow: One to two days

Consideration: The country along the San Juan Skyway is exciting to explore, but safety should always be a major concern. Old and unstable mills, mines, and timber structures may be decaying and hazardous. Be prepared for changing weather both while driving and while hiking. If you are not accustomed to high altitudes, get plenty of rest and resist overdoing activities during your first two days at high altitude. Mountain passes are sometimes closed for an hour or two (sometimes even a day or two) in the case of heavy snowstorms or slides during the winter.

the line was designated a National Historic Civil Engineering Landmark. As it travels along the Animas River amidst majestic mountains, the Durango and Silverton Narrow Gauge Railroad offers scenic vistas and the experience of riding an authentic coal-fired, steam-powered railroad. It is one of southwest Colorado's major attractions and carries more than 200,000 passengers a year.

Recreational: Summer activities include hiking, mountain biking, kayaking, four wheeling, hunting, and fishing. Winter activities include snowshoeing, snowmobiling, and skiing.

Durango Mountain Resort at Purgatory offers downhill skiing and a Nordic center with a groomed track. In summer, the lift takes visitors up the mountain for sightseeing and wildflower viewing. The lift is also a way to get to the top of the mountain biking trail system and to the top of the toboggan-like Alpine Slide.

Highlights:

The following tour begins in Mesa Verde National Park and ends in the town of Ouray. If you are beginning the tour from Ouray, simply begin at the bottom of the list and work your way up.

Mesa Verde National Park: At this park, explore cliff dwellings made by the Anasazi Indians. These dwellings were mysteriously abandoned by the Anasazi approximately 200 years before Columbus discovered America.

Durango: This authentic Old West town, founded in 1880, still retains its Victorian charm. Restored historic landmarks line downtown streets, while nearby ski resorts beckon to adventurous winter travelers.

Silverton: This remote mining community can be reached either by taking the historic Durango and Silverton Narrow Gauge Railroad or by driving over the 10,910-foot Molas Divide Pass. Many of the beautiful Victorian buildings in Silverton are registered as National Historical Sites.

Ghost towns: The ghost towns of Howardsville, Eureka, and Animas Forks are all located within 14 miles of Silverton. At Animas Forks, you can walk through the remnants of a 19th-century mining town or wander through beautiful meadows of wildflowers.

Million Dollar Highway: The section of highway from Silverton to Ouray has been named the Million Dollar Highway because of the immense amounts of silver and gold that were carted through these passes. This road is quite possibly the most beautiful section of byway anywhere in the country and is not to be missed.

Santa Fe Trail Scenic and Historic Byway

Paralleling a historic corridor to the West, modern-day travelers on Colorado's Santa Fe Trail retrace the routes of pioneers, Native Americans, traders, ranchers, and miners. All would still recognize this timeless landscape.

The Santa Fe Trail Scenic and Historic Byway is a rich legacy of the many people who made their way across southeastern Colorado. This transportation route served as a corridor to the West and resulted in the meshing of many cultures and traditions. Today along the byway, festivals and museums honor the many men and women who left a distinctive mark on the area, including early Native Americans, military personnel, ranchers, miners, and railroad passengers.

Cultural: Southeastern Colorado is embedded with Mexican culture; the area was a Mexican territory longer than it has been a part of the United States. Even after the United States acquired Mexico's northern provinces in 1848, the Santa Fe Trail served as a conduit for exchange among Spanish, Native American, and American cultures. Communities along the byway continue to celebrate the diverse inhabitants through traditional celebrations, culturally representative architecture (such as adobe structures), religious folk art, and Hispanic culture at Trinidad's Baca House (located in the Trinidad History Museum) and other museums.

Historical: The Santa Fe Trail Scenic and Historic Byway parallels the Santa Fe Trail, which served as a trade route between Missouri and the Mexican frontiers from 1821 to 1880. Traders, miners, military, and settlers all used this route. Even during the Civil War, the area saw action as Colorado volunteers fought against Confederate troops. With the coming of the railroad, the Santa Fe Trail entered a new phase of its history.

The Santa Fe Trail extended for 900 miles from Missouri to Santa Fe and was instrumental in carrying people and goods across the land. The Mountain Route of the Santa Fe Trail was traveled by caravans of traders, often journeying four horses abreast. Although the Mountain Route was 100 miles longer than the Cimarron Route and included the difficult climb over Raton Pass, the Mountain Route was preferred because water was more

Quick Facts

Length: 188 miles

Time to Allow: Four miles

Consideration: The best time of year to drive this byway is early spring through late fall.

During much of the original adobe fort's 16-year history, Bent's Old Fort was the only major permanent pioneer settlement on the Santa Fe Trail.

accessible and the area was less vulnerable to attacks from Native Americans.

Travel on the trail was beneficial but dangerous for those making the journey. In 1834, Charles and William Bent and Ceran St. Vrain built a fort to protect trading activities among the Americans, Mexicans, and Native Americans. Visitors can go to Bent's Old Fort today and see what fort life was like. Miners heading to California in search of gold often chose the shorter, although more dangerous, route of the Santa Fe Trail rather than the Oregon Trail.

Recreational: The Santa Fe Trail Scenic and Historic Byway offers more than 30,000 acres of public land that supports a variety of recreational activities.

The Arkansas River follows the byway for a good portion of the route, providing many opportunities to enjoy the riverbanks. In addition, the John Martin Reservoir's blue waters give you a chance to enjoy a fun day of swimming, picnicking, camping, boating, water-skiing, sailing, or windsurfing. Fishing is another popular activity both on the lake and in nearby rivers.

An abundance of other wildlife is located along the byway. Desert bighorn sheep, eagles, cranes, pelicans, lesser prairie chickens, and hummingbirds can often be spotted in the area. Hunters come to southeastern Colorado for prime hunting opportunities; in fact, Prowers County is known as the goose hunting capital of the nation.

Highlights:

The Santa Fe Trail historical tour begins at Bent's Old Fort and follows the trail toward Trinidad.

Bent's Old Fort: This National Historical Site is a reconstruction of Bent's Fort, which was built in the 1830s. The fort played an important role as a trading post for trappers and the Plains Indians and also as a supply depot during the Mexican–American War.

Sierra Vista Overlook: For Santa Fe Trail travelers heading south, the changing horizon from plains to mountains was a major milestone on their journey. One of their guiding landmarks was the distant Spanish Peaks, which came into view along this section of the trail. A short walk up the side of a bluff gives you an excellent view of the Rocky Mountains and surrounding prairie, much like what early travelers saw.

Trinidad History Museum: This museum complex, operated by the Colorado Historical Society, houses multiple attractions in one location.

Top of the Rockies Scenic Byway

The Continental Divide and the country's highest-elevation community both lie along this awe-inspiring scenic byway, which cruises the mountaintops amid startling close-ups of 14,000-foot peaks.

The cool mountain air and fresh scent of pine trees beckons you to the Top of the Rockies Scenic Byway. Towering peaks flank the highways, and open lowlands give you a rest from steep mountain passes. However,

The last fields of wildflowers flourish before yielding to the timberline and the majestic peaks of the Rockies.

don't be fooled by these "low-lands" because Leadville, the hub of the byway, is the highest incorporated community in the United States, located 10,200 feet above sea level. Mount Elbert (14,433 feet) and Mount Massive (14,421 feet)—the highest and second highest mountains in Colorado—stand just outside of Leadville.

Historical: Mining shaped a way of life along the Top of the Rockies many years ago. The rich mines of the area led to the growth of communities such as

Twin Lakes, Minturn, Leadville, and Red Cliff. The military presence of the 10th Mountain Division at Camp Hale added another distinct chapter in the history of the byway.

In 1860, the mountains and hills came alive as gold was discovered in California Gulch. Soon, silver was also discovered in the area, bringing individuals such as Horace Tabor, David May, J. J. and Margaret Brown, the Guggenheims, and the Boettchers. Fortunes were made, and communities soon developed

to meet the needs of the growing mining populations. Many of these towns, such as Kokomo, Recen, and Robinson, are now nonexistent, having been destroyed by fires or other natural disasters.

While mining brought many people to the area, when fortunes were harder to come by, many residents turned to farming, and thus the boomtowns remained lively communities. Leadville today maintains the Victorian charm and influence that kept people in town after the mining boom was over.

Other factors contributed to this area's historical development. The 10th Mountain Division, which trained at Camp Hale, fought in the military campaign in Italy during World War II. Camp Hale was the training site of the Invisible Men on Skis. The troops used the high elevation, steep slopes, and winter conditions to train for mountain and winter warfare in the Apennine Mountains of Italy. The 10th Mountain Division saw action during the war, and a memorial to those who lost their lives in this campaign stands at the entrance to Ski Cooper.

Recreational: Recreation along the Top of the Rockies is both diverse and abundant. The many lakes and streams provide rafting and fishing adventures, while the high Rocky Mountains lend themselves to camping, hiking, skiing, or mountain biking. Popular four-wheel drive vehicle trails take you off the beaten track to various destinations. Mount Massive Golf Course outside of Leadville claims the distinction of being the highest golf course on the continent.

The Arkansas and Colorado Rivers give you a chance to enjoy rafting; from high water rapids to float trips, the area has something for everyone. These same rivers boast outstanding fishing. Twin Lakes and Turquoise Lake afford opportunities to fish, camp, and boat along the tranquil shores of the mountain lakes.

These lakes and rivers are set among and near some of the highest mountains in the Rocky Mountains. Near Leadville, the Sawatch Mountain Range has two peaks higher than 14,000 feet, and the Colorado and Continental Divide trails provide many opportunities for hiking. Numerous mountain biking trails are also in the area. Wilderness areas are the perfect place for extensive rugged outdoor adventure, such as backpacking, camping, hunting, horseback riding, four-wheeling, and climbing. You can visit more than 300 miles of hut-to-hut trails associated with the 10th Mountain Hut and Trail System, one of the most extensive backcountry hut-to-hut systems in North America.

World-class skiing facilities along the byway also make this one of the major recreational draws for the area. Both Copper Mountain Ski Resort and Ski Cooper provide opportunities to ski. Other wintertime activities include backcountry skiing, cross-country skiing, and snowmobiling.

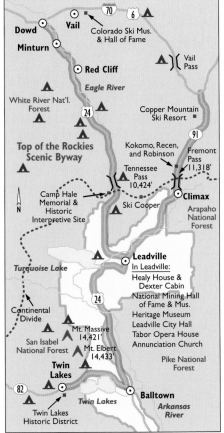

Highlights:

The Top of the Rockies historical tour begins in the town of Dowd, which is about five miles west of Vail along Interstate 70. If you're beginning the tour from Leadville, simply start at the bottom of the list and work your way up.

Dowd and Minturn: The byway passes briefly through these small mountain communities and then quickly gains elevation as it winds its way up and over rugged mountain passes.

Camp Hale Memorial and Historic Interpretive Site: This site is located on the byway near mile-post 160 and features several plaques detailing the history of the 10th Mountain Division that trained here before serving in Europe in World War II.

National Mining Hall of Fame and Museum: Located in Leadville, visitors can see displays of hundreds of fine specimens of gold, silver, ore, and minerals, including spectacular examples loaned from the Smithsonian Institute and the Harvard Mineralogical Museum.

Tabor Opera House: When it opened in 1879, the Tabor Opera House was said to be the finest theater between St. Louis and San Francisco. This building is one of only a few Tabor-associated buildings still standing in Colorado.

Annunciation Church: Started in 1879, this historic church in Leadville was dedicated on New Year's Day, 1880. The church's steeple has become a prominent landmark of this area. It houses a 3,000-plus-pound bell.

Be sure to bring a camera because views of Colorado valleys are incredible, especially in the fall.

Trail Ridge Road/Beaver Meadow Road

The highest continuous paved road in the United States, this byway on the roof of the Rockies offers stirring vistas at every overlook as it climbs through Rocky Mountain National Park.

Sitting in a national park encompassed by national forests, the Trail Ridge Road/Beaver Meadow Road is one of the most beautiful byways in Colorado. The overarching characteristic of the byway is its many overlooks, all of which bestow stirring vistas of 415 square miles of the towering (14,000-plus feet) southern Rockies.

The clear atmosphere of this alpine tundra makes seeing the night sky from one of the overlooks incomparable. Constellations, planets, meteor showers, and phases of the moon

Rocky Mountain National Park encompasses nearly all of the Trail Ridge Road/Beaver Meadow Road and gives a rare opportunity to see up-close alpine tundra.

seem brighter than ever and just beyond arm's reach.

Because this is such a protected area, elk, deer, mountain sheep, coyotes, moose, beavers, ptarmigans, marmots, pikas, eagles, and peregrine falcons can be seen more often than in other (unprotected) areas of Colorado and the nation. Also, the tender tundra wildflowers, which generally peak in July, are an exceptional treat.

Historical: The first Europeans to see this area were French fur traders. In 1859, Joel Estes and his son, Milton, rode into the valley that now bears their name. A few others had settled in this rugged county by 1909 when Enos Mills—a naturalist, writer, and conservationist—began to campaign for preservation of the pristine area, a portion of which became the Rocky Mountain National Park in 1915.

Recreational: The recreational opportunities on this route are varied and excellent. For example, you can enjoy horseback riding, camping, fishing, rock climbing, and numerous winter activities.

Quick Facts

Length: 53 miles

Time to Allow: More than two hours

Consideration: You can't get fuel inside Rocky Mountain National Park so you'll have to fill up in Estes Park or Grand Lake. Beware of vapor lock, a common occurrence for vehicles from low altitudes. Speed limits are generally 35 mph.

Several campgrounds beckon, some of which are open year-round. The Rocky Mountain National Park maintains more than 260 miles of trails for private and commercial horse riders. Hire horses and guides at two locations on the east side of the park or from a number of liveries outside the park boundaries during the summer season.

Four species of trout live in the mountain streams and lakes of Rocky Mountain National Park: German brown, rainbow, brook, and cutthroat trout. These cold waters may not produce large fish, but you do get to enjoy the superb mountain scenery as you fish.

Rocky Mountain National Park also offers a variety of challenging ascents throughout the year for climbers. The Colorado Mountain School is the park's concessionaire, operating a climbing school and guide service.

Winter brings cross-country skiing in the lower valleys and winter mountaineering in the high country. Access roads from the east are kept open and provide you with a panorama of the high mountains.

Highlights:

While visiting the Trail Ridge Road/Beaver Meadow Road, you can take a self-guided tour of the route. If you enter the park from the east (either the Fall River or Beaver Meadows entrance), start at the beginning and move down the list.

Rainbow Curve Overlook: At 10,829 feet, this overlook is more than two vertical miles above sea level. At this elevation, every exposed tree is blasted by wind, ice, and grit into distinctive flag shapes. Tree branches here survive only on the downwind side of tree trunks. Higher still, trees survive only where the severely pruned shrubs are covered and protected by winter snowdrifts.

Forest Canyon Overlook: Here, the erosive force of glacial ice is unmistakable. Although the ice did not reach as high as the overlook, it still lay more

than 1,500 feet thick in a V-shape stream valley. With the grinding of a giant rasp, the ice scoured the valley into the distinctive U-shape of today.

Rock Cut Overlook: Here on the roof of the Rockies, the climate is rigorous. Severe weather can come at any time. Periods of drought may occur in both summer and winter, and winter blizzards are frequent. Temperatures remain below freezing all winter, and they frequently drop below freezing in summer. Wind speeds here can exceed 150 miles per hour in either summer or winter,.

Alpine Visitor Center and Fall River Pass: Beside the visitor center,

there is a gift shop and a short trail to an overlook at 12,003 feet.

Milner Pass: Here, Trail Ridge Road crosses the Continental Divide. At this point, waters enter either the Atlantic or Pacific drainages. The Rockies divide these two great watersheds, but the Continental Divide may be a mountain-top, a ridge, or a pass. From this point, a short trail leads past Poudre Lake, headwaters of the Cache La Poudre River, and up to Old Fall River Road. This road was the original road over the Continental Divide. The trail then connects with another trail leading to Mount Ida, at 12,880 feet. This is a 41/2-mile hike.

Kaibab Plateau–North Rim Parkway

Crossing over a gorgeous high plateau and flanked by rivers and forests, this parkway forms a scenic passage to the North Rim of the Grand Canyon, nature's unsurpassed scenic wonder.

This route crosses over the gorgeous Kaibab Plateau and travels through two forests: the Kaibab National Forest and Grand Canyon National Park. Along the route, you'll find plenty of places to hike and camp. Groves of golden aspen, flowery meadows, ponds, outcrops of limestone, and steep slopes on all sides break up the dominance of the regal coniferous forest. Also, the Colorado River flows right around the byway, so opportunities for water sports abound.

Cultural: The rich cultural diversity of Arizona is proudly displayed on the Kaibab Plateau–North Rim Parkway. Here, you find a diverse cross section of Native Americans and pioneer stock. Visit the local towns of Kanab and Fredonia to see the rich heritage that is still maintained today. From good old country fairs to the vibrant Western Legends Round Up, everyone is sure to have a good time.

Historical: The Kaibab Plateau is rich with the history of preservation and conservation. In 1893, the Grand Canyon Forest Reserve was created, and in the first decade of the 20th century, national forests were designated. Then, in 1906, President Theodore Roosevelt created the Grand Canyon National Game Preserve to protect the Kaibab mule deer, and in 1908, the Grand Canyon Forest Reserve became the Kaibab National Forest.

The historic Jacob Lake Ranger Station was built in 1910 to help administer lands that included what is now Grand Canyon National Park. The ranger station is located along the road that originally led to the North Rim of the Grand Canyon. Eventually, the road to Grand Canyon National Park was moved to its present location, but the Jacob Lake Ranger Station continued to be utilized to administer Kaibab National Forest lands. It is one of the oldest remaining ranger stations in the country and is now an interpretive site presenting the life of a forest ranger.

An awe-inspiring chasm formed over the millennia, the Grand Canyon provides ample opportunity to explore its amazing natural wonders.

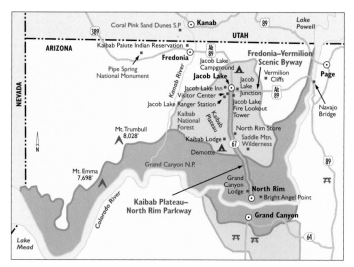

the wilderness and the Grand Canyon National Park trails due to extreme summer temperatures and winter inaccessibility.

The winter season on the Kaibab Plateau is a unique experience. Lodging is available on the plateau at Jacob Lake and Kaibab Lodge. Nordic skiing and snowmobiling are the most popular activities on the plateau in the winter. The area east of Highway 67 is open only to nonmotorized activities. The North Rim is also open only to nonmotorized activities, with no facilities or services during the winter season. All areas west of Highway 67 are open to motorized and nonmotorized activities.

On national forest lands, camping is not limited to campgrounds; instead, camping is permissible off of any dirt road or out of the sight of a paved highway at no charge. Backcountry camping is prohibited within 1/4 mile of water to allow wildlife undisturbed access. Back-country campers also must stay at least 1/2 mile from a developed campground or other facility. Campers are also asked to stay out of meadows, due to the fragile environment.

Highlights:

While visiting the Kaibab Plateau–North Rim Parkway, you can take the following self-guided tour of the byway.

After a devastating wildfire in 1910 burned through much of the Idaho panhandle and parts of western Montana, the United States ushered in an era of fire suppression. Prior to that time, little was done to suppress fires. However, after 1910, fire lookouts and trail systems were developed in earnest throughout the national forest system. The earliest fire lookouts on the Kaibab Plateau consisted of platforms built at the tops of tall trees that were accessed by ladders. Eventually, lookout buildings and lookout buildings and towers were built, including the Jacob Lake Fire Lookout Tower in 1934.

Today, the Jacob Lake Ranger Station and Fire Lookout Tower are on the National Register of Historic Places, and the Jacob Lake Fire Lookout Tower is on the National Register of Fire Lookouts.

Recreational: Nonmotorized and motorized trails are maintained for hikers, walkers, bikers, equestrians, cross-country skiers, four-wheel drivers, and snowmobilers. Fifty miles of the cross-state nonmotorized Arizona Trail traverse the district, providing opportunities for day hiking or multinight trips. Many miles of closed roads provide outstanding mountain biking opportunities for all rider levels. Spring and fall are the best seasons for enjoying both

Jacob Lake Junction: The Jacob Lake Junction is at highway marker 579 or the junction of Highway 67 and State Highway 89A. The Kaibab Plateau Visitor Center offers information and interpretive displays about the natural and cultural resources of the plateau. The visitor center also has books, videos, postcards, and other interpretive sales items through the Public Lands Interpretive Association. At Jacob Lake Campground, you'll find family sites and group sites available.

Jacob Lake Fire Lookout Tower: Get to Jacob Lake Fire Lookout Tower on highway marker 580.3 or one mile south of the Jacob Lake Junction/Highway 67 and State Highway 89A. Visit this historic tower, and find out how fires are detected. Views of the Grand Staircase are visible from the tower. The tower is usually staffed during the day and may be closed for two days during the week; check in at the visitor center for current openings.

Demotte Park Overlook: Find this overlook at highway marker 604 or 22 miles south of the Jacob Lake Junction on the byway. Demotte Park is one of the largest meadows on the Kaibab Plateau, and it's filled with deer,

The Kaibab Plateau provides spectacular views that can be enjoyed by photographers, bird-watchers, hikers, campers, and others.

coyotes, and numerous species of birds. Wildflower enthusiasts will also enjoy the diversity and abundance in this meadow. Near this stop is the historic Kaibab Lodge.

Grand Canyon National Park—North Rim: Forty-four miles south on Highway 67, the end of this scenic parkway leads to a spectacular view of the North Rim of the Grand Canyon. The North Rim Visitor Center is open seven days a week.

Billy the Kid Trail

Infused with the romance of the Wild West, this route through Billy the Kid country rides the trails of outlaws, sheriffs, and cowboys. Bring the kids.

The Lincoln County area surrounding the Billy the Kid Trail is rich in history. It has been home to Billy the Kid, the Lincoln County War, the Mescalero Apache nation, Kit Carson, "Black Jack" Pershing, the Buffalo Soldiers, the world's richest quarter horse race, and Smokey Bear.

Cultural: While many consider Santa Fe the cultural capital of New Mexico, Lincoln County is more than willing to rival this claim. Spectacular annual events showcase the route's cultural dynamics.

Some of the best art in New Mexico can be found in Ruidoso. The Ruidoso Art Festival, held each year in late July, is one of the most outstanding juried art shows in the Southwest. The cool pines create a beautiful mountain setting for spectacular art from more than 125 accomplished, professional artists.

Held at Ruidoso Downs the second weekend of October, the Lincoln County Cowboy Symposium gathers the world's finest cowboy poets, musicians, chuck wagon cooks, and artisans.

For a better glimpse at the real West and American Indian cultures, be sure to see the Mescalero Apache Ceremonial Dances. These ceremonial dances celebrate the Apache Spirit.

The cultural qualities of Lincoln County would be unfinished without mentioning the Spencer Theater for the Performing Arts. Opened in 1997, the Spencer

Sierra Blanca in the Lincoln National Forest takes on a mystical appearance in stormy weather.

Theater creates a year-round venue for world-class performances in theater, music, and dance. An aristocrat among theaters, the 22-million-dollar structure is splendid and elegant, yet intimate and welcoming.

Historical: Henry McCarty, better known as Bonney or Billy the Kid, is the most well-known person from this area. He is believed to have been born in New York City sometime in 1859 or 1860. His family moved to Indiana and then to Wichita, Kansas. In 1874, his mother died, and Billy the Kid was placed in foster homes. He soon ran into trouble with the law and was sent to jail, only to escape through the chimney. Billy the Kid wandered from ranch to ranch and eventually wound up in trouble with the law again when he killed a man at a saloon in Arizona.

When Billy the Kid returned to New Mexico, he and his gang of rustlers became embroiled with the feud going on among James Dolan, John Tunstall, and Alex McSween. Billy the Kid started on Dolan's side, but when he was thrown in jail, he made a deal with Tunstall and became a part of the Regulators, a group that took the law into their own hands after some of their men had been killed. After the Lincoln County War, Billy the Kid made his living by gambling and rustling cattle. He spent his time eluding the law, usually from Pat Garrett, whose job was to hunt for Billy the Kid. After being arrested by Garrett and escaping from jail, Billy the Kid was killed by Garrett in Pete Maxwell's bedroom on July 14, 1881.

One small ferrotype is the only existing authentic photograph of Billy the Kid. Taken by an unknown itinerant photographer outside Beaver Smith's saloon in Old Fort Sumner in 1879, it reveals a young and handsome man. The rumpled hat and layers of utilitarian clothing immediately clash with Hollywood's images of the outlaw. In the photo, he wears a gambler's pinkie ring on his left hand that means he may have cheated at cards. His colt pistol jaunts from his right hip.

Recreational: The Billy the Kid Trail features many recreational opportunities. The historic district of Lincoln, the Hubbard Museum of the American West, Fort Stanton, the Spencer Theater for the Performing Arts, the Ruidoso Downs Racetrack, the Smokey Bear Museum and Park in Capitan, and Ski Apache all lend appeal to the area.

As wild as the West (and kids) can be, the whole family will enjoy the hands-on displays at the Hubbard Museum of the American West.

Highlights:

Consider taking the following historic tour of Billy the Kid country.

Byway Visitor Center: Begin at the Byway Visitor Center located on U.S. Highway 70, and view the exhibits.

Beautiful vistas, vegetation, and wildlife are common along the stops on this byway.

Cemetery and Cave are definite stops along the tour.

Lincoln: After Fort Stanton, drive northeast on U.S. 220 and then southeast U.S. 380 until you arrive in Lincoln. The Lincoln County War started here, and this is also where Billy the Kid made his last escape. Museums and markers are all over this village, which looks almost exactly as it did in the 1850s.

Hubbard Museum of the American West: Right next door to the visitor center is the Hubbard Museum of the American West. Here, exhibits, artifacts, and fine art tell of the special history of the area.

Ruidoso: Heading west on U.S. Highway 70, you pass through the village of Ruidoso, and then turn north on NM Highway 48. Traveling about 26 miles along NM Highway 48, notice the beautiful Sierra Blanca to the west.

Capitan: The next stop of the tour is in Capitan. Here, the Smokey Bear Museum and State Park is a must-see; Smokey is actually buried here. The museum offers exhibits, games, and films about fire safety. There is also a documentary film about Smokey's life.

Fort Stanton: Travel southeast to Fort Stanton. The fort itself is not accessible; however, be sure to stop at the Fort Stanton Post Office and speak with Willie Mae Hobbs, an expert about the Fort Stanton area. The Fort Stanton

El Camino Real

First carved by Spanish explorers, the historic "Royal Highway" follows the Rio Grande from the Mexican border to Santa Fe. Along the way are soaring peaks, American Indian pueblos, and the city of Albuquerque.

One of the most important of the historic trails of New Mexico, El Camino Real is not only the first European road in what is now the United States, but for many years it was also the longest road in North America. The northern portions of El Camino Real followed the Rio Grande Pueblo Indian Trail, which existed for centuries before the Spanish explorers arrived. The land

Pecos National Historical Park preserves nearly 10,000 years of history including fascinating mission ruins.

along El Camino Real has been a meeting ground of peoples and a haven of cultural diversity through the centuries.

El Camino Real follows the Rio Grande River from the U.S.–Mexico border to Santa Fe. It traverses a land rich in history and culture. The scenic beauty of El Camino Real is as varied and colorful as its culture, history, and people. From the low-lying flatlands of the south to the soaring peaks of the northern mountains, the terrain climbs 10,000 feet in altitude, creating a landscape of dramatic contrasts.

Cultural: The cultural landscape along El Camino Real includes a rich variety of people and places. A number of American Indian Pueblos played a significant role in the history of El Camino Real, particularly in establishing trade routes before the arrival of the Spanish. Some pueblos are open to the public year-round and encourage tourism and recreation. Others are open only by invitation during special events (such as feast day celebrations and dances). In addition, the cultural history

of New Mexico and El Camino Real can be enjoyed at a number of museums throughout the byway, including the Maxwell Museum of Anthropology in Albuquerque and the Geronimo Springs Museum in Truth or Consequences.

Historical: El Camino Real, also called the Royal Highway of the Interior Lands, linked New Mexico with New Spain (Mexico) in the Spanish colonial period (1598–1821), the Mexico national period (1821–1848), and the U.S. Territorial period (1848–1912). El Camino Real ran from Mexico City to Chihuahua City, then crossed the desert to El Paso del Norte on what is now the U.S.–Mexico border. After reaching El Paso del Norte, it more or less paralleled the Rio Grande (called

Rio Bravo del Norte) as far as Santa Fe in northern New Mexico.

El Camino Real is one of the most important historic trails in New Mexico. The northern portions of El Camino Real followed the Rio Grande Pueblo Indian Trail, which existed for centuries before the Spanish explorers arrived. This route allowed the Pueblo Indians of New Mexico to have interregional trade with the pre-Columbian Indian civilizations of Mesoamerica.

Recreational: El Camino Real provides a wealth of recreational sites and facilities for visitors to enjoy. Recreational sites lure many outdoor enthusiasts to the Land of Enchantment. Elephant Butte Lake State Park, the largest lake and park in New Mexico, hosts more than a million visitors every year.

Highlights:

This El Camino Real must-see tour begins in Pecos National Historic Park and continues south to Las Cruces. If you're traveling in the other direction, simply start at the bottom of the list and work your way up.

Pecos National Historic Park: A visit to Pecos National Historic Park just south of Santa Fe is a great stop to learn about 10,000 years of history, including the ancient Pueblo of Pecos,

two Spanish colonial missions, and the site of the Civil War battle of Glorieta Pass.

Santa Fe: The town of Santa Fe offers a bevy of sights, sounds, foods, and festivals. Stop for an hour or a week—you'll never tire of the offerings here.

Coronado State Monument and Petroglyph National Monument: Visit two archaeological must-sees before reaching Albuquerque: Coronado State Monument and Petroglyph National Monument.

Isleta Pueblo: Just south of Albuquerque, stop at the Isleta Pueblo. Take time to examine the amazing art produced there, a treat best appreciated in person.

Salinas Pueblo Missions National Monument: A small side trip will bring a great afternoon at the Salinas Pueblo Missions National Monument in Abo.

Truth or Consequences: Stop in the town of Truth or Consequences (T or C, for short). This town has many recreational opportunities.

White Sands National Monument: Back on El Camino Real, head south toward Las Cruces. On Interstate 10, head east toward Alamogordo, where a real treat awaits you at White Sands National Monument.

Historic Route 66

Although much of this icon of American folklore has been absorbed by newer roads, drivers can still get their kicks on parts of Route 66, a blacktop ribbon of adventure across northern New Mexico.

Quick Facts

Length: 604 miles

Time to Allow: 16 hours

Consideration: The busiest seasons are summer and winter. In areas of higher altitude, sweaters and jackets are recommended, even in warmer months.

Many of the early curiosities that made Route 66 intriguing to travelers have fallen victim to interstate highways, but you can still see much of the route's character if you leave the beaten path, both around Albuquerque and on other parts of Historic Route 66. On Albuquerque's eastern edge, you can pick up parts of Route 66 at Tijeras

La Ventana is a large natural arch in the sandstone bluffs on the eastside of El Malpais National Monument.

Canyon, where a serene and rural atmosphere allows you to leave the big city behind. Other parts of Historic Route 66 lead you to quaint and historic sites, enabling you to catch a glimpse into the past.

Cultural: Museums and abandoned pueblos featuring ancient artwork and dress provide byway travelers with reminders of the early culture that thrived for centuries. The Apache, the Navajo, and some nomadic nations all inhabited the desert land; some lived in permanent mud-brick settlements near waterways that were called pueblos when first encountered by Spaniards. The word pueblo also refers to a Native American culture that is unique to the Southwest and not to a particular Native American group. Even though they share many common elements, each pueblo has its own government, social order, religious practices, and language.

The Pueblo people are further distinguished by their art. Each group's jewelry, pottery, weavings, and other art have a different style. Black-on-black

matte pottery, for example, is unique to the San Ildefonso pueblo. Geometric black and white pots are particular to the Acoma. Other non-Pueblo Indians, such as the Navajo and Apaches, are known for their unique and beautiful artwork as well: the Navajos for their weaving and silverwork; the Apaches for their basket weaving.

Spanish conquest is much engrained in early New Mexico's culture. Explorers from Spain in search of riches happened upon the New Mexico area in the early 1540s. Although they didn't find their sought-after gold, they did find thousands of potential Catholic converts. By 1680, Spanish priests had set up more than 80 missions in the area. Although much of the colonization was peaceful, the Spanish culture and Catholic religion imposed on some American

Map labels:
ARIZONA — 666, 371, Navajo I.R., 509, Cont. Divide, Santa Fe N.F., Tent Rocks, Santa Fe, Santa Fe N.F., 25, Las Vegas, Conchas Lake, Conchas Lake S.P., Ute Lake, Ute Lake S.P., Ute Lake S.P., 54, Red Rock S.P., Jemez I.R., Casamero Pueblo Ruins, Las Vegas Nat'l. Wildlife Refuge, 40, Gallup, 605, Bluewater Lake S.P., Petroglyph Nat'l. Mon., 25, 285, 84, Santa Rosa Lake, 104, 602, Cibola N.F., Grants, Albuquerque, Santa Rosa Lake S.P., 40, Cuervo, Tucumcari, 53, 6, Moriarty, Santa Rosa, Sumner Lake, In Tucumcari:, 40, TEXAS, Zuni Pueblo I.R., Laguna I.R., Acoma I.R., Los Lunas, Encino, Vaughn, Blue Hole, 84, Blue Swallow Motel, Mesalands Dinosaur Museum, 209, Ramah Navajo I.R., Acoma Sky Pueblo, Mountainair, 60, Tucumcari Historical Museum, El Malpais Nat'l. Mon., Bandera Volcano and Ice Cave, Cibola N.F., Sumner Lake S.P., Fort Sumner, 268, La Ventana Natural Arch, 25, NEW MEXICO, N, Socorro, N

Indian nations led to the Pueblo Revolt of 1680. Native Americans from all over the area overthrew the settlers, burned churches, and killed priests. The Spanish returned 12 years later and were more attuned to native cultures and religions.

Today's culture is a blend of the Spanish and Native American cultures: Catholicism and indigenous religions, along with festivals and architecture that reflect both cultures. Spanish and Native American art, architecture, and music meshed to create a blend that today is known simply as Southwestern. Mariachi music, pottery, and adobe buildings are cultural reflections of the Southwest that result from a fascinating mixture of many civilizations.

Historical: When incumbent governor A. T. Hannett lost the 1926 New Mexico gubernatorial election to Richard Dillon, he was infuriated over the loss and what he felt was a betrayal by his own party. So he exited with a flamboyant farewell gesture, sending orders to E. B. Bail, the district highway engineer, to assemble all roadbuilding equipment north of U.S. 60 and cut a new road between Santa Rosa and Moriarty before the year (and Hannett's term) ended. Historic Route 66 as we know it today was created.

Hannett, in his 1964 book *Sagebrush Lawyer*, recounts that he conceived of the idea of a shorter route by laying a ruler on the map between Santa

Rosa and Gallup. Of course, the idea was protested not only by chamber of commerce members in Santa Fe (who led a fight to enlarge and straighten a northern route), but also by delegations from the small towns along U.S. 60, a highway that passed through Vaughn, Encino, Mountainair, and Socorro before heading north to Albuquerque. Business leaders in those towns knew that U.S. 60 would have to compete with the new road, but Hannett prevailed because the new shortcut would almost halve the distance from Santa Rosa to Albuquerque.

Plunging ahead, Bail, the district highway engineer, realized the near impossibility of the order. Assembling equipment and organizing road crews would take the rest of November, which meant that the actual construction of 69 miles had to be accomplished in just 31 days. The new cutoff would connect the road seven miles west of Santa Rosa to an existing highway from Moriarty on into Duke City, reducing the distance from 195 miles to 114.

Bail's account of the adventure, first published in 1952 and later appended in Sagebrush Lawyer, credits the road crews with marshaling the motley collection of surplus World War I Caterpillars, tractors, and graders. They did battle against the blowing snow and dense piñon forests. Irate citizens along the southern and northern routes, upset by the impact that reduced traffic would have on their vital tourist business, tried to sabotage the project. Workers found sugar in gas tanks and sand in their engines. Bail brought in blankets so that the workers could sleep next to their equipment at night. Ironically, no one troubled with the most logical way to put a hitch in the project—by fighting it with a lawsuit.

The road was not quite completed by the end of the year so, immediately after taking the oath of office on January 1, 1927, the new governor, Richard Dillon, dispatched an engineer from Santa Fe to halt the venture. However, inclement weather prevented his arrival at the job site before January 3. By then "Hannett's Joke" was complete, and cars drove across the new road. (Hannett denied that his method for accomplishing the project originated as a joke.)

Hannett, whose home base had been Gallup, moved to Albuquerque, practiced law from an office in the Sunshine Building, and wrote a daily column for the *Albuquerque Journal*. Although no monument credits him with the golden thread that helped Albuquerque develop into a metropolitan center, one of the city's streets is named Hannett.

Recreational: Evidence of New Mexico's diversity in culture, climate, and landscape is everywhere, making the area surrounding Historic Route 66 the perfect place to find any type of recreation imaginable.

No trip to the area would be complete without dining in one of the authentic Mexican restaurants. Famous for its fiery-hot chili peppers, New Mexican cuisine is an adventure in itself.

The climate of central New Mexico makes outdoor recreation possible year-round. Summers lend themselves to hiking, camping, biking, and fishing, while New Mexico's winters delight both downhill and cross-country skiers with trails and runs across the state.

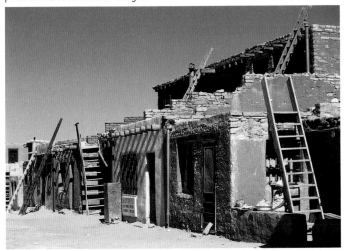

The people of the Acoma Pueblo Village live much like their ancestors did. They reside in the original historic pueblo buildings, and there is no electricity or running water.

New Mexico's Route 66 features historical stops complete with ancient artwork and other cultural landmarks.

The Sandia Mountains, located near Albuquerque, provide exciting recreational opportunities. Travelers enjoy hiking and biking beginner to advanced trails in the summer and skiing the 200 acres of terrain of the Sandia Peak Ski Area in the winter. The ski area's tramway whisks you and your skis or bike to the top of the mountain year-round; just one reason the Sandia Mountains are an excellent place for outdoor adventure.

The geography of the area is unlike any other place. Lush forests, clear lakes, and sporadic mountains break up the desert landscape. Natural caves and rock formations in El Malpais National Monument and Conservation Area are open for tourists to view. Erupted volcanoes, bat caves, and sandstone cliffs

and mesas dot the beautiful area, providing a truly rare chance to see one of the world's most fascinating regions.

If urban entertainment is what you are looking for, New Mexico has that, too. You may want to catch a symphony, attend a hockey game, or shop in unique outdoor markets. The nightlife heats up as the temperatures cool down after dark. Dance clubs, bars, and live music venues around the larger cities come alive at night.

Highlights:

Because Historic Route 66 is more than 600 miles long, the following must-see tour of the byway is split into two sections: one starting near Grants and heading westward into Gallup; the other starting east of Tucumcari and heading westward into Santa Rosa.

Western Must-See Tour

Acoma Sky Pueblo: The first stop along this section is just south of McCarty's, off of exit 96. The Acoma

Sky Pueblo offers a unique view worth seeing—a city atop a 400-foot mesa. The people of the Acoma Pueblo ask that visitors respect the posted warnings and signs and be respectful of residents. Always ask permission to take photos. Also, if you are fortunate to visit on a celebration day or during a dance, remember that dances are prayers and require concentration. Please do not talk to the dancers, walk on the dance plaza, or applaud when a dance ends.

El Malpais National Monument:

The next stop along Route 66 is El Malpais National Monument near Grants. The monument can serve as a central post while visiting several other sites, including La Ventana Natural Arch and Bandera Volcano and Ice Cave.

Bluewater Lake State Park and Casamero Pueblo Ruins: North

of Grants, Bluewater Lake State Park offers a relaxing afternoon of hiking and fishing. The Casamero Pueblo Ruins near McKinley County Road 19 offers a unique view of the area's history. Casamero Pueblo was first recorded by an archaeologist in the mid-1960s. A portion of the site and many smaller sites were reported to have been vandalized prior to this time. Between 1966 and 1975, most of Casamero Pueblo was excavated by archaeologists. In 1976 and 1977, they stabilized the ruins to help prevent deterioration of the walls. Interpretive signs were placed at the site describing the cultural history of the Chacoan Anasazi and the features present at Casamero.

Gallup: The Route 66 Drive-In in Gallup makes a great stop for lunch in keeping with the theme of the drive. Don't forget the Red Rock Museum at Red Rock State Park, just east of Gallup. Also, while in Gallup, finish your trip along western Route 66 by inquiring about ongoing activities at the Gallup McKinley County Chamber of Commerce.

Eastern Must-See Tour

I-40: The modern Route 66 is essentially Interstate 40, although it detours slightly through Tucumcari and Santa Rosa. This section caused quite a lot of trouble back in the early days of Route 66, when the road was narrow and dangerous. This 40-mile stretch of road heading into Tucumcari was poorly maintained and was full of potholes. Driving long hours through this flat countryside often caused motorists to doze off; hitting an unexpected pothole would cause them to lose control. Many people died in collisions on this narrow road. In fact, some of the older residents in the area will tell you that there were "only six inches and a cigarette paper between you and death on 66." Today, I-40 is wider, safer, and well maintained.

Tucumcari: Once in Tucumcari, take exit 335 into town. Historic Route 66 continues along Tucumcari Boulevard. While in Tucumcari, you can easily spend the day shopping or visiting the Blue Swallow Motel (one of the oldest motels in

town and one of the most famous along Route 66), Mesalands Dinosaur Museum, and Tucumcari Historical Museum.

Conchas Lake State Park: At the end of Tucumcari Boulevard, you can choose one of two routes. This tour takes you north on Route 54 toward Conchas home to Conchas Lake State Park, one of New Mexico's largest lakes. The park has a wide variety of water activities, and onshore exploring offers the potential of finding ancient rock formations and American Indian dwellings.

Santa Rosa: Heading farther west along I-40, you pass through Cuervo, and head on to Santa Rosa. The Route 66 Auto Museum is a must-stop for anyone taking in the true spirit of Route 66. The more adventurous will most likely enjoy a dip at Blue Hole, an 81-foot deep clear, natural artesian spring famous for its scuba diving opportunities. A stop at nearby Santa Rosa Lake State Park and Sumner Lake State Park will give the recreationally minded plenty of choices.

The Blue Hole is a natural artesian spring delivering 3,000 gallons of water a minute. At more than 80 feet deep, the pool is amazingly clear nearly to the bottom when undisturbed.

Jemez Mountain Trail

Ghost towns, volcanic rocks, hot springs, American Indian pueblos, camp-grounds, and forests—the Jemez Mountain Trail beckons explorers to a land rich in history, geology, culture, and outdoor recreation.

North of Albuquerque, at the unspoiled village of San Ysidro, begins one of New Mexico's most spectacular scenic drives: the Jemez (pronounced HAY-mez or HAY-mus) Mountain Trail. San Ysidro is a village where you can find the work of local artisans and view the restored Spanish adobe church.

Cultural: The greater Santa Fe area is extremely culturally diverse due to strong Native American and Spanish influences. Of the 19 Native American communities located in New Mexico, eight are in the greater Santa Fe area. All eight are Pueblo Indian nations, and their communities are referred to as pueblos. Many of these pueblos were established centuries ago; the Taos Pueblo, for example, is thought to have been continuously occupied for close to 1,000 years. Each pueblo has its own government, traditions, and ceremonies and is a sovereign and separate entity. The pueblos typically welcome visitors, especially during specific dances and feast days.

A people of great faith, the early Spanish settlers arrived in 1607 with scores of Catholic priests. Just as the Spanish created houses of worship from an adobe mix of mud and straw, they built villages and towns in the same architectural fashion.

Like adobe architecture, art forms practiced by early Spanish settlers were shaped largely from resources they found in their natural environment. Using native aspen and pine, paints derived from natural pigments, and other local materials, they created utilitarian goods and religious objects to adorn their homes and churches. At first, the work echoed the traditional artworks and motifs they had carried with them to the New World from Mexico and Spain. But in time, native artisans developed styles and techniques that were unique to New Mexico alone. Ranging from santos (carved images of saints), furniture, and textiles to works in tin, iron, silver, and straw, the art of the Spanish colonial era

Soda Dam is a large mound of calcium carbonate deposited over millions of years by hot springs bubbling from Earth's interior.

varying degrees of difficulty, biking trails, fishing, and several camping locations. The unique geological features also allow for outdoor adventures; you can visit caves and tunnels.

For the adventurous, Battleship Rock in the Jemez Mountains provides challenging terrain and an intriguing landscape: The trail is covered in shiny black obsidian created from volcanic eruptions five million years ago.

If you enjoy biking, the Jemez Mountain Trail provides several trails. Advanced bikers may want to explore Guacamalla and Paliza Canyons, a steep terrain that offers excellent views of green meadows.

Highlights:

As you travel the Jemez Mountain Trail, consider using this itinerary.

Los Alamos: Your trip through the Jemez Mountains begins in Los Alamos,

remains the art of many Santa Fe-area families. Meanwhile, other artists have carried their ancestors' legacy to new levels of excellence by working in more modern media, including sculpture, photography, painting, jewelry, and literature.

Historical: Jemez State Monument and Bandelier National Monument are popular places to discover more about the history of the area. Both monuments have exhibits and self-and ranger-guided tours.

Recreational: The Jemez Mountain Trail offers all sorts of outdoor recreation. Travelers enjoy hiking trails of

famous as the home of the Los Alamos National Laboratory for its work and historic role in the Manhattan Project and the development of the atomic bomb. The Bradbury Science Museum offers a great deal of information.

Valle Grande: After that, travel east and follow the signs to Valle Grande, the remains of a volcano that erupted 1.4 million years ago. Hot springs and recreational opportunities abound here.

Cuba: After Valle Grande, continue north to Highway 126. This road, all the way to Cuba, is not paved but is well traveled. However, a four-wheel-drive vehicle is recommended for better safety.

Cabezon: After a rest in Cuba, travel south along Interstate 550. A quick detour off of the byway heading west on 197 will take you to Cabezon, a ghost town that was a flourishing city until the 1940s. Back on Interstate 550, head south through the national forest and down toward the many American Indian pueblos. The Zia and Jemez Pueblos have wonderful opportunities for learning and adventure.

Spence Hot Springs: The Jemez State Monument is a perfect getaway in the late afternoon and is highlighted by a dip in the Spence Hot Springs.

Santa Fe Trail

Ride the historic Santa Fe Trail in the footsteps of Western pioneers, Spanish missionaries, and American Indian traders. Start in Santa Fe, and enjoy prairie vistas, rugged landscapes, and the other Las Vegas along the way.

Quick Facts

Length: 381 miles

Time to Allow: Eight hours

Consideration: The best time to drive this route is in the early spring through late fall.

The Santa Fe Trail was the first of America's great trans-Mississippi routes. The trail, including the Mountain and Cimarron routes, traversed more than 1,200 miles from Franklin, Missouri, to Santa Fe, New Mexico. From 1821 to 1880, it was an important two-way avenue for commerce and cultural exchange among Spanish, American Indian, and American cultures.

The area around the Santa Fe Trail boasts more than 20 historic districts and 30 individual sites that are recorded on the National Register of Historic Places.

Cultural: The Santa Fe Trail was the first trail of commerce between the Southwest and the United States. From 1821 to 1880, the Santa Fe Trail was an important two-way avenue for commerce and cultural exchange among Spanish, Native American, and American cultures. You can see evidence of this abounding culture in many of the events and activities on the byway.

Historical: The Santa Fe Trail was the first international trade route, carrying needed materials from Missouri to northern Mexico and taking back silver, furs, mules, and wood to Missouri.

As early as the 1700s, Pueblo and Plains Indian trade fairs at Pecos and Taos introduced Spanish residents to native products. Yet trade between New Mexico and other settlements throughout the West was banned because New Mexico was a colony of Spain and c ould trade only with the mother country. Beginning in 1810 and succeeding in 1821, uprisings in Mexico gave New Mexico freedom to trade with anyone. November 16, 1821, is recognized as the start of legal international trade between New Mexico and the United States; this date also marks the beginning of the Santa Fe Trail.

The Santa Fe Trail passed through the territories and ranges of many Native American nations, including the Pawnee, Arapaho, Cheyenne, Comanche, and the Kiowa, so American Indian traders used it as a commercial route. After the Mexican War (1846–1848), the Jicarillas, Comanches, Kiowas, and other nations became increasingly threatened by the traffic on the trail. With the American promise to the people of New Mexico to subdue the various American Indian nations, an intermittent war began that

In New Mexico's high country, Cimarron Canyon State Park features the Cimarron River and granite cliffs as dominant aspects of the landscape.

Indian pueblo and two 17th-century Franciscan missions.

Las Vegas: Your next stop should be in Las Vegas, New Mexico. It has a great wildlife refuge.

Fort Union National Monument: Going north, still on I-25, you'll pass Buena Vista and come into Fort Union National Monument. The remains of this star-shaped fort are a fantastic sight.

Springer and Clayton: The Santa Fe Trail Museum should be your next stop as you approach the town of Springer and the major highway junction. Enjoy the Kiowa National Grassland as you drive east to the border and the town of Clayton. While here, don't forget to stop and enjoy Clayton Lake State Park, a great place to camp.

Raton: Next, leaving the byway for a few miles, take Highway 64 up to Raton for a fun experience at the Sugarite Canyon State Park. Then, back on the byway, hop on Highway 64 going south through Cimarron. This drive is fantastic and takes you through the Cimarron Canyon State Park. At this point, you may choose to head over to Taos or back to Santa Fe.

ended in the mid-1870s. The American Indian nations of New Mexico were then confined to reservations.

After the Mexican War (and with New Mexico a U.S. Territory), the trail became mainly a military road. It supplied goods to the large contingent of troops in the Southwest, and mercantile goods were still carried into Mexico and New Mexico. After the Civil War, railroads began laying tracks to the West. By 1879, the first locomotive reached Las Vegas, New Mexico, and in 1880, the railroad reached Lamy, essentially ending wagon traffic across the 900 miles of plains.

Recreational: You'll find many recreational activities along the Santa Fe Trail, including fishing, camping, skiing, mountain biking, and hiking. Several state parks and recreational areas are located in northeastern New Mexico. As a matter of fact, outdoor recreation is one of the top four reasons people visit New Mexico.

Highlights:

This Santa Fe Trail tour begins in Santa Fe and heads east to Clayton. With a little backtracking, the trail goes north and enters Colorado over the Raton Pass.

Pecos National Historic Park: Your first stop will be at Pecos National Historic Park, where you'll want to spend some time learning about the ruins of a 14th-century American

Turquoise Trail

Leave the freeway behind to travel the backcountry Turquoise Trail into a four-season mountain wilderness. Then gaze down from the top of a crest to savor some of America's most stunning views.

Back roads often lead to glorious scenery and great discovery, and so it is with the Turquoise Trail. When you leave the freeway and venture onto the scenic and historic Turquoise Trail, you get a chance to see 15,000 square miles of central New Mexico from a bird's-eye view atop Sandia Peak, the magnificent summit of the Sandia Mountains that rises 10,378 feet. From here, you can venture into Sandia Mountain Wilderness and hike through aspen glades and across flowering meadows, coming upon one spectacular view after another.

You can also visit the ghost mining towns of Golden, Madrid, and Cerrillos, towns now with great arts, crafts, theater, music, museums, and restaurants.

Cultural: New Mexico's vibrant history has permeated modern society and left cultural treasures throughout the area. Retaining the flavor of the Southwest, local artisans have saved several of the region's ghost towns and transformed them into artistic communities. Along the byway, you will find shops and galleries filled with paintings, sculpture, pottery, leather goods, jewelry, furniture, beadwork, toys, art wear, and antiques. Some of the old company stores and houses have also been refurbished as restaurants and bed-and-breakfasts.

Historical: Native Americans were the first people to extract gold, silver, lead, zinc, and turquoise from the hills. Indeed, the turquoise found near the Turquoise Trail is considered by some to be the finest in the world. Usually sky

Hundreds of balloons paint a fanciful rainbow of colors in the sky over Albuquerque each year during the annual International Hot Air Balloon Festival.

blue to light greenish blue, turquoise can also be white, dark blue, jade green, reddish brown, and even violet. In the early 1900s, Tiffany's of New York helped to popularize the shade known as robin's egg blue.

When the Native Americans began their mining efforts, the mineral deposits were in pure veins. Early digging implements included stone hammers, chisels, and files. After the minerals had been removed, the native miners would carry the ore and rock outside the mine in reed baskets or buckets made of hide. Spanish explorers estimated that native miners had removed 100,000 tons of rock, based on huge tailing piles and 400-year-old piñon trees growing from the piles.

Although some mining occurred during Spain's (and later Mexico's) ownership of the land, the majority of mining appears to have been done during the territorial expansion of the United States.

Golden began with humble beginnings during the 1825 gold rush, the first gold rush to occur west of the Mississippi. Here, two mining camps were created to mine placer gold (gold extracted from streams or rivers). In 1880, several mining companies moved into the area and renamed the two camps "Golden" to match their high hopes of profiting.

However, these hopes faded by 1884, and the population of Golden steadily decreased.

Another popular New Mexico mining community, Cerrillos, hit its peak in the 1880s, due in part to the arrival of the railroad. The early 1880s quickly expanded the local mines, with more than 2,000 land claims filed on only a few square miles of land. Soon,

Sandia Crest, the summit of the Sandia Mountains, gives a bird's-eye view of the magnificent landscape below.

Recreational: The Turquoise Trail has numerous opportunities to enjoy recreation.

Built in 1966, the Sandia Peak Tramway is the longest continuous jigback tram in the world, which means it has one car going up while another is coming down, and it has the third longest clear span in the world. It is the only place in the United States where visitors traveling on an artificial transportation system are virtually surrounded by a nationally designated wilderness area.

The pristine Sandia Mountain Wilderness is a natural, scenic, and recreational wonder located adjacent to metropolitan Albuquerque. More than 100 miles of recreational trails in the wilderness area offer a wide variety of terrain.

Highlights:

The best way to experience the nature of the Turquoise Trail is to stop at the small towns along the byway and speak with the folks who live there. Here's a sampling of places you may want to stop.

Cerrillos swelled to accommodate 21 saloons and 4 hotels. Sadly, prosperity abandoned Cerrillos within the decade. Today, the Cerrillos Hills Historic Park and the immediately adjacent lands contain approximately 90 vertical or near-vertical shafts, with depths exceeding six feet.

Madrid was founded in the oldest coal-mining region of the state and gradually grew to become the center of the coal-mining industry for the region. Under the direction of the superintendent of mines, employees were to donate from 50 cents to one dollar a month for community causes and were also required to participate in town events such as the Fourth of July celebrations and Christmas light displays. In fact, Madrid became famous for its Christmas light displays. However, the town's Christmas celebrations ended in 1941 with the start of World War II. Eventually, people began choosing natural gas in favor of coal, and the mines near Madrid closed in the early 1950s, causing the town to be abandoned.

Tijeras Pueblo: Between 1948 and 1976, excavations in this area helped scientists learn about the Tijeras Pueblo, a large nation believed to have been in existence between A.D. 1300 and 1600. The pueblo itself includes 200 rooms, a dozen small buildings, and a kiva. After excavation was done, the area was covered again with soil to preserve it.

Sandia Ranger Station: The first stop along the trail is at the Sandia Ranger Station on NM 337. This is a nice way to learn the early history of the area. Inquire about road conditions here as well as special activities that may be planned.

The J. W. Eaves Movie Ranch was built in the late 1960s.

Sandia Peak Tramway: Continue north on 14 out of Tijeras, and turn left on Highway 536 heading toward Sandia Peak. While at Sandia Peak, be sure to stop at the Tinkertown Museum. Continue on to the Sandia Peak Tramway. After the tram, continue to the highpoint of the road and take a quick tour of the Sandia Cave—with your flashlight!

Madrid: Head back down Highway 536, turn left, and continue north on Highway 14. Drive toward Madrid. Expect to spend some time here enjoying the Old Coal Mine Museum and the Engine House Theatre. This town, after being deserted due to a mine shutdown, was listed for sale in *The Wall Street Journal* in 1954 for 250,000 dollars. No one bought it, but the town has been revived since the 1970s by artisans.

Cerrillos: Just north of Madrid and before Cerrillos, be on the lookout for a unique art display. Animal bones and glass are the tools of artist Tammy Jean Lange. A few miles up the road is Cerrillos. Thomas Edison is reported to have stayed here briefly while conducting studies with the area's minerals.

Shona Sol Sculpture Garden and J. W. Eaves Movie Ranch: Five miles past Cerrillos, look for the Shona Sol Sculpture Garden, a gallery of African sculpture. Finally, make a stop at the J. W. Eaves Movie Ranch, home to many famous movies, including *Silverado*.

WEST COAST

From Hawaii to Alaska, the Pacific Northwest to California, this chapter covers America's remarkably diverse West Coast. Drivers along this region's awe-inspiring scenic routes will encounter icy glaciers and ancient volcanoes, arid deserts and crystalline lakes, urban parklands and remote campgrounds, white sand beaches and cool redwood forests. Oregon's Historic Columbia River Highway follows thundering rivers through narrow canyons. California's Big Sur Coast Highway hugs steep sea cliffs as it twists and turns high above the crashing Pacific. Washington's Mountains to Sound Greenway links Puget Sound and Seattle to the soaring peaks of the Cascades. And all along the way, stopovers provide ready access to the multitude of recreational and cultural bounties lying just beyond the byways.

North Shore Oahu/Kamehameha Highway

Ambling along Oahu's tropical and rustic North Shore, the sun-drenched Kamehameha Highway provides a taste of the Hawaii that once was, as well as easy access to some of the world's top surfing beaches.

Away from the urban bustle of Honolulu and the crowds of Waikiki, the road that traverses Oahu's North Shore is a study in pastoral tranquility and rural charm, set against the backdrop of the blue Pacific. The Kamehameha Highway (Route 83)—named for King Kamehameha the Great, who conquered and unified all the Hawaiian islands in the late 18th and early 19th centuries—hugs the Pacific Ocean from the eastern (windward) side of the island going north and then west until it dips south toward Pearl Harbor at the town of Haleiwa. Along the way, it passes a succession of small coves and bays and miles of white sand beaches, some nearly deserted. In summer, the ocean waters tend to be fairly calm and good for swimming. In winter, the waves at Waimea Bay and Sunset Beach may hit 25 to 30 feet or more—the largest surfable waves in the world.

Those who travel Oahu's unspoiled North Shore will soon feel as though they have escaped to the Hawaii of old. Roadside vendors peddle local delicacies such as coconuts, fresh pineapple (the Dole Plantation is farther down Kamehameha Highway to the south), Kahuku sweet corn, and cold shrimp. General stores and food stands offer up some of the islands' most refreshing shaved ice, the exceptionally tasty Hawaiian version of the snow cone; tropical flavors include pineapple, coconut, and passion fruit, and are often served over ice cream or azuki beans. The historic resort town of Haleiwa, the "surf capital of the world," features old-fashioned eateries, intriguing shops, and, of course, the ever-inviting Pacific surf.

As beautiful as the drive is, it's hard to resist stopping at one of the many beaches along the North Shore. Sunset Beach, Ehukai Beach, and Waimea Bay are world famous for their monster

Kualoa Ranch, a historic 4000-acre working cattle ranch, spreads from steep mountain rises to the sparkling ocean waters.

Kuilima Cove
Turtle Bay
Kawela Bay
Sunset Beach
Banzai Beach
Puu O Mahuka Heiau
Waimea Bay
Waimea Bay Beach Park
Haleiwa Beach
Haleiwa
Ehukai Beach
Pipeline
Shark's Cove at
Pupukea Beach Park
Waimea Valley
Adventure Park
Sacred Falls
State Park
Dole Pineapple
Plantation
Kualoa Point
Kualoa Ranch
Kahuku
Malaekahana State Recreation Area
Polynesian Cultural Center
Punaluu
Kahana Bay
Kaaawa Beach
Kualoa Beach Park
Chinaman's Hat
Kaneohe Bay
Kaneohe
Pacific Ocean
North Shore Oahu/
Kamehameha Highway
HAWAII
H2
H3
H1
Honolulu
Pearl Harbor
N

waves and surfing competitions. Malaekahana State Recreation Area has terrific swimming and body surfing. Other beaches, such as Shark's Cove at Pupukea Beach Park, are known for their tide pools and snorkeling. Kawela Bay and Kuilima Cove are uncrowded sandy beaches with safe swimming and snorkeling year-round. In winter, beachgoers might spot humpback whales offshore, migrating south from Alaska to mate.

Highlights:

For those who approach from the windward (eastern) side of Oahu, the North Shore drive begins at Kualoa Point, at the northern end of Kaneohe Bay, which overlooks the conical-shaped island known as Chinaman's Hat and is the site of Kualoa Beach Park. (Those who approach from the leeward or western side, almost due north from Pearl Harbor, will begin the North Shore drive at Haleiwa, so simply reverse the order given here.)

Kualoa Ranch: Kualoa Ranch, a 4,000-acre working ranch just beyond Kualoa Beach Park, has both seafront and a backdrop of steep green mountain cliffs. It offers horseback riding, ranch tours, and other outdoor activities.

Sacred Falls State Park: The highway continues north directly along the windward shore, past Kaaawa Beach, Kahana Bay, and the small resort area of Punaluu. Just beyond Punaluu Beach is Sacred Falls State Park, where a two-mile hiking trail leads through a canyon to the falls, considered Oahu's most beautiful. The trail was closed in 1999, however, due to dangerous rockslides. Check at the entrance for current status.

Polynesian Cultural Center: A bit farther north up the coast in Laie is the Polynesian Cultural Center, said to be Hawaii's most popular paid attraction, which depicts life in Pacific island cultures from Hawaii to Fiji and the Marquesas. Evening luaus and other entertainment are also offered.

Kahuku: Near the northernmost point on the island (Kahuku Point) is the historic sugar plantation town of Kahuku, site of an old sugar mill.

Turtle Bay: As the road dips south-west, an isolated promontory leads to Turtle Bay, surrounded by two protected swimming coves, Kawela Bay and Kuilima Cove. Besides miles of isolated beaches, Turtle Bay is known for winter whale watching and the North Shore's major resort hotel.

Sunset Beach, Ehukai Beach, Pipeline, Banzai Beach, and Pupukea Beach Park: A bit farther west comes a quick succession of world-famous surfing beaches—Sunset Beach, Ehukai Beach, Pipeline, and Banzai Beach—where waves are most powerful in winter. These present the best views of what's called the Banzai Pipeline, where surfers disappear inside the tube-shaped barrel of a "perfect wave" and emerge seconds later when it breaks. (Banzai, a Japanese war cry, refers to the courage to surf there.)

Puu O Mahuka Heiau: Across from Waimea Bay, take a left turn down Pupukea Road to the Puu O Mahuka Heiau—Oahu's largest heiau (sacred temple)—an 18th-century historic landmark perched on a ridge with a spectacular view of Waimea Valley.

Waimea Valley Adventure Park: The next left off the highway, Waimea Valley Road, leads to the 1,800-acre Waimea Valley Adventure Park, which has a botanical garden with thousands of species of tropical plants, a 45-foot waterfall, cliff divers, hula demonstrations, a kids' area, and more.

Waimea Bay Beach Park: Back on Kamehameha Highway, the surf's up again at Waimea Bay Beach Park, where the waves may reach 30 feet or higher in the winter months. In summer, you can swim in calm turquoise waters.

Haleiwa: At the end of this North Shore drive is Haleiwa, established in 1832 on Waialua Bay by Protestant missionaries. The missionaries' original church and the remains of their adobe home still stand, and much of the town has a rustic, early 1900s feel, complete with paniolo (Hawaiian cowboy) architecture.

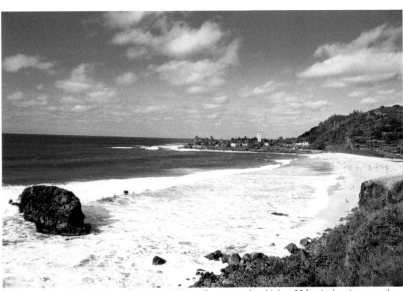

With calm waters in the summer, the waves at Waimea Bay can reach as high as 30 feet in the winter months.

Alaska's Marine Highway

Alaska's Marine Highway is like no other scenic "highway" in America. Riding ferryboats rather than cars, sightseers encounter magnificent views of fjords, glaciers, mountains, islands, waterfalls, and whales—all from the water.

Alaska is best seen from a ferry. The only byway of its kind, Alaska's Marine Highway lets you leave the driving to someone else as you travel scenic coastal routes totaling more than 8,000 miles. From the southern terminus in Bellingham, Washington, the ferries ply waters lined with the lush, green rain forests of British Columbia and Alaska's Inside Passage. Voyagers pass glaciers and fjords in Prince William Sound and the windswept Aleutian Islands, rich in cultural, archaeological, and seismic history.

In southeastern Alaska, northbound travelers can end their sail in Haines or Skagway to connect to the Yukon or other Alaska scenic highways, such as the Haines Highway and the Taylor/Top of the World Highway. Ferryboats travel routes in southcentral Alaska and Prince William Sound.

Cultural: Alaska's native cultures have been joined over the years by Russian and American cultures to create a rich history and a thriving present.

The lives of residents, along with the industries that allow them to survive in the Land of the Midnight Sun, are around every corner as you enjoy the decks of the ferry or the streets of one of Alaska's towns. Alaska's Marine Highway takes you through fishing villages and historic towns.

Nearly every stop on the byway reveals more history of the native Alaskans who have lived here for centuries. The native people celebrate festivals and wear authentic clothing. Feasts and festivals that involve dancing, singing, arts, and crafts traditionally occur during the winter, when all the work of the summer has been done. Many of the festivals are held in honor of animal spirits. The festivals and traditions you witness on

Prince William Sound along Alaska's Marine Highway is situated in the coastal arc of the Chugach Mountain Range.

the byway may be the most memorable part of your trip.

Historical: The history of coastal Alaska dates back to unrecorded times, when the first native Alaskans were just getting used to the beautiful, yet extreme, territory in which they lived. Over many centuries, Alaska has come to be appreciated by different cultures that wanted to stake a claim in the area. As you travel along Alaska's Marine Highway, each port unravels more of the past.

Kodiak Island was the site of the first permanent Russian colony in 1784. The same Russian trappers who were willing to brave the elements in Siberia were also willing to settle the land across the Bering Strait if it meant finding more furs. As settlement progressed, a Russian Orthodox mission was established to keep peace between native peoples and the Russians until the parcel of land was sold to the United States. Today, towns such as Sitka, Unalaska, Seldovia, and many others display pieces of Russian history and influence in Alaska.

Development in Alaska really began in 1867 when "Seward's Icebox" became a U.S. territory. News of gold in the Arctic spread like wildfire, and prospectors gathered in mining communities to try their luck. Ketchikan became the gateway to the Klondike Gold Rush, and Skagway became the destination. Skagway still maintains its reputation as a gold rush town with the Klondike Gold Rush National Historic Park. All through the Inside Passage and into southcentral Alaska, miners established communities in places that promised wealth. Some were successful, and many were not, but stories of Alaska were told far and wide in the lower 48 states.

Recreational: Recreation and adventure go hand in hand, and what is more adventurous than an ocean voyage? From the decks of the ships to the streets of each town to the trails of the forests, you'll find plenty of places to explore along Alaska's Marine Highway. Most of the land along the byway is publicly owned, which makes wilderness experiences and recreational opportunities virtually endless. While you ride the ferry, you can dine, lounge, and even camp on the decks.

One of the benefits of traveling Alaska's Marine Highway is being able to take your favorite recreational activities with you—mountain biking, kayaking, hiking, or whatever other activities beckon along the coast. At each community, you'll find opportunities to get out and explore, with miles of trails, plenty of parks, and places to stay available at every stop.

Highlights:

Alaska's Marine Highway takes you through a variety of towns (listed here from east to west) along the southern Alaskan coastline.

Ketchikan: Ketchikan is known as the Gateway to Alaska and is the state's salmon capital. The community is known for its historic Creek Street district and timber industry.

Petersburg: This town is known as Little Norway due to its Scandinavian roots. It has several festivals to celebrate the heritage of its residents.

Sitka: Numerous volcanic mountains rise out of the ocean and provide a stunning backdrop for this fishing community. Sitka was the Russian capital of North America in the 19th century, as well as the first state capital of Alaska. The community is also a center for Tlingit native culture.

Juneau: Juneau is the capital of Alaska and is a historic community with a range of tourism-oriented services and cultural events. The community was settled as a gold mining district and is now the service hub for southeastern Alaska. It is also the gateway to Glacier Bay National Park.

Skagway: Skagway is a community with a rich history that includes the Klondike Gold Rush. The history of that period is displayed by a National Historic Park site and by the city's historic architecture. The White Pass and Yukon Route historic railway traverses the 3,000-foot mountain pass to the Yukon, Canada.

Haines: Haines is a popular port community. The town is also known for its bald eagle population in the autumn. In October, the world's largest number of bald eagles gather in Haines to take advantage of the late salmon run.

Valdez: Valdez is the terminus of the Trans-Alaskan Pipeline and the Richardson State Scenic Byway. Don't miss the scenic walking trail.

Whittier: Located at the head of Passage Canal, a breathtaking fjord of Prince Williams Sound, Whittier is an

Nestled on the west side of Baranof Island, Sitka is flanked on the east by majestic snow-capped mountains and on the west by the Pacific Ocean.

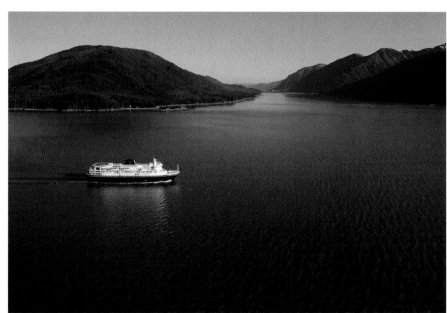

The open waters–including the Pacific Ocean–offer plenty of opportunities for boating.

capital of Russian America. The community is located on Kodiak Island, a national wildlife preserve.

Unalaska/ Dutch Harbor: Located in the Aleutian Islands, Unalaska/Dutch Harbor was the first Russian-American community in Alaska.

important hub connecting the Marine Highway to the Alaska Railroad and to the rest of Alaska.

Seward: If you hear names such as Resurrection Bay and Marathon Mountain, you are probably in the romantic town of Seward. The town was named to honor William H. Seward, who helped the United States purchase Alaska from Russia. Near Seward, you'll find Kenai Fjords National Park and the Chugach National Forest headquarters.

Homer: Homer is the homeport for a large fleet of halibut charter operators fishing the rich and scenic waters of Kachemak Bay. Both commercial fishing boats and leisure fishers gather at The Spit for boating and fishing. Also located in Homer is the Alaska Maritime National Wildlife Refuge. The refuge is home to seabirds, which find a habitat in the rocks and reefs of Alaskan islands.

Kodiak: Kodiak, the nation's largest commercial fishing port, was once the

Glenn Highway

This far-north highway provides passage to a land of native cultures and rugged landscapes as it winds its way from Anchorage toward mountains, rivers, and tundra. Count on long summer days and starry winter nights.

Quick Facts

Length: 135 miles

Time to Allow: Eight years

Consideration: The Glenn Highway is subject to avalanches; when traveling during winter, check road and weather information prior to the trip, and carry appropriate winter gear. Pull-offs are plowed and available for viewing in the winter.

The Glenn Highway is a place where geology, culture, and scenery come together to create a majestic and rugged landscape that can be seen only in Alaska. Winters bring the fascinating Northern Lights among snowcapped mountains. In the spring, hawks, eagles, and falcons can be seen gliding over the Glenn Highway. Summers bring endless days of wildflowers and green forests along the Matanuska River Canyon that runs between the Chugach and Talkeetna Mountains, creating beautiful views all the way.

Among the mountains and the unforgettable seasons lives a distinct Alaskan culture that has been developing for centuries—beginning with the native Alaskan culture that was altered so much with the arrival of Russian fur traders and, later, gold miners from the lower 48 states. The history of all of Alaska's cultures can be seen along the byway in museums and historic places.

Cultural: Cultures from all over the world have combined along the Glenn Highway. Museums, architecture, and

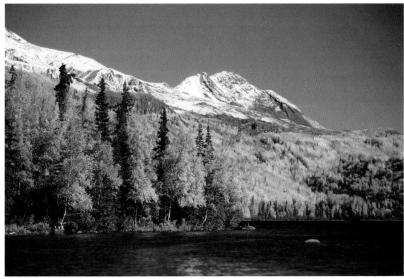

The Mat-Su Valley was shaped by Ice Age glaciers. Today the valley is covered by beautiful trees, here exhibiting vibrant autumn colors, and by tundra spotted with lakes.

historic districts celebrate the unique history of each culture. To discover the original cultures of Alaska, visit the Anchorage Museum or the Alaska Native Heritage Center.

Native society was structured around the family unit. Families hunted together, and when fishing, hunting, or trapping was good, the entire family experienced prosperity. But survival in the Arctic was always a challenge. This way of life remained unchanged for many years, until a new culture emerged during the late 1700s.

When people from Russia began to come to Alaska, they brought their religion with them. Their goal was to introduce the native people of Alaska to Christianity, and one of the rules was that the people could accept the religion only of their own free will. Because of this, the Russian priests who lived in Alaska were extremely dedicated to supporting their parishes during the 100 years they were in Alaska. Yet native Alaskans often combined cultural beliefs: Native people who converted to Orthodoxy would bury the

remains of their dead, but also build a small "spirit house" above the grave.

An economic culture began to grow in Alaska during the 1870s. Rumors of coal, timber, and especially gold brought another significant culture to the land. Mining towns sprung up all over, and Alaska embarked on another great change. Many of those mining towns became the central cities of Alaska; descendants of gold miners became coal miners.

During the 20th century, people continued to gather in Alaska for relief from the Depression or for military strategy during World War II. It was during wartime that the Glenn Highway was constructed as an attempt to better connect Alaska with the lower 48 states.

Historical: Alaska is a romanticized land with a history of gold camps, dog-sled races, and native Alaskans. Native people with the courage and endurance to establish their culture in this rugged

The Eklutna Cemetery has "spirit houses" over the graves of deceased loved ones. The custom comes from a combination of native Alaskan and Russian Orthodox beliefs.

Matanuska Glacier provide opportunities to spot wildlife or get a closer look at a glacier. With the Chugach and Talkeetna Mountains surrounding the byway, you have many opportunities for hiking and exploring these ancient landforms.

In a place where winter engulfs a large part of the year, winter recreation has been perfected. The lodges and roadhouses along the Glenn Highway are perfect places to stop in the winter and enjoy cross-country skiing, snowmobiling, and snowshoeing. You can hardly help enjoying a winter night in Alaska, where the short days lead to extra-long nights. You may want to do some stargazing here or watch for the Northern Lights.

But even in Alaska, the snow melts and summer activities become available to travelers and residents. Alaska is the Land of the Midnight Sun, where, in summer, the long, sunny days make up for the nights of winter. Many people come just to see the wildflowers and watch for wildlife. During March, April, and early May, the air is filled with birds, migrating and moving. A stop at milepost 118 provides an excellent opportunity for viewing birds of prey. The melting rivers and streams are another source of activity. Of course, the fishing in Alaska is superb, but anglers aren't the only ones who enjoy the rivers; raf-

territory settled here nearly 35,000 years ago. Since then, Alaska has maintained its pristine wildernesses, unique wildlife, and exotic atmosphere.

A people known as the Athabascans came from Asia and were the first inhabitants in the lands where the Glenn Highway is now located. The village of Eklutna is a settlement that has been inhabited since the late 1600s by these people. It was not until the 1700s that the land and its people were recorded by Europeans. Explorers James Cook and Vitus Bering opened up European trade between native people in Alaska and their own countries.

In 1867, the United States purchased Alaska from Russia and caused a scandal among the American people. They were mortified at the 7.2-million-dollar price that the government was willing to pay for a frozen wasteland. But with the continued wealth achieved from fur trapping and gold discovered in Alaska, the area's reputation improved in the eyes of Americans, and people from the lower states began to flock to the territory.

Recreational: Getting a good dose of nature isn't difficult when you visit the Glenn Highway. Chugach State Park is accessible from the byway, and places such as the Palmer Hay Flats and the ters and kayakers find places on Alaska rivers to test their skills.

Highlights:

The Glenn Highway takes you through several Alaskan towns (listed here from west to east).

Anchorage: The city of Anchorage began as a ramshackle community of rail workers living in tents. The community, settled in 1915, has grown and evolved into the largest city in Alaska, with 260,000 people. For a look at Alaskan culture, explore the Anchorage Museum or the Alaska Native Heritage Center.

Eagle River: This community, within the municipality of Anchorage, is nestled in the foothills of the Chugach Mountains and provides access to the Old Glenn Highway.

Eklutna: The Athabascan village of Eklutna has a museum, a Russian Orthodox church, and a cemetery with "spirit houses."

Palmer: Palmer is the seat of government for the Matanuska-Susitna Borough, the home of the Alaska State Fair, the center of colonial history, and the heart of Alaska's breadbasket.

Chickaloon: This native community is nestled above the confluence of Moose Creek and the Matanuska River in the Talkeetna Mountains. It is the home of Alaska's first native-maintained school and Katie's Wall, built 60 years ago by Katie Wade to stop the cut slope from eroding. Many of the perennial shrubs she planted are still alive today.

Sutton: This quaint residential community is located in the Talkeetna Mountains. The Alpine Heritage and Cultural Center provides a look into Sutton's past.

Glacier View Community: The Glacier View Community provides several views of the Matanuska Glacier. Matanuska Glacier State Recreation Area lets you walk up next to—or even onto—the glacier.

The Eagle River Nature Center is located just 40 minutes east of downtown Anchorage.

Chinook Scenic Byway

Glacier-covered Mount Rainier is the star attraction of this scenic corridor through the Cascades. Ride to a summer playground or winter wonderland, or just stop to gaze along the way at the regal 14,400-foot volcano.

The Chinook Scenic Byway (also known as the Mather Memorial Parkway) is possibly the most scenic route crossing the Cascade Mountain Range, and it is the most accessible road for viewing Mount Rainier.

The route has a uniquely varied landscape. Traveling east, the route climbs through a closed canopy of Douglas fir. At Chinook Pass, the roadway descends dramatically through the Wenatchee National Forest and along the American River. The road also passes the unique basalt flows of the Columbia Plateau. The byway ends near the fertile agricultural valleys of Yakima County.

Historical: Part of this byway has a unique historic designation: that of a National Historic Landmark District. This district, called the Mount Rainier National Historic Landmark District, was designated so because it is one of the nation's finest collections of "national park rustic" architecture, both in the park's road system and in its historically developed areas.

Recreational: The area surrounding the Chinook Scenic Byway is rife with recreational activities. There are great opportunities for fishing, hunting, hiking, biking, and rafting. Snow sports also abound, given that Mount Rainier and its surrounding area is one of the snowiest places on Earth. Skiing and snowshoeing are the most popular activities.

Highlights:

Chinook Scenic Byway takes you through a variety of sites (listed here from east to west).

Just east of Mount Rainier, Chinook Pass is buried under as much as 50 feet of snow during the winter months.

Boulder Cave National Recreation Trail and Norse Peak: After passing through Cliffdell, the road continues to the Boulder Cave National Recreation Trail and Norse Peak, both known for their beauty and recreational value. Both are within the Mount Baker–Snoqalmie National Forest.

Fifes Peak and Union Creek Waterfall: Here, the road changes to a southwesterly course and passes through the old-growth environment that surrounds Fifes Peak. Union Creek Waterfall is also located in this area.

Edgar Rock Chinook Pass Historic CCC Work Camp, Tipsoo Lake, Chinook Pass Overlook, and Crystal Mountain Ski Resort: Edgar Rock Chinook Pass Historic CCC Work Camp is located at Chinook Pass, where the parkway resumes its northwestern direction. Tipsoo Lake is on the eastern side of the parkway shortly after the pass, followed by the Chinook Pass Overlook and Crystal Mountain Ski Resort.

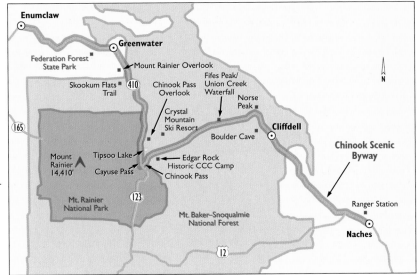

Mount Rainier National Park: Soon after Chinook Pass, you enter Mount Rainier National Park. This national park is known for its recreational, scenic, and natural resources. Goats, chipmunks, and marmots are some wildlife you might see here.

Skookum Flats Trail: Leaving Mount Rainier National Park, the parkway continues through the national forest to the Skookum Flats Trail found at the edge of the forest. A popular viewpoint for Mount Rainier is also located here. The parkway travels through the town of Greenwater and the Federation Forest State Park before continuing on to Enumclaw, where the parkway ends.

Mountains to Sound Greenway (I-90)

A blanket of thick forests puts the "green" in this interstate greenway, which climbs from Seattle's Puget Sound into the Cascades. Hiking trails and sublime views abound along the voyage.

Interstate 90 is the primary east/west highway in Washington. It begins at the historic Seattle waterfront and travels east over the Cascade Mountains to the dry plateaus of eastern Washington. As you travel east along this 100-mile byway, you experience lush green forests, the marine beauty of Puget Sound, pastoral valleys, and a dramatic mountain landscape. You also pass through a complete change in climate, geology, and hometown style.

Each year, more than 20 million vehicles travel this route, making I-90 a popular gateway between Washington's largest city and its diverse and striking landscapes.

Historical: The byway's historic sites demonstrate different eras of modern history. Some sites possess the soul of the Old West, some seem to still embrace the spirit of early industry, and some retain the more obvious past of the last few decades.

The soul of the Old West is possessed in locations such as Fort Tilton, (the site of an 1850s fort and a wildlife wetland), and Meadowbrook Farm (a historic landscape in the dramatic shadow of towering Mount Si). Meadowbrook Farm was the site of a Native American village that became the world's largest hop ranch at the turn of the 19th century. The Klondike Gold Rush Museum, located in the historic Pioneer Square district, houses photos and memorabilia from Seattle's turn-of-the-19th-century boom days. And what would the Old West be without a few mining operations? Catch a glimpse of a 19th-century coal-mining town at Roslyn. The town hasn't changed much in all these years, except for sprucing up the main street for the 1990s TV series *Northern Exposure*.

The spirit of early industry is still embraced in places such as Preston, a turn-of-the-19th-century Scandinavian mill town. Presently, Preston consists of the remnants of a small northwoods logging town along a river, including a number of historic homes and a church. The Historic Thorp Grist Mill, built in 1883,

The Alpine Lakes Wilderness Area includes approximately 394,000 acres accessed by 47 trailheads and 615 miles of trails.

is the oldest industrial artifact in Kittias County. The mill houses a remarkable collection of handmade wooden mill machinery and is open to the public. In addition, Fall City Waterfront was the final upstream landing for early steamboats on the Snoqualmie River, Reinig Road Sycamore Corridor was the tree-lined main street of a former company town, and Mill Pond was the Snoqualmie Mill's former log-holding pond (and is now home to a variety of fish and wildlife).

Recreational: Thousands of miles of recreational trails head from the byway. Most of these trails support hiking, but some of the trails are also great for biking and horseback riding. These trails range in length and difficulty. Some are great for day trips, and others take you deep into the backcountry. Walkers and bicyclists can begin a journey into the mountains from the heart of Seattle on the separated I-90 trail that has its own tunnel and crosses the scenic Lake Washington floating bridge. A series of regional trails lead to the John Wayne Pioneer Trail just south of North Bend (about 40 miles from Seattle). This converted rail/trail crosses

the mountains on a wide and gentle slope and includes a two-mile tunnel under the Snoqualmie Summit on its way to the Columbia River. Another of the more frequented hiking areas is the Burke Gilman Trail, which begins in Seattle and goes to the suburban towns of Bothell, Woodinville, and Redmond and passes farmland before arriving at Marymoore Park.

Another popular hiking area is in the Cougar Mountain Regional Wildland Park, at 4,000 acres, the largest wild park in an urban area in America. This network through wetland and forest passes 19th-century coal-mining shafts

and concrete foundations. Another park, the Squak Mountain State Park, offers excellent hiking because its 2,000 wooded acres are a first-rate wildlife habitat. The Tiger Mountain State Forest has the state's most heavily used trails. This web of trails for hikers, mountain bikers, and equestrians winds through 13,000 acres of working forest and conservation area.

At 4,190 feet, Mount Si towers over the town of North Bend and is a favorite hiking destination with its strenuous eight-mile round-trip trail to the summit or its five-mile round-trip trail to Little Si. Also, the Rattlesnake Ledge Trail climbs steeply (1,175 feet in 1 mile) from Rattlesnake Lake through classic western Washington forests to rock outcrops that provide sweeping views of the Central Cascades and Snoqualmie Valley. The Middle Fork Snoqualmie River Valley, on the edge of the Alpine Lakes Wilderness, has a variety of trails that wind among more than 100,000 acres of both ancient and recently harvested forests. The valley is minutes from North Bend but is lightly visited. Other great places to hike around this byway are Twin Falls State Park, the Asahel Curtis/Annette Lake Trail, the trail to Denny Creek and Franklin Falls, Snoqualmie Pass Summit, the John Wayne/Iron Horse Trail and Snoqualmie Tunnel, and the Coal Mines Trail.

Highlights:

Mountains to Sound Greenway takes you through a variety of towns (listed here from west to east).

Seattle: Start your drive in Seattle, located on Puget Sound. Along the lively waterfront, ferries leave for outlying islands. Seattle is also home to the famous Pike Place Market near the waterfront; the Pioneer Square District (Seattle's original downtown), which includes the Klondike Gold Rush Museum; and the 1962 World's Fair site, featuring the Space Needle and the Monorail.

Alki Beach is a favorite of sunbathers, joggers, and divers, and Discovery Park is an in-city wildlife sanctuary and nature preserve.

Snoqualmie Falls: Head east on I-90 to 268-foot-high Snoqualmie Falls, just before the town of North Bend. A trail leads to the bottom of the falls.

Snoqualmie Valley Historical Museum and Mount Si: In the town of North Bend, the Snoqualmie Valley Historical Museum has displays of pioneer life from the 1890s and other exhibits. Mount Si (4,190 feet) towers over North Bend and features a strenuous eight-mile round-trip hiking trail to its summit.

Snoqualmie Point: As the road continues east there are some excellent viewpoints that look out over the Cascades and even to Puget Sound on a clear day. One is Snoqualmie Point, a promontory with a view to nearby Mount Si and beyond.

Snoqualmie Pass: East of North Bend is 3,022-foot Snoqualmie Pass. In winter, it features downhill skiing and snowboarding, while groomed cross-country trails lead off into the backcountry. (Chains or other traction

The original setting of the Seattle World's Fair, including the landmark Space Needle, has been transformed into a center for heritage, arts, and culture.

devices are often needed to get over the pass in winter.)

Lake Easton State Park: Farther east, near the town of Easton, comes Lake Easton State Park, a good place to camp, with access to hiking and backpacking trails and to cross-country skiing in winter.

Alpine Lakes Wilderness Area: Those seeking more solitude can head to the Alpine Lakes Wilderness Area north of the byway, where miles of hiking and backpacking trails head off amid hundreds of small lakes.

Thorp: At the far eastern end of the greenway is the town of Thorp, home of the Thorp Grist Mill. Built in 1883, the mill is the only one of its kind in the country with its machinery completely intact.

Cascade Lakes Scenic Byway

On a route once forged by mountain explorers, this scenic byway offers a passport to panoramic views of snowcapped peaks and alpine lakes. Hiking, rock climbing, and even late-spring skiing adventures await off-road.

Quick Facts

Length: 66 miles

Time to Allow: Three to five hours

Consideration: The best time of year to drive this byway is from June through October. Winter snowfall closes a portion of the byway from mid-November until late May each year. When parking for more than a few hours near trailhead markers, expect to obtain a permit and pay parking fees.

The towering Cascade Mountains provide the backdrop for this scenic drive. These mountains also offer fabulous hiking and challenging rock climbing. The byway climbs into the Deschutes National Forest, where fishing, hiking, rafting, and other outdoor sports are plentiful. This area is also a winter playground.

As you drive by many bodies of water along the route, it is easy to see why this route was named after the Cascade Lakes. Some of the lakes that you encounter include Todd Lake, Sparks Lake, Cultus Lake, and Crane Prairie Reservoir. As you can imagine, this is an angler's paradise. Anglers can spend hours at the banks of these lakes, fishing for Atlantic salmon and other freshwater fish. Waterfowl and many species of plants thrive here as well.

Historical: This same scenic drive was once traveled by early mountain explorers Kit Carson, John C. Frémont, and Nathaniel J. Wyeth. In the days of horse and buggy, this was a well-worn 100-mile dirt road called the Century Drive.

The Lava River Cave tells the tale of the area's once-active volcanic past. However, it is closed during winter months, and warm clothing is advised when touring the other times of the year.

Recreational: You'll find many recreational activities along the Cascade Lakes Scenic Byway. Due to elevation differences and compact geography, six months out of the year you can ski in the morning and hike, fish, bicycle, or kayak in the afternoon.

Within the Deschutes National Forest and the Three Sisters Wilderness Area, you'll find snowcapped peaks, more than 150 lakes, and a river. With its dependable, dry powder snow and 3,300 foot elevation drop, Mount Bachelor offers the best downhill skiing in the Northwest. The same snow conditions also provide great cross-country skiing, snowmobiling, and dog sledding.

Excellent camping, fishing, boating, bicycling, hiking, backpacking, mountain climbing, and horseback riding are also

Two extinct volcanoes in the Three Sisters Wilderness Area reflect in the beautiful Sparks Lake.

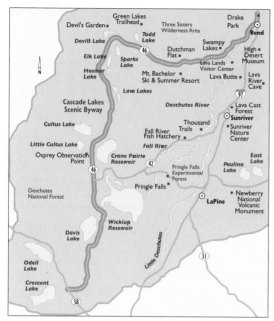

intersection), and explore the charming downtown area. The original site of Bend was selected around this area because it was an easy location for early travelers to cross the Deschutes River.

Swampy Lakes:
Fifteen miles west of Bend on the Cascade Lakes Highway are hiking, mountain biking, and cross-country skiing opportunities at the Swampy Lakes area. From the trailhead at the north end of the parking lot, you can enjoy a variety of marked skiing and hiking trails from two to ten miles in length.

Mount Bachelor Ski and Summer Resort:
Mount Bachelor Ski and Summer Resort is west of the Swampy Lakes, an area where you can spend a whole day relaxing, skiing, or fishing.

Dutchman Flat:
Just west of the entrance to Mount Bachelor, a whole new scenic landscape beckons to be enjoyed and appreciated. By some quirk of nature, the small pumice desert, called Dutchman Flat, has not accumulated enough soil nutrients to sustain the growth of many plants.

Todd Lake, Sparks Lake, Green Lakes Trailhead, and Devil's Garden:
On the byway, you pass Todd Lake, Sparks Lake, and Green Lakes Trailhead, all worthy stops. Continue on west of the Green Lakes Trailhead to a small but scenic area with several springs surfacing from the edge of a huge lava flow, creating a little meadow. Along with the lush meadow grass, you'll find moss, blue lupines, and Native American pictographs. The pictographs are painted on the face of a large dacite boulder, which indicate an ancient trail.

Osprey Observation Point:
Continue on the byway to pass picturesque Devil's Lake, Elk Lake, Hosmer Lake, Lava Lakes, Cultus Lake, and Little Cultus Lake until you come to the Osprey Observation Point. Constructed in 1929, it has become an outstanding fishing area and a breeding ground for the osprey (fish hawk), identified in 1969 as a potentially endangered species.

available. You can also white water raft on the Deschutes River.

Highlights:

The following scenic tour gives you a chance to enjoy the highlights of this byway.

Drake Park:
Starting from Bend and traveling the Cascade Lakes Scenic Byway, you come across Drake Park, at the Highway 97 and Franklin Avenue intersection. Park in Mirror Pond Parking Lot (just west of the Franklin and Wall

Historic Columbia River Highway

Designed to offer incomparable views as it sweeps through the Columbia River Gorge past waterfalls and wildflowers, this engineering marvel is both a scenic highway and historic landmark.

The Historic Columbia River Highway is exquisite: Drive through the Columbia River Gorge for nearly 50 miles, and sweep past majestic waterfalls, including Multnomah Falls. This byway also travels through a spectacular river canyon that you can often view from the tops of cliffs more than 900 feet above the river. During the spring, you experience magnificent wildflower displays, including many plants that exist only in this area.

This is the first scenic highway in the United States to gain the distinction of National Historic Landmark. This highway's construction was considered one of the greatest engineering feats of the modern age. Its engineer, Samuel C. Lancaster, tried not to mar the existing landscape. It was designed from 1913 to 1914 to take advantage of the area's many waterfalls and other beautiful spots.

Make sure to travel the well-known western section of the byway from Troutdale to Dodson and the less-traveled eastern section from Mosier to The Dalles. The difference in vegetation zones and views is amazing.

Historical: The Historic

The Columbia River Gorge is an impressive river canyon carving the only sea-level route through the Cascade Mountain Range.

Columbia River Highway has many nationally significant historic features on the National Register of Historic Places—one of which is the highway itself. It is also a National Historic Civil Engineering Landmark that includes 23 unique bridges. The historic district includes not only the highway, but also the Portland Women's Forum State Scenic Viewpoint, Vista House, Multnomah Falls Lodge, Eagle Creek Recreation Area, and several other waterfall areas.

Recreational: Recreational facilities in the Columbia River Gorge National Scenic Area are also of national significance, including the three major highways (Historic Columbia River Highway, I-84, and Washington State Route 14) that are used extensively for pleasure driving. The highways provide access to many hiking trails, windsurfing sites, and the Mount Hood Railroad, a scenic and historic passenger and freight route up the Hood River Valley.

Highlights:

Begin your must-see tour in Troutdale, the western entry point to the Historic Columbia River Highway. The attractive setting, unique shopping district, and convenient distance from the interstate make this small town a perfect start to your tour of the highway.

Sandy River: The first stop along the tour is Sandy River. An old iron bridge crosses the river at this point. You can even take a side trip to the north to visit Lewis and Clark Park, but be sure to return to the byway to continue your journey east.

Portland Women's Forum State Scenic Viewpoint: If you want a stunning scenic vista, you must stop at Portland Women's Forum State Scenic Viewpoint. It is located about 10 minutes from Troutdale.

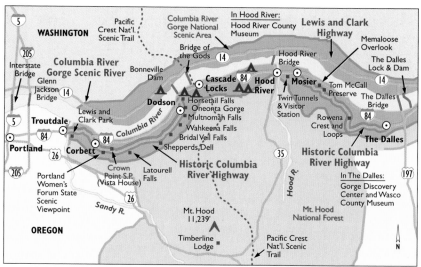

Crown Point and Vista House: Crown Point and historic Vista House are next, about a mile farther east. Take a stroll around the point (carefully—the road curves around the building here), and enjoy yet another wonderful view of the river and the Columbia River Gorge.

Multnomah Falls: Scattered throughout the next few miles are many waterfalls, each with its own history and qualities. Latourell Falls, Shepherd's Dell, Wahkeena Falls, and Bridal Veil Falls each whet your appetite for the most visited waterfall on the byway: Multnomah Falls. This beautiful double-cascade falls more than 620 feet.

Oneonta Gorge: Back on the highway, you shortly encounter Oneonta Gorge. This narrow canyon and its associated stream offer a cool, dark, and shady hike. To enjoy it fully, follow the path to the river crossing, take off your shoes, and wade in the chilly stream.

Bridge of the Gods at Cascade Locks: Continuing east, you rejoin the interstate for a while. The Bridge of the Gods at Cascade Locks connects Oregon to Washington.

Hood River: The city of Hood River, at the confluence of the Hood River and the Columbia River, is the windsurfing capital of the world. Stop and watch expert windsurfers from the riverside or from vantage points at hotels and viewpoints along the river. Or visit the downtown historic district, and stop by The History Museum of Hood River County.

State Trail: Take time to leave your car and walk a portion of the Historic Columbia River Highway between Hood River and Mosier that has been converted to a state trail. Remnants of the original auto highway and railings may still be seen. Or, if you continue in your car along the main highway instead, look for tunnels and roadbed high above you—a visible clue to a tremendous engineering feat.

Memaloose Overlook: As you leave the rain forest of the gorge and enter the drier, wide rolling plains west of Rowena and The Dalles, stop a moment at the Memaloose Overlook near the Tom McCall Preserve. Below you, the highway twists in the hairpin turns of the Rowena Loops. This engineering achievement remains remarkable even by today's standards.

Columbia Gorge Discovery Center & Museum: After you navigate the switchbacks of the Rowena Loops, catch your breath with a stop at the Columbia Gorge Discovery Center & Museum.

Opened in 1997, this museum offers interpretive exhibits about the human and natural history of the Columbia River Gorge.

The Dalles: End your trip on the Historic Columbia River Highway at The Dalles. You can view the nearby Dalles Lock and Dam or tour the historic district of this city.

Multnomah Falls on Oregon's Historic Columbia River Highway is the fifth largest falls in the United States; the waters plummet a total of 620 feet.

Pacific Coast Scenic Byway

As it travels the length of the Oregon coast, this byway by the sea passes fishing ports, oceanfront resorts, rugged cliffs, sandy beaches, dairy farms, windswept dunes, and the occasional migrating whale.

This byway trots along the full length of the Oregon coast. The northern end starts in the shadow of the impressive Astoria–Megler Bridge, where the mouth of the Columbia River gapes wide (Astoria is the oldest U.S. settlement west of the Rockies). Shining beaches and temperate rain forests govern the following dozens of miles. Paralleling the Lewis and Clark Trail, the route stops by attractive places, such as the resort town of Seaside, famous for its two-mile beachfront promenade, and the busy Garibaldi fishing port on Tillamook Bay.

The southern portion of the byway changes a little because it is dominated by rugged cliffs, farms, and sandy beaches. This segment contains some of the most photographed areas in Oregon; photographers often capture Siletz and Depoe Bays, the colorful Oregon skies, lots of dairy land, and the city of Tillamook.

Cultural: Appreciate this area more by taking part in everyday activities to familiarize yourself with the culture. For instance, go to Lincoln City to soar a colorful kite alongside the locals; after that, visit some of Lincoln City's many art galleries. Another popular destination is Bandon, a charming town famous for its lighthouse, giant

Continuing action of storms and ocean waves and years of build-up have left Oregon Dunes National Recreation Area with dunes as far inland as 2.5 miles.

sea stacks, cheese factory, and cranberry harvest.

You might stop in Tillamook and see Oregon's largest cheese factory for a taste-testing tour: something even residents like to do every now and then. This impressive factory has been around for more than 100 years. It boasts of continuing to use the time-tested recipe that has made its cheese famous. Other areas of note include North Bend and Coos Bay, cities that comprise the coast's largest urban area; here, you can find cultural activities galore, such as fantastic symphonies, art galleries, and restaurants.

Historical: The gorgeous and rich Oregon coast has drawn and sustained native people for centuries, and it has done likewise for sightseers and settlers ever since Lewis and Clark praised the area. Each new wave of people who came to live around the route added a new facet of culture and history to it and left their mark through historical and archaeological remains.

Recreational: Beaches along the byway are open to public use. In addition, many state parks can be found on the byway and provide public access to beaches. An abundance of public campsites, motel rooms, beach houses, and eateries along the byway corridor ensure a delightful extended stay along Oregon's Pacific Coast Scenic Byway.

Florence is the gateway to the Oregon Dunes National Recreation Area, a 47-mile sandbox with areas designated for bird-watching and dune riding. Honeyman State Park is a popular place to water ski and camp. As you travel on through the dunes, take a side trip to the Dean Creek Elk Viewing Area at Reedsport. The Oregon Dunes National Recreation Area has more than 31,000 acres.

Tucked in among some of the highest coastal dunes in the world, you'll find plenty of fishing and boating opportunities in small communities such as Winchester Bay and Lakeside. The dunes end near the cities of North Bend and Coos Bay, the coast's largest urban area. As Oregon's deepest natural harbor, Coos Bay has long been a major shipping port for the timber industry and a haven for sport-fishing enthusiasts.

Depoe Bay also offers fishing and whale-watching excursions from the world's smallest navigable harbor.

Flying large, beautiful kites is a common practice all along the coast and is especially popular in Lincoln City. Annual

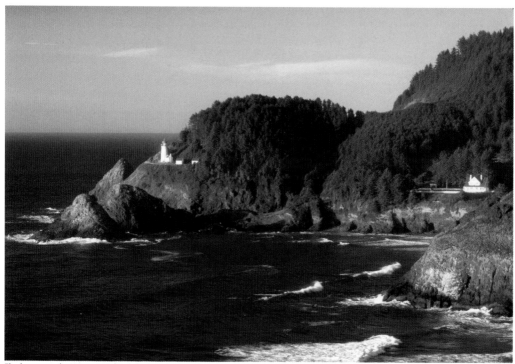

The beacon at the Heceta Head Lighthouse can be seen 21 miles from land and is rated as the strongest on the Oregon coast.

spring and fall kite festivals draw kite enthusiasts from all over. Get out your kite, and watch with the crowds as the delicate crafts are lofted up into the sky by the strong coastal winds.

Highlights:

Consider taking the Pacific Coast Scenic Byway's must-see tour.

Astoria: You will pass through Long Beach and go on to the city of Astoria, the oldest American settlement west of the Rockies. Astoria offers more points of historical interest than any other place on the Oregon coast.

Fort Clatsop National Memorial:

For a glimpse into life on one of the most important expeditions in the nation's history, travel three miles east on Alternate (Old) 101 to Fort Clatsop Road and follow signs to the memorial. It is operated by the National Park Service on the site where the Lewis and Clark Expedition spent the winter of 1805–1806.

Seaside: Next you will reach the city of Seaside, which was Oregon's first seashore resort. The turnaround there is the location of the statue designating the end of the Lewis and Clark Trail. At the south end of the Promenade, you will find the Lewis and Clark Salt Cairn, where members of the expedition made salt from seawater.

Cannon Beach: Cannon Beach is the site of the famous annual Sandcastle Building Contest in early June. The beach was named for the wreckage that washed ashore in 1846 after the wreck of the schooner Shark.

Lincoln City: Lincoln City has miles of ocean beaches known for fine agates and other minerals. There are also ocean cruises and whale-watching trips out of Depoe Bay and Newport. Lincoln City also has Oregon's first factory outlet shopping center.

Yaquina Head Lighthouse: The lighthouse has a museum.

Devil's Churn: The basalt that forms the shore here is penetrated by a split in the rock that narrows to a few feet before finally disappearing into the cliff. Fascinating in summer, it is awe-inspiring during winter storms and is an excellent spot for photographers.

Cape Perpetua Viewpoint: Just south of Devil's Churn you'll find a road going inland. At the branch in the road,

turn left and continue climbing sharply to the Cape Perpetua Viewpoint. There is a fine view of the coast both north and south.

Heceta Head State Park (and Devil's Elbow State Park): This pretty little cove is the place to see Heceta Head Lighthouse State Scenic Viewpoint up close. Just walk up the trail to the former assistant lighthouse keeper's home, Heceta House, and continue on to the lighthouse.

Sea Lion Caves: These natural caves are home to Steller's sea cows.

Florence: There are many delightful shops, restaurants, and galleries near the Siuslaw River in this town.

Oregon Dunes National Recreation Area (NRA): The Oregon Dunes NRA extends from Florence to North Bend with many access points off the byway.

Umpqua River: The Umpqua River Bridge is one of the historic coast bridges. The Umpqua is a major river in Oregon and is navigable by fairly large vessels upstream as far as Scottsburg.

Cape Blanco: Five miles west of the byway, Cape Blanco was discovered by the Spanish explorer Martin de Aguilar in 1603. The lighthouse is located at the westernmost point in Oregon.

Prehistoric Gardens: In the rain forest atmosphere of the Oregon coast, the developers of Prehistoric Gardens have created life-size replicas of dinosaurs.

Cape Blanco's lighthouse is located at the westernmost point in Oregon.

Volcanic Legacy Scenic Byway

This remarkably varied volcano-to-volcano route spans two states as it leads to lava fields, snowcapped peaks, mountain lakes, historic towns, wildlife refuges, forest vistas, and year-round recreation.

Mount Shasta, a dormant volcanic cone, is the second highest volcano in the United States and a major peak in the Cascade Range.

The Volcanic Legacy Scenic Byway stretches from California's Mount Lassen to Oregon's Crater Lake, making this byway America's volcano-to-volcano highway. The volcanic activity of the past has created unique geological formations, such as wavy lava flows and lava tube caves. Surrounding this volcanic landscape is a wide diversity of scenery. The byway travels through or near dense forests, broad wetlands and habitat areas, pastoral grasslands, farms and ranches, and well-managed timber resource lands.

As the byway passes the 90,000 surface-acre Upper Klamath Lake, you can see more than one million birds during peak migrations in the fall. The Klamath Basin is the largest freshwater ecosystem west of the Great Lakes. Six national wildlife refuges in these wetlands were favorite fishing spots of President Theodore Roosevelt.

Cultural: The Klamath nations (more specifically, the Klamaths, Modocs, and Yahooskin) are an integral part of the communities along the byway because they lived here before anyone can remember. Also, the determination and grit they have demonstrated to survive the changes of years, famine, and new settlers have affected positively the attitudes of other groups who have lived in the area, including the groups who caused their setbacks.

The Klamath nations have worked hard to maintain their own culture in spite of difficult circumstances. When the Klamath nations were forced on to reservations in the 1860s, they turned to cattle ranching and made a profitable living. And even though the nations were not federally recognized for about 30 years and had to work without supplemental human services on their reservation land, they have sustained the economy of Klamath County for decades.

Historical: Much of the historical significance of the Volcanic Legacy Scenic Byway arises from its Native American roots, and the byway is dotted with historic mining and logging towns. Many features along the byway are listed as historical landmarks.

Captain Jack's Stronghold, a national monument located in the Lava Beds National Monument, is historically significant because it was the site of the Modoc War. During the Modoc War of 1872–1873, the Modoc nation took advantage of the unique geography of their homelands. Under the guidance of their leader, Kintuashk, who came to be known as Captain Jack, the Modoc people took refuge in a natural lava fortress. The site of the fortress is now

known as Captain Jack's Stronghold. From this secure base, Captain Jack and his group of 53 fighting men and their families held off U.S. Army forces, which numbered up to ten times more than Kintuashk's nation. However, the nation was still able to hold off the Army forces for five months.

Mount Shasta is another site of historical significance along this byway. The major history of the mountain lies in its geological greatness. It also has a spiritual history. Native Americans of the area believed Mount Shasta to be the abode of the Great Spirit. Out of respect, the natives never ascended past the timberline. A long history of mythology surrounds the mountain, including legends of Lemurians, Atlanteans, secret commonwealth citizens, dwarfs, fairies, Bigfoot, and space beings that materialize at will. Mount Shasta draws visitors from all over the world, some seeking spiritual insight, others

Crater Lake is widely known for its brilliant blue color and magnificent views.

searching for the experience of the beauty and wonders that nature has to offer here in this unique alpine region. The upper elevation of Mount Shasta Wilderness was designated in 1976 as a National Natural Historic Landmark.

The Volcanic Legacy Scenic Byway is dotted with historic towns, many of which began as logging communities. McCloud is one example, being a company built mill town, still revealing its colorful railroad and logging history. The town of Weed was also a logging town, built in 1897. The Weed Historic Lumbertown Museum helps to reveal the part Weed played in the logging industry of the time.

Fort Klamath also tells an important story of early settlement. The fort was built in 1863 to protect Oregon Trail pioneers and southern emigrant trains from the nearby Modoc and Klamath nations who were inclined to attack on occasion. Two notable events happened at this fort: one was when Captain Jack was executed at the fort along with three other Modoc warriors in late 1873 (their graves are at the fort); the second was when the fort played an important part in the 1864 Council Grove peace treaty.

Unfortunately, not all of the history along the byway is bright. The Tule Lake Relocation Center was one of ten American concentration camps established during World War II to incarcerate 110,000 persons of Japanese ancestry. The majority of these people were American citizens. A large monument of basalt rock and concrete along the north side of State Highway 139 commemorates the relocation center. The monument, dedicated in 1979, incorporates multiple levels of rock walls, a concrete apron, and a state historical marker. The Tule Lake Relocation Center is located off the byway about ten miles from the town of Tulelake.

Recreational: The Volcanic Legacy Scenic Byway's length and vast diversity of landscapes provide a wide variety of year-round recreational opportunities. In the summer, you can fish, camp, visit a horse and cattle ranch, white water raft, or hike. You can tour a lighted lava tube or spelunk on your own at Lava Beds National Monument, see bubbling mud pots and steam vents at Lassen Volcanic National Park, or drive to an elevation of 7,900 feet on Mount Shasta to view the surrounding landscape. You can also tour the scenic shores of the Upper Klamath Canoe Trail by canoe. Crater Lake National Park is especially good for camping and hiking.

Highlights:

When traveling the byway from north to south, consider following this scenic viewpoints tour. If you're starting from the south, simply read this list from the bottom up.

Walker Mountain: The view from the fire lookout near Chemult extends from Mount Jefferson in central Oregon to Mount Shasta in northern California. There, you're surrounded by a sea of forest land.

Crater Lake National Park: Located 65 miles north of Klamath Falls on Highways 97 and 62, here are the world-renowned views you've seen on postcards and in magazines. Many viewpoints are accessible by wheelchair; some are found at the ends of hiking trails.

Ouxkanee Overlook: A short drive off Highway 97 leads to a picnic area with a stunning overlook of the Williamson River Valley and the surrounding landscape. Scan the horizon as far as Mount Shasta in northern California.

Calimus Butte: This historic, cupola-style lookout was built by the Bureau of Indian Affairs in 1920 and overlooks the scene of the 48-square-mile Lone Pine fire in 1992, as well as Klamath Marsh and Sprague River Valley.

Pelican Butte: The summit offers breathtaking views of Upper Klamath Lake and Sky Lakes Wilderness. Old-growth timber lines the narrow, rough road to the top.

Herd Peak: A gravel road off Highway 97 leads to Herd Peak, where a fire lookout is staffed during the summer months and is open to the public. The summit offers breathtaking views of Mount Shasta and the surrounding area.

Klamath Basin National Wildlife Refuges: Straddling Oregon and California are the Klamath Basin National Wildlife Refuges, home to a remarkable array of birdlife. Those making this drive in October to Novem-

The waters of Burney Falls tumble 129 feet to create a lovely mist-filled basin. The falls are named for a local pioneer settler from the 1850s.

ber can watch for skies filled with geese and ducks; from mid-December to February, for hundreds of bald eagles; and in springtime, for huge flocks of waterfowl and shorebirds.

Lava Beds National Monument: Lava Beds National Monument, south of Tule Lake National Wildlife Refuge, has weird-shaped lava formations, cinder and spatter cones, and undulating beds of volcanic rock, and is honeycombed with nearly 400 lava tube caves (two dozen of which are easily accessible to visitors). Captain Jack's Stronghold, a natural lava fortress where the Modoc Indians held off the U.S. Army during the Modoc War in the early 1870s, is also within the park.

Mount Shasta: Now double back to Highway 97. Vistas on the route south are dominated by mighty Mount Shasta, a 14,162-foot snowcapped volcano. At the town of Mount Shasta (where the byway has briefly joined with I-5), consider a trip east on the Everitt Memorial Highway. It leads halfway up the mountain.

McCloud: Just south of the town of Mount Shasta, take Highway 89 south to the historic town of McCloud, which has a colorful railroad and logging history.

McArthur–Burney Falls Memorial State Park: Continue south on Highway 89. Six miles north of the intersection with Route 299, watch for signs for McArthur–Burney Falls Memorial State Park, site of Burney Falls, which Theodore Roosevelt called the "Eighth Wonder of the World." Two cascades spill 100 million gallons of water a day into a deep emerald pool.

Lassen Volcanic National Park: Though Lassen Volcanic National Park's alpine scenery rivals that of Yosemite, it's far less crowded. Don't miss Bumpass Hell, where boardwalk trails lead past bubbling mudpots. Climbers find

a challenging five-mile-roundtrip trail to the summit of Lassen Peak, which towers over the park at almost 10,500 feet. The trail gains 2,000 feet elevation and has 40 steep switchbacks.

Lake Almanor: Twenty miles southeast of Lassen Park along Highway 89 lies Lake Almanor, a good place to relax with fishing and skiing.

Highway 89 leads farther south to Lassen Volcanic National Park.

Big Sur Coast Highway (Route 1)

With soaring redwoods, windswept cypresses, plunging waterfalls, fog-shrouded cliffs, and barking sea lions, this highway inspires awe and wonder as it winds along the California coast high above the crashing Pacific.

Route 1 from Carmel south to the San Luis Obispo County line follows some of the most spectacular and highly scenic shoreline found along California's coast. Views include rugged canyons and steep sea cliffs, granite shorelines, sea lions and other marine life, windswept cypress trees, and majestic redwood forests.

Cultural: The Big Sur is one example of an area whose culture is largely shaped by the region's geography. The awe-inspiring scenic beauty of the Big Sur has lured and inspired countless artists, authors, and poets.

The Carmel area and the Salinas Valley, less rugged but no less scenic or inspiring, have also had a vital role to play in the area's culture. The area has been home to many artists, none more famous than John Steinbeck, whose novels vividly describe life in the fertile Salinas Valley.

Historical: Written histories regarding the region now known as the Big Sur began to appear in the mid-1500s, when a Portuguese ship passed by the area's coastline. New groups of European explorers approached the area throughout the late 1500s and early 1600s, many anchoring for a time

Quick Facts

Length: 72 miles

Time to Allow: Five hours

Consideration: There are occasional mudslides during severe rainstorms. Also, fill your gas tank in Carmel before heading south or in San Simeon before heading north on Route 1 because you'll encounter few gas stations along the way. The road is narrow and curvy, and in some places it has narrow shoulders and sharp drop-offs to the ocean far below.

in Monterey Bay. However, it wasn't until 1770 that the first permanent settlement was established, when a Spanish group started a mission in Carmel. The Spaniards first called the area south of the Carmel settlement El Pais Grande del Sur, or "the Big Country of the South."

Before the Europeans arrived at the Big Sur,

The Bixby Bridge, built in 1932, is an engineering marvel known for its environmental sensitivity and aesthetically pleasing design.

the Esselen Indians had thrived in the area as hunters and gathers. By the early 18th century, other Spanish missions followed the Carmel Mission. In the late 1700s, the Spanish missionaries and soldiers forced many of the Esselen and other native peoples to leave their villages and move into the missions. Smallpox, cholera, and other European diseases from foreign settlers almost completely wiped out the Esselen people.

Until the late 1800s, a small, rough trail served as the best overland route to Monterey from the Big Sur. Eventually, the trail widened into a road of sorts, which was still frequently lost in landslides. This widening allowed the journey to Monterey to be made in just 11 hours, as opposed to the three or four days it had taken previously. After many years of difficult passage over poor roads between the Big Sur and the rest of central California, Route 1 was completed in 1937. By its completion, 15 years of labor and nine million dollars had been expended.

Recreational: The Big Sur's beaches offer a wide variety of recreational possibilities. Even during the summer, beaches are subject to generally cool weather. Sunny days are sporadic because a blanket of seasonal fog often hugs the coastline, dropping the temperature in the process. To be prepared, bring a pair of sturdy shoes—getting to the Big Sur's beaches requires at least a short hike.

Several state park and U.S. Forest Service beaches are open to the public year-round. These beaches are recommended due to easy access and breathtaking scenery.

Highlights:

The Big Sur Coast Highway runs along Route 1 from northwest of San Simeon to Carmel.

Ragged Point: On a promontory 400 feet above the Pacific, Ragged Point has incredible ocean views; a waterfall; and a steep trail to a secluded beach.

Rocky shores, sandy beaches, and brilliant turquoise waves are found throughout this Pacific Ocean byway.

Lucia: Northwest of Ragged Point is the tiny hamlet of Lucia. Lucia has an incredible vantage point looking out over the Pacific.

Limekiln State Park: Not far after Ragged Point, the byway enters Los Padres National Forest, traveling north to Limekiln State Park, which has camp-sites in the redwoods and wonderful coastal views.

Julia Pfeiffer Burns State Park: Julia Pfeiffer Burns State Park has trails through the redwoods and a short trail to a spectacular waterfall that plunges 80 feet into the Pacific.

Pfeiffer Beach: Secluded Pfeiffer Beach is one popular stop for those who can find it. Watch for paved and ungated but unmarked Sycamore Can-yon Road, located on the western side of Route 1 one mile south of Pfeiffer Big Sur State Park.

Pfeiffer Big Sur State Park: Pfeiffer Big Sur State Park makes a good central base for exploring the area. The park has a lodge and campgrounds in the redwoods, while hiking trails follow the Big Sur River to an inland waterfall.

Andrew Molera State Park and Point Sur State Historic Park: Next up is Andrew Molera State Park, the larg-est park along the Big Sur Coast, where a mile-long trail crosses rugged headlands to a stretch of wild beach. Just north is Point Sur State Historic Park.

Bixby Bridge: The Bixby Bridge follows Point Sur. Built in 1932 and spanning a 100-foot-wide canyon, it's one of the ten highest single-span bridges in the world at 260 feet above the sea.

Carmel: In addition to a picture-perfect beach and intriguing shops, the resort town of Carmel is known for its beautiful Spanish-style mission, founded in 1770 by Father Junípero Serra.

Point Lobos Reserve: Often called the "crown jewel" of the state park sys-tem, Point Lobos has rocky headlands to hike, hidden coves, and rich marine life, including sea otters and sea lions.

Death Valley Scenic Byway

The surprising splendors of the desert—from spring wildflowers to towering cacti, "painted" rocks to windswept dunes—come alive on this fascinating drive through historic Death Valley National Park.

In Death Valley, the lowest elevation in the Western Hemisphere is contrasted with mountain ridges rising from the valley.

Quick Facts

Length: 81.5 miles

Time to Allow: Three hours

Consideration: The best times to drive this route are in the winter and spring, spring being the busiest. Be aware of extreme heat, lack of water, and occasional flash floods. Access to Death Valley National Park can be limited by winter snowstorms when traveling from the west over the Sierra Nevada in California on Routes 108 and 120 and on Route 160 from Las Vegas to the east in Nevada.

Death Valley National Park contains the hottest, driest, lowest point in North America. It has 3.3 million acres of spectacular desert scenery, interesting and rare desert wildlife, complex geology, undisturbed wilderness, and sites of historical and cultural interest.

Located in one of the most remote parts of California, travelers from all over the world use the Death Valley Scenic Byway (Route 190) as the gateway to Death Valley. International visitors see Death Valley as part of the grand tour of California—more than 75 percent of the summer visitors in this area come from abroad. Even scientists and researchers come to study and explore the park's unique resources.

Historical: A tale of the valley's history must include one brief but important period that started when some of the '49ers, who were heading for the California gold fields, took an ill-advised detour through Death Valley. This began the boom-and-bust era of Death Valley, a period that involved more bust than boom. Borax, the "white gold of the desert," was the only significant "gold" found in Death Valley.

Eventually, the prospectors lost hope of finding gold in the desert. Likewise, the miners eventually deserted their borax mines. In the 1870s, for example, Darwin was a thriving mining town. Now, the historical city has but a few

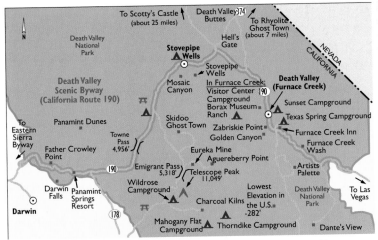

Furnace Creek: When you stop at Zabriskie Point, about eight miles past the entrance, you'll enter the heart of Death Valley—Furnace Creek. This area is full of history and is a recommended base camp for visiting Death Valley.

Stovepipe Wells: After spending the heat of the day indoors, take an afternoon drive farther north along Route 190 to Harmony Borax Works and Salt Creek. Catch the sunset near the sand dunes, and then head back into Furnace Creek or on to Stovepipe Wells.

Charcoal Kilns or Scotty's Castle: Take a day to explore the southern end of the park, including Devil's Golf Course, Artists Palette, and Golden Canyon. In the summer, take a detour through Emigrant Pass and on up the road to see the Charcoal Kilns. Or head north to Scotty's Castle for a great tour.

residences, a post office, and a phone booth. Rhyolite, once the largest town in the Death Valley area during the mining boom, is now home to a train depot, a jail, a two-story schoolhouse, the ruins of a three-story bank building, and a house built completely of bottles. Skidoo was one of the last gold-mining camps in Death Valley. This ghost town is a marvel of mining engineering that existed from 1906 to 1922.

Recreational: One of the best ways to discover Death Valley National Park is to get out of the car and take a hike. Due to the extreme elevation changes and climate, however, many of the hikes within Death Valley may be too difficult for the average visitor, but several very easy to moderate hikes are accessible to just about everyone.

Highlights:

Consider taking this scenic tour of Death Valley, beginning in the early morning from the east.

Death Valley National Park: Enter Death Valley National Park on Route 190 about three miles northwest of Death Valley Junction.

Furnace Creek Wash: Traveling north along Route 190, you'll notice that you're following along the Furnace Creek Wash. There may or may not be any water, but watch for thunderstorms—water rises fast in this area!

Tioga Road/Big Oak Flat Road

California's highest-elevation automobile pass slices through Yosemite National Park's dramatic Sierra Nevada high country, complete with vistas of granite peaks, pristine mountain lakes, wildflower-covered meadows, and lush evergreen forests.

Tioga Road/Big Oak Flat Road offers one of the most spectacular passages over the Sierra Nevada, making it the highest automobile pass in California, with an elevation change of more than one mile from west to east. Along the route, views include towering peaks, exquisite lakes, vibrant meadows, and lush forests with giant sequoia groves.

The byway provides motorists with an opportunity to experience this scenery from a vehicle. For hiking enthusiasts, it offers some of the most beautiful High Sierra backcountry trails.

Historical: The area now encompassed by Yosemite National Park was once home to various nations of Native Americans. By the mid-1800s, when American explorers first caught sight of the area, the natives were primarily of Southern Miwok ancestry and called themselves the Ahwaneechee. These earliest inhabitants of Yosemite soon found themselves at odds with the new settlers of the area. The Gold Rush of 1849 brought thousands of settlers to Yosemite, many crossing over the Sierra Nevada in search of their dreams.

The missing half of Half Dome in Yosemite National Park is assumed to have been sheered off during the Ice Age when glaciers passed through the area.

Conflict between the natives and the new settlers followed, and eventually California authorized the organization of the Mariposa Battalion to gather the Ahwaneechee and relocate them to various other places in the state. Thus the Yosemite valley opened for tourism, which today brings more than three million visitors annually.

The many new visitors to the beautiful area did not come without impact, so citizens began a campaign to preserve the area. On June 30, 1864, President Abraham Lincoln signed a bill granting Yosemite Valley and the Mariposa Grove of Giant Sequoias to the state of California as an inalienable public trust. This marked the first time in history that the federal government set aside scenic lands simply to protect them and to allow for their enjoyment by all people. This act also paved the way for the establishment of the nation's first national park, Yellowstone, in 1872. Later, a concerned and energetic conservationist, John Muir, brought about the creation of Yosemite National Park on October 1, 1890.

Recreational: For more than a century, Yosemite National Park has been a premier destination for recreation. Its unique natural qualities and breathtaking scenery provide the perfect backdrop for outdoor recreational activities.

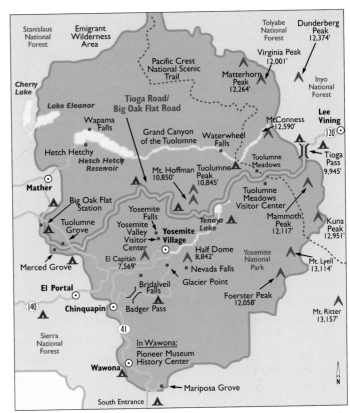

The summer season, although short along the Sierra Nevada, offers the most accommodating environment for recreation. Hiking, fishing, camping, wildlife viewing, mountain and rock climbing, backpacking, and photography are some activities available in the park.

In the winter, Yosemite's high country is a serene, white wonderland. The land is covered by deep, undisturbed snow, creating a landscape far different from the summer's. The winter months in Yosemite are seeing increased numbers of mountaineering activities.

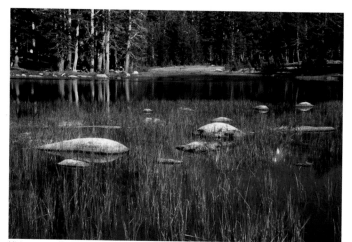

Visitors see tall grass in up-close views of the wetlands of Tuolumne Meadows. Beyond this photo are magnificent vistas of the mountains in the distance.

Highlights:

Consider taking this tour of Yosemite National Park, beginning on the east end by ascending the Tioga Pass and entering the park.

Tuolumne Meadows: Enjoy the drive as you approach Tuolumne Meadows. Expect to spend several hours learning and exploring through tours and tram rides. You can also take advantage of the concessions offered by the park.

Tenaya Lake: Fifteen to 20 miles past Tuolumne Meadows, look to the south and notice Tenaya Lake. Look up to the north, and you see the towering peaks of Mount Hoffmann and Tuolumne Peak.

Tuolumne and Merced Groves: As you approach the junction of the Tioga and Big Oak Flat Roads, chances are you'll want to get out and enjoy the sights. The Junction at Crane Flat is a good stopping place. To the north is Tuolumne Grove, a short hike onto a pretty grove of sequoia trees with a self-guided nature trail. A little down the road and to the south is Merced Grove.

Big Oak Flat Station: As you near the end of the byway at the Big Oak Flat Station, be sure to stop and gather information about Yosemite. As you exit the park, you may wish to turn to the north and take a side trip up to Hetch Hetchy Reservoir. This is an especially great idea if you like the outdoors and backcountry trails. Fishing is available at the reservoir.

Yosemite Valley: After a visit to the reservoir, turn back toward Big Oak Flat Road and head down into the Yosemite Valley, about 40 miles to the south. Stop at the visitor center for up-to-date information about activities and sights, including the famous Half Dome, El Capitán, and Bridalveil Falls. Hotels and restaurants are plentiful here, which makes the area an excellent place to stay the night.

Wawona: Continue south along Highway 41 (Wawona Road) into Wawona. Although smaller than Yosemite Valley, plenty of amenities are still to be found here, including the Pioneer Museum History Center. If you visit in the summer, hop on the free shuttle bus at the Wawona store, which will take you seven miles away to the Mariposa Grove. The grove is famous for the "drive through trees," the giant sequoias.

Sierra National Forest: The tour ends as you head south and out the South Entrance toward Fish Camp and into the Sierra National Forest, which is a whole new treasure to discover.

San Luis Obispo North Coast Byway (Route 1)

Pastoral countryside, golden beaches, rocky coves, serene hills, clean air, the blue Pacific, even an American castle in the sky—this California coastal byway is an enchanted pathway for daydreamers and nature lovers.

Route 1 in north San Luis Obispo County winds past and through some of the finest views in the western United States. The byway blends the rural beauty associated with much of Route 1 in the northern portion of the state with the convenience and amenities found in the more heavily populated southern sections of California.

Historical: The city of San Luis Obispo had its beginnings in the 1772 founding of the Mission San Luis Obispo de Tolosa by Father Junípero Serra; it was named for the Franciscan saint known as Louis, Bishop of Toulouse (France). Built on a knoll beside a sparkling creek, the mission became the hub of a growing settlement, serving as the center of both the community and the county. Many considered Mission San Luis Obispo to be the most beautiful of all California missions.

During the 1880s, the Southern Pacific Railroad built a railroad south from San Jose. After a five-year delay, the railroad came to San Luis Obispo in 1894. Construction of the railroad helped bring both industry and variety to the small community and changed the face of the city.

Hearst Castle, or the Hearst San Simeon State Historical Monument, is just off the byway. The castle, a living monument to the area's early 20th-century history, was built by publisher William Randolph Hearst, who entertained the rich and famous there. He intended it to be an elaborate getaway, complete with fine art and architecture. This historic treasure now provides a look into the windows of the past; it is one of the most heavily visited facilities in the California State Park System.

Bird-watching, golfing, sailing, and hiking are just some of the recreational opportunities you can enjoy at Morro Bay.

Recreational: The San Luis Obispo corridor is blessed with pristine opportunities for outdoor recreation. Visitors may hike, cycle, surf, ride horses, watch birds, windsurf, hang glide, kayak, and fly kites, among many other activities. The excellent climate of the area allows for year-round recreation.

The byway's close proximity to countless cycling routes makes it a desirable destination for cyclists. The highway itself generally has generous shoulders and makes for a great bike ride.

Perhaps the best way to take in the immense scenic opportunities of the byway is to hike or ride horses right along the coastline. Coastal access adjacent to the southern boundary of the Monterey Bay National Marine Sanctuary, for example, gives you the opportunity to experience the magnificence of the Pacific Ocean.

The Harmony Coast contains unique opportunities to explore rocky coastal inlets by kayak. Just north of the California beach community of Cayucos on rural Route 1, rocky sections support some of the state's richest and most extensive tide pool habitat areas. Kayaking allows for in-depth exploration of these intriguing natural habitats.

Highlights

Begin your tour at the Mission San Luis Obispo de Tolosa, and end at Hearst San Simeon State Historical Monument.

Mission San Luis Obispo de Tolosa and Ah Louis Store: Starting at the southern end of the route in San Luis Obispo, visit the 1772 Mission San Luis Obispo de Tolosa, the fifth of California's historic Franciscan missions. Just up the street is the Ah Louis Store, a center of San Luis Obispo's 19th-century Chinese community.

Montaña de Oro State Park: Montaña de Oro State Park is a spectacular stretch of coastline and mountain

parkland that includes beaches, tide pools, hiking trails, and camping. It's eight miles south of Morro Bay via Los Osos Valley Road.

Morro Bay: Morro Bay is home to an estuary and 576-foot dome-shaped Morro Rock, known as the "Gibraltar of the Pacific." Drive to its base to watch the many seabirds that congregate there. Nearby is Morro Bay State Park, popular for boating, fishing, picnicking, and camping.

Cambria: Continuing north from Morro Bay on Route 1, consider stopping at the pretty little town of Cambria to shop, eat, or spend the night.

Hearst San Simeon State Historical Monument: Farther north on the route is Hearst San Simeon State Historical Monument, better known as Hearst Castle. The fabulous estate has 165 rooms and 127 acres of gardens, terraces, walkways, and pools. Several different tours are available.